PHARM.D. SCHOOL PROFILES

Pharmacy School
Admissions Data and Analysis

Rachel A. Winston, Ph.D.

ISBN 978-1946432469 (hardback); 978-1946432452 (paperback); 978-1946432476 (e-book);

LCCN: 2021924178

Lizard Publishing* 7700 Irvine Center Drive, Suite 800 Irvine, CA 92618 *www.lizard-publishing.com*

Lizard Publishing creates, designs, produces, and distributes books and resources to provide academic, admissions, and career information. Our mental process is fueled by three tenets:

- Ignite the hunger to learn and the passion to make a difference

- Illuminate the expanse of knowledge by sharing cutting edge thinking

- Innovate to create a world that makes the transition from dreams to reality

We work with academic leaders who transform the educational landscape to publish relevant content and advise students of their educational and professional options, with the aim of developing 21st-century learners and leaders. We also work with students to publish their books and present widely diverse ideas to the college/graduate school-bound community. With headquarters in Irvine, California, Lizard Publishing works virtually with authors to edit, publish, and distribute both hard copy and paperback books.

This book was published in the U.S.A. Lizard Publishing is a premium quality provider of educational reference, career guidance, and motivational publications/merchandise for global learners, educators, and stakeholders in education.

Book design by Michelle Tahan *www.michelletahan.com*

Book formatting by Obinna Chinemerem Ozuo

Book website: *www.medschoolexpert.com*

LIZARD PUBLISHING

This book is dedicated to students who seek to become patient-centered physicians and are passionately devoted to their pursuit of compassionate, ethical, and service-oriented medicine. This book was inspired by Marina Eryan, Jackie Xu, Rick Ruiz, Greg Kelley, Lola Knicker, Riki Kucheck, and Chenoa Robbins.

Working at hospitals and conducting research in neurobiochemistry at Upstate Medical School and genetics at Syracuse University, I was surrounded by pre-med hopeful students eagerly pursuing their medical career. Subsequently, I spent most of my life helping students gain admission to medical school and working with authors who wrote books on medical school admission and MCAT prep.

Surrounded by students and teaching college for thirty-five years provided a keen insight into the student pursuit. I have also completed more than a dozen degrees and certificates and know the challenge and rigor of meshing rigorous coursework with a full complement of activities. Supporting students in their quest to attend medical school further inspired me to continuously adapt to changes in medical school admissions as well as investigate the broader picture of cutting-edge medical research.

ACKNOWLEDGMENTS

There is never enough room to acknowledge every person. Many people contributed to my perspective about medicine, assisted in the development of my knowledge base, or taught me indelible lessons. In a lifetime of experiences working with students, I am wiser and more worldly.

I gratefully acknowledge Michelle Tahan, Jasmine Jhunjhnuwala, and E. Liz Kim, as well as my family, friends, colleagues, and professors. It is with profound gratitude that I mention and acknowledge the many physicians I have known.

As a faculty member in the UCLA College Counseling Certificate Program, I met numerous dedicated counselors who spend their life serving and supporting students. Meaningful contributions to the book have been made indirectly by admissions representatives, college counselors, faculty members who took a special interest in this book's success.

I would also like to thank the thousands of students I have taught, counseled, or supported in my nearly four decades of service.

> *"If I see so far, it is because I stand on the shoulders of giants."*
> *– Isaac Newton*

Isaac Newton once said, "If see so far, it is because I stand on the shoulders of giants."

A few of those giants whose broad shoulders lifted me higher and helped teach invaluable lessons include: David Waugh, Zenobia Miro, and Sandra Savage.

Finally, there would be no book on pharmacy school and no career college admissions counseling, without the support of Robert Helmer whose tireless efforts support me every single day.

ABOUT THE AUTHIOR

D r. Rachel A. Winston is a tireless student advocate. She has served the educational community as a university professor, college advisor, statistician, researcher, author, cryptanalyst, motivational speaker, publishing executive, and lifelong student. As one of the leading experts in college counseling and an award-winning faculty member, Dr. Winston has spent her lifetime learning, teaching, mentoring, and coaching students. Much of her counseling practice is focused on admissions to medical, dental, vet, and engineering schools.

She started college at thirteen and graduated from college programs in such widely ranging disciplines as chemistry, mathematics, computers, liberal arts, international relations, negotiation, conflict resolution, peacebuilding, business administration, higher education leadership, interpreting, college counseling, and publishing. Throughout her education, she attended and graduated from Harvard, University of Chicago, GWU, UCLA, Syracuse, CSUF, CSUDH, Pepperdine, Claremont Graduate University, and Gallaudet University.

Her position working in Washington, D.C. on Capitol Hill and with the White House in the 1980s took her to approximately a hundred universities training campaign managers at colleges from Colorado to California, thoroughly dotting the western states. Later, she led college tours with students and their families on road trips throughout the United States. She has taught or counseled thousands of students over her career and speaks at conferences and academic programs throughout the world.

As a professor and avid writer for numerous publications, she won the 2012 McFarland Literary Achievement Award, Bletchley Park Cryptanalyst Award, and numerous other awards, including Faculty Member of the Year, Leadership Tomorrow Leader of the Year, and college service and leadership awards. While studying Human Capital at Claremont Graduate University, she was a scholarship recipient at the Drucker School of Management. She was also elected to the statewide Board of Governors for the Faculty Association for California Community Colleges, where she served on their executive committee.

She served as a faculty member for the UCLA College Counselor Certificate Program, the Director of Mathematics at Brandman University, and Embry Riddle Aeronautical University, Chapman University, Cal State Fullerton, and a handful of California Community Colleges, including Cerro Coso College where she also served as the Academic Senate President and retired in 2016. Over her career, she taught mathematics online, on television, live interactive satellite, telecourses, and in large and small lecture halls.

AUTHORS' NOTE

You are reading this book because you are considering admission to pharmacy school. Whatever route you took to get to this point, you are in the right place. Right now, you need to gather information to make informed decisions.

While many people offer advice, suggestions differ. Friends will tell you the 'right' way or the way their neighbor was accepted. Graciously accept this anecdotal information while you commit to learning more. This opportunity to pursue the healthcare profession is your future.

Dig deeper to consider both expert and current information from counselors who have worked with hundreds of students. Changes in programs, curricula, requirements, and links happen each year.

Double-check each program's specifics yourself. This guide is current as of September 2021, with each school's profile information. However, since researching this book, changes may have taken place.

> *"We are what we think. All that we are arises with our thoughts. With our thoughts, we make the world."*
> *— Buddha*

There are other pharmacy school books written by talented and experienced counselors. We admire and cheer on their efforts.

This set of profiles and lists is different in that it also provides and unique tidbits. We hope you find this information valuable. Your job is to begin early by assembling information for the schools you are considering. Create a road map and set yourself on a clear path.

If you see an error in this book or even a suggestion for a future edition, please write to Rachel Winston at collegeguide@yahoo.com. We will fix the entry with the next printed version. All of that said, this book was written for you in mind.

There is a wealth of information on the Internet with free downloads, FAQs, testimonials, and offers to help you with your applications. Some of these advisors are knowledgeable and could help you. Students and parents hunt around the web, searching for a tremendous number of hours to seek the information they need.

This book of profiles was designed to make your search easier. For now, though, we will assume that you are reasonably confident that you want to attend pharmacy school and are exploring this avenue as a possible way to take advantage of a program that will get you on your way toward your goal.

We assume that you are a highly academic candidate who is willing to work very hard. You may be fascinated with the human body, human physiology, chemistry, or holistic health. Selflessly serving others is virtually a prerequisite for pharmacy programs. This book will help you get to your goal. Applying to PharmD schools and writing essays for each program will require a persistent effort. Research the schools that are the best fit for your future goals.

While you might believe that pharmacy school programs are relatively similar, each program's nuances make them very different. These small differences may seem confusing. My goal with this book is to demystify this information and your application process.

CONTENTS

CHAPTER 1

INTRODUCTION

WHY CHOOSE A CAREER IN PHARMACY?

If you love science and want to help people, pharmacy is a stable field with a promising future. Whether you are fascinated by the brain, lungs, heart, kidneys, skin, reproductive organs, or circulatory system, pharmacy school covers the whole arena of human and animal biology. Pharmacists are experts in medication, patient support, and healthcare. However, pharmacists are also knowledgeable about the physical properties of pharmaceuticals, how they are manufactured, and the socio-cultural and ethical aspects of drug use. Your comprehensive study of chemistry, biology, environmental science, psychology, and socioeconomics offers diverse skills and directions as you continue on your pursuit of a PharmD.

You are in charge. You have specialized knowledge that other healthcare practitioners do not have. With your expertise, other people in the medical field will come to you and rely on you for your opinion. Over the course of your studies, you will listen to lectures regarding a wide range of diseases and procedures, know cutting-edge medicines and clinical trials, and be aware of medications that can stop the spread of diseases and improve a patient's quality of life.

With 144 PharmD schools, there are many schools from which you can choose, with a couple of additional schools in candidate and precandidate accreditation status according to the Accreditation Council for Pharmacy

Education (ACPE). According to the Bureau of Labor Statistics, the percent change in pharmacy employment from 2020-2030 is negative 2.2%. The median wage for pharmacists is $128,710, with 0.9% self-employed.[1]

WHAT DIRECTION WILL YOU CHOOSE?

Pharmacists dispense prescription medications and explain over-the-counter medicines to patients. Communication is essential as pharmacists provide knowledge and expertise, but they also relieve stress and offer clarity about pharmaceutical products that can benefit and harm individuals. Pharmacists help patients relieve symptoms, improve their health, and enhance their overall wellbeing. Culturally aware and good communicators, pharmacists work directly with patients and are highly respected in their communities. In addition, pharmacists can provide immunizations, some types of scanning, screening tests, consultation, and other healthcare services. Thorough knowledge of human biology is a necessity, as is an understanding of environmental and chemical influences confounding the benefits of medicinal use.

Your goal may be to become a pharmacist in a traditional pharmacy. This pharmacy may be in a drug store, grocery store, or healthcare facility. However, there are also numerous specialties you may choose to pursue. For those who like fast-paced environments, emergency room, surgical wards, or poison control are options. Others might prefer a more patient-centered area like working with geriatric patients, children, cancer patients, or psychiatric patient. Some choose to work in a hospital's pharmacy dispensary or at a veterinary medical clinic.

On the other hand, you might also go into other career pathways like public advocacy regarding medicines, organizational outreach, the law, student empowerment, or a professorship. Pharmaceutical companies also hire pharmacists. As a professional in the field, you will have a thorough knowledge of preparing and dispensing prescriptions, understanding dosages that fit various types of conditions, and what medications counteract one another. Your specialized knowledge of chemistry, anatomy, and physiology is invaluable.

Additionally, with the U.S. government's commitment to spending billions of dollars for medicine distribution worldwide, you may choose to work for a non-governmental agency, non-profit, or government-affiliated organization to

---

1   U.S. Bureau of Labor Statistics, "Employment Projections," *U.S. Bureau of Labor Statistics*, 2020, https://www.bls.gov/emp/tables/occupational-projections-and-characteristics.htm

do global service dispensing medicines. Knowledge of pharmacy is required for all human as well as non-human beings. From newborns and children to senior citizens and those with terminal illnesses, there are always people in need of your services.

PHARMD SCHOOLS AND THE PANDEMIC

During the COVID-19 pandemic, life as we knew it changed. The public health crisis impacted colleges worldwide, including the way classes were taught, as well as training for PharmD students, and undergraduate and graduate admissions. Admissions offices granted some flexibility to applicants throughout the process as local, state, and national requirements for masking, vaccines, distancing, and classroom access shifted with the winds.

As schools adapted, students and applicants adapted as well. Students attempted to take the Pharmacy College Admission Test (PCAT) multiple times as test centers opened and closed. Research facilities did not allow lab assistants to work in the building, resulting in discussion-based journal clubs to suffice for laboratory experiences. Some attempted to gain work and volunteer experiences with limited success. Even getting letters of recommendation became difficult as professors refused to write letters for students they had never met in person.

Resilience cannot be understated. PharmD school applicants could not base their future on their past as the ground shifted underneath. With schools going test-optional, schools offering classes online, and, volunteer opportunities shutting down, virtually all of the traditional requirements changed. Work experience is nearly a prerequisite for some pharmacy schools. However, healthcare facilities had to adjust to patient needs and government regulations which often barred families of patients from entering and volunteers from assisting. Suddenly there was a 'new normal' with ever-changing rules.

Similarly, faculty needed to continue 'as usual' in transformed classroom environments that alternated from online and back to in-person as students, faculty, and staff depended upon COVID-19 results. Weekly and sometimes daily rapid COVID tests were administered. Meanwhile, classrooms were filled with masked faces of socially distanced students managing their own challenges while complying with those of schools

Admissions officers who presented at college fairs now discussed their schools virtually. Those representatives who traveled to colleges to meet with prospective students or gave tours on campus needed to find alternatives. Most interviews were conducted virtually, some with multiple interviewees in group interview days. Every participant in the PharmD admissions ecosystem needed to find new ways to both reach out to student applicants and interview candidates.

One of the most interesting aspects taking hold at some schools was using artificial intelligence for the initial, computerized screening of applicants. In addition, a few PharmD schools do not meet their candidates virtually or in person and choose students without an interview. While these changes may or may not stick, they are with us now at some schools and are likely to take root in the new normal of PharmD school admissions.

Pass/Fail Grades – Most PharmD schools are accepting P/F grades for specific terms only. Check with each school.

Online Prerequisite Courses – Courses that transitioned to online during specific terms only will be counted. Otherwise, online courses may not be accepted for credit.

Standardized Tests – Some schools are test-optional, and some still require the PCAT. The test does not need to be submitted with the initial application to allow students to find a convenient time to take the test.

With the uncertainty over the pandemic and concern about completing chemical laboratory classes online, enrollments in pharmacy programs declined. According to the American Association of Colleges of Pharmacy (AACP), enrollment in first-degree pharmacy students dropped to 60,594 (5.1 percent from 2019 to 2020) with 64.6 percent women and 18.4 percent underrepresented minorities.[2] Approximately 12.3 percent of the students have dropped out of their program per year in recent years. This statistic could be due to a variety of factors, one being the challenging curriculum, although undoubtedly the pandemic impacted enrollment.

APPLICATION AND ADMISSION TO PHARMACY SCHOOL

To become a pharmacist, you must earn a 4-year professional degree (PharmD), though some programs are shorter, combined with summer clinical opportunities, or are paired with an undergraduate school. Pharmacists must be licensed, passing two exams to complete the licensure requirements.

---

2   American Association of Colleges of Pharmacy (AACP), "Academic Pharmacy's Vital Statistics," *American Association of Colleges of Pharmacy* (AACP), January 2021, https://www.aacp.org/article/academic-pharmacys-vital-statistics

Nearly all applicants have a bachelor's degree. Exceptions might include military medics who earned most of their degree in the service, but could not complete the requirements. Other possible exceptions are nurses or medical technicians who did not need an entire bachelor's degree for their job but have worked in their field for a decade.

The American Association of Colleges of Pharmacy (AACP) is an excellent resource for your pursuit. The AACP offers up-to-date tables, like the Pharmacy School Admissions Requirements in PharmCAS. There are other excellent reference books as well from those who have earned a PharmD. Some are outdated, which is partly why this profile book current as of the 2021-2022 admissions cycle may be very helpful for you.

Acceptance rates are fairly high for pharmacy school. This higher percentage is partly due to the overabundance of schools and partly due to the lower number of applicants. Particularly when compared to the number of applicants to med school, osteopathic medical school, physician assistant school, and vet school, pharmacy has a greater supply and a lower demand.

In 2021, there were 144 U.S. pharmacy schools. Sixty-eight are public universities supported by state taxes, and seventy-six are private universities with a total student enrollment count of 60,594 and individual school enrollments of 56 to 1,569 students starting in the fall of 2020.[3] There are nearly 7,000 full and part-time faculty members. Serving as a professor of pharmacy is another potential job option.

Many colleges provide this type of data. However, just for a sample, I included data from the University of Washington with its 2020 43.4% acceptance rate below.[4]

3   American Association of Colleges of Pharmacy (AACP), "Academic Pharmacy's Vital Statistics," *American Association of Colleges of Pharmacy* (AACP), January 2021, https://www.aacp.org/article/academic-pharmacys-vital-statistics

4   University of Washington School of Pharmacy, "Why US PharmD?," *University of Washington School of Pharmacy,* 2020, https://sop.washington.edu/pharmd/uw/

University of Washington Pharmacy School Admissions Data					
Entry Year	2016	2017	2018	2019	2020
Washington State Residents	70%	61%	64%	64%	77%
Percent BS or BA Degrees	94%	94%	94%	90%	86%
Cumulative Mean GPA	3.56	3.47	3.45	3.41	3.45
Applied	401	366	403	344	376
Offered Admission	132	153	151	154	163
Enrolled	106	105	108	105	108

Percent Acceptance to A Few of the Top Schools

Note that there are many pharmacy schools with admissions rates above seventy percent. However, these universities are a few schools with somewhat lower percentages.

1. University of North Carolina - Chapel Hill: 31%
2. UCSF: 25.4%
3. University of Michigan - Ann Arbor: 28%
4. University of Florida: ~ 40 %
5. University of Kentucky: 49%
6. Ohio State University: 27%
7. Purdue University: 37.5 %
8. University of Illinois - Chicago: 29%
9. University of Texas – Austin 31%

When you are ready to apply, you will complete the Pharmacy College Application Service (PharmCAS) application. Check the requirements for each of the colleges to which you are applying since they may vary. Every school will require background checks and drug testing. Since you are working in a field with access to drugs that are dangerous to people's health, colleges include this as part of admissions and enrollment requirements.

Finally, international students may enroll in pharmacy programs in the United States with variations in requirements at each school. More information is contained in my book on pharmacy school admission, *Pharm.D. School: Preparation, Application, Admissions*.

BUREAU OF LABOR STATISTICS DATA (UPDATED SEPTEMBER 2021)[5]

Pharmacists Median Pay $128,710 ($61.88/hour) – Doctoral degree (PharmD)

Number of Jobs in 2020 – 322,200 (Expected decline from 2020-2030 of 2%)

Despite this decline, 11,300 new openings are projected each year. Some pharmacists transfer to new jobs and leadership positions in the community or with the government, while others retire or are unable to work due to health, family, or other life circumstances.

PROFILES AND LISTS

The profiles and tables in this book include information available in the summer of 2021 for the fall of 2022. Outside of fee increases and new programs, changes in admission are unlikely to be significant through 2024 since many students who apply in 2024 were in college in 2020 and 2021 in which the pandemic impacted coursework.

Notably, the demand for PharmD candidacy and the desire for students to pursue pharmacy school varies from school to school and, with new schools opening and applications stable, the chances for admission are higher now than in previous years. Given the number of schools and the importance of valuable information about schools, lists, and profiles, this book will prove extremely helpful to those wanting to make solid decisions.

With data about applicants, admitted students, and entering classes, along with tests, requirements, and contacts, you have the information here at your fingertips. The companion book to this profile book offers more specific information about pharmacy school planning, GPA, electronic letters of recommendation, resumes, healthcare experiences, research, prerequisites, timelines, applications, essays, international programs, financial aid, and scholarships. PharmD school is the right place for you if you have a keen interest in anatomy and physiology, disease diagnostics, healthcare, and chemistry.

The profiles are laid out by region with location markers in the general location of the school. Some of the PharmD schools are in more rural regions, while others are in cities. Whether you work for a drug store, clinic, hospital, or association, you will find a career waiting for you when you graduate.

---

5   U.S. Bureau of Labor Statistics, "Pharmacists," *U.S. Bureau of Labor Statistics,* 2020, https://www.bls.gov/ooh/healthcare/pharmacists.htm

5
Regions

144
Programs

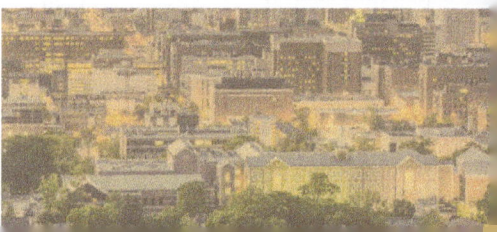

COLLEGE PROFILES AND REQUIREMENTS

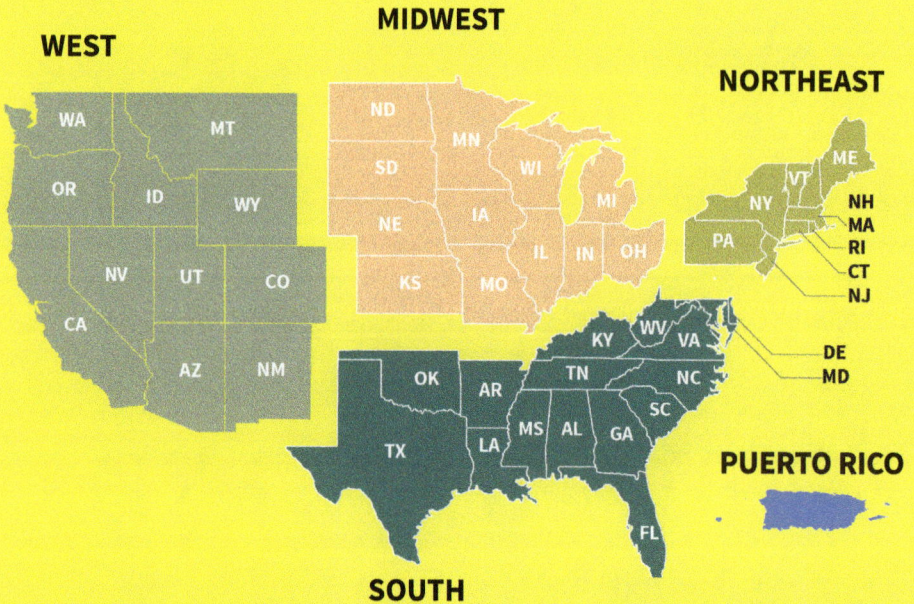

WEST

MIDWEST

NORTHEAST

PUERTO RICO

SOUTH

PHARMD PROGRAMS BY REGION
U.S. CENSUS BUREAU CLASSIFICATIONS

REGION 1 – NORTHEAST

Connecticut, Maine, Massachusetts, New Hampshire, New Jersey, New York, Pennsylvania, Rhode Island, and Vermont

REGION 2 – MIDWEST

Illinois, Indiana, Iowa, Kansas, Michigan, Minnesota, Missouri, Nebraska, North Dakota, Ohio, South Dakota, and Wisconsin

REGION 3 – SOUTH

Alabama, Arkansas, Delaware, District of Columbia, Florida, Georgia, Kentucky, Louisiana, Maryland, Mississippi, North Carolina, Oklahoma, South Carolina, Tennessee, Texas, Virginia, and West Virginia

REGION 4 – WEST

Alaska, Arizona, California, Colorado, Hawaii, Idaho, Montana, Nevada, New Mexico, Oregon, Utah, Washington, and Wyoming

REGION 5 – U.S. TERRRITORIES

Puerto Rico

LIST OF PHARM.D. PROGRAMS

The programs listed in the following pages include Pharm.D. programs. This book also provides lists of MD, DO, dental, physician assistant, and vet schools, since many students interested in medical school are also interested in healthcare. There are many facets of the healthcare world. One of these other areas might be a good option for you.

Pharmacy school is not for everyone.

Thus, this book aims to provide you with a more comprehensive set of lists so that you can explore your options. Keep the book handy. You may find that even after you begin college, if you choose a traditional pre-pharmacy path, you may find the additional programs in the back a good option for you.

Creating lists is often tedious and cumbersome. These lists were gathered to help you with this task.

These descriptions of the college programs, tuition, requirements, and deadlines are accurate as of April 2021. Requirements may have changed somewhat due to the pandemic, but all of this information is a great place to start!

Note: To simplify the text and fit information into the charts and descriptions, abbreviations were used as well as shortened sentences and acronyms.

CONNECTICUT

MAINE

MASSACHUSETTS

NEW HAMPSHIRE

NEW JERSEY

NEW YORK

PENNSYLVANIA

RHODE ISLAND

VERMONT

CHAPTER 2

REGION ONE

NORTHEAST

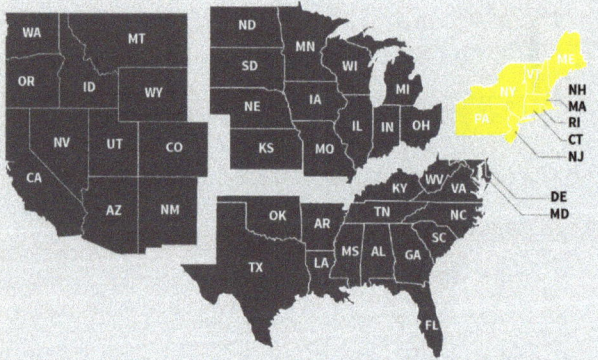

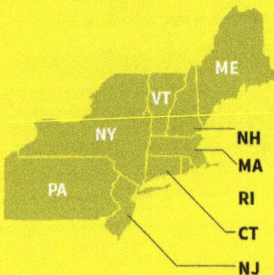

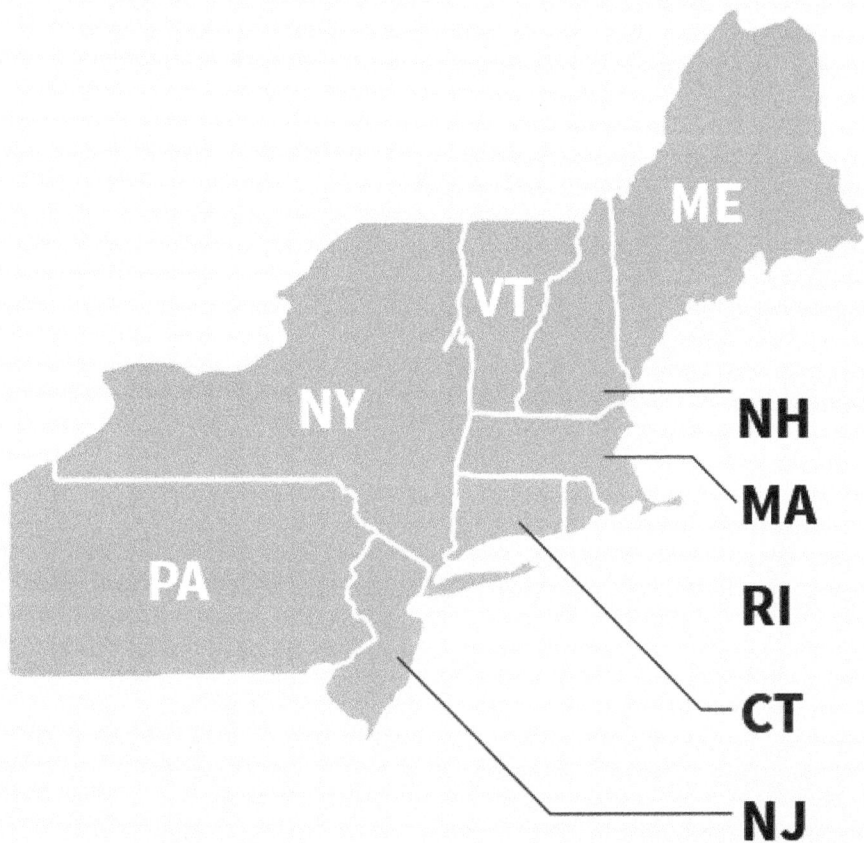

1. *CT – University of Connecticut School of Pharmacy*
2. *CT - University of Saint Joseph School of Pharmacy and Physician Assistant Studies*
3. *ME - Husson University School of Pharmacy*
4. *ME - University of New England College of Pharmacy*
5. *MA - MCPHS University School of Pharmacy – Boston**
6. *MA - MCPHS University School of Pharmacy - Worcester*
7. *MA - Northeastern University Bouvé College of Health Sciences School of Pharmacy*
8. *MA - Western New England University College of Pharmacy*
9. *NJ - Fairleigh Dickinson University School of Pharmacy*
10. *NJ - Rutgers, the State University of New Jersey Ernest Mario School of Pharmacy*
11. *NY - Albany College of Pharmacy and Health Sciences School of Pharmacy and Pharmaceutical Sciences*
12. *NY - Binghamton University State University of New York School of Pharmacy and Pharmaceutical Sciences*
13. *NY - D'Youville College School of Pharmacy*
14. *NY - Long Island University Arnold and Marie Schwartz College of Pharmacy and Health Sciences*
15. *NY - St. John Fisher College Wegmans School of Pharmacy*
16. *NY - St. John's University College of Pharmacy and Health Sciences**
17. *NY - Touro New York College of Pharmacy*
18. *NY - University at Buffalo The State University of New York School of Pharmacy & Pharmaceutical Sciences*
19. *PA - Duquesne University School of Pharmacy*
20. *PA - Lake Erie College of Osteopathic Medicine School of Pharmacy*
21. *PA - Temple University School of Pharmacy*
22. *PA - Thomas Jefferson University Jefferson College of Pharmacy*
23. *PA - University of Pittsburgh School of Pharmacy**
24. *PA - University of the Sciences Philadelphia College of Pharmacy*
25. *PA - Wilkes University Nesbitt School of Pharmacy*
26. *RI - University of Rhode Island College of Pharmacy**

PHARMACY PROGRAMS

Pharmacy School	Ave. GPA & PCAT (%) Early Decision (ED): Yes/No Int'l Students: Yes/No	Admissions Statistics	Science Req. Other than Gen Chem, OChem, Physics, Bio
University of Connecticut 69 North Eagleville Road, Storrs, CT 06269	3.2 PCAT: 72 ED: No Int'l Student: Yes	(2019) Apps Received: 283 Interviews Offered: N/A Admission Offered: 85 Number Enrolled: N/A Admitted Rate: 30% (2020) Apps Received: 133 Interviews Offered: N/A Admission Offered: N/A Number Enrolled: 65 Admitted Rate: 48.9%	Calc. Physio. & Anatomy Microbio. Biochem.
University of Saint Joseph* 1678 Asylum Ave, West Hartford, CT 06117	3.45 PCAT: Optional ED: Yes Int'l Student: Yes	(2019) Apps Received: 243 Interviews Offered: N/A Admission Offered: N/A Number Enrolled: 70 Admitted Rate: 28.8% (2020) Apps Received: 118 Interviews Offered: N/A Admission Offered: N/A Number Enrolled: 60 Admitted Rate: 50.9%	Microbio. w/ Lab Human Anatomy & Physio. w/ Lab Calc. Stats. Health-related science Behav. Sciences *This is an accelerated 3-year PharmD program.
Husson University 1 College Circle, Bangor, ME 04401	3.5 PCAT: Optional ED: No Int'l Student: Yes	(2019) Apps Received: 92 Interviews Offered: N/A Admission Offered: 65 Number Enrolled: 55 Admitted Rate: 59.8%% (2020) Apps Received: 42 Interviews Offered: N/A Admission Offered: N/A Number Enrolled: 33 Admitted Rate: 78.6%	Human Anatomy & Physio. w/ Lab Calc. Stats. Psych./Sociology

PHARMACY PROGRAMS

Pharmacy School	Ave. GPA & PCAT (%) Early Decision (ED): Yes/No Int'l Students: Yes/No	Admissions Statistics	Science Req. Other than Gen Chem, OChem, Physics, Bio
University of New England 716 Stevens Avenue, Portland, ME 04103	3.2 PCAT: Not Req. ED: Yes Int'l Student: Yes	(2019) Apps Received: 275 Interviews Offered: N/A Admission Offered: N/A Number Enrolled: 58 Admitted Rate: 21.1% (2020) Apps Received: 75 Interviews Offered: N/A Admission Offered: N/A Number Enrolled: 42 Admitted Rate: 56.0%	Cell Bio. w/ Lab Human Anatomy & Physio. w/ Lab Microbio. Calc. Stats. for Life Sciences Social sciences
MCPHS University – Boston* 179 Longwood Avenue, Boston, MA 02115	3.4 PCAT: Not Req. ED: Yes Int'l Student: Yes	(2019) Apps Received: 1,626 Interviews Offered: N/A Admission Offered: N/A Number Enrolled: 275 Acceptance Rate: 16.9% (2020) Apps Received: 802 Interviews Offered: N/A Admission Offered: N/A Number Enrolled: 287 Admitted Rate: 35.8%	.*This program is a Direct Entry PharmD program (0-6 program) intended for high school applicants.
MCPHS University – Worcester* 19 Foster Street, Worcester, MA 01608	3.4 PCAT: Not Req. ED: Yes Int'l Student: Yes	(2019) Apps Received: 1,266 Interviews Offered: N/A Admission Offered: N/A Number Enrolled: N/A Acceptance Rate: N/A (2020) Apps Received: 666 Interviews Offered: N/A Admission Offered: N/A Number Enrolled: 201 Admitted Rate: 30.2%	Microbio. w/ Lab Math/Comp. Sci elective Stats. *This is an accelerated 3-year PharmD program.

NORTHEAST

PHARMACY PROGRAMS

Pharmacy School	Ave. GPA & PCAT (%) Early Decision (ED): Yes/No Int'l Students: Yes/No	Admissions Statistics	Science Req. Other than Gen Chem, OChem, Physics, Bio
Northeastern University Bouvé 360 Huntington Avenue, Boston, MA 02115	3.5 PCAT: Optional ED: Yes Int'l Student: Yes	(2019) Apps Received: 1,089 Interviews Offered: N/A Admission Offered: N/A Number Enrolled: 130 Acceptance Rate: 11.9% (2020) Apps Received: 716 Interviews Offered: N/A Admission Offered: N/A Number Enrolled: 110 Admitted Rate: 15.4%	Biochem. Calc/Stats. Social Sciences Human Anatomy & Physio.
Western New England University 1215 Wilbraham Road, Springfield, MA 01119	3.2 PCAT: Not Req. ED: Yes Int'l Student: Yes	(2019) Apps Received: 255 Interviews Offered: N/A Admission Offered: N/A Number Enrolled: 66 Acceptance Rate: 25.9% (2020) Apps Received: 119 Interviews Offered: N/A Admission Offered: N/A Number Enrolled: 51 Admitted Rate: 42.9%	Fairleigh Dickinson University 230 Park Avenue, Florham Park, NJ 07932
Fairleigh Dickinson University 230 Park Avenue, Florham Park, NJ 07932	N/A PCAT/GRE: Optional ED: Yes Int'l Student: Yes	(2019) Apps Received: 362 Interviews Offered: N/A Admission Offered: N/A Number Enrolled:74 Acceptance Rate: 20.4% (2020) Apps Received: 282 Interviews Offered: N/A Admission Offered: N/A Number Enrolled: 86 Admitted Rate: 30.5%	Anatomy & Physio. w/ Lab Biochem. Calc. Stats.

Pharmacy School	Ave. GPA & PCAT (%) Early Decision (ED): Yes/No Int'l Students: Yes/No	Admissions Statistics	Science Req. Other than Gen Chem, OChem, Physics, Bio
Rutgers, the State University of New Jersey* 160 Frelinghuysen Rd, Piscataway, NJ 08854	3.5 PCAT: Optional for 2021 ED: Yes Int'l Student: Yes	(2019) Apps Received: 2,660 Interviews Offered: N/A Admission Offered: N/A Number Enrolled: 212 Acceptance Rate: 8% (2020) Apps Received: 1,935 Interviews Offered: N/A Admission Offered: N/A Number Enrolled: 214 Admitted Rate: 11.1%	Anatomy & Physio. Calc. Research Stats. Microecon. Social Sci./Humanities Elect. *This is a Direct Entry PharmD program (0-6 program) intended for high school students.
Albany College of Pharmacy and Health Sciences 106 New Scotland Avenue, Albany, NY 12208	3.2 PCAT: Not Req. ED: Yes Int'l Student: Yes	(2019) Apps Received: 909 Interviews Offered: N/A Admission Offered: N/A Number Enrolled: 191 Acceptance Rate: 60% (2020) Apps Received: 558 Interviews Offered: N/A Admission Offered: N/A Number Enrolled: 173 Admitted Rate: 31%	Stats. Microbio. w/ Lab Social Science Elective
Binghamton University SUNY 96 Corliss Avenue, Johnson City, NY 13790	N/A PCAT: N/A ED: Yes Int'l Student: Yes	(2019) Apps Received: 300 Interviews Offered: N/A Admission Offered: N/A Number Enrolled: 90 Acceptance Rate: 30% (2020) Apps Received: 230 Interviews Offered: N/A Admission Offered: N/A Number Enrolled: 91 Admitted Rate: 39.6%	Microbio. Anatomy & Physio. Calc. Stats. Social/Behav. Science

NORTHEAST

PHARMACY PROGRAMS

Pharmacy School	Ave. GPA & PCAT (%) Early Decision (ED): Yes/No Int'l Students: Yes/No	Admissions Statistics	Science Req. Other than Gen Chem, OChem, Physics, Bio
D'Youville College 320 Porter Avenue, Buffalo, NY 14201	N/A PCAT: Optional ED: Yes Int'l Student: Yes	(2019) Apps Received: 276 Interviews Offered: N/A Admission Offered: N/A Number Enrolled: 71 Acceptance Rate: 25.7% (2020) Apps Received: 171 Interviews Offered: N/A Admission Offered: N/A Number Enrolled: 58 Admitted Rate: 33.9%	Calc. Stats.
Long Island University 75 Dekalb Avenue, Brooklyn, NY 11201	3.2 PCAT: (recommended) ED: Yes Int'l Student: Yes N/A	(2019) Apps Received: 547 Interviews Offered: N/A Admission Offered: N/A Number Enrolled: 217 Acceptance Rate: 39.7% (2020) Apps Received: N/A Interviews Offered: N/A Admission Offered: N/A Number Enrolled: N/A Admitted Rate: N/A	N/A
St. John Fisher College 3690 East Avenue, Rochester, NY 14618	3.3 PCAT: Optional ED: Yes Int'l Student: Yes	(2019) Apps Received: 334 Interviews Offered: N/A Admission Offered: N/A Number Enrolled: 58 Acceptance Rate: 17.4% (2020) Apps Received: 450 Interviews Offered: N/A Admission Offered: N/A Number Enrolled: 200 Admitted Rate: 44.4%	Calc. Stats.

Pharmacy School	Ave. GPA & PCAT (%) / Early Decision (ED): Yes/No / Int'l Students: Yes/No	Admissions Statistics	Science Req. Other than Gen Chem, OChem, Physics, Bio
St. John's University* 8000 Utopia Parkway, Queens, NY 11439	N/A PCAT: Not Req. ED: N/A Int'l Student: Yes	(2019) Apps Received: 1,096 Interviews Offered: N/A Admission Offered: N/A Number Enrolled: 285 Acceptance Rate: 26% (2020) Apps Received: 404 Interviews Offered: N/A Admission Offered: N/A Number Enrolled: 67 Admitted Rate: 16.6%	*This is a Direct Entry PharmD program (0-6 program) intended for high school students.
Touro New York College of Pharmacy 230 W. 125th St., New York, NY 10027	3.3 PCAT: Optional ED: Yes Int'l Student: Yes N/A	(2019) Apps Received: 373 Interviews Offered: ~185 (50% interviewed) Admission Offered: N/A Number Enrolled: 47 Acceptance Rate: 12.6% (2020) Apps Received: 277 Interviews Offered: N/A Admission Offered: N/A Number Enrolled: 55 Admitted Rate: 19.9%	Biochem. Human Anatomy w/ Lab Physio. w/ Lab (see Chart) Microbio. w/ Lab Calc. Social/Behav. Sci.

NORTHEAST

PHARMACY PROGRAMS

Pharmacy School	Ave. GPA & PCAT (%) Early Decision (ED): Yes/No Int'l Students: Yes/No	Admissions Statistics	Science Req. Other than Gen Chem, OChem, Physics, Bio
University at Buffalo SUNY 285 Pharmacy Building, Buffalo, NY 14214	3.0 PCAT: 50 (if GPA < 3.0) ED: Yes Int'l Student: Yes	(2019) Apps Received: 300 Interviews Offered: N/A Admission Offered: N/A Number Enrolled: 125 Acceptance Rate: 41.7% (2020) Apps Received: 294 Interviews Offered: N/A Admission Offered: N/A Number Enrolled: 125 Admitted Rate: 42.5%	Microbio. Biochem. Anatomy Physio. Calc. Stats.
Duquesne University* 600 Forbes Avenue, Pittsburgh, PA 15282	3.5 PCAT: 33 ED: No Int'l Student: Yes	(2019) Apps Received: 374 Interviews Offered: N/A Admission Offered: N/A Number Enrolled:219 Acceptance Rate: 58.6% (2020) Apps Received: 323 Interviews Offered: N/A Admission Offered: N/A Number Enrolled: 145 Admitted Rate: 44.9%	Stats. Soc. Sci. *This is a Direct Entry PharmD program (0-6 program) intended for high school students.
Lake Erie College of Osteopathic Medicine School of Pharmacy* 1858 West Grandview Boulevard, Erie, PA 16509	3.4 PCAT: Not Req. ED: Yes Int'l Student: Yes	(2019) Apps Received: 1,789 Interviews Offered: N/A Admission Offered: N/A Number Enrolled: 170 Acceptance Rate: 9.5% (2020) Apps Received: 524 Interviews Offered: N/A Admission Offered: N/A Number Enrolled: 143 Admitted Rate: 27.3%	Calc. Stats. Psych./Sociology/Anthrop. *This is an accelerated 3-year PharmD program.

Pharmacy School	Ave. GPA & PCAT (%) Early Decision (ED): Yes/No Int'l Students: Yes/No	Admissions Statistics	Science Req. Other than Gen Chem, OChem, Physics, Bio
Temple University 3307 North Broad Street, Philadelphia, PA 19140	3.4 PCAT: Not Req. ED: Yes Int'l Student: Yes	(2019) Apps Received: 569 Interviews Offered: N/A Admission Offered: N/A Number Enrolled:156 Acceptance Rate: 27.4% (2020) Apps Received: 536 Interviews Offered: N/A Admission Offered: N/A Number Enrolled: 152 Admitted Rate: 28.4%	Anatomy/Physio. Stats. Soc. Sci.
Thomas Jefferson University 901 Walnut Street, Philadelphia, PA 19107	3.0 PCAT: Optional ED: Yes Int'l Student: Yes	(2019) Apps Received: 444 Interviews Offered: N/A Admission Offered: N/A Number Enrolled: 63 Acceptance Rate: 14.2% (2020) Apps Received: 386 Interviews Offered: N/A Admission Offered: N/A Number Enrolled: 68 Admitted Rate: 17.6%	Anatomy & Physio. Calc. Microbio. Soc. Sci.
University of Pittsburgh 3501 Terrace Street, Pittsburgh, PA 15261	3.6 PCAT: 81 ED: Yes Int'l Student: Yes	(2019) Apps Received: 335 Interviews Offered: 200 Admission Offered: N/A Number Enrolled: 113 Acceptance Rate: 33.7% (2020) Apps Received: 244 Interviews Offered: N/A Admission Offered: N/A Number Enrolled: 115 Admitted Rate: 47.1%	Calc. (Analytic Geom. & Calc.) Stats. Soc./Behav. Sci

NORTHEAST

PHARMACY PROGRAMS

Pharmacy School	Ave. GPA & PCAT (%) Early Decision (ED): Yes/No Int'l Students: Yes/No	Admissions Statistics	Science Req. Other than Gen Chem, OChem, Physics, Bio
University of the Sciences Philadelphia* 600 South 43rd Street, Philadelphia, PA 19104	3.5 PCAT: Not Req. ED: Yes Int'l Student: Yes	(2019) Apps Received: 197 Interviews Offered: N/A Admission Offered: N/A Number Enrolled: 81 Acceptance Rate: 41.2% (2020) Apps Received: 209 Interviews Offered: N/A Admission Offered: N/A Number Enrolled: 120 Admitted Rate: 57.4%	Human Anatomy & Physio. Microbio. w/ Lab Stats. Soc./Behav. Sci *This is a Direct Entry PharmD program (0-6 program) intended for high school students.
Wilkes University 84 West South Street, Wilkes-Barre, PA 18766	3.6 PCAT: N/A ED: No Int'l Student: Yes	(2019) Apps Received: 85 Interviews Offered: N/A Admission Offered: N/A Number Enrolled: 67 Acceptance Rate: 78.8% (2020) Apps Received: 90 Interviews Offered: N/A Admission Offered: N/A Number Enrolled: 67 Admitted Rate: 74.4%	Stats. Calc. Microecon.
University of Rhode Island* 7 Greenhouse Road, Kingston, RI 02881	2.5 PCAT: Not Req. ED: No Int'l Student: Yes	(2019) Apps Received: 631 Interviews Offered: N/A Admission Offered: N/A Number Enrolled: 117 Acceptance Rate: 18.5% (2020) Apps Received: 432 Interviews Offered: N/A Admission Offered: N/A Number Enrolled: 130 Admitted Rate: 30.1%	*This is a Direct Entry PharmD program (0-6 program) intended for high school students.

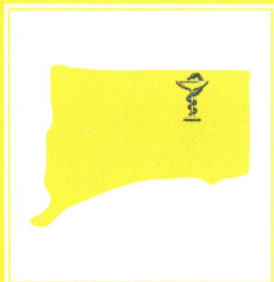

CONNECTICUT

MAINE

MASSACHUSETTS

NEW HAMPSHIRE

NEW JERSEY

NEW YORK

PENNSYLVANIA

RHODE ISLAND

VERMONT

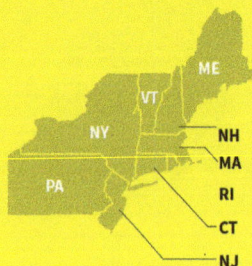

UNIVERSITY OF CONNECTICUT SCHOOL OF PHARMACY

Address: 69 North Eagleville Road, Storrs, CT 06269
Website: *https://pharmacy.uconn.edu/*
Contact: *https://pharmacy.uconn.edu/contact-us/*
Phone: (860) 486-2129

COST OF ATTENDANCE

In-State Tuition and Fees: $27,238
Additional Expenses: $16,686
Total: $43,924

Out-of-State Tuition and Fees: $55,410
Additional Expenses: $16,686
Total: $72,096

Financial Aid: https://financialaid.uconn.edu/

ADDITIONAL INFORMATION

Interesting tidbit: Beyond the core curriculum, UConn SOP offers specialized learning tracks to allow students to pursue their passions and maximize their course of study - LEADERS Track, Urban Service Track, Pediatric Pharmacy Track, Pharmaceutical Sciences Track, and Honors Track.

Important Updates due to COVID-19: Accept all general education completed during spring 2020 as Pass/Fail.

Were tests required? No.

Are tests expected next year? No.

What international experiences are available? N/A

What dual degree options exist? PharmD/MBA, PharmD/MPH, and PharmD/PhD. For more information, visit: https://pharmacy.uconn.edu/Admission-academics/dual-joint-degrees/

What service learning opportunities exist? Urban Service Track. For more information, visit: https://pharmacy.uconn.edu/Admission-academics/pharm-d-degree/urban-service-track/

What percent of graduates place in postgraduate training? 74.5% (2019)

NAPLEX First-Time Pass Rate: 90.48% (2020)

MPJE First-Time Pass Rate: 69.70% (2020)

Other: Early Assurance Program available. For more information, visit: https://pharmacy.uconn.edu/Admission-academics/bs-pharmacy-studies/early-assurance/

UNIVERSITY OF SAINT JOSEPH SCHOOL OF PHARMACY AND PHYSICIAN ASSISTANT STUDIES

Address: 1678 Asylum Ave, West Hartford, CT 06117
Website: *https://www.usj.edu/academics/academic-schools/sppas/*
Contact: *https://www.usj.edu/academics/academic-schools/sppas/
pharmacy/pharmacy-Admissions-information/contact-us/*
Phone: (860) 232-4571

COST OF ATTENDANCE

Tuition and Fees: $52,086
Additional Expenses: N/A
Total: $52,086*

***Note:** This figure does not reflect estimated housing/living expenses.

Financial Aid: https://www.usj.edu/Admissions-financial-aid/
tuition-and-financial-aid/pharmacy-financial-aid/

ADDITIONAL INFORMATION

Interesting tidbit: USJ offers a three-year distinctive and innovative modified-block curriculum, moving students into the workforce a full year earlier than traditional four-year Doctor of Pharmacy programs.

Important Updates due to COVID-19: Virtual Interview

Were tests required? No.

Are tests expected next year? No.

What international experiences are available? N/A

What dual degree options exist? No dual degree options listed.

What service learning opportunities exist? Community service required to graduate.

What percent of graduates place in postgraduate training? 39% (2020)

NAPLEX First-Time Pass Rate: 71.93% (2020)

MPJE First-Time Pass Rate: 59.46% (2020)

Other: 3+3 PharmD Program available.

CONNECTICUT

MAINE

MASSACHUSETTS

NEW HAMPSHIRE

NEW JERSEY

NEW YORK

PENNSYLVANIA

RHODE ISLAND

VERMONT

NORTHEAST

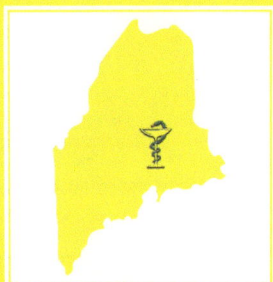

CONNECTICUT

MAINE

MASSACHUSETTS

NEW HAMPSHIRE

NEW JERSEY

NEW YORK

PENNSYLVANIA

RHODE ISLAND

VERMONT

HUSSON UNIVERSITY SCHOOL OF PHARMACY

Address: 1 College Circle, Bangor, ME 04401
Website: *https://www.husson.edu/pharmacy/*
Contact: *http://www.hussonu.com/gradrfi.html?*
Phone: (207) 941-7000

COST OF ATTENDANCE

Tuition and Fees: $35,376
Additional Expenses: 21,080
Total: $56,456

Financial Aid: https://www.husson.edu/pharmacy/about-the-school-of-pharmacy/cost-of-attendance

ADDITIONAL INFORMATION

Interesting tidbit: Husson students are offered guaranteed Admission to the pharmacy program if they meet the following criteria: (a) math/science pre-pharmacy GPA of 3.30 or greater, (b) PCAT Composite Score of 50th Percentile or higher, and (c) completion of a successful interview.

Important Updates due to COVID-19: Virtual Interview

Were tests required? PCAT required.

Are tests expected next year? Yes.

What international experiences are available? N/A

What dual degree options exist? PharmD/MBA. For more information, visit: https://www.husson.edu/pharmacy/about-the-school-of-pharmacy/dual-degree-programs

What service learning opportunities exist? N/A

What percent of graduates place in postgraduate training? 17.1% (2020)

NAPLEX First-Time Pass Rate: 69.39% (2020)

MPJE First-Time Pass Rate: 69.23% (2020)

Other: Guaranteed interview for applicants with 3.5+ GPA in math/science and 80th percentile or higher on the PCAT.

ME

VT

NY

NH

MA

RI

CT

NJ

PA

UNIVERSITY OF NEW ENGLAND COLLEGE OF PHARMACY

Address: 716 Stevens Avenue, Portland, ME 04103
Website: *https://www.une.edu/pharmacy*
Contact: *https://www.une.edu/Admissions/grad-inquiry*
Phone: (207) 221-4225

COST OF ATTENDANCE

Tuition and Fees: $42,220
Additional Expenses: $25,094
Total: $67,314

Financial Aid: https://www.une.edu/sfs/graduate/financing-your-education/scholarships-and-grants

ADDITIONAL INFORMATION

Interesting tidbit: As a UNE Pharm.D. student, you'll have the opportunity to pursue tracks in Pharmaceutical Sciences, Wellness and Integrative Medicine, and Health Data Analytics giving you advanced training at no extra cost.

Important Updates due to COVID-19: Virtual Interview

Were tests required? No.

Are tests expected next year? No.

What international experiences are available? Contact the Global Education office: https://www.une.edu/global/ed

What dual degree options exist? No dual degree options listed.

What service learning opportunities exist? N/A

What percent of graduates place in postgraduate training? 13% (2020)

NAPLEX First-Time Pass Rate: 58.21% (2020)

MPJE First-Time Pass Rate: 64.52% (2020)

Other: Health Data Analytics track. For more information, visit: https://www.une.edu/pharmacy/program/health-data-analytics-track

Wellness and Integrative Medicine Track: https://www.une.edu/pharmacy/program/wellness-and-integrative-medicine-track

CONNECTICUT

MAINE

MASSACHUSETTS

NEW HAMPSHIRE

NEW JERSEY

NEW YORK

PENNSYLVANIA

RHODE ISLAND

VERMONT

NORTHEAST

MCPHS UNIVERSITY SCHOOL OF PHARMACY – BOSTON

Address: 179 Longwood Avenue, Boston, MA 02115
Website: *https://www.mcphs.edu/*
Contact: *https://www.mcphs.edu/Admission-and-aid/request-information?*
Phone: (617) 879-5964

COST OF ATTENDANCE

Tuition and Fees: $40,800
Additional Expenses: N/A
Total: $40,800*

*Note: This figure does not reflect estimated housing/living expenses.

Financial Aid: https://www.mcphs.edu/Admission-and-aid/financial-services/financial-aid/graduate-financial-aid

ADDITIONAL INFORMATION

Interesting tidbit: MCPHS - Boston offers the Direct Entry PharmD program, which is a full-time, six-year direct entry to Doctor of Pharmacy program. The program includes a two-year pre-professional phase that combines the liberal arts, communications, and basic sciences followed by a four-year professional phase that focuses on the pharmaceutical sciences and pharmacy practice.

Important Updates due to COVID-19: Virtual Interview

Were tests required? No.

Are tests expected next year? No.

What international experiences are available? N/A

What dual degree options exist? N/A, accelerated programs available. See below.

What service learning opportunities exist? N/A

What percent of graduates place in postgraduate training? 18% (2019)

NAPLEX First-Time Pass Rate: 82.38% (2020)

MPJE: 70.43% (2020)

Other: Accelerated PharmD available. Students in the Boston PharmD program may elect to apply for the 5-Year Accelerated PharmD Pathway and complete the professional phase of their degree in three years (instead of four) by transferring to the Worcester or Manchester campus after the initial two years of pre-professional study in Boston. For more information, visit: https://www.mcphs.edu/academics/school-of-pharmacy/pharmacy/pharmacy-pharmd-accelerated

Other: PharmD Honors Program available. The Doctor of Pharmacy Honors Program offers highly motivated and academically talented students the opportunity to pursue their professional interests and advance their skills and talents beyond the level possible in the standard PharmD curriculum.

CONNECTICUT

MAINE

MASSACHUSETTS

NEW HAMPSHIRE

NEW JERSEY

NEW YORK

PENNSYLVANIA

RHODE ISLAND

VERMONT

MCPHS UNIVERSITY SCHOOL OF PHARMACY - WORCESTER

Address: 19 Foster Street, Worcester, MA 01608
Website: *https://www.mcphs.edu/*
Contact: *https://www.mcphs.edu/Admission-and-aid/request-information?*
Phone: (508) 373-5607

Other locations: Manchester, NH

COST OF ATTENDANCE

Tuition and Fees: $54,810
Additional Expenses: $19,073
Total: $73,833

Financial Aid: https://www.mcphs.edu/Admission-and-aid/financial-services/financial-aid/graduate-financial-aid

ADDITIONAL INFORMATION

Interesting tidbit: Offered on the Worcester campus is the year-round, three-year Accelerated PharmD program. It provides students who've completed prerequisites the opportunity to start practicing ahead of their peers. Situated in the heart of the second-largest city in Massachusetts, the MCPHS–Worcester campus offers an energetic culture and rich history, and incredible housing options dot the campus.

Important Updates due to COVID-19: Virtual Interview

Were tests required? No.

Are tests expected next year? No.

What international experiences are available? N/A

What dual degree options exist? No dual degree options listed.

What percent of applicants place in postgraduate training? N/A

What service learning opportunities exist? N/A

What percent of graduates place in postgraduate training? 7.7% (2019)

NAPLEX First-Time Pass Rate: 73.27% (2020)

MPJE First-Time Pass Rate: 68.67% (2020)

Other: The Boston campus has a Direct Entry 6-year program for high school applicants.

Other: The Manchester campus offers an identical three-year Accelerated PharmD program.

CONNECTICUT

MAINE

MASSACHUSETTS

NEW HAMPSHIRE

NEW JERSEY

NEW YORK

PENNSYLVANIA

RHODE ISLAND

VERMONT

NORTHEAST

CONNECTICUT

MAINE

MASSACHUSETTS

NEW HAMPSHIRE

NEW JERSEY

NEW YORK

PENNSYLVANIA

RHODE ISLAND

VERMONT

NORTHEASTERN UNIVERSITY BOUVÉ COLLEGE OF HEALTH SCIENCES SCHOOL OF PHARMACY

Address: 360 Huntington Avenue, Boston, MA 02115
Website: *https://bouve.northeastern.edu/pharmacy/*
Contact: *https://bouve.northeastern.edu/pharmacy/contact-2/*
Phone: (617) 373-7000

COST OF ATTENDANCE

Tuition and Fees: $44,236
Additional Expenses: N/A
Total: $44,236*

*Indirect costs information is not available.

Financial Aid: https://studentfinance.northeastern.edu/applying-for-aid/graduate/

ADDITIONAL INFORMATION

Interesting tidbit: Students in the PharmD program participate in Northeastern University's signature cooperative education (co-op) program, which provides up to three 4-month full-time work experiences alternating with full-time campus-based academic work. The school offers the only pharmacy co-op program in the country.

Important Updates due to COVID-19: Virtual Interview

Were tests required? No.

Are tests expected next year? No.

What international experiences are available? N/A

What dual degree options exist? PharmD/MPH program. For more information, visit: https://bouve.northeastern.edu/health-sciences/programs/pharmd-mph/

What service learning opportunities exist? N/A

What percent of graduates place in postgraduate training? 39% (2019)

NAPLEX First-Time Pass Rate: 98.15% (2020)

MPJE First-Time Pass Rate: 78.85% (2020)

Other: Early Assurance Pathway for high school applicants. For more information, visit: https://bouve.northeastern.edu/pharmacy/programs/pharmd-freshman/

WESTERN NEW ENGLAND UNIVERSITY COLLEGE OF PHARMACY

Address: 1215 Wilbraham Road, Springfield, MA 01119
Website: *https://www1.wne.edu/pharmacy-and-health-sciences/*
Contact: *https://www1.wne.edu/pharmacy-and-health-sciences/Admissions/pharmd/request-information.cfm*
Phone: (413) 796-2113

COST OF ATTENDANCE

Tuition and Fees: $46,275
Additional Expenses: $10,000
Total: $56,274

Financial Aid: https://www1.wne.edu/pharmacy-and-health-sciences/cost-and-aid/scholarships.cfm

ADDITIONAL INFORMATION

Interesting tidbit: The Class of 2020 ranked second best in the nation for postgraduate residency program match rate. Its 2020 Phase 1 match rate is the highest match rate in the New England region and second nationally only to the University of California – San Francisco.

Important Updates due to COVID-19: Virtual Interview

Were tests required? No.

Are tests expected next year? No.

What international experiences are available? International opportunities in Thailand and China.

What dual degree options exist? PharmD/MBA: https://www1.wne.edu/pharmacy-and-health-sciences/academics/pharmd-mba/index.cfm

PharmD/MSOL: https://www1.wne.edu/pharmacy-and-health-sciences/academics/pharmd-msol/index.cfm

What service learning opportunities exist? Service learning through Advanced Pharmacy Practice Experiences (APPEs) in various settings.

What percent of graduates place in postgraduate training? 82.4% (2020)

NAPLEX First-Time Pass Rate: 93.22% (2020)

MPJE First-Time Pass Rate: 78.57% (2020)

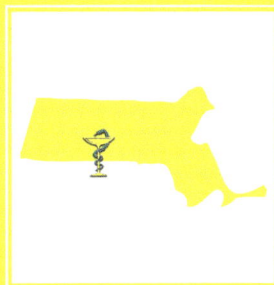

CONNECTICUT

MAINE

MASSACHUSETTS

NEW HAMPSHIRE

NEW JERSEY

NEW YORK

PENNSYLVANIA

RHODE ISLAND

VERMONT

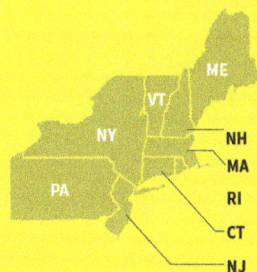

NORTHEAST

FAIRLEIGH DICKINSON UNIVERSITY SCHOOL OF PHARMACY

Address: 230 Park Avenue, Florham Park, NJ 07932
Website: *https://view2.fdu.edu/academics/pharmacy/*
Contact: *https://view2.fdu.edu/academics/pharmacy/indicate-your-interest/*
Phone: (973) 443-8401

COST OF ATTENDANCE

Tuition and Fees: $41,534
Additional Expenses: N/A
Total: $41,534*

*Note: This figure does not reflect estimated housing/living expenses .

Financial Aid: https://view2.fdu.edu/academics/pharmacy/financial-aid/scholarships/

ADDITIONAL INFORMATION

Interesting tidbit: The Fairleigh Dickinson University School of Pharmacy and Health Sciences is one of only two degree-granting pharmacy schools in New Jersey, and is the first in the state to be associated with a private university.

Important Updates due to COVID-19: Virtual Interview

Were tests required? No.

Are tests expected next year? No.

What international experiences are available? Global healthcare and opportunities to learn abroad.

What dual degree options exist? Several options, including PharmD/MBA, MS, MPA, MHS, or MA in various areas. For more information, visit: https://view2.fdu.edu/academics/pharmacy/dual-degrees/

What service learning opportunities exist? Service learning through experiential education with various populations.

What percent of graduates place in postgraduate training? N/A

NAPLEX First-Time Pass Rate: 81.82% (2020)

MPJE First-Time Pass Rate: 65.22% (2020)

CONNECTICUT

MAINE

MASSACHUSETTS

NEW HAMPSHIRE

NEW JERSEY

NEW YORK

PENNSYLVANIA

RHODE ISLAND

VERMONT

RUTGERS, THE STATE UNIVERSITY OF NEW JERSEY ERNEST MARIO SCHOOL OF PHARMACY

Address: 160 Frelinghuysen Rd, Piscataway, NJ 08854
Website: *https://pharmacy.rutgers.edu/*
Contact: *https://pharmacy.rutgers.edu/contact-us/*
Phone: (848) 445-2675

COST OF ATTENDANCE

In-State Tuition and Fees: $18,938
Additional Expenses: $12,386
Total: $31,324

Out-of-State Tuition and Fees: $41,013
Additional Expenses: $12,386
Total: $53,399

Financial Aid: https://financialaid.rutgers.edu/

ADDITIONAL INFORMATION

Interesting tidbit: The PharmD program at Rutgers is a six-year PharmD program, which begins with two years of pre-professional study and moves seamlessly into four years of professional training. Students can enter directly from high school or transfer from a two- or four-year college into the first professional year.

Important Updates due to COVID-19: For Fall 2021 Admission Only, the PCAT is optional, but strongly encouraged.

Were tests required? SAT or ACT required. PCAT optional.

Are tests expected next year? Yes.

What international experiences are available? N/A

What dual degree options exist? PharmD/MD, MPH, MBA, or PhD. For more information, visit: https://pharmacy.rutgers.edu/programs/professional-degree-program-doctor-of-pharmacy-pharmd/dual-degree-options-for-pharmd-students/

What service learning opportunities exist? N/A

What percent of graduates place in postgraduate training? 25% (2020)

NAPLEX First-Time Pass Rate: 86.96% (2020)

MPJE First-Time Pass Rate: 80.92% (2020)

Other: BS/PharmD program available to high school applicants. Rutgers also has partnerships with the following undergraduate partner schools: Montclair State University, Saint Peter's University, and Stockton University. For more information, visit: https://pharmacy.rutgers.edu/programs/apply/

CONNECTICUT

MAINE

MASSACHUSETTS

NEW HAMPSHIRE

NEW JERSEY

NEW YORK

PENNSYLVANIA

RHODE ISLAND

VERMONT

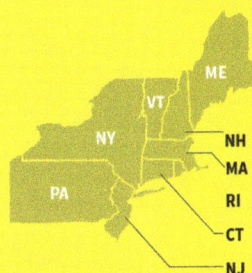

NORTHEAST

CONNECTICUT

MAINE

MASSACHUSETTS

NEW HAMPSHIRE

NEW JERSEY

NEW YORK

PENNSYLVANIA

RHODE ISLAND

VERMONT

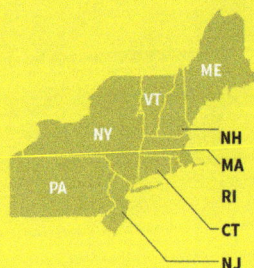

ALBANY COLLEGE OF PHARMACY AND HEALTH SCIENCES SCHOOL OF PHARMACY AND PHARMACEUTICAL SCIENCES

Address: 106 New Scotland Avenue, Albany, NY 12208
Website: *https://www.acphs.edu/*
Contact: *https://www.acphs.edu/requestinfo*
Phone: (518) 694-7200

Other locations: Colchester, VT

COST OF ATTENDANCE

Tuition and Fees: $41,780
Additional Expenses: $14,461
Total: $56,241

Financial Aid: https://www.acphs.edu/professional-pharmacy-students-p1

ADDITIONAL INFORMATION

Interesting tidbit: At ACPH, students can gain firsthand experience in a student-operated pharmacy and obtain your pharmacy intern permit and help immunize patients after the P1 year.

Important Updates due to COVID-19: Accept grades of "Pass" and "Credit" (from Pass/Fail and Credit/No Credit grading policies) for courses completed during the Spring 2020, Fall 2020, and Spring 2021 semester. Due to the COVID-19 pandemic, for both the 2020-2021 and 2021-2022 application cycles, the PCAT is optional. Beyond Fall 2022 entry, the PCAT will be recommended for students with a GPA less than 3.0.

Were tests required? No.

Are tests expected next year? No.

What international experiences are available? Advanced rotation (APPE) sites abroad, in locations such as England, Switzerland, and Italy. Other service learning trips in South America.

What dual degree options exist? No dual degree options listed.

What service learning opportunities exist? See international experiences.

What percent of graduates place in postgraduate training? 22.5% (2020)

NAPLEX First-Time Pass Rate: 85.87% (2020)

MPJE First-Time Pass Rate: 85.85% (2020)

Other: The 4-year program is located in Albany, NY. The 3-year Accelerated program is located in Colchester, VT.

Early Assurance Program available to high school applicants. PCAT not required. For more information, visit: https://www.acphs.edu/early-assurance

BINGHAMTON UNIVERSITY STATE UNIVERSITY OF NEW YORK SCHOOL OF PHARMACY AND PHARMACEUTICAL SCIENCES

Address: 96 Corliss Avenue, Johnson City, NY 13790
Website: *https://www.binghamton.edu/pharmacy-and-pharmaceutical-sciences/*
Contact: *https://www.binghamton.edu/pharmacy-and-pharmaceutical-sciences/students/future/request-information.html*
Phone: (607) 777-2151

COST OF ATTENDANCE

In-State Tuition and Fees: $30,309
Additional Expenses: N/A
Total: $30,309*

Out-of-State Tuition and Fees: $49,999
Additional Expenses: N/A
Total: $49,999*

*Note: These figures do not reflect estimated housing/living expenses.

Financial Aid: https://www.binghamton.edu/pharmacy-and-pharmaceutical-sciences/students/future/fin-aid-scholarships.html

ADDITIONAL INFORMATION

Interesting tidbit: 2020-21 marked the first year possible for Binghamton University School of Pharmacy and Pharmaceutical Sciences students to apply for residencies and six were matched.

Important Updates due to COVID-19: Virtual Interview

Were tests required? PCAT required.

Are tests expected next year? Yes.

What international experiences are available? Students may complete a global health experience as part of their Advanced Pharmacy Practice Experiences (APPEs).

What dual degree options exist? No dual degree options listed.

What service learning opportunities exist? Service learning through experiential education. For more information, visit: https://www.binghamton.edu/pharmacy-and-pharmaceutical-sciences/departments/experiential-education/index.html

What percent of graduates place in postgraduate training? 6.6% (2021)

NAPLEX First-Time Pass Rate: N/A

MPJE First-Time Pass Rate: N/A

Other: Pharmacy Early Acceptance Program (PEA) for current Binghamton first-year students or Educational Opportunity Program second-year students. For more information, visit: https://www.binghamton.edu/pharmacy-and-pharmaceutical-sciences/students/future/application.html

3+4 and 2+4 degree programs available. For more information, visit: https://www.binghamton.edu/pharmacy-and-pharmaceutical-sciences/students/future/3-plus-4-programs.html

CONNECTICUT

MAINE

MASSACHUSETTS

NEW HAMPSHIRE

NEW JERSEY

NEW YORK

PENNSYLVANIA

RHODE ISLAND

VERMONT

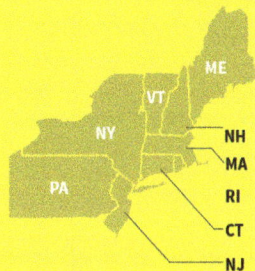

NORTHEAST

CONNECTICUT

MAINE

MASSACHUSETTS

NEW HAMPSHIRE

NEW JERSEY

NEW YORK

PENNSYLVANIA

RHODE ISLAND

VERMONT

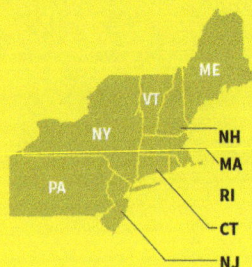

D'YOUVILLE COLLEGE SCHOOL OF PHARMACY

Address: 320 Porter Avenue, Buffalo, NY 14201
Website: *http://www.dyc.edu/academics/schools-and-departments/pharmacy/*
Contact: *http://www.dyc.edu/academics/schools-and-departments/pharmacy/about-the-school/contact.aspx*
Phone: (716) 829-8000

COST OF ATTENDANCE

Tuition and Fees: $38,112
Additional Expenses: N/A
Total: $38,112*

*Note: This figure does not reflect estimated housing/living expenses.

Financial Aid: http://www.dyc.edu/Admissions/financial-aid-scholarships/types-of-aid/scholarships/graduate.aspx

ADDITIONAL INFORMATION

Interesting tidbit: D'Youville's unique interdisciplinary education lab offers the opportunity for you to practice treating patients (played by actors) alongside a team of students from 7 other healthcare majors at D'Youville - all under the supervision of a skilled instructor.

Important Updates due to COVID-19: Virtual Interview

Were tests required? No.

Are tests expected next year? No.

What international experiences are available? International exchange programs. For more information, visit: http://www.dyc.edu/academics/schools-and-departments/pharmacy/about-the-school/advocacy-and-service.aspx

What dual degree options exist? No dual degree options listed.

What service learning opportunities exist? Community outreach programs. For more information, visit: http://www.dyc.edu/academics/schools-and-departments/pharmacy/about-the-school/advocacy-and-service.aspx

What percent of graduates place in postgraduate training? N/A

NAPLEX First-Time Pass Rate: 75.93% (2020)

MPJE First-Time Pass Rate: 78.38% (2020)

Other: Early Assurance Program (2+4) available. For more information, visit: http://www.dyc.edu/academics/schools-and-departments/pharmacy/programs-and-degrees/pre-pharmacy.aspx

LONG ISLAND UNIVERSITY ARNOLD AND MARIE SCHWARTZ COLLEGE OF PHARMACY AND HEALTH SCIENCES

Address: 75 Dekalb Avenue, Brooklyn, NY 11201
Website: *https://liu.edu/Pharmacy*
Contact: *https://apply.liu.edu/form/inquiry.aspx?id=1*
Phone: (718) 488-1234

COST OF ATTENDANCE

Tuition and Fees: $52,832
Additional Expenses: N/A
Total: $52,832*

*Note: This figure does not reflect estimated housing/living expenses.

Financial Aid: https://www.liu.edu/Brooklyn/Enrollment-Services/Financial-Aid

ADDITIONAL INFORMATION

Interesting tidbit: LIU Pharmacy offers a six-year Doctor of Pharmacy (Pharm.D.) degree program. The program consists of two years of preprofessional studies (offered through LIU Brooklyn's Richard L. Conolly College of Liberal Arts and Sciences) and four years of professional studies.

Important Updates due to COVID-19: Due to the coronavirus pandemic, applicants do not need approval from the Admissions office to take online coursework to fulfill prerequisite courses for the 2020-21 academic year.

Were tests required? No.

Are tests expected next year? No.

What international experiences are available? N/A

What dual degree options exist? PharmD/MBA and PharmD/MPH. For more information, visit: https://liu.edu/Pharmacy/Programs

What service learning opportunities exist? N/A

What percent of graduates place in postgraduate training? 18.2% (2020)

NAPLEX First-Time Pass Rate: 82.61% (2020)

MPJE First-Time Pass Rate: 75.68% (2020)

Other: Early Assurance Admission pathway available. For more information, visit: https://liu.edu/Pharmacy/Admissions/PharmD/Admissions-Pathways

CONNECTICUT

MAINE

MASSACHUSETTS

NEW HAMPSHIRE

NEW JERSEY

NEW YORK

PENNSYLVANIA

RHODE ISLAND

VERMONT

NORTHEAST

CONNECTICUT

MAINE

MASSACHUSETTS

NEW HAMPSHIRE

NEW JERSEY

NEW YORK

PENNSYLVANIA

RHODE ISLAND

VERMONT

ST. JOHN FISHER COLLEGE WEGMANS SCHOOL OF PHARMACY

Address: 3690 East Avenue, Rochester, NY 14618
Website: *https://www.sjfc.edu/schools/school-of-pharmacy/*
Contact: *https://www.sjfc.edu/Admissions-aid/request-information/*
Phone: (585) 385-8000

COST OF ATTENDANCE

Tuition and Fees: $42,975
Additional Expenses: N/A
Total: $42,975*

*Note: This figure does not reflect estimated housing/living expenses.

Financial Aid: https://www.sjfc.edu/Admissions-aid/financial-aid/

ADDITIONAL INFORMATION

Interesting tidbit: The Wegmans School of Pharmacy opened in fall 2006 with an inaugural class of 55 students, nine faculty, and two staff. Since its beginning, the School has grown to include over 300 students in four classes and over 40 faculty and staff.

Important Updates due to COVID-19: For the 2021-2022 Admission cycle, the Wegmans School of Pharmacy is not requiring PCAT.

Were tests required? No.

Are tests expected next year? Yes.

What international experiences are available? Medical mission trips to El Salvador. For more information, visit: https://www.sjfc.edu/graduate-programs/doctor-of-pharmacy-pharmd/service-experiences/

What dual degree options exist? PharmD/MBA. For more information, visit: https://www.sjfc.edu/graduate-programs/doctor-of-pharmacy-pharmd/program-requirements/joint-pharmdmba/

What service learning opportunities exist? Various opportunities. For more information, visit: https://www.sjfc.edu/graduate-programs/doctor-of-pharmacy-pharmd/service-experiences/

What percent of graduates place in postgraduate training? 35.4% (2020)

NAPLEX First-Time Pass Rate: 87.84% (2020)

MPJE First-Time Pass Rate: 82.26% (2020)

Other: Early Assurance Program available. For more information, visit: https://www.sjfc.edu/major-minors/pre-health-professions/pharmacy-early-assurance-program/

ST. JOHN'S UNIVERSITY COLLEGE OF PHARMACY AND HEALTH SCIENCES

Address: 8000 Utopia Parkway, Queens, NY 11439
Website: *https://www.stjohns.edu/academics/programs/doctor-pharmacy*
Contact: *https://www.stjohns.edu/academics/schools/college-pharmacy-and-health-sciences/contact*
Phone: (718) 990-6362

COST OF ATTENDANCE

Tuition and Fees: $77,888
Additional Expenses: $20,485
Total: $98,373

Financial Aid: https://www.stjohns.edu/Admission/tuition-and-financial-aid

ADDITIONAL INFORMATION

Interesting tidbit: Pharm.D. students gain hands-on experience at St. John's more than 160 Affiliated Clinical Pharmacy Sites around the New York metropolitan area.

Important Updates due to COVID-19: Virtual Interview

Were tests required? No.

Are tests expected next year? No.

What international experiences are available? Study abroad experiences in Rome, Italy and Paris, France. For more information, visit: https://www.stjohns.edu/academics/programs/doctor-pharmacy

What dual degree options exist? No dual degree options listed.

What service learning opportunities exist? Service initiatives: https://www.stjohns.edu/academics/schools/college-pharmacy-and-health-sciences/about/service-initiatives

What percent of graduates place in postgraduate training?
15.3% (2019)

NAPLEX First-Time Pass Rate: 90.64% (2020)

MPJE First-Time Pass Rate: 83.24% (2020)

Note: This program is intended for high school applicants.

CONNECTICUT

MAINE

MASSACHUSETTS

NEW HAMPSHIRE

NEW JERSEY

NEW YORK

PENNSYLVANIA

RHODE ISLAND

VERMONT

NORTHEAST

TOURO NEW YORK COLLEGE OF PHARMACY

Address: 230 W. 125th St., New York, NY 10027
Website: *https://tcop.touro.edu/*
Contact: *https://tcop.touro.edu/request-more-information/*
Phone: (646) 981-4700

COST OF ATTENDANCE

Tuition and Fees: $43,000
Additional Expenses: $43,308
Total: $92,308

Financial Aid: https://tcop.touro.edu/Admissions--aid/financial-aid/

ADDITIONAL INFORMATION

Interesting tidbit: At TCOP, students can focus their education by selecting one of three tracks offered - research track, managed care track, and advanced patient track. If you know early on in your PharmD education (i.e., as you enter your second year) where your interests lie, you can focus your electives with one of the three tracks.

Important Updates due to COVID-19: Virtual Interview

Were tests required? No.

Are tests expected next year? No.

What international experiences are available? International APPE in Geneva with the WHO or Global Health Mission in Haiti, Ghana, or India.

What dual degree options exist? No dual degree options listed.

What service learning opportunities exist? See international experiences.

What percent of graduates place in postgraduate training? N/A

NAPLEX First-Time Pass Rate: 83.93% (2020)

MPJE First-Time Pass Rate: 69.23% (2020)

Other: Linkage agreements offering direct pathways/early Admission to Touro College of Pharmacy. For more information, visit: https://tcop.touro.edu/Admissions--aid/linkage-agreements/

CONNECTICUT

MAINE

MASSACHUSETTS

NEW HAMPSHIRE

NEW JERSEY

NEW YORK

PENNSYLVANIA

RHODE ISLAND

VERMONT

UNIVERSITY AT BUFFALO - THE STATE UNIVERSITY OF NEW YORK SCHOOL OF PHARMACY & PHARMACEUTICAL SCIENCES

Address: 285 Pharmacy Building, Buffalo, NY 14214
Website: *http://pharmacy.buffalo.edu/*
Contact: *http://pharmacy.buffalo.edu/about-us/contact-us.html*
Phone: (716) 645-2823

COST OF ATTENDANCE

In-State Tuition and Fees: $26,450
Additional Expenses: $22,512
Total: $48,962

Out-of-State Tuition and Fees: $37,140
Additional Expenses: $22,512
Total: $59,652

Financial Aid: http://pharmacy.buffalo.edu/academic-programs/pharmd/cost-financial-aid-awards.html

ADDITIONAL INFORMATION

Interesting tidbit: Micro-credential programs at UB School of Pharmacy and Pharmaceutical Sciences provide PharmD students with specialized knowledge in research, teaching, and professional development beyond that provided by the core curriculum, preparing you for postgraduate training. Students apply to these programs during the second professional year. There is no added time to degree.

Important Updates due to COVID-19: Virtual Interview

Were tests required? PCAT required for applicants with a math and science prerequisite GPA of less than 3.0.

Are tests expected next year? PCAT required for applicants with a math and science prerequisite GPA of less than 3.0.

What international experiences are available? Service trips abroad. For more information, visit: http://pharmacy.buffalo.edu/academic-programs/experiential-education/global-health.html

What dual degree options exist? Several options. For more information, visit: http://pharmacy.buffalo.edu/academic-programs/pharmd/combined-degrees.html

What service learning opportunities exist? Service learning through experiential education. For more information, visit: http://pharmacy.buffalo.edu/academic-programs/experiential-education.html

What percent of graduates place in postgraduate training? 76% (2020)

NAPLEX First-Time Pass Rate: 97.32% (2020)

MPJE First-Time Pass Rate: 93.51% (2020)

Other: Early Assurance (2+4) program available for high school applicants. For more information, visit: http://pharmacy.buffalo.edu/academic-programs/pharmd/early-assurance.html

International partnerships, combined programs, and various pathways. For more information, visit: http://pharmacy.buffalo.edu/academic-programs/pharmd/3_4_agreements.html

CONNECTICUT

MAINE

MASSACHUSETTS

NEW HAMPSHIRE

NEW JERSEY

NEW YORK

PENNSYLVANIA

RHODE ISLAND

VERMONT

NORTHEAST

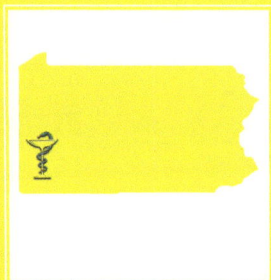

CONNECTICUT

MAINE

MASSACHUSETTS

NEW HAMPSHIRE

NEW JERSEY

NEW YORK

PENNSYLVANIA

RHODE ISLAND

VERMONT

DUQUESNE UNIVERSITY SCHOOL OF PHARMACY

Address: 600 Forbes Avenue, Pittsburgh, PA 15282
Website: *https://www.duq.edu/academics/schools/pharmacy*
Contact: *https://www.duq.edu/contact*
Phone: (412) 396-6393

COST OF ATTENDANCE

Tuition and Fees: $61,017
Additional Expenses: N/A
Total: $61,017*

*Note: This figure does not reflect estimated housing/living expenses.

Financial Aid: https://www.duq.edu/Admissions-and-aid/financial-aid

ADDITIONAL INFORMATION

Interesting tidbit: Students earn a Doctor of Pharmacy, (Pharm.D.) in six years at the Duquesne University School of Pharmacy. All students accepted into the School of Pharmacy as freshmen automatically enter the Early Assurance Program, essentially guaranteeing a spot in the professional phase of the program after meeting a few basic requirements. Also, students can transfer from accredited two and four-year colleges by applying for Admission into the first professional year of the PharmD.

Important Updates due to COVID-19: Virtual Interview

Were tests required? PCAT required.

Are tests expected next year? Yes.

What international experiences are available? Experiential education available in Italy.

What dual degree options exist? PharmD/MBA and PharmD/MS. For more information on the PharmD/MBA, visit: https://www.duq.edu/academics/schools/pharmacy/pharmd/pharmd/mba

What service learning opportunities exist? Experiential opportunities locally, nationally, and internationally. For more information, visit: https://www.duq.edu/academics/schools/pharmacy/pharmd/experiental-education

What percent of graduates place in postgraduate training? N/A

NAPLEX First-Time Pass Rate: 89.81% (2020)

MPJE First-Time Pass Rate: 90.40% (2020)

Other: Early Assurance Admission available to high school students. For more information, visit: https://www.duq.edu/academics/schools/pharmacy/pharmd/early-assurance

LAKE ERIE COLLEGE OF OSTEOPATHIC MEDICINE SCHOOL OF PHARMACY

Address: 1858 West Grandview Boulevard, Erie, PA 16509
Website: *https://lecom.edu/academics/school-of-pharmacy/*
Contact: *https://lecom.edu/contact-us/*
Phone: (814) 866-6641

Other locations: Bradenton, FL 4-Year Pathway. For more information, visit: https://lecom.edu/academics/school-of-pharmacy/pharmacy-pathways/pharmacy-four-year-pathway-bradenton/

COST OF ATTENDANCE

Tuition and Fees: $29,705
Additional Expenses: $31,431
Total: $61,136

Financial Aid: https://lecom.edu/Admissions/tuition-and-financial-aid/tuition-overview/financial-aid-lecom-scholarship-program/

ADDITIONAL INFORMATION

Interesting tidbit: LECOM is a single school of pharmacy operating out of two locations (Erie and Bradenton campuses). Three distinct learning pathways are offered for the PharmD degree providing students the option of choosing a pathway most suited to their learning needs - three-year Accelerated Pathway (Erie campus), four-year Florida Pathway (Bradenton campus), and four-year Distance Education Pathway.

Important Updates due to COVID-19: Virtual Interview

Were tests required? No.

Are tests expected next year? No.

What international experiences are available? N/A

What dual degree options exist? No dual degree options listed.

What service learning opportunities exist? Poison Prevention Education, Relay for Life, Health Fairs, and more.

What percent of graduates place in postgraduate training? N/A

NAPLEX First-Time Pass Rate: 84.43% (2020)

MPJE First-Time Pass Rate: 84.48% (2020)

CONNECTICUT

MAINE

MASSACHUSETTS

NEW HAMPSHIRE

NEW JERSEY

NEW YORK

PENNSYLVANIA

RHODE ISLAND

VERMONT

NORTHEAST

CONNECTICUT

MAINE

MASSACHUSETTS

NEW HAMPSHIRE

NEW JERSEY

NEW YORK

PENNSYLVANIA

RHODE ISLAND

VERMONT

TEMPLE UNIVERSITY SCHOOL OF PHARMACY

Address: 3307 North Broad Street, Philadelphia, PA 19140
Website: *https://pharmacy.temple.edu/*
Contact: *http://pharmacyinfo.temple.edu/inquiryform*
Phone: (215) 707-4900

COST OF ATTENDANCE

In-State Tuition and Fees: $35,644
Additional Expenses: N/A
Total: $35,644*

Out-of-State Tuition and Fees: $38,172
Additional Expenses: N/A
Total: $37,878*

*Note: These figures do not reflect estimated housing/living expenses.

Financial Aid: https://pharmacy.temple.edu/Admissions/tuition-and-financial-aid

ADDITIONAL INFORMATION

Interesting tidbit: During your third year of professional study at TUSP, students can begin to differentiate your degree by choosing electives in one of the following tracks - Clinical Trials, Business, Drug Safety and Advanced Clinical Practice.

Important Updates due to COVID-19: Virtual Interview

Were tests required? No.

Are tests expected next year? No.

What international experiences are available? N/A

What dual degree options exist? PharmD/MBA and PharmD/MS.

What service learning opportunities exist? N/A

What percent of graduates place in postgraduate training? 33% (2019)

NAPLEX First-Time Pass Rate: 94.26% (2020)

MPJE First-Time Pass Rate: 74.00% (2020)

THOMAS JEFFERSON UNIVERSITY
JEFFERSON COLLEGE OF PHARMACY

Address: 901 Walnut Street, Philadelphia, PA 19107
Website: *https://www.jefferson.edu/university/pharmacy.html*
Contact: *http://explore.jefferson.edu/inquiryform*
Phone: (215) 503-8890

COST OF ATTENDANCE

Tuition and Fees: $39,655
Additional Expenses: $14,494
Total: $54,149

Financial Aid: https://www.jefferson.edu/university/pharmacy/Admissions/tuition.html

ADDITIONAL INFORMATION

Interesting tidbit: As part of Thomas Jefferson University, the largest freestanding academic medical center in Philadelphia, the Jefferson College of Pharmacy (JCP) is a partner in one of the country's most successful and highly recognized interprofessional healthcare learning environments. JCP students will get first-hand experience in a Department of Pharmacy renowned as one of the world's most contemporary health system pharmacy practices.

Important Updates due to COVID-19: Virtual Interview

Were tests required? No.

Are tests expected next year? No.

What international experiences are available? Elective rotations may be at an international site.

What dual degree options exist? PharmD/MPH. For more information, visit: https://www.jefferson.edu/academics/colleges-schools-institutes/population-health/degrees-programs/degrees-graduate-certificates/public-health/Pathways/dual-degrees/PharmDMPH.html

What service learning opportunities exist? Service learning through experiential education.

What percent of graduates place in postgraduate training? 34% (2019)

NAPLEX First-Time Pass Rate: 98.08% (2020)

MPJE First-Time Pass Rate: 87.50% (2020)

CONNECTICUT

MAINE

MASSACHUSETTS

NEW HAMPSHIRE

NEW JERSEY

NEW YORK

PENNSYLVANIA

RHODE ISLAND

VERMONT

NORTHEAST

CONNECTICUT

MAINE

MASSACHUSETTS

NEW HAMPSHIRE

NEW JERSEY

NEW YORK

PENNSYLVANIA

RHODE ISLAND

VERMONT

UNIVERSITY OF PITTSBURGH SCHOOL OF PHARMACY

Address: 3501 Terrace St, Pittsburgh, PA 15261
Website: *https://www.pharmacy.pitt.edu/*
Contact: *https://www.pharmacy.pitt.edu/about/contact_us.php*
Phone: (412) 624-5240

COST OF ATTENDANCE

In-State Tuition and Fees: $33,812
Additional Expenses: N/A
Total: $33,812*

Out-of-State Tuition and Fees: $39,220
Additional Expenses: N/A
Total: $39,220*

*Note: These figures do not reflect estimated housing/living expenses.

Financial Aid: https://students.pharmacy.pitt.edu/list-of-scholarships//

ADDITIONAL INFORMATION

Interesting tidbit: Each PharmD student at PittPharmacy maintains an electronic portfolio, building its contents with evolving career plans, evidence of developing knowledge and skills, unique experiences and accomplishments, and self-reflections as he or she progresses through the curriculum. The portfolio serves as the focus for personalized mentoring and career planning conversations held twice annually with a faculty advisor.

Important Updates due to COVID-19: Virtual Interview

Were tests required? PCAT required.

Are tests expected next year? Yes.

What international experiences are available? Service learning and global health concentration. For more information, visit: https://www.pharmacy.pitt.edu/programs/GlobalHealth/global_health.php

What dual degree options exist? PharmD/PhD.

What service learning opportunities exist? Community Leadership and Innovation in Practice Center. For more information, visit: https://www.clip.pharmacy.pitt.edu/

What percent of graduates place in postgraduate training? 79% (2020)

NAPLEX First-Time Pass Rate: 95.41% (2020)

MPJE First-Time Pass Rate: 95.18% (2020)

Other: Pharmacy Guarantee pathway available for high school applicants. For more information, visit: https://pages.pharmacy.pitt.edu/pharmdhandbook/the-pharmd-student-handbook/Admissions/types-of-Admission/

UNIVERSITY OF THE SCIENCES
PHILADELPHIA COLLEGE OF PHARMACY

Address: 600 South 43rd Street, Philadelphia, PA 19104
Website: *https://www.usciences.edu/philadelphia-college-of-pharmacy/*
Contact: *https://www.usciences.edu/Admission/request-information/index.html*
Phone: (215) 596-8800

COST OF ATTENDANCE

Tuition and Fees: $35,000
Additional Expenses: $16,813
Total: $51,813

Financial Aid: https://www.usciences.edu/philadelphia-college-of-pharmacy/pharmacy-pharmd/cost-financial-aid.html

ADDITIONAL INFORMATION

Interesting tidbit: Philadelphia College of Pharmacy (PCP) is the first college of pharmacy in North America. It offers three admission pathways - direct-entry freshman, transfer or graduate student. During the four-year professional phase of the curriculum, students will complete 14 Integrated Pharmacy Sciences, Disease, and Therapeutics (iPSDT) modules and hands-on simulations from PioneerRX pharmacy software.

Important Updates due to COVID-19: Virtual Interview

Were tests required? No.

Are tests expected next year? No.

What international experiences are available? Pharmacy rotations abroad.

What dual degree options exist? No dual degree options listed.

What service learning opportunities exist? Service learning through experiential education. For more information, visit: https://www.usciences.edu/philadelphia-college-of-pharmacy/pharmacy-pharmd/experiential-opportunities.html

What percent of graduates place in postgraduate training? 37% (2020)

NAPLEX First-Time Pass Rate: 84.03% (2020)

MPJE First-Time Pass Rate: 85.71% (202)

Other: Direct entry (6-year program) available for high school students. For more information, visit: https://www.usciences.edu/philadelphia-college-of-pharmacy/pharmacy-pharmd/direct-entry-Admission.html

CONNECTICUT

MAINE

MASSACHUSETTS

NEW HAMPSHIRE

NEW JERSEY

NEW YORK

PENNSYLVANIA

RHODE ISLAND

VERMONT

NORTHEAST

WILKES UNIVERSITY NESBITT SCHOOL OF PHARMACY

Address: 84 West South Street, Wilkes-Barre, PA 18766
Website: *https://www.wilkes.edu/academics/colleges/nesbitt-school-of-pharmacy/index.aspx*
Contact: *https://www.wilkes.edu/campus-directory/*
Phone: (800) 945-5378

COST OF ATTENDANCE

Tuition and Fees: $42,448
Additional Expenses: N/A
Total: $42,448*

*Note: This figure does not reflect estimated housing/living expenses.

Financial Aid: https://www.wilkes.edu/academics/graduate-programs/graduate-Admissions/financial-aid-graduate/index.aspx

ADDITIONAL INFORMATION

Interesting tidbit: All pharmacy students enter a formal four-year program in communication skills as well as in team building and team leadership. Students will reinforce their ability to articulate their knowledge with health professionals, administrators and patients and to work effectively as part of a healthcare team.

Important Updates due to COVID-19: Virtual Interview

Were tests required? PCAT required.

Are tests expected next year? Yes.

What international experiences are available? N/A

What dual degree options exist? PharmD/MBA. For more information, visit: https://wilkes.edu/pharmDmba

What service learning opportunities exist? Public Health Concentration available. For more information, visit: https://www.wilkes.edu/academics/colleges/nesbitt-school-of-pharmacy/program-information/dual-degrees-concentrations-and-minors/pharmd-public-health-concentration.aspx

What percent of graduates place in postgraduate training? 73.1% (PGY1) and 80% (PGY2) for 2020

NAPLEX First-Time Pass Rate: 95.83% (2020)

MPJE First-Time Pass Rate: 100% (2020)

Other: Guaranteed Seat Program for high school applicants available. For more information, visit: https://www.wilkes.edu/academics/colleges/nesbitt-school-of-pharmacy/program-information/pre-pharmacy-guaranteed-seat-program/index.aspx

CONNECTICUT

MAINE

MASSACHUSETTS

NEW HAMPSHIRE

NEW JERSEY

NEW YORK

PENNSYLVANIA

RHODE ISLAND

VERMONT

UNIVERSITY OF RHODE ISLAND COLLEGE OF PHARMACY

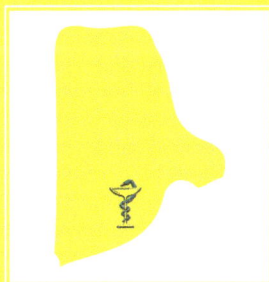

Address: 7 Greenhouse Road, Kingston, RI 02881
Website: *https://web.uri.edu/pharmacy/*
Contact: *https://Admissions.uri.edu/register/request-information*
Phone: (401) 874-2761

COST OF ATTENDANCE

In-State Tuition and Fees: $15,332
Additional Expenses: $17,014
Total: $32,346

Out-of-State Tuition and Fees: $33,354
Additional Expenses: $17,014
Total: $51,066

NE Regional Tuition and Fees: $25,270*
Additional Expenses: $17,014
Total: $67,554

*New England residents pay NE regional tuition.

Financial Aid: https://web.uri.edu/enrollment/financial-aid/

ADDITIONAL INFORMATION

Interesting tidbit: The URI offers a six-year entry-level Doctor of Pharmacy (Pharm.D.) degree. Students come to us directly from high school, through application to the zero-6 program. University Admissions is currently not accepting transfer applications for the Pharm.D. program.

Important Updates due to COVID-19: Virtual Interview

Were tests required? SAT or ACT required.

Are tests expected next year? Yes.

What international experiences are available? Study abroad opportunities available. For more information, visit: https://web.uri.edu/pharmacy/students/international-experiences/

What dual degree options exist? PharmD/MBA and PharmD/MS. For more information, visit: https://web.uri.edu/pharmacy/academics/

What service learning opportunities exist? Outreach opportunities available. For more information, visit: https://web.uri.edu/pharmacy/services/

What percent of graduates place in postgraduate training? 72% (2020)

NAPLEX First-Time Pass Rate: 93.75% (2020)

MPJE First-Time Pass Rate: 86.67% (2020)

Note: This program is intended for high school applicants, although a limited number of transfer students are accepted

CONNECTICUT

MAINE

MASSACHUSETTS

NEW HAMPSHIRE

NEW JERSEY

NEW YORK

PENNSYLVANIA

RHODE ISLAND

VERMONT

NORTHEAST

CHAPTER 3

REGION TWO

MIDWEST

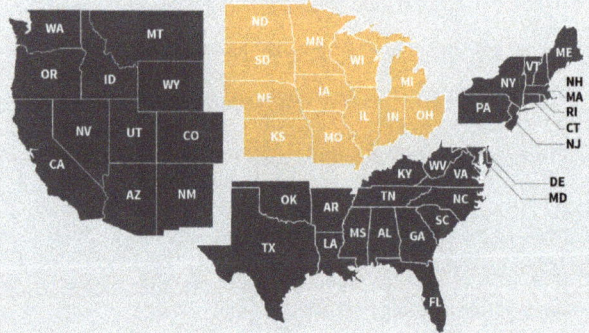

ILLINOIS

INDIANA

IOWA

KANSAS

MICHIGAN

MINNESOTA

MISSOURI

NEBRASKA

NORTH DAKOTA

OHIO

SOUTH DAKOTA

WISCONSIN

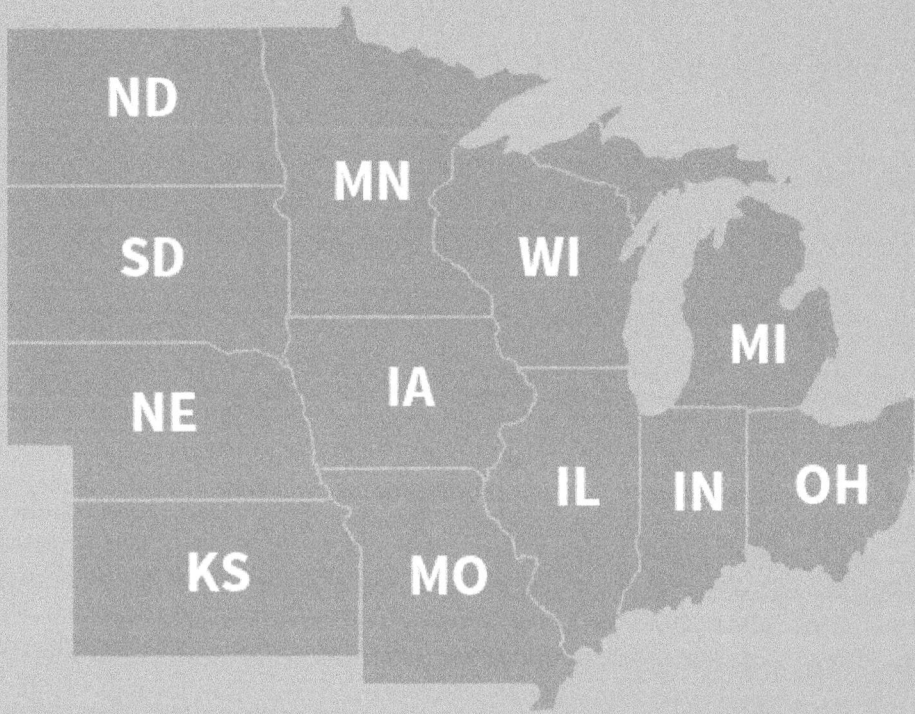

32 Programs | 12 States

1. IL – Chicago State University College of Pharmacy
2. IL - Midwestern University Chicago College of Pharmacy
3. IL - Roosevelt University College of Pharmacy
4. IL - Rosalind Franklin University of Medicine and Science College of Pharmacy
5. IL - Southern Illinois University Edwardsville School of Pharmacy
6. IL - University of Illinois at Chicago College of Pharmacy
7. IN - Butler University College of Pharmacy and Health Sciences
8. IN - Manchester University College of Pharmacy, Natural and Health Sciences
9. IN - Purdue University College of Pharmacy
10. IA - Drake University College of Pharmacy and Health Sciences
11. IA - University of Iowa College of Pharmacy
12. KS - University of Kansas School of Pharmacy
13. MI - Ferris State University College of Pharmacy
14. MI - University of Michigan College of Pharmacy
15. MI - Wayne State University Eugene Applebaum College of Pharmacy and Health Sciences
16. MN - University of Minnesota College of Pharmacy
17. MO - St. Louis College of Pharmacy
18. MO - University of Missouri-Kansas City School of Pharmacy
19. NE - Creighton University School of Pharmacy and Health Professions
20. NE - University of Nebraska Medical Center College of Pharmacy
21. ND - North Dakota State University College of Health Professions School of Pharmacy
22. OH - Cedarville University School of Pharmacy
23. OH - Northeast Ohio Medical University College of Pharmacy
24. OH - Ohio Northern University Raabe College of Pharmacy
25. OH - Ohio State University College of Pharmacy
26. OH - University of Cincinnati James L. Winkle College of Pharmacy
27. OH - University of Findlay College of Pharmacy
28. OH - University of Toledo College of Pharmacy and Pharmaceutical Sciences
29. SD - South Dakota State University College of Pharmacy and Allied Health Professions
30. WI - Concordia University Wisconsin School of Pharmacy
31. WI - Medical College of Wisconsin School of Pharmacy
32. WI - University of Wisconsin-Madison School of Pharmacy

PHARMACY PROGRAMS

Pharmacy School	Ave. GPA & PCAT (%) / Early Decision (ED): Yes/No / Int'l Students: Yes/No	Admissions Statistics	Science Req. Other than Gen Chem, OChem, Physics, Bio
Chicago State University 9501 S. King Dr., Chicago, IL 60628	3.10 PCAT: Not Req. ED: Yes Int'l Student: Yes	(2019) Apps Received: 389 Interviews Offered: N/A Admission Offered: N/A Number Enrolled: 65 Admitted Rate: 16.7% (2020) Apps Received: 216 Interviews Offered: N/A Admission Offered: N/A Number Enrolled: 48 Admitted Rate: 22.2%	Anatomy w/ Lab Calc. Stats. Psych./Sociology
Midwestern University Chicago* 555 31st Street, Downers Grove, IL 60515	3.10 PCAT: Not Req. ED: Yes Int'l Student: Yes	(2019) Apps Received: 744 Interviews Offered: N/A Admission Offered: N/A Number Enrolled: 146 Admitted Rate: 19.6% (2020) Apps Received: 496 Interviews Offered: N/A Admission Offered: N/A Number Enrolled: 108 Admitted Rate: 21.8%	Human/Vertebrate Anatomy Soc.Behav. Science Electives Calc. Stats. *This is an accelerated 3-year PharmD program.
Roosevelt University* 1400 N Roosevelt Blvd, Schaumburg, IL 60173	3.15 (overall) 3.01 (math/science) PCAT: 33 ED: No Int'l Student: Yes	(2019) Apps Received: 389 Interviews Offered: N/A Admission Offered: N/A Number Enrolled: 72 Admitted Rate: 18.5% (2020) Apps Received: 279 Interviews Offered: N/A Admission Offered: N/A Number Enrolled: 56 Admitted Rate: 20.1%	Anatomy & Physio. w/ Lab Stats. Social/Behav. Sci. *This is an accelerated 3-year PharmD program.

Pharmacy School	Ave. GPA & PCAT (%) / Early Decision (ED): Yes/No / Int'l Students: Yes/No	Admissions Statistics	Science Req. Other than Gen Chem, OChem, Physics, Bio
Rosalind Franklin University 3333 Green Bay Rd, North Chicago, IL 60064	3.16 (overall) 2.60 (math/science) PCAT: 397.2 ED: Yes Int'l Student: Yes	(2019) Apps Received: 404 Interviews Offered: N/A Admission Offered: N/A Number Enrolled: 65 Admitted Rate: 18.3% (2020) Apps Received: 315 Interviews Offered: N/A Admission Offered: N/A Number Enrolled: 63 Admitted Rate: 20.0%	Anatomy/Anatomy & Physio. w/ Lab Calc. Social/Behav. Sci
Southern Illinois University Edwardsville 200 University Park Dr., Edwardsville, IL 62025	3.60 PCAT: Not Req. ED: Yes Int'l Student: Yes	(2019) Apps Received: 218 Interviews Offered: N/A Admission Offered: N/A Number Enrolled: 82 Admitted Rate: 37.6% (2020) Apps Received: 175 Interviews Offered: N/A Admission Offered: N/A Number Enrolled: 74 Admitted Rate: 42.3%	Anatomy & Physio. w/ Lab Microbio./Bacteriology Calc. Stats. Behav./Soc. Sci
University of Illinois at Chicago 833 S. Wood Street, Chicago, IL 60612	3.50 PCAT: Optional ED: Yes Int'l Student: Yes	(2019) Apps Received: 668 Interviews Offered: 400 Admission Offered: N/A Number Enrolled: 196 Admitted Rate: 29.3% (2020) Apps Received: 454 Interviews Offered: N/A Admission Offered: N/A Number Enrolled: 176 Admitted Rate: 38.8%	Anatomy & Physio. Microbio. w/ Lab Biochem. Calc. Stats. Social/Behav. Sci

MIDWEST

PHARMACY PROGRAMS

Pharmacy School	Ave. GPA & PCAT (%) / Early Decision (ED): Yes/No / Int'l Students: Yes/No	Admissions Statistics	Science Req. Other than Gen Chem, OChem, Physics, Bio
Butler University 4600 Sunset Ave, Indianapolis, IN 46208	3.50 PCAT: Not Req. ED: No Int'l Student: Yes	(2019) Apps Received: 286 Interviews Offered: N/A Admission Offered: N/A Number Enrolled: 132 Admitted Rate: 46.2% (2020) Apps Received: 217 Interviews Offered: N/A Admission Offered: N/A Number Enrolled: 110 Admitted Rate: 50.7%	Cell Bio. Microbio. w/ Lab Anatomy & Physio. Calc.
Manchester University 604 E College Ave, North Manchester, IN 46962	3.11 PCAT: Not Req. ED: Yes Int'l Student: Yes	(2019) Apps Received: 449 Interviews Offered: N/A Admission Offered: 114 Number Enrolled: 63 Admitted Rate: 14% (2020) Apps Received: 231 Interviews Offered: N/A Admission Offered: N/A Number Enrolled: 69 Admitted Rate: 29.9%	Anatomy & Physio. Microbio. w/ Lab Stats. Calc. Social Sci.
Purdue University 575 Stadium Mall Dr., West Lafayette, IN 47907	3.40 PCAT: Not Req. ED: No Int'l Student: Yes	(2019) Apps Received: 401 Interviews Offered: N/A Admission Offered: 275 Number Enrolled: 153 Admitted Rate: 38.2% (2020) Apps Received: 377 Interviews Offered: N/A Admission Offered: N/A Number Enrolled: 148 Admitted Rate: 39.3%	Anatomy & Physio. w/ Lab Calc. Microbio. Immunology Biochem. Stats.

PHARMACY PROGRAMS

Pharmacy School	Ave. GPA & PCAT (%) / Early Decision (ED): Yes/No / Int'l Students: Yes/No	Admissions Statistics	Science Req. Other than Gen Chem, OChem, Physics, Bio
Drake University 2802 Forest Ave., Des Moines, IA 50311	3.50 PCAT: N/A ED: Yes Int'l Student: Yes	(2019) Apps Received: 202 Interviews Offered: N/A Admission Offered: N/A Number Enrolled: 87 Admitted Rate: 43% (2020) Apps Received: 163 Interviews Offered: N/A Admission Offered: N/A Number Enrolled: 77 Admitted Rate: 47.2%	Microbio. w/ Lab Stats. Calc.
University of Iowa 180 South Grand Avenue, Iowa City, IA 52242	(2019) Apps Received: 267 Interviews Offered: N/A Admission Offered: N/A Number Enrolled: 100 Admitted Rate: 37.5% (2020) Apps Received: 184 Interviews Offered: N/A Admission Offered: N/A Number Enrolled: 100 Admitted Rate: 54.3%	(2019) Apps Received: 267 Interviews Offered: N/A Admission Offered: N/A Number Enrolled: 100 Admitted Rate: 37.5% (2020) Apps Received: 184 Interviews Offered: N/A Admission Offered: N/A Number Enrolled: 100 Admitted Rate: 54.3%	Stats. Calc. Anatomy Physio. Biochem. Microbio.

MIDWEST

PHARMACY PROGRAMS

Pharmacy School	Ave. GPA & PCAT (%) Early Decision (ED): Yes/No Int'l Students: Yes/No	Admissions Statistics	Science Req. Other than Gen Chem, OChem, Physics, Bio
University of Kansas 2010 Becker Dr., Lawrence, KS 66047	3.50 PCAT: 65 ED: Yes Int'l Student: Yes	(2019) Apps Received: 207 Interviews Offered: N/A Admission Offered: N/A Number Enrolled: 148 Admitted Rate: 71.5% (2020) Apps Received: 236 Interviews Offered: N/A Admission Offered: N/A Number Enrolled: 132 Admitted Rate: 55.9%	Calc. Microbio. Anatomy Physio. Molecular/Cell. Bio. Social Sci./Humanities Stats.
Ferris State University 220 Ferris Dr., Big Rapids, MI 49307	3.37 (overall) 3.17 (math/science) PCAT: Not Req. ED: Yes Int'l Student: Yes	(2019) Apps Received: 377 Interviews Offered: N/A Admission Offered: N/A Number Enrolled: 142 Admitted Rate: 37.7% (2020) Apps Received: 219 Interviews Offered: N/A Admission Offered: N/A Number Enrolled: 97 Admitted Rate: 44.3%	Biochem. Anatomy & Physio. Microbio. w/ Lab Genetics Calc. Stats. Psych./Sociology
University of Michigan 428 Church St., Ann Arbor, MI 48109	3.40 PCAT: Not Req. ED: Yes Int'l Student: Yes	(2019) Apps Received: 305 Interviews Offered: N/A Admission Offered: N/A Number Enrolled: 92 Admitted Rate: 30.2% (2020) Apps Received: 231 Interviews Offered: N/A Admission Offered: N/A Number Enrolled: 85 Admitted Rate: 36.8%	Biochem. Calc. Genetics Human Anatomy Human Physio. Microbio. w/ Lab Stats. Social Science

PHARMACY PROGRAMS

Pharmacy School	Ave. GPA & PCAT (%) — Early Decision (ED): Yes/No — Int'l Students: Yes/No	Admissions Statistics	Science Req. Other than Gen Chem, OChem, Physics, Bio
Wayne State University 259 Mack Ave., Detroit, MI 48201	3.70 PCAT: 75 ED: Yes Int'l Student: Yes	(2019) Apps Received: 258 Interviews Offered: N/A Admission Offered: 160 Number Enrolled: 103 Admitted Rate: 39.9% (2020) Apps Received: 211 Interviews Offered: N/A Admission Offered: N/A Number Enrolled: 96 Admitted Rate: 45.5%	Biochem. Calc. Stats. Anatomy & Physio. Microbio. w/ Lab
University of Minnesota 232 Life Science, 1110 Kirby Dr., Duluth, MN 55812	3.34 (overall) 3.19 (science) PCAT: 70 ED: Yes Int'l Student: Yes	(2019) Apps Received: 444 Interviews Offered: N/A Admission Offered: N/A Number Enrolled: 172 Admitted Rate: 38.7% (2020) Apps Received: 293 Interviews Offered: N/A Admission Offered: N/A Number Enrolled: 147 Admitted Rate: 50.2%	Microbio. (w/ lab pref.) Human/Comparative Anatomy (w/ lab pref) Human/Comparative Physio. (w/ lab pref) Advanced Bio. Calc. Stats. Soc./Behav. Sciences

MIDWEST

PHARMACY PROGRAMS

Pharmacy School	Ave. GPA & PCAT (%) Early Decision (ED): Yes/No Int'l Students: Yes/No	Admissions Statistics	Science Req. Other than Gen Chem, OChem, Physics, Bio
St. Louis College of Pharmacy 1 Pharmacy Place St. Louis, Missouri 63110	3.50 PCAT: N/A ED: Yes Int'l Student: Yes	(2019) Apps Received: 295 Interviews Offered: N/A Admission Offered: N/A Number Enrolled: 209 Admitted Rate: 70.8% (2020) Apps Received: 251 Interviews Offered: N/A Admission Offered: N/A Number Enrolled: 131 Admitted Rate: 52.2%	Biochem. Human Anatomy & Physio. w/ Lab Microbio. w/ Lab Calc. Stats. Psych./Sociology
University of Missouri-Kansas City 2464 Charlotte St., Kansas City, MO 64108	3.50 PCAT: 65 ED: Yes Int'l Student: Yes	(2019) Apps Received: 275 Interviews Offered: N/A Admission Offered: 193 Number Enrolled: 151 Admitted Rate: 54.9% (2020) Apps Received: 208 Interviews Offered: N/A Admission Offered: N/A Number Enrolled: 146 Admitted Rate: 70.2%	Calc. w/ Analytical Geom. Human Anatomy w/ Lab Microbio. w/ Lab Medical Terminology Stats. Cell Bio.
Creighton University 2500 California Plaza, Omaha, NE 68178	3.30 PCAT: Not Req. ED: Yes Int'l Student: Yes	(2019) Apps Received: 1,000 Interviews Offered: N/A Admission Offered: N/A Number Enrolled: 146 Admitted Rate: 14.6% (2020) Apps Received: 453 Interviews Offered: N/A Admission Offered: N/A Number Enrolled: 141 Admitted Rate: 31.1%	Human Anatomy Calc. Psych.

PHARMACY PROGRAMS

Pharmacy School	Ave. GPA & PCAT (%) / Early Decision (ED): Yes/No / Int'l Students: Yes/No	Admissions Statistics	Science Req. Other than Gen Chem, OChem, Physics, Bio
University of Nebraska 42nd and Emile, Omaha, NE 68198	3.60 PCAT: Not Req. (but preferred) ED: Yes Int'l Student: Yes	(2019) Apps Received: 119 Interviews Offered: N/A Admission Offered: N/A Number Enrolled: 63 Admitted Rate: 52.9% (2020) Apps Received: 77 Interviews Offered: N/A Admission Offered: N/A Number Enrolled: 63 Admitted Rate: 81.8%	Biochem. Anatomy Physio. Calc. Stats./Biostats.
North Dakota State University 1401 Albrecht Blvd., Fargo, ND 58102	3.70 PCAT: 63 ED: No Int'l Student: Yes	(2019) Apps Received: N/A Interviews Offered: N/A Admission Offered: N/A Number Enrolled: N/A Admitted Rate: N/A (2020) Apps Received: 453 Interviews Offered: N/A Admission Offered: N/A Number Enrolled: 74 Admitted Rate: 16.3%	Anatomy & Physio. w/ Lab Microbio. w/ Lab Biochem. Stats. Calc. Soc./Behav. Sci
Cedarville University 251 N. Main St., Cedarville, OH 45314	N/A PCAT: Not Req. ED: Yes Cedarville University 251 N. Main St., Cedarville, OH 45314 Int'l Student: Yes	(2019) Apps Received: 96 Interviews Offered: 40 Admission Offered: N/A Number Enrolled: 25 Admitted Rate: 26% (2020) Apps Received: 81 Interviews Offered: N/A Admission Offered: N/A Number Enrolled: 42 Admitted Rate: 51.9%	Anatomy & Physio. w/ Lab Microbio. w/ Lab Cell Bio. Advanced Physio.

MIDWEST

PHARMACY PROGRAMS

Pharmacy School	Ave. GPA & PCAT (%) / Early Decision (ED): Yes/No / Int'l Students: Yes/No	Admissions Statistics	Science Req. Other than Gen Chem, OChem, Physics, Bio
Northeast Ohio Medical University 4209 St., Rootstown, OH 44272	N/A PCAT: Optional ED: Yes Int'l Student: Yes	(2019) Apps Received: 569 Interviews Offered: N/A Admission Offered: N/A Number Enrolled: 98 Admitted Rate: 17.2% (2020) Apps Received: 304 Interviews Offered: N/A Admission Offered: N/A Number Enrolled: 92 Admitted Rate: 30.3%	Anatomy & Physio. Microbio. Biochem. Calc. Stats.
Ohio Northern University* 525 South Main Street, Ada, OH 45810	3.50 PCAT: Not Req. ED: No Int'l Student: Yes	(2019) Apps Received: 617 Interviews Offered: N/A Admission Offered: N/A Number Enrolled: 146 Admitted Rate: 23.7% (2020) Apps Received: 361 Interviews Offered: N/A Admission Offered: N/A Number Enrolled: 129 Admitted Rate: 35.7%	Anatomy & Physio. w/ Lab Calc. Stats. *This is a Direct Entry PharmD program (0-6 program) intended for high school students.
Ohio State University 500 West 12th Ave., Columbus, OH 43210	3.50 PCAT: Not Req. ED: Yes Int'l Student: Yes	(2019) Apps Received: 460 Interviews Offered: 200 Admission Offered: N/A Number Enrolled: 128 Admitted Rate: 27.8% (2020) Apps Received: 282 Interviews Offered: N/A Admission Offered: N/A Number Enrolled: 137 Admitted Rate: 48.6%	Calc. Human Anatomy w/ Lab Microbio. w/ Lab Stats. Biochem. Human Physio.

PHARMACY PROGRAMS

Pharmacy School	Ave. GPA & PCAT (%) / Early Decision (ED): Yes/No / Int'l Students: Yes/No	Admissions Statistics	Science Req. Other than Gen Chem, OChem, Physics, Bio
University of Cincinnati 3255 Eden Ave., Cincinnati, OH 45229	3.5 PCAT: 71 ED: Yes Int'l Student: Yes	(2019) Apps Received: 222 Interviews Offered: N/A Admission Offered: N/A Number Enrolled: 92 Admitted Rate: 41.4% (2020) Apps Received: 153 Interviews Offered: N/A Admission Offered: N/A Number Enrolled: 83 Admitted Rate: 54.2%	Stats. Microbio. Calc. Anatomy & Physio. Biochem.
University of Findlay 1000 N. Main St., Findlay, OH 45840	3.30 PCAT: Not Req. ED: No Int'l Student: Yes	(2019) Apps Received: 362 Interviews Offered: N/A Admission Offered: N/A Number Enrolled: 47 Admitted Rate: 13% (2020) Apps Received: 253 Interviews Offered: N/A Admission Offered: N/A Number Enrolled: 44 Admitted Rate: 17.4%	Cell/Molecular Bio. w/ Lab Immunology Human Genetics w/ Lab Microbio. w/ Lab Health Care Ethics Calc. Stats. and Data Analysis
University of Toledo 3000 Arlington Ave, Toledo, OH 43614	3.30 PCAT: Not Req. ED: No Int'l Student: Yes	(2019) Apps Received: 300 Interviews Offered: N/A Admission Offered: N/A Number Enrolled: 76 Admitted Rate: 25.3% (2020) Apps Received: 290 Interviews Offered: N/A Admission Offered: N/A Number Enrolled: 94 Admitted Rate: 32.4%	Calc. Physio. or Anatomy & Physio. Stats.

MIDWEST

Pharmacy School	Ave. GPA & PCAT (%) / Early Decision (ED): Yes/No / Int'l Students: Yes/No	Admissions Statistics	Science Req. Other than Gen Chem, OChem, Physics, Bio
South Dakota State University Avera Health Science Center, Brookings, SD 57007	3.70 PCAT: N/A ED: No Int'l Student: Yes	(2019) Apps Received: 137 Interviews Offered: N/A Admission Offered: N/A Number Enrolled: 82 Admitted Rate: 59.9% (2020) Apps Received: 91 Interviews Offered: N/A Admission Offered: N/A Number Enrolled: 65 Admitted Rate: 71.4%	Calc. Microbio. w/ Lab Human Anatomy w/ Lab Human Physio. w/ Lab Stats.
Concordia University Wisconsin 12800 N Lake Shore Drive, Mequon, WI 53097	3.20 PCAT: Optional ED: Yes Int'l Student: Yes	(2019) Apps Received: 317 Interviews Offered: N/A Admission Offered: N/A Number Enrolled: 80 Admitted Rate: 25.2% (2020) Apps Received: 163 Interviews Offered: N/A Admission Offered: N/A Number Enrolled: 55 Admitted Rate: 33.7%	Advanced Science Elective Calc. Stats.
Medical College of Wisconsin* 8701 Watertown Plank Rd., Milwaukee, WI 53226	N/A PCAT: Not Req. ED: Yes Int'l Student: Yes	(2019) Apps Received: 187 Interviews Offered: N/A Admission Offered: N/A Number Enrolled: 50 Admitted Rate: 26.7% (2020) Apps Received: 108 Interviews Offered: N/A Admission Offered: N/A Number Enrolled: 44 Admitted Rate: 40.7%	Advanced Bio. Stats. Calc. *This is an accelerated 3-year PharmD program.

PHARMACY PROGRAMS

Pharmacy School	Ave. GPA & PCAT (%) Early Decision (ED): Yes/No Int'l Students: Yes/No	Admissions Statistics	Science Req. Other than Gen Chem, OChem, Physics, Bio
University of Wisconsin-Madison 777 Highland Avenue, Madison, WI 53705	3.60 PCAT: Optional ED: Yes Int'l Student: Yes	(2019) Apps Received: 361 Interiews Offered: N/A Admission Offered: N/A Number Enrolled: 138 Admitted Rate: 38.2% (2020) Apps Received: 220 Interviews Offered: N/A Admission Offered: N/A Number Enrolled: 128 Admitted Rate: 58.2%	Calc. Microbio. Human Physio. or Anatomy & Physio. Stats.

MIDWEST

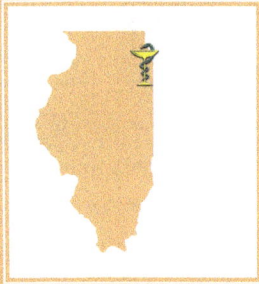

ILLINOIS

INDIANA

IOWA

KANSAS

MICHIGAN

MINNESOTA

MISSOURI

NEBRASKA

NORTH DAKOTA

OHIO

SOUTH DAKOTA

WISCONSIN

CHICAGO STATE UNIVERSITY COLLEGE OF PHARMACY*

Address: 9501 S. King Dr., Chicago, IL 60628
Website: *https://www.csu.edu/collegeofpharmacy/*
Contact: *https://www.csu.edu/collegeofpharmacy/contact.htm*
Phone: (773) 821-2500

COST OF ATTENDANCE

In-State Tuition and Fees: $28,273
Additional Expenses: $17,106
Total: $45,379

Out-of-State Tuition and Fees: $40,225
Additional Expenses: $17,106
Total: $57,331

Financial Aid: https://www.csu.edu/financialaid/

ADDITIONAL INFORMATION

*Please note the following: As of October 2021, Chicago State University College of Pharmacy is currently accredited with probation. For updates, please check:https://www.acpe-accredit.org/faq-item/Chicago-State-University-College-of-Pharmacy-PharmD/

Interesting tidbit: The CSU-COP PharmD program requires a minimum of six years of course work, the first two years at CSU or another college and the final four years at CSU-COP. Effective Fall 2020, newly admitted students (Class of 2024) and beyond will follow a redesigned curriculum.

Important Updates due to COVID-19: The PCAT requirement is waived for 2020-21 application cycle.

Were tests required? No.

Are tests expected next year? Yes.

What international experiences are available? N/A

What dual degree options exist? No dual degree options listed.

What service learning opportunities exist? N/A

What percent of graduates place in postgraduate training? N/A

NAPLEX First-Time Pass Rate: 56.82% (2020)

MPJE First-Time Pass Rate: 79.41% (2020)

MIDWESTERN UNIVERSITY CHICAGO COLLEGE OF PHARMACY

Address: 555 31st Street, Downers Grove, IL 60515
Website: *https://www.midwestern.edu/academics/degrees-and-programs/doctor-of-pharmacy-il.xml*
Contact: *https://online.midwestern.edu/public/reqinfo.cgi*
Phone: (630) 515-6171

COST OF ATTENDANCE

Tuition and Fees: $65,529
Additional Expenses: $27,492
Total: $93,021

Financial Aid: https://www.midwestern.edu/academics/degrees-and-programs/doctor-of-pharmacy-il/scholarships.xml

ADDITIONAL INFORMATION

Interesting tidbit: Midwestern University Chicago COP PharmD program is an accelerated three-year curriculum. Midwestern University's sole focus is to provide healthcare education. In the PharmD curriculum, students will have the opportunity to work with other healthcare profession students to practice communication across disciplines, as well as collaboration.

Important Updates due to COVID-19: Virtual Interview

Were tests required? No.

Are tests expected next year? No.

What international experiences are available? International rotations available.

What dual degree options exist? No dual degree options listed.

What service learning opportunities exist? Student organizations dedicated to community outreach.

What percent of graduates place in postgraduate training? 28% (2020)

NAPLEX First-Time Pass Rate: 86.47% (2020)

MPJE First-Time Pass Rate: 74.77% (2020)

Other: Early Assurance Program available for high school applicants or first-year college undergraduates. For more information, visit: https://www.midwestern.edu/academics/degrees-and-programs/doctor-of-pharmacy-il/early-assurance-programs.xml

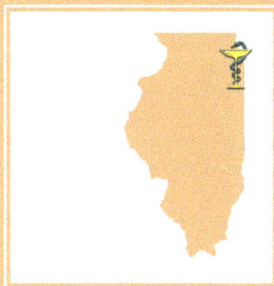

ILLINOIS

INDIANA

IOWA

KANSAS

MICHIGAN

MINNESOTA

MISSOURI

NEBRASKA

NORTH DAKOTA

OHIO

SOUTH DAKOTA

WISCONSIN

MIDWEST

ILLINOIS

INDIANA

IOWA

KANSAS

MICHIGAN

MINNESOTA

MISSOURI

NEBRASKA

NORTH DAKOTA

OHIO

SOUTH DAKOTA

WISCONSIN

ROOSEVELT UNIVERSITY COLLEGE OF PHARMACY

Address: 1400 N Roosevelt Blvd, Schaumburg, IL 60173
Website: *https://www.roosevelt.edu/colleges/pharmacy*
Contact: *https://applyru.roosevelt.edu/register/pharmacy*
Phone: (847) 330-4500

COST OF ATTENDANCE

Tuition and Fees: $51,920
Additional Expenses: $14,837
Total: $66,757

Financial Aid: https://www.roosevelt.edu/colleges/pharmacy/pharmacy-tuition-aid

ADDITIONAL INFORMATION

Interesting tidbit: The Roosevelt University College of Pharmacy Doctor of Pharmacy (Pharm.D.) degree program is an accelerated three-year curriculum.

Important Updates due to COVID-19: Due to the COVID-19 pandemic, the PCAT is optional through the 2020-2021 admissions cycle.

Were tests required? No.

Are tests expected next year? Yes.

What international experiences are available? N/A

What dual degree options exist? PharmD/MBA: https://catalog.roosevelt.edu/graduate/pharmacy/pharmd-mba-dual-degree-program/

What service learning opportunities exist? Contact the Office of Experiential Education for offerings in service learning and community outreach. For more information, visit: https://www.roosevelt.edu/colleges/pharmacy/office-of-the-dean/experiential-education

What percent of graduates place in postgraduate training? 54% (2020)

NAPLEX First-Time Pass Rate: 74.42% (2020)

MPJE First-Time Pass Rate: 78.13% (2020)

SOUTHERN ILLINOIS UNIVERSITY EDWARDSVILLE SCHOOL OF PHARMACY

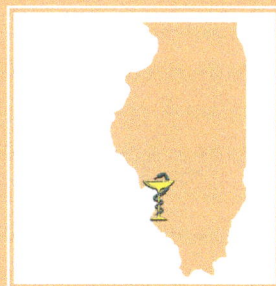

Address: 200 University Park Dr., Edwardsville, IL 62025
Website: *https://www.siue.edu/pharmacy/*
Contact: *https://www.siue.edu/contact/index.shtml*
Phone: (800) 447-7483

COST OF ATTENDANCE

Tuition and Fees: $27,598
Additional Expenses: N/A
Total: $27,598*

*Note: These figures do not reflect estimated housing/living expenses.

Financial Aid: https://www.siue.edu/financial-aid/

ADDITIONAL INFORMATION

Interesting tidbit: For students interested in a specific area of pharmacy, specializations are available to provide concentrated training and focus through designated didactic electives and advanced practice experience electives - Acute Care Pharmacy, Education Pharmacy, and Pediatrics Pharmacy.

Important Updates due to COVID-19: Virtual Interview

Were tests required? No.

Are tests expected next year? No.

What international experiences are available? Global programs in Costa Rica, Guatemala, Haiti, India, and Jamaica. For more information, visit: https://www.siue.edu/pharmacy/degrees-programs-research/global-opportunities/

What dual degree options exist? PharmD/MBA: https://www.siue.edu/academics/graduate/degrees-and-programs/pharmd-mba/index.shtml

PharmD/MSHI: https://www.siue.edu/academics/graduate/degrees-and-programs/pharmd-healthcare-informatics/index.shtml

What service learning opportunities exist? Service learning through experiential education. For more information, visit: https://www.siue.edu/academics/graduate/degrees-and-programs/pharmacy-practice/hands-on-learning.shtml

What percent of graduates place in postgraduate training? N/A

NAPLEX First-Time Pass Rate: 94.87% (2020)

MPJE First-Time Pass Rate: 80.70% (2020)

Other: Conditional Entry Program available to high school applicants. For more information, visit: https://www.siue.edu/pharmacy/admission/conditional-entry.shtml

ILLINOIS

INDIANA

IOWA

KANSAS

MICHIGAN

MINNESOTA

MISSOURI

NEBRASKA

NORTH DAKOTA

OHIO

SOUTH DAKOTA

WISCONSIN

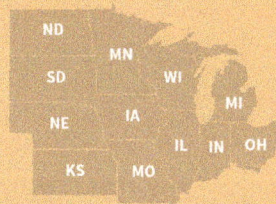

MIDWEST

ILLINOIS

INDIANA

IOWA

KANSAS

MICHIGAN

MINNESOTA

MISSOURI

NEBRASKA

NORTH DAKOTA

OHIO

SOUTH DAKOTA

WISCONSIN

UNIVERSITY OF ILLINOIS AT CHICAGO
COLLEGE OF PHARMACY

Address: 833 S. Wood Street, Chicago, IL 60612
Website: *https://pharmacy.uic.edu/*
Contact: *https://applygrad.uic.edu/register/pharmd-rfi*
Phone: (312) 996-7242

Other Location: 1601 Parkview Avenue, Rockford, IL 61107

COST OF ATTENDANCE

In-State Tuition and Fees: $29,698
Additional Expenses: N/A
Total: $29,698*

Out-of-State Tuition and Fees: $45,216
Additional Expenses: N/A
Total: $45,216*

*Note: These figures do not reflect estimated housing/living expenses.

Financial Aid: https://pharmacy.uic.edu/programs/pharmd/scholarships/

ADDITIONAL INFORMATION

Interesting tidbit: The UIC College of Pharmacy is made up of two campuses, Chicago and Rockford. UIC-COP concentrations in Rural Pharmacy (RPHARM on Rockford campus) and Urban Pharmacy (UPHARM on Chicago campus) allow students to focus their degree even further.

Important Updates due to COVID-19: Virtual Interview

Were tests required? No, PCAT is optional starting with Fall 2021 admission (2020 application cycle).

Are tests expected next year? No.

What international experiences are available? Pharmacy practice sites in Taiwan, India, and Malta.

What dual degree options exist? PharmD/MBA, PharmD/PhD, PharmD/MSCTS (MS in Clinical and Translational Science) and PharmD/MSHI (MS in Health Informatics). For more information, visit: https://pharmacy.uic.edu/programs/pharmd/requirements/admission-pathways/joint-degree-programs/

What service learning opportunities exist? Pharmacy practice sites in D.C., New Mexico, and Alaska.

What percent of graduates place in postgraduate training? For Class of 2021, 66% (PGY1) and 92% (PGY2).

NAPLEX First-Time Pass Rate: 89.51% (2020)

MPJE First-Time Pass Rate: 81.08% (2020)

Other: Guaranteed Professional Program Admissions (GPPA) guarantees selected UIC undergraduate students a place in the PharmD program. For more information, visit: https://gppa.uic.edu/

BUTLER UNIVERSITY COLLEGE OF PHARMACY AND HEALTH SCIENCES

Address: 4600 Sunset Ave, Indianapolis, IN 46208
Website: *https://www.butler.edu/cophs*
Contact: *https://www.butler.edu/contact*
Phone: (317) 940-9322

COST OF ATTENDANCE

Tuition and Fees: $45,040
Additional Expenses: $15,341
Total: $60,381

Financial Aid: https://www.butler.edu/admission/affordability-aid

ADDITIONAL INFORMATION

Interesting tidbit: To better equip our graduates with the requisite linguistic and cultural competence skills necessary for providing quality care to the growing Hispanic/Latino community, the College of Pharmacy and Health Sciences has developed a Spanish language and culture concentration as part of its Doctor of Pharmacy Curriculum.

Important Updates due to COVID-19: VIrtual Interview

Were tests required? No.

Are tests expected next year? No.

What international experiences are available? N/A

What dual degree options exist? PharmD/MBA and PharmD/MSPS (Pharmaceutical Science). For more information, visit: https://www.butler.edu/cophs/pharmd-programs

What service learning opportunities exist? N/A

What percent of graduates place in postgraduate training? 34% (2019)

NAPLEX First-Time Pass Rate: 92.93% (2020)

MPJE First-Time Pass Rate: 92.31% (2020)

Other: Medical Spanish Track. For more information, visit: https://www.butler.edu/cophs/Medical-Spanish-Track

ILLINOIS

INDIANA

IOWA

KANSAS

MICHIGAN

MINNESOTA

MISSOURI

NEBRASKA

NORTH DAKOTA

OHIO

SOUTH DAKOTA

WISCONSIN

MIDWEST

ILLINOIS

INDIANA

IOWA

KANSAS

MICHIGAN

MINNESOTA

MISSOURI

NEBRASKA

NORTH DAKOTA

OHIO

SOUTH DAKOTA

WISCONSIN

MANCHESTER UNIVERSITY COLLEGE OF PHARMACY, NATURAL AND HEALTH SCIENCES

Address: 604 E College Ave, North Manchester, IN 46962
Website: *https://www.manchester.edu/academics/colleges/college-of-pharmacy-natural-health-sciences*
Contact: *http://bestself.manchester.edu/inquiryform*
Phone: (800) 852-3648

COST OF ATTENDANCE

Tuition and Fees: $39,738
Additional Expenses: $16,426
Total: $56,164

Financial Aid: https://www.manchester.edu/academics/colleges/college-of-pharmacy-natural-health-sciences/academic-programs/pharmacy/admissions/costs-and-financial-aid/financial-aid

ADDITIONAL INFORMATION

Interesting tidbit: If applicants submit their PharmCAS application by September 1, they may be considered to attend the Instant Decision Day. Candidates who attend Instant Decision Day will know their admission decision before leaving campus that afternoon. They will earn a $300 seat deposit waiver and receive a first year rotation schedule before the rest of the class.

Important Updates due to COVID-19: VIrtual Interview

Were tests required? No.

Are tests expected next year? No.

What international experiences are available? International rotations.

What dual degree options exist? PharmD/MS in Pharmacogenics. For more information, visit: https://www.manchester.edu/academics/colleges/college-of-pharmacy-natural-health-sciences/academic-programs/pharmacy/pharmacy-pharmacogenomics-dual-degree-program

What service learning opportunities exist? All students are required to participate in 2+ service events per year. For more information, visit: https://www.manchester.edu/academics/colleges/college-of-pharmacy-natural-health-sciences/academic-programs/pharmacy/student-life/service-learning/service-opportunities

What percent of graduates place in postgraduate training? 28% (2021)

NAPLEX First-Time Pass Rate: 89.66% (2020)

MPJE First-Time Pass Rate: 83.33% (2020)

Other: Early Assurance Program. For more information, visit: https://www.manchester.edu/academics/colleges/college-of-pharmacy-natural-health-sciences/academic-programs/pharmacy/admissions/admission-requirements/early-assurance-program

PURDUE UNIVERSITY COLLEGE OF PHARMACY

Address: 575 Stadium Mall Dr., West Lafayette, IN 47907
Website: *https://www.pharmacy.purdue.edu/*
Contact: *https://www.pharmacy.purdue.edu/contact-us*
Phone: (765) 494-1361

COST OF ATTENDANCE

In-State Tuition and Fees: $11,008
Additional Expenses: N/A
Total: $11,008*

Out-of-State Tuition and Fees: $20,138
Additional Expenses: $12,790
Total: $20,138*

*Note: These figures do not reflect estimated housing/living expenses.

Financial Aid: https://www.pharmacy.purdue.edu/oss/scholarships

ADDITIONAL INFORMATION

Interesting tidbit: Purdue College of Pharmacy boasts an extremely distinguished 85-member faculty renowned for both its cutting-edge work in pharmaceutical research and for developing educational curricula used in pharmacy programs around the world.

Important Updates due to COVID-19: VIrtual Interview

Were tests required? No.

Are tests expected next year? No.

What international experiences are available? N/A

What dual degree options exist? No dual degree options listed.

What service learning opportunities exist? For more information, visit:

What percent of graduates place in postgraduate training? 47.2% (2019)

NAPLEX First-Time Pass Rate: 93.89% (2020)

MPJE First-Time Pass Rate: 83.70% (2020)

ILLINOIS

INDIANA

IOWA

KANSAS

MICHIGAN

MINNESOTA

MISSOURI

NEBRASKA

NORTH DAKOTA

OHIO

SOUTH DAKOTA

WISCONSIN

MIDWEST

ILLINOIS

INDIANA

IOWA

KANSAS

MICHIGAN

MINNESOTA

MISSOURI

NEBRASKA

NORTH DAKOTA

OHIO

SOUTH DAKOTA

WISCONSIN

DRAKE UNIVERSITY COLLEGE OF PHARMACY AND HEALTH SCIENCES

Address: 2802 Forest Ave., Des Moines, IA 50311
Website: *https://www.drake.edu/cphs/*
Contact: *https://www.drake.edu/cphs/contactus/*
Phone: (515) 271-1814

COST OF ATTENDANCE

Tuition and Fees: $43,430
Additional Expenses: $11,989
Total: $55,419

Financial Aid: https://www.drake.edu/pharmacy/scholarships/

ADDITIONAL INFORMATION

Interesting tidbit: Doctor of Pharmacy (PharmD) students participate in a variety of experiences not only in Des Moines, but throughout the country and the world. Students can participate in high quality experiential sites that prepare you for your career.

Important Updates due to COVID-19: VIrtual Interview

Were tests required? PCAT (or any graduate-level standardized test, such as GRE/MCAT/DAT) required.

Are tests expected next year? Yes.

What international experiences are available? Study abroad opportunities during January Term (J-Term) or the summer.

What dual degree options exist? PharmD/JD, PharmD/MBA, PharmD/MPH, and PharmD/MS in Leadership Development. For more information, visit: https://www.drake.edu/pharmacy/dualdegreesconcentrations/

What service learning opportunities exist? Students are required to participate in community outreach events such as health fairs, immunization clinics, and other activities.

What percent of graduates place in postgraduate training? 81.13% (2021)

NAPLEX First-Time Pass Rate: 85.56% (2020)

MPJE First-Time Pass Rate: 75.00% (2020)

UNIVERSITY OF IOWA COLLEGE OF PHARMACY

Address: 180 South Grand Avenue, Iowa City, IA 52242
Website: *https://pharmacy.uiowa.edu/*
Contact: *https://pharmacy.uiowa.edu/contact-us*
Phone: (319) 335-8795

COST OF ATTENDANCE

In-State Tuition and Fees: $28,599
Additional Expenses: N/A
Total: $28,599*

Out-of-State Tuition and Fees: $45,075
Additional Expenses: N/A
Total: $45,075*

*Note: These figures do not reflect estimated housing/living expenses.

Financial Aid: https://pharmacy.uiowa.edu/scholarship-opportunities

ADDITIONAL INFORMATION

Interesting tidbit: The college's close proximity to other healthcare colleges and University of Iowa Hospitals and Clinics (UIHC) allows students to engage in inter-professional experiences with students and practitioners from many disciplines.

Important Updates due to COVID-19: VIrtual Interview

Were tests required? No.

Are tests expected next year? No.

What international experiences are available? UI-Rotary service project in Mexico and palliative care in India. For more information, visit: https://pharmacy.uiowa.edu/global-student-opportunities

What dual degree options exist? PharmD/MPH: https://pharmacy.uiowa.edu/PharmD-MPH

PharmD/MSHI or MHIIM (Health Informatics): https://pharmacy.uiowa.edu/pharmd-informatics

What service learning opportunities exist? All students are required to complete service and leadership hours. This can be achieved through student organizations, volunteering with local hospitals/mobile clinics, or volunteering at immunization events.

What percent of graduates place in postgraduate training? 45% (2020)

NAPLEX First-Time Pass Rate: 87.88% (2020)

MPJE First-Time Pass Rate: 75.00% (2020)

Other: Certificate in Palliative Care available. For more information, visit: https://pharmacy.uiowa.edu/palliative-certificate

Certificate in Global Health Certificate available. For more information, visit: https://clas.uiowa.edu/global-health-studies/certificate

Assured Admissions pathway available for high school applicants: https://pharmacy.uiowa.edu/prospective-students/doctor-pharmacy/admissions-pharmd

ILLINOIS

INDIANA

IOWA

KANSAS

MICHIGAN

MINNESOTA

MISSOURI

NEBRASKA

NORTH DAKOTA

OHIO

SOUTH DAKOTA

WISCONSIN

MIDWEST

ILLINOIS

INDIANA

IOWA

KANSAS

MICHIGAN

MINNESOTA

MISSOURI

NEBRASKA

NORTH DAKOTA

OHIO

SOUTH DAKOTA

WISCONSIN

UNIVERSITY OF KANSAS SCHOOL OF PHARMACY

Address: 2010 Becker Dr., Lawrence, KS 66047
Website: *https://pharmacy.ku.edu/*
Contact: *https://deptsec.ku.edu/~pharmforms/forms/form/12*
Phone: (785) 864-3591
Other locations: Wichita, KS

COST OF ATTENDANCE

In-State Tuition and Fees: $23,420
Additional Expenses: N/A
Total: $23,420*

Out-of-State Tuition and Fees: $43,250
Additional Expenses: N/A
Total: $43,250*

*Note: These figures do not reflect estimated housing/living expenses.

Financial Aid: https://pharmacy.ku.edu/financial-aid

ADDITIONAL INFORMATION

Interesting tidbit: The KU School of Pharmacy offers the Pharm. D. Program on the Lawrence (home campus) and Wichita campuses. After the interviews, accepted students are ranked, and the top students get their first choice of campus.

Important Updates due to COVID-19: Accept Credit/No Credit grades for all pre-pharmacy courses completed during the Spring 2020, Summer 2020, Fall 2020 and Spring 2021 semesters.

Were tests required? PCAT required.

Are tests expected next year? Yes.

What international experiences are available? Study abroad

What dual degree options exist? PharmD/MBA. For more information, visit: https://business.ku.edu/mba-doctor-pharmacy-mba-pharmd

What service learning opportunities exist? Service learning through experiential education in pharmacy rotations. For more information, visit: https://pharmacy.ku.edu/experiential-education

What percent of graduates place in postgraduate training? N/A

NAPLEX First-Time Pass Rate: 94.74% (2020)

MPJE First-Time Pass Rate: 99.12% (2020)

FERRIS STATE UNIVERSITY COLLEGE OF PHARMACY

Address: 220 Ferris Dr., Big Rapids, MI 49307
Website: *https://www.ferris.edu/pharmacy/*
Contact: *https://forward.ferris.edu/request-info*
Phone: (231) 591-3780

COST OF ATTENDANCE

Tuition and Fees: $24,276
Additional Expenses: $15,110
Total: $39,386

Financial Aid: https://www.ferris.edu/pharmacy/
PharmacyScholarships.htm

ADDITIONAL INFORMATION

I**nteresting tidbit:** The first two years of the program are conducted at the Big Rapids campus site. The third year of the program is conducted at the new Grand Rapids facility. The fourth year of the program is comprised of field experiences in multiple pharmacy practice settings throughout the state of Michigan, with opportunities to concentrate the student experience in one of the following geographic areas -- Grand Rapids, Lansing, Kalamazoo, Flint/Saginaw, Traverse City and Marquette.

Important Updates due to COVID-19: VIrtual Interview

Were tests required? No.

Are tests expected next year? No.

What international experiences are available? International rotations.

What dual degree options exist? PharmD/MBA and PharmD/MPH.

What service learning opportunities exist? Various opportunities, including international rotations.

What percent of graduates place in postgraduate training? N/A

NAPLEX First-Time Pass Rate: 93.50% (2020)

MPJE First-Time Pass Rate: 87.18% (2020)

Other: Honors Guaranteed Admissions Program available to students who are enrolled in the pre-pharmacy Honors Program at Ferris State. For more information, visit: https://www.ferris.edu/pharmacy/admissions/Honors.htm

ILLINOIS

INDIANA

IOWA

KANSAS

MICHIGAN

MINNESOTA

MISSOURI

NEBRASKA

NORTH DAKOTA

OHIO

SOUTH DAKOTA

WISCONSIN

MIDWEST

ILLINOIS

INDIANA

IOWA

KANSAS

MICHIGAN

MINNESOTA

MISSOURI

NEBRASKA

NORTH DAKOTA

OHIO

SOUTH DAKOTA

WISCONSIN

UNIVERSITY OF MICHIGAN COLLEGE OF PHARMACY

Address: 428 Church St., Ann Arbor, MI 48109
Website: *https://pharmacy.umich.edu/*
Contact: *https://pharmacy.umich.edu/academic-research-about/about-college/department-contact-info*
Phone: (866) 990-0111

COST OF ATTENDANCE

In-State Tuition and Fees: $32,926
Additional Expenses: N/A
Total: $32,926*

Out-of-State Tuition and Fees: $38,670
Additional Expenses: N/A
Total: $38,670*

*Note: These figures do not reflect estimated housing/living expenses.

Financial Aid: https://pharmacy.umich.edu/prospective-students/admissions/funding-your-education

ADDITIONAL INFORMATION

Interesting tidbit: U-M Pharmacy is a small school within one of the world's most prestigious universities and is affiliated with the University of Michigan Health System – a world-class health care and research organization. PharmD students are required to complete a major research project.

Important Updates due to COVID-19: VIrtual Interview

Were tests required? No.

Are tests expected next year? No.

What international experiences are available? Month-long trip to Africa.

What dual degree options exist? PharmD/PhD, PharmD/MBA, and PharmD/MPH. For more information, visit: https://pharmacy.umich.edu/prospective-students/programs/dual-programs

What service learning opportunities exist? Longitudinal Early Practice Experience (LEPE). For more information, visit: https://pharmacy.umich.edu/prospective-students/discover/community-engagement/CommunityOutreach

What percent of graduates place in postgraduate training? 71% (2019)

NAPLEX First-Time Pass Rate: 95.95% (2020)

MPJE First-Time Pass Rate: 90.20% (2020)

WAYNE STATE UNIVERSITY EUGENE APPLEBAUM COLLEGE OF PHARMACY AND HEALTH SCIENCES

Address: 259 Mack Ave., Detroit, MI 48201
Website: *https://cphs.wayne.edu/*
Contact: *https://cphs.wayne.edu/about/contact.php*
Phone: (313) 577-1716

COST OF ATTENDANCE

In-State Tuition and Fees: $27,379
Additional Expenses: N/A
Total: $27,379*

Out-of-State Tuition and Fees: $52,697
Additional Expenses: N/A
Total: $52,697*

*Note: These figures do not reflect estimated housing/living expenses.

Financial Aid: https://cphs.wayne.edu/admissions/scholarships.php

ADDITIONAL INFORMATION

Interesting tidbit: The PharmD program at Wayne State University is administered by two departments in the Eugene Applebaum College of Pharmacy and Health Sciences: Pharmacy Practice and Pharmaceutical Sciences. Oversight of the program occurs through the associate dean of pharmacy, who serves as the Doctor of Pharmacy program director.

Important Updates due to COVID-19: Virtual Interview

Were tests required? PCAT required.

Are tests expected next year? PCAT required.

What international experiences are available? World Health Student Organization

What dual degree options exist? PharmD/PhD. Students may enroll in this program only after starting the PharmD. It requires a separate application.

What service learning opportunities exist? Community Homeless Interprofessional Program (CHIP), Diabetes Education and Wellness Clinic (DEW), and several others. For more information, visit: https://cphs.wayne.edu/about/community-engagement.php

What percent of graduates place in postgraduate training? 25% (2020)

NAPLEX First-Time Pass Rate: 92.63% (2020)

MPJE First-Time Pass Rate: 92.22% (2020)

ILLINOIS

INDIANA

IOWA

KANSAS

MICHIGAN

MINNESOTA

MISSOURI

NEBRASKA

NORTH DAKOTA

OHIO

SOUTH DAKOTA

WISCONSIN

MIDWEST

ILLINOIS

INDIANA

IOWA

KANSAS

MICHIGAN

MINNESOTA

MISSOURI

NEBRASKA

NORTH DAKOTA

OHIO

SOUTH DAKOTA

WISCONSIN

UNIVERSITY OF MINNESOTA COLLEGE OF PHARMACY

Address: 232 Life Science, 1110 Kirby Dr., Duluth, MN 55812
Website: *https://www.pharmacy.umn.edu/*
Contact: *https://www.pharmacy.umn.edu/about/contact*
Phone: (612) 624-9490
Other Locations: 308 Harvard Street S.E., Minneapolis, MN 55455

COST OF ATTENDANCE

In-State Tuition and Fees: $29,826
Additional Expenses: $15,924
Total: $45,665

Out-of-State Tuition and Fees: $42,668
Additional Expenses: $15,924
Total: $58,592

Financial Aid: https://www.pharmacy.umn.edu/degrees-and-programs/doctor-pharmacy/admissions/costs-aid

ADDITIONAL INFORMATION

Interesting tidbit: The only college of pharmacy in the state, the University of Minnesota College of Pharmacy PharmD program is conveniently offered on two campuses: Duluth and the Twin Cities. Campus assignment occurs after the admissions committee determines whether or not to admit an applicant.

Important Updates due to COVID-19: During the COVID-19 pandemic, PCAT scores will be optional for Fall 2022 applications (2021-22 application cycle).

Were tests required? No.

Are tests expected next year? PCAT required.

What international experiences are available? Global engagement opportunities. For more information, visit: https://www.pharmacy.umn.edu/about/global-pharmacy-engagement

What dual degree options exist? PharmD/MBA, PharmD/MPH, and PharmD/Masters in Health Informatics. For more information, visit: https://www.pharmacy.umn.edu/degrees-and-programs/doctor-pharmacy/curriculum/dual-degree-programs

What service learning opportunities exist? Service learning through experiential education in rotations. For more information, visit: https://www.pharmacy.umn.edu/degrees-and-programs/doctor-pharmacy/experiential-education-program

What percent of graduates place in postgraduate training? 55.5% (2020)

NAPLEX First-Time Pass Rate: 97.37% (2020)

MPJE First-Time Pass Rate: 86.55% (2020)

ST. LOUIS COLLEGE OF PHARMACY

Address: 1 Pharmacy Place St. Louis, Missouri 63110
Website: *https://www.stlcop.edu/*
Contact: *https://www.stlcop.edu/contact.html*
Phone: (314) 367-8700

COST OF ATTENDANCE

Tuition and Fees: $40,112
Additional Expenses: $16,725
Total: $56,837

Financial Aid: https://www.stlcop.edu/financialaid/scholarships/index.html

ADDITIONAL INFORMATION

Interesting tidbit: St. Louis College of Pharmacy is the third-oldest and 10th-largest college of pharmacy in the United States. Electives in the pharmacy curriculum have areas of focus that allow students to tailor their elective courses offerings to their interests - Clinical Services, Community Care, Disease State Management, Health Care Management and Entrepreneurship, Health System Pharmacy, Pharmaceutical Sciences, and Public Health.

Important Updates due to COVID-19: VIrtual Interview

Were tests required? PCAT required.

Are tests expected next year? PCAT required.

What international experiences are available? Students may study abroad, participate in international APPE rotations, or participate in on-campus events to learn about global health issues. For more information, visit: https://www.stlcop.edu/academics/international/index.html

What dual degree options exist? PharmD/MBA. For more information, visit: https://www.stlcop.edu/academics/graduate/mba.html

What service learning opportunities exist? C.A.R.E.S. event, Outreach and Advocacy Day, educational summer programs, and various other opportunities. For more information, visit: https://www.stlcop.edu/campuslife/activities/service.html

What percent of graduates place in postgraduate training? 53% (2020)

NAPLEX First-Time Pass Rate: 83.87% (2020)

MPJE First-Time Pass Rate: 74.47% (2020)

ILLINOIS

INDIANA

IOWA

KANSAS

MICHIGAN

MINNESOTA

MISSOURI

NEBRASKA

NORTH DAKOTA

OHIO

SOUTH DAKOTA

WISCONSIN

MIDWEST

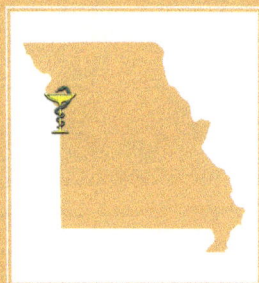

ILLINOIS

INDIANA

IOWA

KANSAS

MICHIGAN

MINNESOTA

MISSOURI

NEBRASKA

NORTH DAKOTA

OHIO

SOUTH DAKOTA

WISCONSIN

UNIVERSITY OF MISSOURI-KANSAS CITY SCHOOL OF PHARMACY

Address: 2464 Charlotte St., Kansas City, MO 64108
Website: *https://pharmacy.umkc.edu/*
Contact: *https://pharmacy.umkc.edu/contact-us/*
Phone: (816) 235-1609

Other Locations: Columbia, MO; Springfield, MO

COST OF ATTENDANCE

In-State Tuition and Fees: $25,509
Additional Expenses: N/A
Total: $25,509*

Out-of-State Tuition and Fees: $58,858
Additional Expenses: N/A
Total: $58,858*

*Note: These figures do not reflect estimated housing/living expenses.

Financial Aid: https://pharmacy.umkc.edu/pharm-d/financing-your-pharmacy-education/

ADDITIONAL INFORMATION

Interesting tidbit: PharmD program students may attend the program at one of our three campus sites — Kansas City, Columbia, or Springfield. Applicants indicate their campus site preferences on the application. Ninety-five percent of the students are accepted to their first choice of the campus site.

Important Updates due to COVID-19: VIrtual Interview

Were tests required? PCAT required.

Are tests expected next year? PCAT required.

What international experiences are available? N/A

What dual degree options exist? PharmD/MBA. For more information, visit: https://bloch.umkc.edu/graduate-program/pmba/pharm-d-mba-joint-program/

What service learning opportunities exist? N/A

What percent of graduates place in postgraduate training? 39% (2020)

NAPLEX First-Time Pass Rate: 94.62% (2020)

MPJE First-Time Pass Rate: 88.70% (2020)

Other: Early Assurance Program ensures a seat in the PharmD program for up to 40 incoming college undergraduates. For more information, visit: https://pharmacy.umkc.edu/pharm-d/current-high-school-students/

CREIGHTON UNIVERSITY SCHOOL OF PHARMACY AND HEALTH PROFESSIONS

Address: 2500 California Plaza, Omaha, NE 68178
Website: *https://spahp.creighton.edu/*
Contact: *https://choose.creighton.edu/register/inquiry-form*
Phone: (402) 280-2700

Other locations: Phoenix, AZ

COST OF ATTENDANCE

Tuition and Fees: $39,514
Additional Expenses: $23,423
Total: $62,9347

Financial Aid: https://spahp.creighton.edu/future-students/scholarships-aid

ADDITIONAL INFORMATION

Interesting tidbit: Creighton University offers three pathways to obtain your Doctor of Pharmacy degree in our Omaha Pathway, Distance Pathway, and Phoenix Hybrid Pathway. In 2001, the School initiated the first distance-based Doctor of Pharmacy degree (PharmD) pathway in the United States and it is the first accredited PharmD program in the United States.

Important Updates due to COVID-19: VIrtual Interview

Were tests required? No.

Are tests expected next year? No.

What international experiences are available? ILAC Summer Program, China Honors Immersion Program (CHIP), etc. For more information, visit: https://spahp.creighton.edu/academics/pharmacy-departments/international-opportunities

What dual degree options exist? PharmD/MBA and PharmD/MS in Pharmaceutical Sciences. For more information on the PharmD/MBA, visit: https://www.creighton.edu/program/pharmacy-business-administration-dual-degree

What service learning opportunities exist? Project Homeless Connect, Elementary School Outreach, etc. For more information, visit: https://spahp.creighton.edu/future-students/service-opportunities

What percent of graduates place in postgraduate training? 22% (2020)

NAPLEX First-Time Pass Rate: 94.70% (2020)

MPJE First-Time Pass Rate: 96.55% (2020)

ILLINOIS

INDIANA

IOWA

KANSAS

MICHIGAN

MINNESOTA

MISSOURI

NEBRASKA

NORTH DAKOTA

OHIO

SOUTH DAKOTA

WISCONSIN

MIDWEST

ILLINOIS

INDIANA

IOWA

KANSAS

MICHIGAN

MINNESOTA

MISSOURI

NEBRASKA

NORTH DAKOTA

OHIO

SOUTH DAKOTA

WISCONSIN

UNIVERSITY OF NEBRASKA MEDICAL CENTER COLLEGE OF PHARMACY

Address: 42nd and Emile, Omaha, NE 68198
Website: *https://www.unmc.edu/pharmacy/*
Contact: *https://www.unmc.edu/contact/*
Phone: (402) 559-4333

COST OF ATTENDANCE

In-State Tuition and Fees: $26,220
Additional Expenses: N/A
Total: $26,220*

Out-of-State Tuition and Fees: $32,712
Additional Expenses: N/A
Total: $32,712*

*Note: These figures do not reflect estimated housing/living expenses.

Financial Aid: https://www.unmc.edu/pharmacy/programs/pharmd/Scholarships.html

ADDITIONAL INFORMATION

Interesting tidbit: In 1976, the College of Pharmacy initiated a new pharmacy curriculum, the Doctor of Pharmacy (PharmD) Program, becoming only the third pharmacy school in the nation to offer the PharmD as the sole degree of the professional program when the Bachelor of Science in Pharmacy was the principal professional degree offered by all of the remaining colleges and schools of pharmacy.

Important Updates due to COVID-19: VIrtual Interview

Were tests required? No, PCAT is no longer required for Fall 2021 applicants (2020-21 application cycle).

Are tests expected next year? No.

What international experiences are available? N/A

What dual degree options exist? PharmD/MBA and PharmD/MPH. For more information, visit: https://www.unmc.edu/pharmacy/programs/dual%20degree/index.html

What service learning opportunities exist? N/A

What percent of graduates place in postgraduate training? 37.5% (2020)

NAPLEX First-Time Pass Rate: 100% (2020)

MPJE First-Time Pass Rate: 98.04% (2020)

Other: Early Acceptance Programs available, including the Rural Health Opportunities Program (RHOP), the Rural Pharmacy Practice Educational Initiative, and the Kearney Health Opportunities Program (KHOP). For more information, visit: http://catalog.unmc.edu/pharmacy/early-acceptance-programs/

NORTH DAKOTA STATE UNIVERSITY COLLEGE OF HEALTH PROFESSIONS SCHOOL OF PHARMACY

Address: 1401 Albrecht Blvd., Fargo, ND 58102
Website: *https://www.ndsu.edu/pharmacy/*
Contact: *https://www.ndsu.edu/pharmacy/contact/*
Phone: (701) 231-7456

COST OF ATTENDANCE

In-State Tuition and Fees: $19,550
Additional Expenses: N/A
Total: $19,550*

Out-of-State Tuition and Fees: $28,969
Additional Expenses: N/A
Total: $28,969*

***Note:** These figures do not reflect estimated housing/living expenses.

Financial Aid: https://www.ndsu.edu/healthprofessions/ scholarships/

ADDITIONAL INFORMATION

Interesting tidbit: Starting in 2021, NDSU SOP is debuting a new, streamlined pathway to its PharmD program called the Post-Baccalaureate Admissions Pathway. May 2021 graduates with a bachelor's degree in a health or STEM field are eligible to apply through this pathway, which has fewer requirements.

Important Updates due to COVID-19: VIrtual Interview

Were tests required? PCAT or MCAT required.

Are tests expected next year? Yes.

What international experiences are available? Medical missions abroad.

What dual degree options exist? PharmD/MBA, PharmD/MPH, and PharmD/PhD. For more information, visit: https://www.ndsu.edu/ pharmacy/dual_degrees/

What service learning opportunities exist? N/A

What percent of graduates place in postgraduate training? 60% PGY1 match (2020)

NAPLEX First-Time Pass Rate: 92.59% (2020)

MPJE First-Time Pass Rate: 89.80% (2020)

Other: Early Admission Pathway (EAP) available to high school applicants. For more information, visit: https://www.ndsu.edu/ pharmacy/pharmd/app_eap/

ILLINOIS

INDIANA

IOWA

KANSAS

MICHIGAN

MINNESOTA

MISSOURI

NEBRASKA

NORTH DAKOTA

OHIO

SOUTH DAKOTA

WISCONSIN

MIDWEST

ILLINOIS

INDIANA

IOWA

KANSAS

MICHIGAN

MINNESOTA

MISSOURI

NEBRASKA

NORTH DAKOTA

OHIO

SOUTH DAKOTA

WISCONSIN

CEDARVILLE UNIVERSITY SCHOOL OF PHARMACY

Address: 251 N. Main St., Cedarville, OH 45314
Website: *https://www.cedarville.edu/Academic-Schools-and-Departments/Pharmacy.aspx*
Contact: *https://www.cedarville.edu/Admissions/Undergraduate/Request-Information.aspx*
Phone: (800) 233-2784

COST OF ATTENDANCE

Tuition and Fees: $37,542
Additional Expenses: $12,512
Total: $50,054

Financial Aid: https://www.cedarville.edu/Academic-Schools-and-Departments/Pharmacy/Pre-Pharmacy/Cost-and-Financial-Aid.aspx

ADDITIONAL INFORMATION

Interesting tidbit: Cedarville University is distinctly Christ-centered. Cedarville's commitment to the authority of the Bible is the basis for discussions on medical ethics, the sanctity of life, origins, and the balanced integration of faith and learning.

Important Updates due to COVID-19: VIrtual Interview

Were tests required? No.

Are tests expected next year? No.

What international experiences are available? Pharmacy Missions. For more information, visit: https://www.cedarville.edu/Academic-Schools-and-Departments/Pharmacy/Experiential-Program/Missions.aspx

What dual degree options exist? PharmD/MBA. For more information, visit: https://www.cedarville.edu/Academic-Programs/PharmD-MBA-Dual-Degree.aspx

What service learning opportunities exist? Service learning through experiential education. For more information, visit: https://www.cedarville.edu/Academic-Schools-and-Departments/Pharmacy/Experiential-Program.aspx

What percent of graduates place in postgraduate training? 69% (2018)

NAPLEX First-Time Pass Rate: 89.13% (2020)

MPJE First-Time Pass Rate: 79.41% (2020)

Other: Preferred Admission available to high school applicants or transfer students. For more information, visit: https://www.cedarville.edu/Academic-Schools-and-Departments/Pharmacy/Pre-Pharmacy/Admission.aspx

NORTHEAST OHIO MEDICAL UNIVERSITY COLLEGE OF PHARMACY

Address: 4209 St., Rootstown, OH 44272
Website: *https://www.neomed.edu/pharmacy/*
Contact: *https://www.neomed.edu/pharmacy/about/contact/*
Phone: (800) 686-2511

COST OF ATTENDANCE

In-State Tuition and Fees: $27,181
Additional Expenses: $31,153
Total: $58,334

Out-of-State Tuition and Fees: $38,695
Additional Expenses: $31,639
Total: $70,334

Financial Aid: https://www.neomed.edu/financialaid/

ADDITIONAL INFORMATION

Interesting tidbit: At NEOMED COP, the curriculum is organized to give each year a central theme that serves as a foundation for each successive year. The College of Pharmacy curriculum is undergoing a transformation, which will provide better opportunities for interprofessional training of students

Important Updates due to COVID-19: VIrtual Interview

Were tests required? No.

Are tests expected next year? No.

What international experiences are available? N/A

What dual degree options exist? Dual degrees are not conferred jointly, however related degrees may be pursued concurrently (i.e., PhD, MBA, and MS).

What service learning opportunities exist? N/A

What percent of graduates place in postgraduate training? 30% (2019)

NAPLEX First-Time Pass Rate: 86.67% (2020)

MPJE First-Time Pass Rate: 87.32% (2020)

Other: Early Assurance Program for high school applicants. For more information, visit: https://www.neomed.edu/pharmacy/admissions/paths/early-assurance-high-school/

Early Assurance Program for undergraduate applicants in their first or second years. For more information, visit: https://www.neomed.edu/pharmacy/admissions/paths/early-assurance-undergrad/

ILLINOIS

INDIANA

IOWA

KANSAS

MICHIGAN

MINNESOTA

MISSOURI

NEBRASKA

NORTH DAKOTA

OHIO

SOUTH DAKOTA

WISCONSIN

MIDWEST

OHIO NORTHERN UNIVERSITY RAABE COLLEGE OF PHARMACY

Address: 525 South Main Street, Ada, OH 45810
Website: *https://www.onu.edu/college-pharmacy*
Contact: *https://connect.onu.edu/register/student_information_request*
Phone: (419) 772-2275

COST OF ATTENDANCE

Tuition and Fees: $39,570
Additional Expenses: $16,260
Total: $55,830

Financial Aid: https://www.onu.edu/financial-aid

ADDITIONAL INFORMATION

Interesting tidbit: ONU's rural location and focus on rural healthcare provide ample opportunities for faculty and students to have an impact on the health of our community. The faculty's research provides students the opportunity to sharpen problem-solving skills and develop as clinician-scientists while studying topics like protecting cardiac muscle during a heart attack, identifying anti-cancer medicines in wild potatoes, and the impact pharmacists can make on the health and wellness of our community.

Important Updates due to COVID-19: VIrtual Interview

Were tests required? No.

Are tests expected next year? No.

What international experiences are available? N/A

What dual degree options exist? No dual degree options listed.

What service learning opportunities exist? On-Campus Pharmacy, Mobile Clinic, and more opportunities through student organizations.

What percent of graduates place in postgraduate training? 41% entering PGY1 (2020)

NAPLEX First-Time Pass Rate: 90.00% (2020)

MPJE First-Time Pass Rate: 91.82% (2020)

Other: The Rural and Underserved Health Scholars Program provides students with the training to work with underserved populations.

The Direct Entry (0-6) program is available to high school applicants. The entering class for this program typically has an average GPA of 3.5 and an ACT score of 27. This program receives approximately 400-500 applications and the final class size is 165 students.

ILLINOIS

INDIANA

IOWA

KANSAS

MICHIGAN

MINNESOTA

MISSOURI

NEBRASKA

NORTH DAKOTA

OHIO

SOUTH DAKOTA

WISCONSIN

ND

MN

SD

WI

MI

NE

IA

IL   IN   OH

KS   MO

OHIO STATE UNIVERSITY COLLEGE OF PHARMACY

Address: 500 West 12th Ave., Columbus, OH 43210
Website: *https://pharmacy.osu.edu/*
Contact: *https://pharmacy.osu.edu/contact*
Phone: (614) 292-2266

COST OF ATTENDANCE

In-State Tuition and Fees: $25,213
Additional Expenses: N/A
Total: $24,261*

Out-of-State Tuition and Fees: $48,909
Additional Expenses: N/A
Total: $47,957*

*Note: These figures do not reflect estimated housing/living expenses.

Financial Aid: https://pharmacy.osu.edu/financial-aid-scholarships

ADDITIONAL INFORMATION

Interesting tidbit: Ohio State has seven health science colleges and is located in the center of a comprehensive, nationally-ranked medical center. Student pharmacists have access to world-class faculty members in the College of Pharmacy, where they can learn from scientists and clinicians who are discovering tomorrow's cures and treating today's most complex diseases.

Important Updates due to COVID-19: Accept a grade of pass for any coursework completed in Fall 2020 or Spring 2021 terms.

Were tests required? No.

Are tests expected next year? No.

What international experiences are available? Study abroad experiences and coursework focused on global pharmacy initiatives.

What dual degree options exist? PharmD/MBA and PharmD/PhD. For more information, visit: https://pharmacy.osu.edu/combined-pharmd-programs

What service learning opportunities exist? Service learning through student organizations and health outreach (e.g., Podemos and Buckeyes without Borders). For more information, visit: https://pharmacy.osu.edu/experiential-program

What percent of graduates place in postgraduate training? 47% (2020)

NAPLEX First-Time Pass Rate: 91.74% (2020)

MPJE First-Time Pass Rate: 85.87% (2020)

Other: Early Assurance Program (EAP) available for high school applicants. For more information, visit: https://pharmacy.osu.edu/early-assurance-program

ILLINOIS

INDIANA

IOWA

KANSAS

MICHIGAN

MINNESOTA

MISSOURI

NEBRASKA

NORTH DAKOTA

OHIO

SOUTH DAKOTA

WISCONSIN

MIDWEST

ILLINOIS

INDIANA

IOWA

KANSAS

MICHIGAN

MINNESOTA

MISSOURI

NEBRASKA

NORTH DAKOTA

OHIO

SOUTH DAKOTA

WISCONSIN

UNIVERSITY OF CINCINNATI JAMES L. WINKLE COLLEGE OF PHARMACY

Address: 3255 Eden Ave., Cincinnati, OH 45229
Website: *https://pharmacy.uc.edu/*
Contact: *https://pharmacy.uc.edu/about/college-directory.html*
Phone: (513) 558-3784

COST OF ATTENDANCE

In-State Tuition and Fees: $24,418
Additional Expenses: $12,294*
Total: $36,712*

Out-of-State Tuition and Fees: $37,346
Additional Expenses: $12,294*
Total: $49,640*

*Note: These figures do not reflect estimated housing/living expenses.

Financial Aid: https://pharmacy.uc.edu/for-students/financial-aid-scholarships.html

ADDITIONAL INFORMATION

Interesting tidbit: Renewed PharmD curriculum includes new courses, such as clinical pharmacogenomics, modified basic science courses with a stronger foundation in immunology and pharmacogenomics, more time devoted to key practice issues, such as provider status, and an increase in the exposure to ability-based courses such as pharmacy practice skills development. The new curriculum also includes a new, exciting partnership with the College of Medicine whereby medical students and pharmacy students are learning and applying key principles in collaborative practice and team-based care.

Important Updates due to COVID-19: PCAT is optional for 2020-2021 & 2021-2022 application cycles.

Were tests required? No.

Are tests expected next year? No.

What international experiences are available? International rotations and trips abroad available. For more information, visit: https://pharmacy.uc.edu/academic-programs/pharmd/international-experiences.html

What dual degree options exist? No dual degree options listed.

What service learning opportunities exist? Service learning through international opportunities and experiential education during APPEs. For more information on experiential education, visit: https://pharmacy.uc.edu/academic-programs/pharmd/experiential-education.html

What percent of graduates place in postgraduate training? N/A

NAPLEX First-Time Pass Rate: 95.24% (2020)

MPJE First-Time Pass Rate: 95.65% (2020)

UNIVERSITY OF FINDLAY COLLEGE OF PHARMACY

Address: 1000 N. Main St., Findlay, OH 45840
Website: *https://www.findlay.edu/pharmacy/*
Contact: *https://www.findlay.edu/admissions/request-information*
Phone: (800) 472-9502

COST OF ATTENDANCE

Tuition and Fees: $46,188
Additional Expenses: $13,008
Total: $59,1906

Financial Aid: https://www.findlay.edu/pharmacy/scholarships

ADDITIONAL INFORMATION

Interesting tidbit: the University of Findlay was established through a joint partnership between the Churches of God, General Conference, and the city of Findlay, and thus is firmly grounded in faith.

Important Updates due to COVID-19: Virtual Interview

Were tests required? No.

Are tests expected next year? No.

What international experiences are available? International experiential rotations.

What dual degree options exist? PharmD/MBA: https://www.findlay.edu/pharmacy/pharm-d-mba

PharmD/MSHI (Health Informatics): https://www.findlay.edu/pharmacy/pharm-d-health-informatics

What service learning opportunities exist? Various service organizations, including Oilers Serving Abroad, Habitat for Humanity, and the international experiential rotations.

What percent of graduates place in postgraduate training? N/A

NAPLEX First-Time Pass Rate: 88.37% (2020)

MPJE First-Time Pass Rate: 93.75% (2020)

Note: This is a Direct Entry (0-6) program intended for high school applicants. However, the University of Findlay accepts transfer students into the first three years.

ILLINOIS

INDIANA

IOWA

KANSAS

MICHIGAN

MINNESOTA

MISSOURI

NEBRASKA

NORTH DAKOTA

OHIO

SOUTH DAKOTA

WISCONSIN

MIDWEST

ILLINOIS

INDIANA

IOWA

KANSAS

MICHIGAN

MINNESOTA

MISSOURI

NEBRASKA

NORTH DAKOTA

OHIO

SOUTH DAKOTA

WISCONSIN

UNIVERSITY OF TOLEDO COLLEGE OF PHARMACY AND PHARMACEUTICAL SCIENCES

Address: 3000 Arlington Ave, Toledo, OH 43614
Website: *https://www.utoledo.edu/pharmacy/*
Contact: *https://www.utoledo.edu/pharmacy/Contact_us.html*
Phone: (419) 530-2010

COST OF ATTENDANCE

In-State Tuition and Fees: $18,489
Additional Expenses: N/A
Total: $18,489*

Out-of-State Tuition and Fees: $27,849
Additional Expenses: N/A
Total: $27,849*

*Note: These figures do not reflect estimated housing/living expenses.

Financial Aid: https://www.utoledo.edu/pharmacy/prospective/scholarships.html

ADDITIONAL INFORMATION

Interesting tidbit: UToledo PharmD is a six-year program - two years of pre-professional course work and four years of professional PharmD. Students spend the first two years on UToledo's Main Campus and the next four professional years just a few miles away on the Health Science Campus. Pharmacy students at UToledo enjoy the personal attention of a small college with the resources and opportunities of a large university.

Important Updates due to COVID-19: Virtual Interview

Were tests required? No.

Are tests expected next year? No.

What international experiences are available? International rotations.

What dual degree options exist? PharmD/MBA, PharmD/PhD, and PharmD/MS in Health Outcomes and Socioeconomic Sciences. For more information, visit: https://www.utoledo.edu/pharmacy/academic-programs/#dual-degree

What service learning opportunities exist? N/A

What percent of graduates place in postgraduate training? 31% (2019)

NAPLEX First-Time Pass Rate: 89.90% (2020)

MPJE First-Time Pass Rate: 90.91% (2020)

Other: Contingent Admission (0-6) available to high school applicants and Early Admission (1+5) for UToledo first-year students who did not gain Contingent Admission are also available. For more information, visit: https://www.utoledo.edu/pharmacy/academic_programs/pharmdprogram/pathways.html

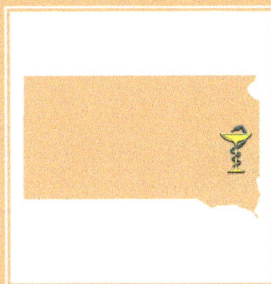

SOUTH DAKOTA STATE UNIVERSITY COLLEGE OF PHARMACY AND ALLIED HEALTH PROFESSIONS

Address: Avera Health Science Center, Brookings, SD 57007
Website: *https://www.sdstate.edu/pharmacy-allied-health-professions*
Contact: *Contact via email: sdsu.pharmacy@sdstate.edu*
Phone: (605) 688-6197

COST OF ATTENDANCE

In-State Tuition and Fees: $20,337
Additional Expenses: N/A
Total: $20,337*

Out-of-State Tuition and Fees: $31,875
Additional Expenses: N/A
Total: $31,875*

*Note: These figures do not reflect estimated housing/living expenses.

Financial Aid: https://www.sdstate.edu/admissions/office-financial-aid

ADDITIONAL INFORMATION

Interesting tidbit: When South Dakota State College attained university status in 1964, the Division of Pharmacy became the College of Pharmacy. In 1994, 50 students were the first to be admitted into the professional program and graduated in 1998.

Important Updates due to COVID-19: VIrtual Interview

Were tests required? PCAT required.

Are tests expected next year? Yes.

What international experiences are available? Study abroad during clinical experience.

What dual degree options exist? PharmD/MPH and PharmD/PhD. For more information on the PharmD/PhD, visit: https://www.sdstate.edu/pharmacy-and-allied-health-professions/phd-pharmaceutical-sciences

What service learning opportunities exist? Service learning through experiential education during APPEs. For more information, visit: https://www.sdstate.edu/pharmacy-allied-health-professions/doctor-pharmacy-pharmd/office-experiential-education

In addition, students are often involved in government outreach at the state level, provide health screenings, and provide immunizations.

What percent of graduates place in postgraduate training? 47% (2021)

NAPLEX First-Time Pass Rate: 97.33% (2020)

MPJE First-Time Pass Rate: 98.15% (2020)

Other: Pre-Admission Program available to high school applicants. For more information, visit: https://www.sdstate.edu/pharmacy-allied-health-professions/doctor-pharmacy-pharmd/pre-admission-program

ILLINOIS

INDIANA

IOWA

KANSAS

MICHIGAN

MINNESOTA

MISSOURI

NEBRASKA

NORTH DAKOTA

OHIO

SOUTH DAKOTA

WISCONSIN

MIDWEST

ILLINOIS

INDIANA

IOWA

KANSAS

MICHIGAN

MINNESOTA

MISSOURI

NEBRASKA

NORTH DAKOTA

OHIO

SOUTH DAKOTA

WISCONSIN

CONCORDIA UNIVERSITY WISCONSIN SCHOOL OF PHARMACY

Address: 12800 N Lake Shore Drive, Mequon, WI 53097
Website: *https://www.cuw.edu/academics/schools/pharmacy/index.html*
Contact: *https://www.cuw.edu/admissions/contact.html*
Phone: (877) 289-1897

COST OF ATTENDANCE

Tuition and Fees: $40,122
Additional Expenses: N/A
Total: $40,122*

*Note: This figure does not reflect estimated housing/living expenses.

Financial Aid: https://www.cuw.edu/academics/schools/pharmacy/admissions/financial-aid.html

ADDITIONAL INFORMATION

Interesting tidbit: As a Lutheran institution, CUW SOP is committed to helping students develop in mind, body, and spirit for service to Christ in the Church and the world. At CUW SOP, 40 percent of program learning happens in real-life clinical settings.

Important Updates due to COVID-19: VIrtual Interview

Were tests required? No.

Are tests expected next year? No.

What international experiences are available? Study abroad.

What dual degree options exist? PharmD/MBA, PharmD/MPH, and PharmD/MS in Pharmaceutical/Chemical Product Development. For more information, visit: https://www.cuw.edu/academics/schools/pharmacy/programs.html

What service learning opportunities exist? Community engagement, volunteering, and service to local communities.

What percent of graduates place in postgraduate training? 34% (year unspecified)

NAPLEX First-Time Pass Rate: 83.08% (2020)

MPJE First-Time Pass Rate: 74.51% (2020)

Other: Early Assurance pathway available for high school applicants. For more information, visit: https://www.cuw.edu/academics/schools/pharmacy/admissions/early-assurance.html

MEDICAL COLLEGE OF WISCONSIN SCHOOL OF PHARMACY

Address: 8701 Watertown Plank Rd., Milwaukee, WI 53226
Website: *https://www.mcw.edu/education/pharmacy-school*
Contact: *https://www.mcw.edu/contact-us*
Phone: (414) 955-7476

COST OF ATTENDANCE

Tuition and Fees: $50,234
Additional Expenses: N/A
Total: $50,234*

*Note: This figure does not reflect estimated housing/living expenses.

Financial Aid: https://www.mcw.edu/education/pharmacy-school/prospective-students/tuition-and-fees

ADDITIONAL INFORMATION

Interesting tidbit: The MCW Pharmacy School offers a three-year, year round curriculum that begins in July. MCW Pharmacy School students may pursue an academic concentration. In Year 1, students may apply to pursue an academic concentration in one of the following areas - Research, Population Health, Specialized Pharmacy Practice, and Entrepreneurship & Leadership.

Important Updates due to COVID-19: VIrtual Interview

Were tests required? No.

Are tests expected next year? No.

What international experiences are available? N/A

What dual degree options exist? No dual degree options listed.

What service learning opportunities exist? Community engagement opportunities such as the Saturday Clinic for the Uninsured. For more information, visit: https://www.mcw.edu/departments/community-engagement

What percent of graduates place in postgraduate training? N/A

NAPLEX First-Time Pass Rate: 97.30% (2020)

MPJE First-Time Pass Rate: 84.62% (2020)

Other: 0-6 Program and other pathways available. For more information, visit: https://www.mcw.edu/education/pharmacy-school/prospective-students/undergraduate-dual-degree-programs

ILLINOIS

INDIANA

IOWA

KANSAS

MICHIGAN

MINNESOTA

MISSOURI

NEBRASKA

NORTH DAKOTA

OHIO

SOUTH DAKOTA

WISCONSIN

MIDWEST

UNIVERSITY OF WISCONSIN-MADISON
SCHOOL OF PHARMACY

Address: 777 Highland Avenue, Madison, WI 53705
Website: *https://pharmacy.wisc.edu/*
Contact: *https://pharmacy.wisc.edu/request-info/request-info-about-pharmd/*
Phone: (608) 262-6234

COST OF ATTENDANCE

In-State Tuition and Fees: $25,711
Additional Expenses: N/A
Total: $25,711*

Out-of-State Tuition and Fees: $43,554
Additional Expenses: N/A
Total: $43,554*

*Note: This figure does not reflect estimated housing/living expenses.

Financial Aid: https://pharmacy.wisc.edu/academics/pharmd/financial-aid/

ADDITIONAL INFORMATION

Interesting tidbit: The University of Wisconsin–Madison PharmD curriculum blends foundational knowledge from biomedical, pharmaceutical, and clinical sciences approaches. With over 10 PharmD specializations available, students can distinguish themselves in their career interests.

Important Updates due to COVID-19: VIrtual Interview

Were tests required? No.

Are tests expected next year? No.

What international experiences are available? International trips and APPE clerkship. For more information, visit: https://pharmacy.wisc.edu/about-us/offices/global-health/opportunities/

What dual degree options exist? PharmD/MPH For more information, visit: https://pharmacy.wisc.edu/academics/pharmd/dual-degree-programs/

What service learning opportunities exist? Second-year PharmD service learning trips. For more information, visit: https://pharmacy.wisc.edu/about-us/offices/global-health/opportunities/second-year-pharmd-service-learning-opportunities/

What percent of graduates place in postgraduate training? 56% (2020)

NAPLEX First-Time Pass Rate: 93.65% (2020)

MPJE First-Time Pass Rate: 97.98% (2020)

ILLINOIS
INDIANA
IOWA
KANSAS
MICHIGAN
MINNESOTA
MISSOURI
NEBRASKA
NORTH DAKOTA
OHIO
SOUTH DAKOTA
WISCONSIN

ALABAMA

ARKANSAS

DELAWARE

DISTRICT OF
COLUMBIA

FLORIDA

GEORGIA

KENTUCKY

LOUISIANA

MARYLAND

MISSISSIPPI

NORTH CAROLINA

OKLAHOMA

SOUTH CAROLINA

TENNESSEE

TEXAS

VIRGINIA

WEST VIRGINIA

CHAPTER 4

REGION THREE
SOUTH

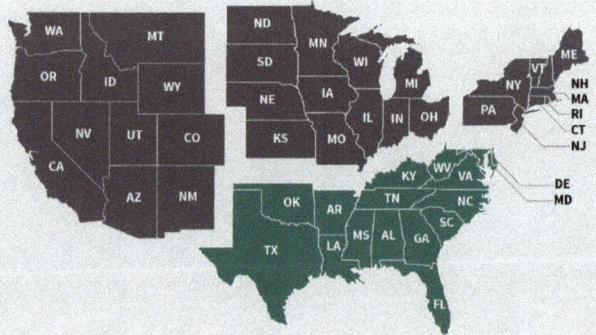

55 *Programs* | 16 *States*

1. AL – Auburn University Harrison School of Pharmacy
2. AL - Samford University McWhorter School of Pharmacy
3. AR - Harding University College of Pharmacy
4. AR - University of Arkansas for Medical Sciences College of Pharmacy
5. DC - Howard University College of Pharmacy
6. FL - Florida Agricultural & Mechanical University College of Pharmacy and Pharmaceutical Sciences
7. FL - Larkin University College of Pharmacy
8. FL - Nova Southeastern University College of Pharmacy
9. FL - Palm Beach Atlantic University Lloyd L. Gregory School of Pharmacy
10. FL - University of Florida College of Pharmacy
11. FL - University of South Florida Health Taneja College of Pharmacy
12. GA - Mercer University College of Pharmacy
13. GA - Philadelphia College of Osteopathic Medicine - Georgia School of Pharmacy
14. GA - South University School of Pharmacy
15. GA - University of Georgia College of Pharmacy
16. KY - Sullivan University College of Pharmacy
17. KY - University of Kentucky College of Pharmacy
18. LA - University of Louisiana at Monroe College of Pharmacy
19. LA - Xavier University of Louisiana College of Pharmacy
20. MD - Notre Dame of Maryland University School of Pharmacy
21. MD - University of Maryland Eastern Shore School of Pharmacy and Health Professions
22. MD - University of Maryland School of Pharmacy
23. MS - University of Mississippi School of Pharmacy
24. MS - William Carey University School of Pharmacy
25. NC - Campbell University College of Pharmacy and Health Sciences
26. NC - High Point University Fred Wilson School of Pharmacy
27. NC - University of North Carolina Eshelman School of Pharmacy
28. NC - Wingate University School of Pharmacy
29. OK - Southwestern Oklahoma State University College of Pharmacy
30. OK - University of Oklahoma College of Pharmacy
31. SC - Medical University of South Carolina College of Pharmacy
32. SC - Presbyterian College School of Pharmacy
33. SC - University of South Carolina College of Pharmacy
34. TN - Belmont University College of Pharmacy
35. TN - East Tennessee State University Bill Gatton College of Pharmacy
36. TN - Lipscomb University College of Pharmacy and Health Sciences
37. TN - South College School of Pharmacy
38. TN - Union University College of Pharmacy
39. TN - University of Tennessee Health Science Center College of Pharmacy
40. TX - Texas A & M University Health Science Center Irma Lerma Rangel College of Pharmacy
41. TX - Texas Southern University College of Pharmacy and Health Sciences
42. TX - Texas Tech University Health Sciences Center Jerry H. Hodge School of Pharmacy
43. TX - University of Houston College of Pharmacy
44. TX - University of North Texas Health Science Center UNT System College of Pharmacy
45. TX - University of Texas at Austin College of Pharmacy
46. TX - University of Texas at El Paso School of Pharmacy
47. TX - University of Texas at Tyler Ben and Maytee Fisch College of Pharmacy
48. TX - University of the Incarnate Word Feik School of Pharmacy
49. VA - Appalachian College of Pharmacy
50. VA - Hampton University School of Pharmacy
51. VA - Shenandoah University Bernard J. Dunn School of Pharmacy
52. VA - Virginia Commonwealth University at the Medical College of Virginia Campus School of Pharmacy
53. WV - Marshall University School of Pharmacy
54. WV - University of Charleston School of Pharmacy
55. WV - West Virginia University School of Pharmacy

PHARMACY PROGRAMS

Pharmacy School	Ave. GPA & PCAT (%) / Early Decision (ED): Yes/No / Int'l Students: Yes/No	Admissions Statistics	Science Req. Other than Gen Chem, OChem, Physics, Bio
Auburn University Harrison 2316 Walker Building, AL 36849	3.4 PCAT: Optional ED: Yes Int'l Student: Yes	(2019) Apps Received: 365 Interviews Offered: N/A Admission Offered: N/A Number Enrolled: 153 Admitted Rate: 41.3% (2020) Apps Received: 281 Interviews Offered: N/A Admission Offered: N/A Number Enrolled: 148 Admitted Rate: 52.7%	Biochem. Microbio. w/ Lab Calc. Physio. Stats. Social/Behav. Sci
Samford University McWhorter 800 Lakeshore Dr., Birmingham, AL 35229	3.2 PCAT: Not Req. ED: Yes Int'l Student: Yes	(2019) Apps Received: 314 Interviews Offered: N/A Admission Offered: N/A Number Enrolled: 123 Admitted Rate: 32.9% (2020) Apps Received: 238 Interviews Offered: N/A Admission Offered: N/A Number Enrolled: 127 Admitted Rate: 53.4%	Calc. Human Anatomy & Physio. Microbio. Elementary Stats. Sociology/Psych.
Harding University* 915 E. Market Ave., Searcy, AR 72149	3.4 PCAT: Optional ED: Yes Int'l Student: Yes	(2019) Apps Received: 141 Interviews Offered: N/A Admission Offered: N/A Number Enrolled: 36 Admitted Rate: 25.5% (2020) Apps Received: 62 Interviews Offered: N/A Admission Offered: N/A Number Enrolled: 39 Admitted Rate: 62.9%	Biochem. Microbio. w/ Lab Calc. Stats. Psych./Sociology Bio. coursework (see Chart) *This is a 3.5 yr program, starting with a summer semester.

PHARMACY PROGRAMS

Pharmacy School	Ave. GPA & PCAT (%) / Early Decision (ED): Yes/No / Int'l Students: Yes/No	Admissions Statistics	Science Req. Other than Gen Chem, OChem, Physics, Bio
University of Arkansas for Medical Sciences 4301 W Markham St., Little Rock, AR 72205	3.7 PCAT: 80 ED: Yes Int'l Student: No	(2019) Apps Received: 218 Interviews Offered: N/A Admission Offered: N/A Number Enrolled: 97 Admitted Rate: 44.5% (2020) Apps Received: 139 Interviews Offered: N/A Admission Offered: N/A Number Enrolled: 75 Admitted Rate: 54.0%	College Algebra Microbio. w/ Lab Stats. Psych. Advanced Science Selectives (See Chart)
Howard University 2300 4th Street NW, Washington, DC 20059	3.3 PCAT: Recommended ED: Yes Int'l Student: Yes	(2019) Apps Received: 340 Interviews Offered: N/A Admission Offered: N/A Number Enrolled: 39 Admitted Rate: 11.5% (2020) Apps Received: 266 Interviews Offered: N/A Admission Offered: N/A Number Enrolled: 79 Admitted Rate: 29.7%	Calc. Socio-Behav. Sciences Anatomy/Physio. Biochem.
Florida Agricultural & Mechanical University 1415 S. Martin Luther King, Jr. Blvd., Tallahassee, FL 32307	3.5 PCAT: Not Req. ED: No Int'l Student: Yes	(2019) Apps Received: 366 Interviews Offered: N/A Admission Offered: N/A Number Enrolled: 145 Admitted Rate: 39.6% (2020) Apps Received: 266 Interviews Offered: N/A Admission Offered: N/A Number Enrolled: 87 Admitted Rate: 38.5%	Larkin University* 18301 N Miami Ave, Miami, FL 33169

SOUTH

PHARMACY PROGRAMS

Pharmacy School	Ave. GPA & PCAT (%) Early Decision (ED): Yes/No Int'l Students: Yes/No	Admissions Statistics	Science Req. Other than Gen Chem, OChem, Physics, Bio
Larkin University* 18301 N Miami Ave, Miami, FL 33169	N/A PCAT: Recommended ED: Yes Int'l Student: No	(2019) Apps Received: 310 Interviews Offered: N/A Admission Offered: N/A Number Enrolled: N/A Admitted Rate: N/A (2020) Apps Received: 226 Interviews Offered: N/A Admission Offered: N/A Number Enrolled: 87 Admitted Rate: 38.5%	Anatomy & Physio. Calc. Stats. Advanced Science Courses Psych./Sociology Humanities or Soc./Behav. Sciences *This is an accelerated 3-year PharmD program.
Nova Southeastern University 3301 College Ave., Fort Lauderdale, FL 33314	3.5 PCAT: Recommended ED: Yes Int'l Student: Yes	(2019) Apps Received: 896 Interviews Offered: N/A Admission Offered: N/A Number Enrolled: 209 Admitted Rate: 23.3% (2020) Apps Received: 761 Interviews Offered: N/A Admission Offered: N/A Number Enrolled: 219 Admitted Rate: 28.8%	Anatomy & Physio. Soc./Behav. Sciences Calc. Advanced Sciences (see Chart)
Palm Beach Atlantic University 901 S Flagler Dr., West Palm Beach, FL 33401	3.4 PCAT: 72 ED: Yes Int'l Student: Yes	(2019) Apps Received: 321 Interviews Offered: N/A Admission Offered: N/A Number Enrolled: 83 Admitted Rate: 25.9% (2020) Apps Received: 243 Interviews Offered: N/A Admission Offered: N/A Number Enrolled: 75 Admitted Rate: 30.9%	Stats. Calc. Human Anatomy & Physio. w/ Lab Microbio. w/ Lab Biochem.

Pharmacy School	Ave. GPA & PCAT (%) Early Decision (ED): Yes/No Int'l Students: Yes/No	Admissions Statistics	Science Req. Other than Gen Chem, OChem, Physics, Bio
University of Florida 1225 Center Drive, Gainesville, FL 32610	3.4 PCAT: 65 ED: Yes Int'l Student: Yes	(2019) Apps Received: 612 Interviews Offered: N/A Admission Offered: N/A Number Enrolled: 280 Admitted Rate: 45.8% (2020) Apps Received: 449 Interviews Offered: N/A Admission Offered: N/A Number Enrolled: 248 Admitted Rate: 55.2%	Analytical Geom. w/ Calc. Soc./Behav. Sciences Anatomy/Physio w/ Lab Biochem. Microbio. Stats.
University of South Florida 12901 Bruce B. Downs Blvd., Tampa, FL 33612	N/A PCAT: N/A ED: Yes Int'l Student: No	(2019) Apps Received: 428 Interviews Offered: N/A Admission Offered: N/A Number Enrolled: 101 Admitted Rate: 23.6% (2020) Apps Received: 305 Interviews Offered: N/A Admission Offered: N/A Number Enrolled: 92 Admitted Rate: 30.2%	Calc. Biochem. Genetics Psych./Sociology Stats. Microbio. Human Anatomy & Physio. Cell or Molecular Bio.
Mercer University 3001 Mercer University Dr., Atlanta, GA 30341	3.3 PCAT: Optional ED: Yes Int'l Student: Yes	(2019) Apps Received: 442 Interviews Offered: N/A Admission Offered: N/A Number Enrolled: 135 Admitted Rate: 30.5% (2020) Apps Received: 449 Interviews Offered: N/A Admission Offered: N/A Number Enrolled: 122 Admitted Rate: 27.2%	Anatomy & Physio. Microbio. Biochem. Calc. Stats. Soc./Behav. Science Elective

SOUTH

PHARMACY PROGRAMS

Pharmacy School	Ave. GPA & PCAT (%) — Early Decision (ED): Yes/No — Int'l Students: Yes/No	Admissions Statistics	Science Req. Other than Gen Chem, OChem, Physics, Bio
PCOM - Georgia 625 Old Peachtree Road NW, Suwanee, GA 30024	2.86 (overall) 2.65 (science) PCAT: 28 ED: Yes Int'l Student: Yes	(2019) Apps Received: 553 Interviews Offered: N/A Admission Offered: N/A Number Enrolled: 93 Admitted Rate: 16.8% (2020) Apps Received: 340 Interviews Offered: N/A Admission Offered: 203 Number Enrolled: 91 Admitted Rate: 26.8%	Calc. Stats. Soc./Behav. Sciences
South University* 709 Mall Blvd, Savannah, GA 31406	3.3 PCAT: Not Req. ED: Yes Int'l Student: Yes	(2019) Apps Received: 607 Interviews Offered: N/A Admission Offered: N/A Number Enrolled: 90 Admitted Rate: 9.9% (2020) Apps Received: N/A Interviews Offered: N/A Admission Offered: N/A Number Enrolled: 76 Admitted Rate: N/A	Microbio. Anatomy & Physio. Psych./Sociology Calc. Stats. *This is an accelerated 3-year PharmD program.
University of Georgia 250 W. Green Street Athens, GA 30602	3.4 PCAT: 80 ED: Yes Int'l Student: Yes	(2019) Apps Received: 401 Interviews Offered: 210-250 Admission Offered: N/A Number Enrolled: 157 Admitted Rate: 39.2% (2020) Apps Received: 358 Interviews Offered: N/A Admission Offered: N/A Number Enrolled: 146 Admitted Rate: 40.8%	Calc. Stats. Soc.Behav. Sciences Microbio. Biochem. Anatomy & Physio.

PHARMACY PROGRAMS

Pharmacy School	Ave. GPA & PCAT (%) Early Decision (ED): Yes/No Int'l Students: Yes/No	Admissions Statistics	Science Req. Other than Gen Chem, OChem, Physics, Bio
Sullivan University 3101 Bardstown Rd., Louisville, KY 40205	3.3 PCAT: Optional ED: Yes Int'l Student: Yes	(2019) Apps Received: 251 Interviews Offered: 150-200 Admission Offered: N/A Number Enrolled: 65 Admitted Rate: 25.9% (2020) Apps Received: 117 Interviews Offered: N/A Admission Offered: N/A Number Enrolled: 48 Admitted Rate: 41.0%	Calc. Microbio. w/ Lab Human Anatomy & Physio. Stats. *This is an accelerated 3-year PharmD program
University of Kentucky 789 South Limestone, Lexington, KY 40536	3.6 PCAT: Not Req. ED: Yes Int'l Student: Yes	(2019) Apps Received: 282 Interviews Offered: N/A Admission Offered: N/A Number Enrolled: 134 Admitted Rate: 47.5% (2020) Apps Received: 252 Interviews Offered: N/A Admission Offered: N/A Number Enrolled: 140 Admitted Rate: 55.6%	Microbio. w/ Lab Anatomy Physio. Stats. Math
University of Louisiana at Monroe 1800 Bienville Dr., Monroe, LA 71201	3.5 PCAT: 56 ED: Yes Int'l Student: Yes	(2019) Apps Received: 208 Interviews Offered: N/A Admission Offered: N/A Number Enrolled: 86 Admitted Rate: 41.3% (2020) Apps Received: 122 Interviews Offered: N/A Admission Offered: N/A Number Enrolled: 84 Admitted Rate: 68.9%	Stats. Microbio. w/ Lab Anatomy & Physio. w/ Lab Cell Bio./Cell Physio. Genetics Calc. Biochem. Social Sciences

SOUTH

PHARMACY PROGRAMS

Pharmacy School	Ave. GPA & PCAT (%) Early Decision (ED): Yes/No Int'l Students: Yes/No	Admissions Statistics	Science Req. Other than Gen Chem, OChem, Physics, Bio
Xavier University of Louisiana 1 Drexel Dr., New Orleans, LA 70125	3.3 PCAT: Not Req. ED: No Int'l Student: Yes	(2019) Apps Received: 335 Interviews Offered: N/A Admission Offered: N/A Number Enrolled: 155 Admitted Rate: 43.6% (2020) Apps Received: 250 Interviews Offered: N/A Admission Offered: N/A Number Enrolled: 158 Admitted Rate: 63.2%	Microbio. w/ Lab Calc. Biostats. Psych./Sociology
Notre Dame of Maryland University 4701 North Charles Street, Baltimore, MD 21210	3.2 PCAT: Not Req. ED: Yes Int'l Student: Yes	(2019) Apps Received: 265 Interviews Offered: 93 (approx.) Admission Offered: N/A Number Enrolled: 65 Admitted Rate: 24.5% (2020) Apps Received: 186 Interviews Offered: N/A Admission Offered: N/A Number Enrolled: 52 Admitted Rate: 28.0%	Anatomy & Physio. w/ Lab Psych./Social Science Calc. Stats. Microbio. w/ Lab
University of Maryland Eastern Shore 11868 College Backbone Rd, Princess Anne, MD 21853	N/A PCAT: N/A ED: Yes Int'l Student: Yes	(2019) Apps Received: 209 Interviews Offered: N/A Admission Offered: N/A Number Enrolled: 50 Admitted Rate: 23.9% (2020) Apps Received: 159 Interviews Offered: N/A Admission Offered: N/A Number Enrolled: 49 Admitted Rate: 30.8%	Anatomy & Physio. w/ Lab Microbio. w/ Lab Calc. Stats. Humanities/Social Sciences *This is an accelerated 3-year PharmD program.

PHARMACY PROGRAMS

Pharmacy School	Ave. GPA & PCAT (%) Early Decision (ED): Yes/No Int'l Students: Yes/No	Admissions Statistics	Science Req. Other than Gen Chem, OChem, Physics, Bio
University of Maryland 20 North Pine St., Baltimore, MD 21201	3.5 PCAT: Not Req. ED: Yes Int'l Student: Yes	(2019) Apps Received: 632 Interviews Offered: N/A Admission Offered: N/A Number Enrolled: 132 Admitted Rate: 20.9% (2020) Apps Received: 380 Interviews Offered: N/A Admission Offered: N/A Number Enrolled: 125 Admitted Rate: 32.9%	Calc. Microbio. w/ Lab Stats. Human Anatomy & Physio.
University of Mississippi Thad Cochran Research Center, University Ave, University, MS 38677	3.2 PCAT: Not Req. ED: Yes Int'l Student: Yes	(2019) Apps Received: 153 Interviews Offered: N/A Admission Offered: N/A Number Enrolled: 107 Admitted Rate: 69.9% (2020) Apps Received: 152 Interviews Offered: N/A Admission Offered: N/A Number Enrolled: 109 Admitted Rate: 71.7%	Bioethics. Biochem. Human Physio. Medical Microbio. Genetics Calc. Human Anatomy Social Sciences
William Carey University 19640 Highway 67, Biloxi, MS 39532	N/A PCAT: Not Req. ED: Yes Int'l Student: Yes	(2019) Apps Received: 134 Interviews Offered: N/A Admission Offered: N/A Number Enrolled: 44 Admitted Rate: 32.9% (2020) Apps Received: 121 Interviews Offered: N/A Admission Offered: N/A Number Enrolled: 51 Admitted Rate: 42.1%	Human Anatomy & Phsyio. w/ Lab Calc. Stats. Social Sciences *This is an accelerated 3-year PharmD program.

SOUTH

PHARMACY PROGRAMS

Pharmacy School	Ave. GPA & PCAT (%) Early Decision (ED): Yes/No Int'l Students: Yes/No	Admissions Statistics	Science Req. Other than Gen Chem, OChem, Physics, Bio
Campbell University 143 Main Street, Buies Creek, NC 27506	3.3 (overall) 3.09 (science) PCAT: 50 ED: Yes Int'l Student: Yes	(2019) Apps Received: 357 Interviews Offered: N/A Admission Offered: N/A Number Enrolled: 97 Admitted Rate: 27.2% (2020) Apps Received: 254 Interviews Offered: N/A Admission Offered: N/A Number Enrolled: 74 Admitted Rate: 29.1%	Calc. Microbio. w/ Lab Human Anatomy & Physio. w/ Lab Stats.
High Point University One University Parkway High Point North Carolina 27268	N/A PCAT: N/A ED: Yes Int'l Student: Yes	(2019) Apps Received: 233 Interviews Offered: N/A Admission Offered: N/A Number Enrolled: 61 Admitted Rate: 26.2% (2020) Apps Received: 149 Interviews Offered: N/A Admission Offered: N/A Number Enrolled: 60 Admitted Rate: 40.3%	Physio. w/ Lab Microbio. w/ Lab Calc. Soc./Behav. Science
University of North Carolina 301 Pharmacy Lane, CB 7355, Chapel Hill, NC 27599	3.5 PCAT: 86 ED: Yes Int'l Student: Yes	(2019) Apps Received: 492 Interviews Offered: ~200 Admission Offered: N/A Number Enrolled: 146 Admitted Rate: 29.7% (2020) Apps Received: 453 Interviews Offered: N/A Admission Offered: N/A Number Enrolled: 130 Admitted Rate: 28.7%	Calc. Stats. Human Anatomy & Physio. w/ Lab Microbio. w/ Lab Biochem.

PHARMACY PROGRAMS

Pharmacy School	Ave. GPA & PCAT (%) Early Decision (ED): Yes/No Int'l Students: Yes/No	Admissions Statistics	Science Req. Other than Gen Chem, OChem, Physics, Bio
Wingate University 220 N Camden St Wingate, NC 28174	3.5 PCAT: Optional ED: Yes Int'l Student: Yes	(2019) Apps Received: 349 Interviews Offered: ~150 Admission Offered: N/A Number Enrolled: 83 Admitted Rate: 23.8% (2020) Apps Received: 269 Interviews Offered: N/A Admission Offered: N/A Number Enrolled: 75 Admitted Rate: 27.9%	Calc. Stats. Anatomy & Physio. w/ Lab Microbio. w/ Lab
Southwestern Oklahoma State University 100 Campus Dr., Weatherford, OK 73096	3.6 PCAT: Not Req. ED: No Int'l Student: No	(2019) Apps Received: 133 Interviews Offered: N/A Admission Offered: N/A Number Enrolled: 76 Admitted Rate: 57.1% (2020) Apps Received: 89 Interviews Offered: N/A Admission Offered: N/A Number Enrolled: 73 Admitted Rate: 82.0%	Calc. Anatomy w/ Lab Psych. Microbio. w/ Lab
University of Oklahoma 1110 N. Stonewall Ave., Oklahoma City, OK 73117	3.45 (overall) 3.20 (science) 3.35 (math) PCAT: ED: Yes Int'l Student: No	(2019) Apps Received: 139 Interviews Offered: N/A Admission Offered: N/A Number Enrolled: 61 Admitted Rate: 42.9% (2020) Apps Received: 90 Interviews Offered: N/A Admission Offered: N/A Number Enrolled: 58 Admitted Rate: 64.4%	Medical University of South Carolina 280 Calhoun Street, Charleston, SC 29425

SOUTH

PHARMACY PROGRAMS

Pharmacy School	Ave. GPA & PCAT (%) / Early Decision (ED): Yes/No / Int'l Students: Yes/No	Admissions Statistics	Science Req. Other than Gen Chem, OChem, Physics, Bio
Medical University of South Carolina 280 Calhoun Street, Charleston, SC 29425	3.6 PCAT: Optional ED: Yes Int'l Student: Yes	(2019) Apps Received: 215 Interviews Offered: N/A Admission Offered: N/A Number Enrolled: 69 Admitted Rate: 32.1% (2020) Apps Received: 152 Interviews Offered: N/A Admission Offered: N/A Number Enrolled: 67 Admitted Rate: 44.1%	Calc. Stats. Psych. Human Anatomy Human Physio. Microbio.
Presbyterian College 307 North Broad St., Clinton, SC 29325	N/A PCAT: Not Req. ED: Yes Int'l Student: Yes	(2019) Apps Received: 164 Interviews Offered: N/A Admission Offered: N/A Number Enrolled: 67 Admitted Rate: 40.9% (2020) Apps Received: 107 Interviews Offered: N/A Admission Offered: N/A Number Enrolled: 56 Admitted Rate: 52.3%	Microbio. w/ Lab Human Anatomy & Physio. Stats. Calc. Psych./Sociology
University of South Carolina 715 Sumter St., Columbia, SC 29208	3.6 PCAT: 68 ED: Yes Int'l Student: Yes	(2019) Apps Received: 271 Interviews Offered: N/A Admission Offered: N/A Number Enrolled: 114 Admitted Rate: 42.1% (2020) Apps Received: 227 Interviews Offered: N/A Admission Offered: N/A Number Enrolled: 110 Admitted Rate: 48.5%	Calc. Stats. Human Anatomy & Physio. Microbio. Soc./Behav. Science

PHARMACY PROGRAMS

Pharmacy School	Ave. GPA & PCAT (%) Early Decision (ED): Yes/No Int'l Students: Yes/No	Admissions Statistics	Science Req. Other than Gen Chem, OChem, Physics, Bio
Belmont University 1900 Belmont Blvd, Nashville, TN 37212	3.3 PCAT: Optional ED: Yes Int'l Student: Yes	(2019) Apps Received: 535 Interviews Offered: N/A Admission Offered: N/A Number Enrolled: 93 Admitted Rate: 17.4% (2020) Apps Received: 275 Interviews Offered: N/A Admission Offered: N/A Number Enrolled: 90 Admitted Rate: 32.7%	Calc. Stats. Soc. Sciences
East Tennessee State University Gatton College of Pharmacy, Maple Ave, Johnson City, TN 37604	3.3 PCAT: Not Req. ED: Yes Int'l Student: Yes	(2019) Apps Received: 610 Interviews Offered: N/A Admission Offered: N/A Number Enrolled: 84 Admitted Rate: 13.8% (2020) Apps Received: 370 Interviews Offered: N/A Admission Offered: N/A Number Enrolled: 78 Admitted Rate: 21.1%	Microbio. w/ Lab Bio. Elective Calc. Stats. Social Sciences/Humanities Electives
Lipscomb University 1 University Park Dr., Nashville, TN 37204	3.3 PCAT: Optional ED: Yes Int'l Student: Yes	(2019) Apps Received: 349 Interviews Offered: N/A Admission Offered: N/A Number Enrolled: 77 Admitted Rate: 22.1% (2020) Apps Received: 288 Interviews Offered: N/A Admission Offered: N/A Number Enrolled: 68 Admitted Rate: 23.6%	Microbio. w/ Lab Stats. Calc. Social Science/Humanities Electives

SOUTH

PHARMACY PROGRAMS

Pharmacy School	Ave. GPA & PCAT (%) Early Decision (ED): Yes/No Int'l Students: Yes/No	Admissions Statistics	Science Req. Other than Gen Chem, OChem, Physics, Bio
South College* 3904 Lonas Dr., Knoxville, TN 37909	N/A PCAT: Not Req. ED: Yes Int'l Student: Yes	(2019) Apps Received: 395 Interviews Offered: N/A Admission Offered: N/A Number Enrolled: 100 Admitted Rate: 25.3% (2020) Apps Received: 354 Interviews Offered: N/A Admission Offered: N/A Number Enrolled: 99 Admitted Rate: 28.0%	Anatomy & Physio. w/ Lab Microbio. w/ Lab Calc. Stats. *This is an accelerated 3-year PharmD program.
Union University 1050 Union University Dr., Jackson, TN 38305	N/A PCAT: Optional ED: Yes Int'l Student: Yes	(2019) Apps Received: 198 Interviews Offered: N/A Admission Offered: N/A Number Enrolled: 53 Admitted Rate: 26.8% (2020) Apps Received: 105 Interviews Offered: N/A Admission Offered: N/A Number Enrolled: 41 Admitted Rate: 39.0%	Human Anatomy & Physio. w/ Lab Microbio. w/ Lab Calc. Stats. Soc. Science Electives
University of Tennessee 881 Madison Ave., Memphis, TN 38163	3.4 PCAT: Not Req. ED: Yes Int'l Student: Yes	(2019) Apps Received: 654 Interviews Offered: N/A Admission Offered: N/A Number Enrolled: 202 Admitted Rate: 30.9% (2020) Apps Received: 484 Interviews Offered: N/A Admission Offered: N/A Number Enrolled: 198 Admitted Rate: 40.9%	Microbio. w/ Lab Anatomy & Physio. w/ Lab Calc. Stats. Social Sciences

PHARMACY PROGRAMS

Pharmacy School	Ave. GPA & PCAT (%) Early Decision (ED): Yes/No Int'l Students: Yes/No	Admissions Statistics	Science Req. Other than Gen Chem, OChem, Physics, Bio
Texas A&M University Health Science Center 1010 W. Avenue B, Kingsville, TX 78363	3.4 PCAT: 60 ED: Yes Int'l Student: Yes	(2019) Apps Received: 395 Interviews Offered: N/A Admission Offered: N/A Number Enrolled: 108 Admitted Rate: 27.3% (2020) Apps Received: 310 Interviews Offered: N/A Admission Offered: N/A Number Enrolled: 112 Admitted Rate: 36.1%	Calc. Microbio. w/ Lab Molecular Bio. or Genetics Stats. Sociology/Psych/Econ/ Comp. Sci
Texas Southern University 3100 Cleburne Street Houston, TX 77004	3.4 PCAT: 48 ED: Yes Int'l Student: Yes	(2019) Apps Received: 447 Interviews Offered: N/A Admission Offered: N/A Number Enrolled: 86 Admitted Rate: 19.2% (2020) Apps Received: 231 Interviews Offered: N/A Admission Offered: N/A Number Enrolled: 70 Admitted Rate: 30.3%	Microbio. w/ Lab Human Anatomy & Physio. w/ Lab Stats. Calc. Soc./Behav. Sciences
Texas Tech University Health Sciences Center 3601 4th Street, Lubbock TX 79430	3.5 PCAT: 73 ED: Yes Int'l Student: Yes	(2019) Apps Received: 489 Interviews Offered: N/A Admission Offered: N/A Number Enrolled: 151 Admitted Rate: 30.9% (2020) Apps Received: 296 Interviews Offered: N/A Admission Offered: N/A Number Enrolled: 157 Admitted Rate: 53.0%	Microbio. w/ Lab Calc. Stats. Humanities/Social Sciences

SOUTH

PHARMACY PROGRAMS

Pharmacy School	Ave. GPA & PCAT (%) Early Decision (ED): Yes/No Int'l Students: Yes/No	Admissions Statistics	Science Req. Other than Gen Chem, OChem, Physics, Bio
University of Houston 4849 Calhoun, Houston, TX 77204	3.6 PCAT: 78 ED: Yes Int'l Student: Yes	Microbio. w/ Lab Genetics Calc. Stats.	Microbio. w/ Lab Genetics Calc. Stats.
University of North Texas Health Science Center 3500 Camp Bowie Blvd. Fort Worth, TX 76107	3.4 PCAT: Not Req. ED: Yes Int'l Student: No	(2019) Apps Received: 527 Interviews Offered: N/A Admission Offered: N/A Number Enrolled: 114 Admitted Rate: 21.6% (2020) Apps Received: 348 Interviews Offered: N/A Admission Offered: N/A Number Enrolled: 88 Admitted Rate: 25.3%	Microbio. w/ Lab Human Anatomy & Physio. w/ Lab Genetics Calc. Stats. Social/Behav. Science Elective
University of Texas at Austin 2409 University Ave., Austin, TX, 78712	3.7 PCAT: 84 ED: Yes Int'l Student: Yes	(2019) Apps Received: 408 Interviews Offered: N/A Admission Offered: N/A Number Enrolled: 127 Admitted Rate: 31.1% (2020) Apps Received: 318 Interviews Offered: N/A Admission Offered: N/A Number Enrolled: 125 Admitted Rate: 39.3%	Microbio. w/ Lab Genetics Calc. Stats.

PHARMACY PROGRAMS

Pharmacy School	Ave. GPA & PCAT (%) Early Decision (ED): Yes/No Int'l Students: Yes/No	Admissions Statistics	Science Req. Other than Gen Chem, OChem, Physics, Bio
University of Texas at El Paso 1101 N. Campbell St., El Paso, TX 79902	N/A PCAT: N/A ED: Yes Int'l Student: Yes	(2019) Apps Received: 131 Interviews Offered: N/A Admission Offered: N/A Number Enrolled: 57 Admitted Rate: 43.5% (2020) Apps Received: 91 Interviews Offered: N/A Admission Offered: N/A Number Enrolled: 57 Admitted Rate: 62.6%	Human Anatomy & Physio. w/ Lab Genetics Biochem. Microbio. w/ Lab
University of Texas at Tyler 3900 University Blvd., Tyler, TX 75799	N/A PCAT: Not Req. ED: Yes Int'l Student: Yes	(2019) Apps Received: 280 Interviews Offered: 143 Admission Offered: N/A Number Enrolled: 75 Admitted Rate: 26.8% (2020) Apps Received: 213 Interviews Offered: N/A Admission Offered: N/A Number Enrolled: 75 Admitted Rate: 35.2%	Microbio. w/ Lab Calc. Human Anatomy & Physio. w/ Lab

SOUTH

PHARMACY PROGRAMS

Pharmacy School	Ave. GPA & PCAT (%) Early Decision (ED): Yes/No Int'l Students: Yes/No	Admissions Statistics	Science Req. Other than Gen Chem, OChem, Physics, Bio
University of the Incarnate Word 4301 Broadway, San Antonio, TX 78209	3.6 PCAT: Optional ED: Yes Int'l Student: Yes	(2019) Apps Received: 310 Interviews Offered: N/A Admission Offered: N/A Number Enrolled: 117 Admitted Rate: 37.7% (2020) Apps Received: 198 Interviews Offered: N/A Admission Offered: N/A Number Enrolled: 92 Admitted Rate: 46.5%	Calc. Stats. Microbio. w/ Lab Anatomy & Physio. w/ Lab Social Science
Appalachian College of Pharmacy* 1060 Dragon Road, Oakwood, VA 24631	3.2 PCAT: Not Req. ED: Yes Int'l Student: Yes	(2019) Apps Received: 421 Interviews Offered: N/A Admission Offered: N/A Number Enrolled: 75 Admitted Rate: 17.8% (2020) Apps Received: 282 Interviews Offered: N/A Admission Offered: N/A Number Enrolled: 72 Admitted Rate: 25.5%	Human Anatomy/Physio. Microbio. Calc. Social/Behav. Science *This is an accelerated 3-year PharmD program.
Hampton University 121 William R. Harvey Way, Hampton, VA 23668	3.3 PCAT: 82 ED: No Int'l Student: Yes	(2019) Apps Received: 83 Interviews Offered: N/A Admission Offered: N/A Number Enrolled: 38 Admitted Rate: 45.8% (2020) Apps Received: N/A Interviews Offered: N/A Admission Offered: N/A Number Enrolled: N/A Admitted Rate: N/A	Calc. Stats. Social Science Microbio. (Lab pref.) Microbio./Immunology Human Anatomy w/ Lab Human Physio. w/ Lab Genetics

Pharmacy School	Ave. GPA & PCAT (%) Early Decision (ED): Yes/No Int'l Students: Yes/No	Admissions Statistics	Science Req. Other than Gen Chem, OChem, Physics, Bio
Shenandoah University Bernard J. Dunn 1775 N Sector Ct, Winchester, VA 22601	3.3 PCAT: 52 ED: Yes Int'l Student: Yes	(2019) Apps Received: 394 Interviews Offered: N/A Admission Offered: N/A Number Enrolled: 86 Admitted Rate: 21.8% (2020) Apps Received: 200 Interviews Offered: N/A Admission Offered: N/A Number Enrolled: 74 Admitted Rate: 37.0%	Calc. Stats. Microbio. Human Anatomy & Physio. Adv. Bio. Science Social/Behav. Science
Virginia Commonwealth University 410 N. 12th St., Richmond, VA 23298	3.6 PCAT: 70 ED: Yes Int'l Student: Yes	(2019) Apps Received: 400 Interviews Offered: N/A Admission Offered: N/A Number Enrolled: 138 Admitted Rate: 34.5% (2020) Apps Received: 259 Interviews Offered: N/A Admission Offered: N/A Number Enrolled: 103 Admitted Rate: 39.8%	Microbio. Biochem. Calc. Stats. Human Anatomy Human Physio.
Marshall University 1 John Marshall Drive, Huntington, WV 25701	N/A PCAT: Not Req. ED: Yes Int'l Student: Yes	(2019) Apps Received: 276 Interviews Offered: N/A Admission Offered: N/A Number Enrolled: 60 Admitted Rate: 21.7% (2020) Apps Received: 175 Interviews Offered: N/A Admission Offered: N/A Number Enrolled: 54 Admitted Rate: 30.9%	Calc. Stats. Human Anatomy w/ Lab Human Physio. w/ Lab Social Science Elective

SOUTH

PHARMACY PROGRAMS

Pharmacy School	Ave. GPA & PCAT (%) Early Decision (ED): Yes/No Int'l Students: Yes/No	Admissions Statistics	Science Req. Other than Gen Chem, OChem, Physics, Bio
University of Charleston 2300 MacCorkle Ave SE, Charleston, WV 25396	3.2 PCAT: 51 ED: Yes Int'l Student: Yes	(2019) Apps Received: 169 Interviews Offered: N/A Admission Offered: N/A Number Enrolled: 53 Admitted Rate: 31.4% (2020) Apps Received: 156 Interviews Offered: N/A Admission Offered: N/A Number Enrolled: 50 Admitted Rate: 32.1%	Human Anatomy w/ Lab Human Physio. w/ Lab Microbio. w/ Lab Calc. Stats. Psych./Sociology
West Virginia University 64 Medical Center Dr., Morgantown, WV 26506	3.5 PCAT: 51 ED: Yes Int'l Student: Yes	(2019) Apps Received: 226 Interviews Offered: N/A Admission Offered: N/A Number Enrolled: 79 Admitted Rate: 35.0% (2020) Apps Received: 122 Interviews Offered: N/A Admission Offered: N/A Number Enrolled: 65 Admitted Rate: 53.3%	Stats. Calc. Microbio. Biochem.

ALABAMA

ARKANSAS

DELAWARE

DISTRICT OF COLUMBIA

FLORIDA

GEORGIA

KENTUCKY

LOUISIANA

MARYLAND

MISSISSIPPI

NORTH CAROLINA

OKLAHOMA

SOUTH CAROLINA

TENNESSEE

TEXAS

VIRGINIA

WEST VIRGINIA

AUBURN UNIVERSITY HARRISON SCHOOL OF PHARMACY

Address: 2316 Walker Building, Auburn, AL 36849
Website: *https://pharmacy.auburn.edu/*
Contact: *Email – hsopcomm@auburn.edu*
Phone: (334) 844-8348

COST OF ATTENDANCE

In-State Tuition and Fees: $10,080
Additional Expenses: $12,282*
Total: $22,362*

Out-of-State Tuition and Fees: $30,240
Additional Expenses: $12,282*
Total: $42,522*

*Note: These figures do not reflect estimated housing/living expenses.

Financial Aid: http://www.auburn.edu/academic/pharmacy/apply/finance.html

ADDITIONAL INFORMATION

Interesting tidbit: The School has campuses both in Auburn and in Mobile, Alabama. The Mobile campus, created in 2006, is housed within the University of South Alabama Research Park. Auburn University has implemented a new Doctor of Pharmacy (PharmD) curriculum, the Practice Ready Curriculum (PRC).

Important Updates due to COVID-19: Virtual Interview

Were tests required? No.

Are tests expected next year? No.

What international experiences are available? International rotation in Thailand.

What dual degree options exist? PharmD/MPH and PharmD/PhD. For more information, visit: https://www.auburn.edu/academic/pharmacy/students/dual.html

What service learning opportunities exist? Numerous outreach opportunities. For more information, visit: http://www.auburn.edu/academic/pharmacy/outreach/index.html

What percent of graduates place in postgraduate training? 31.57% placed in PGY1 (2020) & 9.6% placed in PGY2 (2020)

NAPLEX First-Time Pass Rate: 87.02% (2020)

MPJE First-Time Pass Rate: 85.86% (2020)

Other: Early Assurance program. For more information, visit: http://www.auburn.edu/academic/pharmacy/apply/early.html

SAMFORD UNIVERSITY MCWHORTER SCHOOL OF PHARMACY

Address: 800 Lakeshore Dr., Birmingham, AL 35229
Website: *https://www.samford.edu/pharmacy/*
Contact: *https://www.samford.edu/pharmacy/contact*
Phone: (205) 726-2011

COST OF ATTENDANCE

Tuition and Fees: $41,539
Additional Expenses: N/A
Total: $41,539*

*Note: This figure does not reflect estimated housing/living expenses.

Financial Aid: https://www.samford.edu/pharmacy/scholarships

ADDITIONAL INFORMATION

Interesting tidbit: At McWhorter School of Pharmacy, students can personalize their Pharm.D curriculum, graduating with a competitive advantage in the area of pharmacy they are most interested in. Certificate programs are integrated into its curriculum, enabling students to become certified in areas like medication therapy management and immunizations before they graduate.

Important Updates due to COVID-19: Virtual Interview

Were tests required? No.

Are tests expected next year? No.

What international experiences are available? International rotations, service learning trips, and study abroad courses available in Taiwan, Ecuador, Thailand, Italy, and Honduras.

What dual degree options exist? PharmD/MBA, PharmD/MPH, PharmD/MS in Health Informatics, and PharmD/MS in Law with a Concentration in Health Law and Policy. For more information, visit: https://www.samford.edu/pharmacy/dual-degrees

What service learning opportunities exist? See international experiences.

What percent of graduates place in postgraduate training? 35% (2020)

NAPLEX First-Time Pass Rate: 95.56% (2020)

MPJE First-Time Pass Rate: 92.98% (2020)

Other: Early Assurance pathway for high school applicants. For more information, visit: https://www.samford.edu/pharmacy/early-assurance-program

ALABAMA

ARKANSAS

DELAWARE

DISTRICT OF COLUMBIA

FLORIDA

GEORGIA

KENTUCKY

LOUISIANA

MARYLAND

MISSISSIPPI

NORTH CAROLINA

OKLAHOMA

SOUTH CAROLINA

TENNESSEE

TEXAS

VIRGINIA

WEST VIRGINIA

SOUTH

ALABAMA

ARKANSAS

DELAWARE

DISTRICT OF COLUMBIA

FLORIDA

GEORGIA

KENTUCKY

LOUISIANA

MARYLAND

MISSISSIPPI

NORTH CAROLINA

OKLAHOMA

SOUTH CAROLINA

TENNESSEE

TEXAS

VIRGINIA

WEST VIRGINIA

HARDING UNIVERSITY COLLEGE OF PHARMACY

Address: 915 E. Market Ave., Searcy, AR 72149
Website: *https://www.harding.edu/academics/colleges-departments/pharmacy*
Contact: *https://grad.harding.edu/pharmacyinquiry/inquiryform/*
Phone: (501) 279-5528

COST OF ATTENDANCE

Tuition and Fees: $35,300
Additional Expenses: N/A
Total: $35,300*

*Note: This figure does not reflect estimated housing/living expenses.

Financial Aid: See "Scholarships": https://www.harding.edu/academics/colleges-departments/pharmacy/admissions

ADDITIONAL INFORMATION

Interesting tidbit: Starting Summer 2021, Harding University College of Pharmacy (HUCOP) is introducing a new condensed 3.5-yr PharmD curriculum. The first class in the new curriculum begins in June 2021.

Important Updates due to COVID-19: Virtual Interview

Were tests required? No.

Are tests expected next year? No.

What international experiences are available? N/A

What dual degree options exist? PharmD/MBA: https://www.harding.edu/academics/colleges-departments/pharmacy/complementary-degrees

What service learning opportunities exist? Bone Marrow Drive, Day of Caring, Immunization Clinic, etc. For more information, visit: https://www.harding.edu/community/medical-counseling

What percent of graduates place in postgraduate training? N/A

NAPLEX First-Time Pass Rate: 92.00% (2020)

MPJE First-Time Pass Rate: N/A

Other: Early Assurance pathway available to high school applicants. For more information, visit: https://www.harding.edu/academics/colleges-departments/pharmacy/early-assurance-program

UNIVERSITY OF ARKANSAS FOR MEDICAL SCIENCES COLLEGE OF PHARMACY

Address: 4301 W Markham St., Little Rock, AR 72205
Website: https://pharmacy.uams.edu/
Contact: https://pharmacy.uams.edu/aboutus/contact-us/
Phone: (501) 686-8889

COST OF ATTENDANCE

In-State Tuition and Fees: $22,424
Additional Expenses: N/A
Total: $22,424*
Out-of-State Tuition and Fees: $41,704
Additional Expenses: N/A
Total: $41,704*
Border State Tuition and Fees: $24,100**
Additional Expenses: N/A
Total: $24,100*
**Border state tuition rates for admitted applicants who reside in any of the six bordering states (MO, MS, LA, OK, TN, TX) to Arkansas.
Financial Aid: https://pharmacy.uams.edu/prospective-students/doctor-of-pharmacy-program/financial-information-2/scholarships-3/

ADDITIONAL INFORMATION

Interesting tidbit: UAMS College of Pharmacy is one of only 10 schools in the country offering the Nuclear Pharmacy Specialty Track. All College of Pharmacy students complete the first two years of the program on the Little Rock Campus, with 25% transitioning to the Northwest Regional Campus for the final two years of the program.
Important Updates due to COVID-19: Virtual Interview
Were tests required? PCAT required for applicants who have lower than a cumulative GPA of 3.3
Are tests expected next year? PCAT required for applicants who have lower than a cumulative GPA of 3.3
Note: The MCAT, GRE, and DAT may be accepted in lieu of the PCAT. Applicants with a cumulative GPA of 3.3+ are not required to take the PCAT. The minimum composite percentile is 30 to be considered for an interview.
What international experiences are available? International rotations during P4. International locations include Italy, Taiwan, Thailand, Peru, and Ecuador. For more information, visit: https://pharmacy.uams.edu/current-students/academic-programs/experiential-education/program-overview/
What dual degree options exist? PharmD/JD, PharmD/MBA, PharmD/MPH, and PharmD/PhD.
For more information on the PharmD/MBA and PharmD/MPH, visit: https://pharmacy.uams.edu/prospective-students/doctor-of-pharmacy-program/dual-degree-programs/
For more information on the PharmD/JD, visit: https://ualr.edu/law/academics/juris-doctordoctor-of-pharmacy/
For more information on the PharmD/PhD, visit: https://pharmacy.uams.edu/prospective-students/graduate/pspstrack/
What service learning opportunities exist? Service learning through experiential education. For more information, visit: https://pharmacy.uams.edu/current-students/academic-programs/experiential-education/program-overview/
What percent of graduates place in postgraduate training? N/A
NAPLEX First-Time Pass Rate: 93.75% (2020)
MPJE First-Time Pass Rate: N/A
Other: Early Assurance pathway available to high school applicants. For more information, visit: Nuclear Pharmacy Program available. For more information, visit: https://nuclearpharmacy.uams.edu/

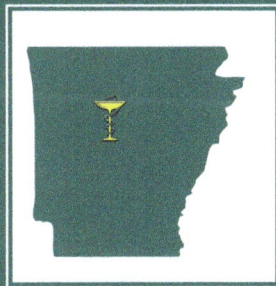

ALABAMA

ARKANSAS

DELAWARE

DISTRICT OF COLUMBIA

FLORIDA

GEORGIA

KENTUCKY

LOUISIANA

MARYLAND

MISSISSIPPI

NORTH CAROLINA

OKLAHOMA

SOUTH CAROLINA

TENNESSEE

TEXAS

VIRGINIA

WEST VIRGINIA

SOUTH

ALABAMA

ARKANSAS

DELAWARE

DISTRICT OF
COLUMBIA

FLORIDA

GEORGIA

KENTUCKY

LOUISIANA

MARYLAND

MISSISSIPPI

NORTH CAROLINA

OKLAHOMA

SOUTH CAROLINA

TENNESSEE

TEXAS

VIRGINIA

WEST VIRGINIA

HOWARD UNIVERSITY COLLEGE OF PHARMACY

Address: 2300 4th Street NW, Washington, DC 20059
Website: *http://pharmacy.howard.edu/*
Contact: *http://pharmacy.howard.edu/contact*
Phone: (202) 806-6100

COST OF ATTENDANCE

Tuition and Fees: $30,842
Additional Expenses: $35,665
Total: $66,497

Financial Aid: http://pharmacy.howard.edu/students/scholarships

ADDITIONAL INFORMATION

Interesting tidbit: The mission of Howard University College of Pharmacy is to provide pharmacy education of excellent quality, with particular emphasis upon the recruitment, retention, and graduation of promising African American and other ethnically diverse minority students.

Important Updates due to COVID-19: Virtual Interview

Were tests required? No.

Are tests expected next year? No.

What international experiences are available? Experiential education in 9 countries.

What dual degree options exist? PharmD/MBA. For more information, visit: http://pharmacy.howard.edu/academic-programs/five-year-pharmdmba-program

What service learning opportunities exist? Experiential education in 250+ sites across the nation. For more information, visit: http://pharmacy.howard.edu/departments/experiential-and-external-programs

What percent of graduates place in postgraduate training? N/A

NAPLEX First-Time Pass Rate: 77.78% (2020)

MPJE First-Time Pass Rate: 28.57% (2020)

Other: 7-year BS/PharmD program available. For more information, visit: http://pharmacy.howard.edu/academic-programs/bspharmd-program

FLORIDA AGRICULTURAL & MECHANICAL UNIVERSITY COLLEGE OF PHARMACY AND PHARMACEUTICAL SCIENCES

Address: 1415 S. Martin Luther King, Jr. Blvd., Tallahassee, FL 32307
Website: *https://pharmacy.famu.edu/*
Contact: *https://pharmacy.famu.edu/contact/*
Phone: (850) 599-3301

COST OF ATTENDANCE

In-State Tuition and Fees: $25,228
Additional Expenses: $17,786
Total: $43,014

Out-of-State Tuition and Fees: $36,322
Additional Expenses: $17,786
Total: $54,108

Financial Aid: https://www.famu.edu/index.cfm?FinancialAid&Welcome

ADDITIONAL INFORMATION

Interesting tidbit: In 2009, the College of Pharmacy was presented The President's Honor Roll Award for outstanding community service provided by its Pharm.D. students. Community service is part of COPPS' mission and provides a rich environment for student training and life-long experiences.

Important Updates due to COVID-19: Virtual Interview

Were tests required? No.

Are tests expected next year? No.

What international experiences are available? N/A

What dual degree options exist? PharmD/MBA. For more information, visit: https://pharmacy.famu.edu/office-of-student-services/dual-degree-program/

What service learning opportunities exist? N/A

What percent of graduates place in postgraduate training? 10% (2020)

NAPLEX First-Time Pass Rate: 83.33% (2020)

MPJE First-Time Pass Rate: 74.73% (2020)

ALABAMA
ARKANSAS
DELAWARE
DISTRICT OF COLUMBIA
FLORIDA
GEORGIA
KENTUCKY
LOUISIANA
MARYLAND
MISSISSIPPI
NORTH CAROLINA
OKLAHOMA
SOUTH CAROLINA
TENNESSEE
TEXAS
VIRGINIA
WEST VIRGINIA

SOUTH

ALABAMA

ARKANSAS

DELAWARE

DISTRICT OF
COLUMBIA

FLORIDA

GEORGIA

KENTUCKY

LOUISIANA

MARYLAND

MISSISSIPPI

NORTH CAROLINA

OKLAHOMA

SOUTH CAROLINA

TENNESSEE

TEXAS

VIRGINIA

WEST VIRGINIA

LARKIN UNIVERSITY COLLEGE OF PHARMACY

Address: 18301 N Miami Ave, Miami, FL 33169
Website: *https://ularkin.org/pharmacy/*
Contact: *https://ularkin.org/student-affairs-and-admissions/contact-us/*
Phone: (305) 760-7500

COST OF ATTENDANCE

Tuition and Fees: $37,122
Additional Expenses: $27,240
Total: $64,362

Financial Aid: http://ularkin.org/financial-services/

ADDITIONAL INFORMATION

*Please note the following: As of October 2021, Larkin University College of Pharmacy is currently a candidate for accreditation. For updates, please check:https://www.acpe-accredit.org/faq-item/Larkin-University-College-of-Pharmacy-PharmD/

Interesting tidbit: Larkin University was created to support the education and health care needs of the diverse communities of South Florida. The College of Pharmacy offers a graduate Doctor of Pharmacy degree that was granted Candidate status by the Accreditation Council for Pharmacy Education (ACPE) on June 24, 2017. Its PharmD is an accelerated 3-year program.

Important Updates due to COVID-19: Virtual Interview

Were tests required? No.

Are tests expected next year? No.

What international experiences are available? N/A

What dual degree options exist? No dual degree options listed.

What service learning opportunities exist? N/A

What percent of graduates place in postgraduate training? N/A

NAPLEX First-Time Pass Rate: 57.38% (2020)

MPJE First-Time Pass Rate: 72.55% (2020)

NOVA SOUTHEASTERN UNIVERSITY COLLEGE OF PHARMACY

Address: 3301 College Ave., Fort Lauderdale, FL 33314
Website: *https://pharmacy.nova.edu/index.html*
Contact: *https://apply.nova.edu/Ellucian.Erecruiting.Web.External/Pages/prospectinquiry.aspx*
Phone: (800) 541-6682

COST OF ATTENDANCE

In-State Tuition and Fees: $35,455**
Additional Expenses: N/A
Total: $35,455*

Out-of-State Tuition and Fees: $40,471
Additional Expenses: N/A
Total: $40,471*

*Note: These figures do not reflect estimated housing/living expenses.

****In-state tuition applies to Florida and Puerto Rico residents.

Financial Aid: N/A

ADDITIONAL INFORMATION

Interesting tidbit: During 2000-2001, the PharmD program extended to Palm Beach, Florida, and Puerto Rico. Students can earn degrees on three campuses - Fort Lauderdale/Davie, Florida; Palm Beach, Florida; San Juan, Puerto Rico. Puerto Rico residents are charged at the out-of-state tuition rate and receive a pharmacy program discount to the in-state tuition rate.

Important Updates due to COVID-19: Virtual Interview

Were tests required? No.

Are tests expected next year? No.

What international experiences are available? N/A

What dual degree options exist? PharmD/MBA, PharmD/MPH, and PharmD/MS in Biomedical Informatics. For more information, visit: https://pharmacy.nova.edu/graduate/concurrent-degrees.html

What service learning opportunities exist? Asthma 101, Immunization awareness, etc. For more information, visit: https://pharmacy.nova.edu/outreach/index.html

What percent of graduates place in postgraduate training? 51% PGY1 match rate (2020)

NAPLEX First-Time Pass Rate: 82.87% (2020)

MPJE First-Time Pass Rate: 84.00% (2020)

Other: Dual Admission pathway available to high school applicants. For more information, visit: https://www.nova.edu/undergraduate/academics/dual-admission/pharmacy.html

ALABAMA

ARKANSAS

DELAWARE

DISTRICT OF COLUMBIA

FLORIDA

GEORGIA

KENTUCKY

LOUISIANA

MARYLAND

MISSISSIPPI

NORTH CAROLINA

OKLAHOMA

SOUTH CAROLINA

TENNESSEE

TEXAS

VIRGINIA

WEST VIRGINIA

SOUTH

ALABAMA

ARKANSAS

DELAWARE

DISTRICT OF COLUMBIA

FLORIDA

GEORGIA

KENTUCKY

LOUISIANA

MARYLAND

MISSISSIPPI

NORTH CAROLINA

OKLAHOMA

SOUTH CAROLINA

TENNESSEE

TEXAS

VIRGINIA

WEST VIRGINIA

PALM BEACH ATLANTIC UNIVERSITY LLOYD L. GREGORY SCHOOL OF PHARMACY

Address: 901 S Flagler Dr., West Palm Beach, FL 33401
Website: *https://www.pba.edu/academics/schools/gregory-pharmacy/index.html*
Contact: *https://www.pba.edu/contact.html*
Phone: (561) 803-2122

COST OF ATTENDANCE

Tuition and Fees: $33,872
Additional Expenses: N/A
Total: $33,872*

*Note: This figure does not reflect estimated housing/living expenses.

Financial Aid: https://www.pba.edu/academics/schools/gregory-pharmacy/financial-aid/index.html

Other: Some students receive a $5,000 or $16,000 scholarship upon acceptance. The applicant profile of this type of student is typically 3.5+ GPA and a 60+ PCAT.

ADDITIONAL INFORMATION

Interesting tidbit: PBA's PharmD courses are infused with Christian values to provide students with a solid foundation for ethical conduct as a healthcare provider. Students will learn from Christian faculty who are experts in their fields, and alongside fellow students who share values, amplify each student's skills and inspire them to follow their passions.

Important Updates due to COVID-19: Virtual Interview

Were tests required? PCAT required.

Are tests expected next year? Yes.

What international experiences are available? Medical mission trips to locations such as the Amazon, Belize, Guatemala, Zambia, and more. For more information, scroll down to "Be the Change": https://www.pba.edu/academics/schools/gregory-pharmacy/index.html

What dual degree options exist? PharmD/MBA. For more information, visit: https://www.pba.edu/academics/programs/pharmacy-business-adminisatration-pharmd-mba.html

What service learning opportunities exist? See international experiences.

What percent of graduates place in postgraduate training? N/A

NAPLEX First-Time Pass Rate: 89.39% (2020)

MPJE First-Time Pass Rate: 85.19% (2020)

Other: Early Assurance pathway available to current PBA undergraduates. For more information, visit: https://www.pba.edu/academics/schools/gregory-pharmacy/admissions/early-assurance.html

UNIVERSITY OF FLORIDA COLLEGE OF PHARMACY

Address: 1225 Center Drive, Gainesville, FL 32610
Website: *https://pharmacy.ufl.edu/*
Contact: *https://admissions.pharmacy.ufl.edu/why-pharmacy/contacts/*
Phone: (352) 273-6217

Other Locations: Jacksonville, FL; Orlando, FL

COST OF ATTENDANCE

In-State Tuition and Fees: $23,860
Additional Expenses: $18,374
Total: $42,234

Out-of-State Tuition and Fees: $41,860
Additional Expenses: $18,374
Total: $54,374

Financial Aid: https://admissions.pharmacy.ufl.edu/financial-aid/scholarships/

ADDITIONAL INFORMATION

Interesting tidbit: As one of the Top 5, National Institutes of Health-funded pharmacy colleges nationally, the UF College of Pharmacy features preeminent researchers who are leading major medical breakthroughs in areas such as drug discovery and development, pharmacometrics and systems pharmacology, and precision medicine. The Pharm.D. program is taught at three Florida campuses - Gainesville, Jacksonville, and Orlando.

Important Updates due to COVID-19: Accept a pass, satisfactory, or a letter grade of "C" or better for any prerequisite courses. Accept all required prerequisite lectures and labs that have transitioned completely to online for spring, summer, and fall 2020.

Were tests required? PCAT required.

Are tests expected next year? Yes.

What international experiences are available? International APPEs, study abroad programs, health outreach trips, etc. For more information, visit: https://admissions.pharmacy.ufl.edu/why-pharmacy/international-opportunities/

What dual degree options exist? PharmD/MBA, PharmD/MPH, and PharmD/PhD. For more information, visit: https://pharmacy.ufl.edu/education/combination-degree-programs/

What service learning opportunities exist? See international experiences.

What percent of graduates place in postgraduate training? N/A

NAPLEX First-Time Pass Rate: 88.93% (2020)

MPJE First-Time Pass Rate: 85.05% (2020)

Other: Early Assurance pathway available to high school applicants. For more information, visit: https://admissions.pharmacy.ufl.edu/planning-to-succeed/early-assurance-program/

ALABAMA
ARKANSAS
DELAWARE
DISTRICT OF COLUMBIA
FLORIDA
GEORGIA
KENTUCKY
LOUISIANA
MARYLAND
MISSISSIPPI
NORTH CAROLINA
OKLAHOMA
SOUTH CAROLINA
TENNESSEE
TEXAS
VIRGINIA
WEST VIRGINIA

SOUTH

ALABAMA

ARKANSAS

DELAWARE

DISTRICT OF
COLUMBIA

FLORIDA

GEORGIA

KENTUCKY

LOUISIANA

MARYLAND

MISSISSIPPI

NORTH CAROLINA

OKLAHOMA

SOUTH CAROLINA

TENNESSEE

TEXAS

VIRGINIA

WEST VIRGINIA

UNIVERSITY OF SOUTH FLORIDA HEALTH TANEJA COLLEGE OF PHARMACY

Address: 12901 Bruce B. Downs Blvd., Tampa, FL 33612
Website: *https://health.usf.edu/pharmacy*
Contact: *https://health.usf.edu/pharmacy/contact*
Phone: (813) 974-5699

COST OF ATTENDANCE

In-State Tuition and Fees: $19,905
Additional Expenses: N/A
Total: $19,905*

Out-of-State Tuition and Fees: $38,537
Additional Expenses: N/A
Total: $38,537*

*Note: These figures do not reflect estimated housing/living expenses.

Financial Aid: https://health.usf.edu/well/financial-aid

ADDITIONAL INFORMATION

Interesting tidbit: For an active learning environment, the USF TCOP's pharmaceutical skills course utilizes PioneerRx Pharmacy Software as one of several innovative learning technologies in the course series. Students apply their knowledge in simulated, real-world functions using this pharmacy management system to prepare them for life outside of the classroom and future ownership.

Important Updates due to COVID-19: The PCAT is not required for the 2020-2021 Admissions cycle (optional).

Were tests required? No.

Are tests expected next year? Yes.

What international experiences are available? International site in Spain for P4 students, as well as medical mission, trips over Spring Break through student organizations.

What dual degree options exist? PharmD/MBA, PharmD/MPH, and PharmD/MSPN. For more information, visit: https://health.usf.edu/pharmacy/graduate-programs/concurrent-degree-programs-concentrations/concurrent-degrees

What service learning opportunities exist? Student-run free clinic for low-income patients and National Prescription Drug Takeback Day.

What percent of graduates place in postgraduate training? N/A

NAPLEX First-Time Pass Rate: 87.37% (2020)

MPJE First-Time Pass Rate: 88.37% (2020)

Other: 0-7 BS/PharmD program available in partnership with USF Honors College.

MERCER UNIVERSITY COLLEGE OF PHARMACY

Address: 3001 Mercer University Dr., Atlanta, GA 30341
Website: *https://pharmacy.mercer.edu/*
Contact: *https://pharmacy.mercer.edu/about-us/contact-us/*
Phone: (678) 547-6232

COST OF ATTENDANCE

Tuition and Fees: $38,484
Additional Expenses: N/A
Total: $38,484*

*Note: This figure does not reflect estimated housing/living expenses.

Financial Aid: https://pharmacy.mercer.edu/admissions/pharm-d/tuition-and-aid/

ADDITIONAL INFORMATION

Interesting tidbit: Exclusive to Mercer for first- and second-year students interested in the pharmaceutical industry, managed care, health outcomes research or health policy are internships at UCB biopharmaceutical company, the Medical Affairs Company, InPharmD drug information service, North Georgia Rheumatology and Mercer's Center for Clinical Outcomes Research and Education. Furthermore, unique to Mercer's Pharm.D. Program are opportunities for students during the fourth professional year, such as Advanced Clinical Track, Global Medical Missions, Indian Health Service, and International Pharmacy Program.

Important Updates due to COVID-19: Virtual Interview

Were tests required? No.

Are tests expected next year? No.

What international experiences are available? International rotations and medical mission trips.

What dual degree options exist? PharmD/PhD, PharmD/MBA, PharmD/MPH, and PharmD/MS in Health Informatics. For more information, visit: https://pharmacy.mercer.edu/academic-programs/combined-degrees/

What service learning opportunities exist? N/A

What percent of graduates place in postgraduate training? N/A

NAPLEX First-Time Pass Rate: 91.85% (2020)

MPJE First-Time Pass Rate: 93.39% (2020)

ALABAMA

ARKANSAS

DELAWARE

DISTRICT OF COLUMBIA

FLORIDA

GEORGIA

KENTUCKY

LOUISIANA

MARYLAND

MISSISSIPPI

NORTH CAROLINA

OKLAHOMA

SOUTH CAROLINA

TENNESSEE

TEXAS

VIRGINIA

WEST VIRGINIA

SOUTH

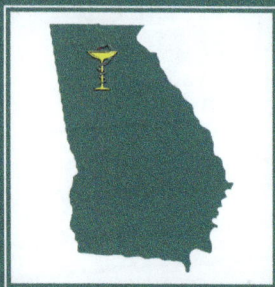

ALABAMA

ARKANSAS

DELAWARE

DISTRICT OF
COLUMBIA

FLORIDA

GEORGIA

KENTUCKY

LOUISIANA

MARYLAND

MISSISSIPPI

NORTH CAROLINA

OKLAHOMA

SOUTH CAROLINA

TENNESSEE

TEXAS

VIRGINIA

WEST VIRGINIA

PHILADELPHIA COLLEGE OF OSTEOPATHIC MEDICINE - GEORGIA SCHOOL OF PHARMACY

Address: 625 Old Peachtree Road NW, Suwanee, GA 30024
Website: *https://www.pcom.edu/academics/programs-and-degrees/doctor-of-pharmacy/*
Contact: *https://www.pcom.edu/contact.html*
Phone: (678) 225-7500

COST OF ATTENDANCE

Tuition and Fees: $40,344
Additional Expenses: $26,532
Total: $66,876

Financial Aid: https://www.pcom.edu/about/departments/financial-aid/types-of-aid/scholarships/

ADDITIONAL INFORMATION

Interesting tidbit: PCOM School of Pharmacy offers concentrations in three different pharmacy practice areas - acute care pharmacy, ambulatory care pharmacy and managed care pharmacy.

Important Updates due to COVID-19: Virtual Interview

Were tests required? No.

Are tests expected next year? No.

What international experiences are available? N/A

What dual degree options exist? PharmD/MBA and PharmD/MS in Healthcare Informatics. For more information, visit: https://www.pcom.edu/academics/programs-and-degrees/doctor-of-pharmacy/dual-degree-programs/

What service learning opportunities exist? All PCOM students are required to participate in service learning. For more information, visit: https://www.pcom.edu/academics/programs-and-degrees/doctor-of-pharmacy/service-learning.html

What percent of graduates place in postgraduate training? 40% residency match (2020)

NAPLEX First-Time Pass Rate: 71.08% (2020)

MPJE First-Time Pass Rate: 72.58% (2020)

Other: Early Assurance Program available for college freshmen, sophomore, and junior applicants. For more information, visit: https://www.pcom.edu/academics/programs-and-degrees/doctor-of-pharmacy/early-assurance.html

Note: MCAT, GRE, OAT, and the DAT may be submitted in lieu of the PCAT.

SOUTH UNIVERSITY SCHOOL OF PHARMACY

Address: 709 Mall Blvd, Savannah, GA 31406
Website: *https://www.southuniversity.edu/degree-programs/pharmacy*
Contact: *http://pharmacy.southuniversity.edu/inquiryform*
Phone: (912) 201-8000

Other Locations: Columbia, SC

COST OF ATTENDANCE

Tuition and Fees: $49,821
Additional Expenses: N/A
Total: $49,821*

***Note:** This figure does not reflect estimated housing/living expenses.

Financial Aid: https://www.southuniversity.edu/paying-for-college

ADDITIONAL INFORMATION

Interesting tidbit: On June 14, 2010, South University opened the doors to the second campus in Columbia, South Carolina, offering the Doctor of Pharmacy degree program. The School has integrated Medicinal Chemistry, Pharmacology, and Therapeutics into one combined continuing course sequence, allowing a rigorous comprehensive didactic component in a 3-year curriculum that contains 12 months of full-time rotations.

Important Updates due to COVID-19: Virtual Interview

Were tests required? No.

Are tests expected next year? No.

What international experiences are available? N/A

What dual degree options exist? PharmD/MBA. For more information, visit: http://catalog.southuniversity.edu/preview_program.php?catoid=16&poid=1656&returnto=866

What service learning opportunities exist? N/A

What percent of graduates place in postgraduate training? 9% (2018)

NAPLEX First-Time Pass Rate: 83.33% (2020)

MPJE First-Time Pass Rate: 77.59% (2020)

ALABAMA

ARKANSAS

DELAWARE

DISTRICT OF COLUMBIA

FLORIDA

GEORGIA

KENTUCKY

LOUISIANA

MARYLAND

MISSISSIPPI

NORTH CAROLINA

OKLAHOMA

SOUTH CAROLINA

TENNESSEE

TEXAS

VIRGINIA

WEST VIRGINIA

SOUTH

ALABAMA

ARKANSAS

DELAWARE

DISTRICT OF COLUMBIA

FLORIDA

GEORGIA

KENTUCKY

LOUISIANA

MARYLAND

MISSISSIPPI

NORTH CAROLINA

OKLAHOMA

SOUTH CAROLINA

TENNESSEE

TEXAS

VIRGINIA

WEST VIRGINIA

UNIVERSITY OF GEORGIA COLLEGE OF PHARMACY

Address: 250 W. Green St., Athens, GA 30602
Website: *https://rx.uga.edu/*
Contact: *https://rx.uga.edu/about/contact-us/*
Phone: (706) 542-1911

Other Locations: Albany, NY; Augusta, GA; Savannah, GA

COST OF ATTENDANCE

In-State Tuition and Fees: $16,636
Additional Expenses: N/A
Total: $16,636*

Out-of-State Tuition and Fees: $37,344
Additional Expenses: N/A
Total: $37,344*

*Note: This figure does not reflect estimated housing/living expenses.

Financial Aid: https://osfa.uga.edu/

ADDITIONAL INFORMATION

Interesting tidbit: All students complete their coursework in Athens for the first and second years of the Pharm.D program. In the third year of the curriculum, some students move to our extended campuses in Albany, Augusta, or Savannah, Georgia. A matching system is used during the third year to assign students. Students are assigned to one area for the entire fourth year.

Important Updates due to COVID-19: For the 2020-2021 application cycle, the PCAT exam is recommended, but not required.

Were tests required? No.

Are tests expected next year? Yes.

What international experiences are available? N/A

What dual degree options exist? PharmD/MPH and PharmD/MBA. For more information, visit: https://rx.uga.edu/academic-programs/dual-degree/

What service learning opportunities exist? Service learning through experiential education during APPEs. In addition, student organizations often participate in health fairs, fundraising events, nationwide charities, and more. Last, students may also participate in the Farm Worker Family Health Program where students provide healthcare assistance to farm workers and their families.

What percent of graduates place in postgraduate training? 35% (2019)

NAPLEX First-Time Pass Rate: 95.38% (2020)

MPJE First-Time Pass Rate: 83.48% (2020)

SULLIVAN UNIVERSITY COLLEGE OF PHARMACY

Address: 3101 Bardstown Rd., Louisville, KY 40205
Website: *https://www.sullivan.edu/colleges/college-of-pharmacy-and-health-sciences*
Contact: *https://www.sullivan.edu/contact-us*
Phone: (502) 456-6505

COST OF ATTENDANCE

Tuition and Fees: $54,060
Additional Expenses: $20,381
Total: $74,441

Financial Aid: https://www.sullivan.edu/college-of-pharmacy-and-health-sciences/tuition-financial-aid/

ADDITIONAL INFORMATION

Interesting tidbit: The Sullivan University PharmD consists of a three-calendar-year professional program offered at the Louisville campus. The College's curriculum prepares graduates to be APPE-, team-, and practice-ready.

Important Updates due to COVID-19: Virtual Interview

Were tests required? No.

Are tests expected next year? No.

Note: Although the PCAT is preferred (not required), the GRE, MCAT, and DAT may be considered.

What international experiences are available? International rotation in Honduras and Puerto Rico.

What dual degree options exist? PharmD/MBA.

What service learning opportunities exist? Service learning through experiential education.

What percent of graduates place in postgraduate training? N/A

NAPLEX First-Time Pass Rate: 83.75% (2020)

MPJE First-Time Pass Rate: 84.85% (2020)

ALABAMA
ARKANSAS
DELAWARE
DISTRICT OF COLUMBIA
FLORIDA
GEORGIA
KENTUCKY
LOUISIANA
MARYLAND
MISSISSIPPI
NORTH CAROLINA
OKLAHOMA
SOUTH CAROLINA
TENNESSEE
TEXAS
VIRGINIA
WEST VIRGINIA

SOUTH

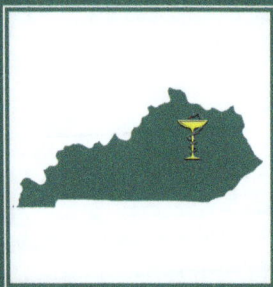

ALABAMA

ARKANSAS

DELAWARE

DISTRICT OF
COLUMBIA

FLORIDA

GEORGIA

KENTUCKY

LOUISIANA

MARYLAND

MISSISSIPPI

NORTH CAROLINA

OKLAHOMA

SOUTH CAROLINA

TENNESSEE

TEXAS

VIRGINIA

WEST VIRGINIA

UNIVERSITY OF KENTUCKY COLLEGE OF PHARMACY

Address: 789 South Limestone, Lexington, KY 40536
Website: *https://pharmacy.uky.edu/*
Contact: *https://pharmacy.uky.edu/contact-us*
Phone: (859) 323-7601

COST OF ATTENDANCE

In-State Tuition and Fees: $28,662
Additional Expenses: N/A
Total: $28,662*

Out-of-State Tuition and Fees: $53,686
Additional Expenses: N/A
Total: $53,686*

*Note: These figures do not reflect estimated housing/living expenses.

Financial Aid: https://pharmacy.uky.edu/pharmd-professional-program/tuition-financial-aid/scholarships

ADDITIONAL INFORMATION

Interesting tidbit: UKY COP provides an iPad to each student upon their arrival, which they keep upon successful graduation from its program. The iPad Initiative was started in 2016 to provide a common computing platform for its students.

Important Updates due to COVID-19: Virtual Interview

Were tests required? No.

Are tests expected next year? No.

What international experiences are available? International rotations and short-term medical outreach abroad. For more information, visit: https://pharmacy.uky.edu/pharmd-professional-program/international-education-opportunities

What dual degree options exist? PharmD/MBA, PharmD/MPA, PharmD/MPH, and PharmD/MS in Pharmaceutical Sciences. For more information, visit: https://pharmacy.uky.edu/pharmd-professional-program/dual-degrees-and-certificates

What service learning opportunities exist? Community Service Learning (CSL) involves students collaborating with a non-profit community partner. For more information, visit: https://pharmacy.uky.edu/ukcop-effect

What percent of graduates place in postgraduate training? 55% (2020)

NAPLEX First-Time Pass Rate: 91.79% (2020)

MPJE First-Time Pass Rate: 94.39% (2020)

UNIVERSITY OF LOUISIANA AT MONROE COLLEGE OF PHARMACY

Address: 1800 Bienville Dr., Monroe, LA 71201
Website: *https://www.ulm.edu/pharmacy/*
Contact: *https://www.ulm.edu/pharmacy/contact.html*
Phone: (318) 342-3800

COST OF ATTENDANCE

In-State Tuition and Fees: $24,164
Additional Expenses: $15,269
Total: $39,433

Out-of-State Tuition and Fees: $36,264
Additional Expenses: $15,269
Total: $51,533

Financial Aid: https://www.ulm.edu/financialaid/index.html

ADDITIONAL INFORMATION

Interesting tidbit: The University Of Louisiana Monroe College Of Pharmacy is Louisiana's College of Pharmacy and is the only publicly supported center for pharmacy education and research in the state.

Important Updates due to COVID-19: Virtual Interview

Were tests required? PCAT required.

Are tests expected next year? Yes.

What international experiences are available? Medical Outreach Experience course.

What dual degree options exist? PharmD/MBA. For more information, visit: https://www.ulm.edu/pharmacy/pharmdmba.html

What service learning opportunities exist? Service learning through experiential education and student organizations.

What percent of graduates place in postgraduate training? 14% (year unspecified)

NAPLEX First-Time Pass Rate: 89.16 % (2020)

MPJE First-Time Pass Rate: 90.54% (2020)

Other: Provisional Entry Program available to high school applicants. For more information, visit: https://www.ulm.edu/pharmacy/prospective/pep.html

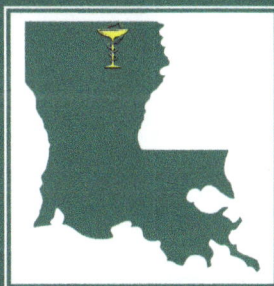

ALABAMA
ARKANSAS
DELAWARE
DISTRICT OF COLUMBIA
FLORIDA
GEORGIA
KENTUCKY
LOUISIANA
MARYLAND
MISSISSIPPI
NORTH CAROLINA
OKLAHOMA
SOUTH CAROLINA
TENNESSEE
TEXAS
VIRGINIA
WEST VIRGINIA

SOUTH

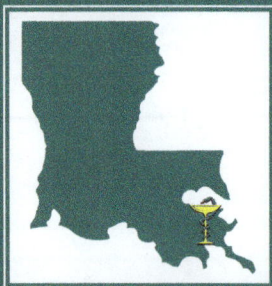

ALABAMA

ARKANSAS

DELAWARE

DISTRICT OF
COLUMBIA

FLORIDA

GEORGIA

KENTUCKY

LOUISIANA

MARYLAND

MISSISSIPPI

NORTH CAROLINA

OKLAHOMA

SOUTH CAROLINA

TENNESSEE

TEXAS

VIRGINIA

WEST VIRGINIA

XAVIER UNIVERSITY OF LOUISIANA COLLEGE OF PHARMACY

Address: 1 Drexel Dr., New Orleans, LA 70125
Website: *https://www.xula.edu/collegeofpharmacy*
Contact: *https://www.xula.edu/copcontacts*
Phone: (504) 520-7500

COST OF ATTENDANCE

Tuition and Fees: $42,436
Additional Expenses: N/A
Total: $42,436*

***Note:** This figure does not reflect estimated housing/living expenses.

Financial Aid: https://www.xula.edu/financialaid

ADDITIONAL INFORMATION

Interesting tidbit: Xavier retains its distinction as the only historically Black, Catholic University in the United States. The Xavier University College of Pharmacy is dedicated to bringing minority youth into the learned profession of pharmacy.

Important Updates due to COVID-19: Virtual Interview

Were tests required? No.

Are tests expected next year? No.

What international experiences are available? International global health elective.

What dual degree options exist? No dual degree options listed.

What service learning opportunities exist? Service learning through experiential education.

What percent of graduates place in postgraduate training? 48% (2020)

NAPLEX First-Time Pass Rate: 75.00% (2020)

MPJE First-Time Pass Rate: 67.02% (2020)

Other: Contingent Admit Program available to high school applicants. For more information, visit: https://www.xula.edu/contingentadmitprogram

NOTRE DAME OF MARYLAND UNIVERSITY SCHOOL OF PHARMACY

Address: 4701 North Charles Street, Baltimore, MD 21210
Website: *https://www.ndm.edu/colleges-schools/school-pharmacy*
Contact: *https://www.ndm.edu/request-info*
Phone: (410) 435-0100

COST OF ATTENDANCE

Tuition and Fees: $41,500
Additional Expenses: N/A
Total: $41,500*

*Note: This figure does not reflect estimated housing/living expenses.

Financial Aid: https://www.ndm.edu/colleges-schools/school-pharmacy/admissions/scholarships

ADDITIONAL INFORMATION

Interesting tidbit: The School of Pharmacy (offering the Pharm.D.) opened in 2009 and is Notre Dame's first professional degree program. Although NDMU remains a women's college, its graduate and professional programs are open to women and men alike.

Important Updates due to COVID-19: Virtual Interview

Were tests required? No.

Are tests expected next year? No.

What international experiences are available? N/A

What dual degree options exist? No dual degree options listed.

What service learning opportunities exist? Service learning through experiential education.

What percent of graduates place in postgraduate training? 23% (2020)

NAPLEX First-Time Pass Rate: 90.32% (2020)

MPJE First-Time Pass Rate: 84.21% (2020)

Other: Notre Dame of Maryland has affiliations with several schools for 3+4 and 4+4 programs. For more information, visit: https://www.ndm.edu/colleges-schools/school-pharmacy/admissions/pre-pharmacy-pathways

ALABAMA
ARKANSAS
DELAWARE
DISTRICT OF COLUMBIA
FLORIDA
GEORGIA
KENTUCKY
LOUISIANA
MARYLAND
MISSISSIPPI
NORTH CAROLINA
OKLAHOMA
SOUTH CAROLINA
TENNESSEE
TEXAS
VIRGINIA
WEST VIRGINIA

SOUTH

ALABAMA

ARKANSAS

DELAWARE

DISTRICT OF
COLUMBIA

FLORIDA

GEORGIA

KENTUCKY

LOUISIANA

MARYLAND

MISSISSIPPI

NORTH CAROLINA

OKLAHOMA

SOUTH CAROLINA

TENNESSEE

TEXAS

VIRGINIA

WEST VIRGINIA

UNIVERSITY OF MARYLAND EASTERN SHORE SCHOOL OF PHARMACY AND HEALTH PROFESSIONS

Address: 11868 College Backbone Rd, Princess Anne, MD 21853
Website: *https://www.umes.edu/pharmacy/*
Contact: *https://www.umes.edu/ContactUMES/*
Phone: (410) 651-2200

COST OF ATTENDANCE

In-State Tuition and Fees: $32,761
Additional Expenses: N/A
Total: $32,761*

Out-of-State Tuition and Fees: $62,085
Additional Expenses: N/A
Total: $62,085*

Regional Tuition and Fees: $50,089**
Additional Expenses: N/A
Total: $50,089*

*Note: These figures do not reflect estimated housing/living expenses.

**Regional tuition applies to residents of Delaware and eastern shore of Virginia.

Financial Aid: https://www.umes.edu/PharmD/Content/Financial-Aid/

ADDITIONAL INFORMATION

Interesting tidbit: The University of Maryland Eastern Shore (UMES) is a land-grant, historically black college founded in 1886, and is a member of the University of Maryland System. The Doctor of Pharmacy Program at UMES is the first professional pharmacy program on the Delmarva (Delaware, Maryland, and Virginia) Peninsula, and the only pharmacy program in Maryland where students can receive their PharmD in 3 years.

Important Updates due to COVID-19: The PCAT is not required for the 2020-2021 admissions cycle.

Were tests required? No.

Are tests expected next year? Yes.

What international experiences are available? N/A

What dual degree options exist? No dual degree options listed.

What service learning opportunities exist? Service learning through experiential education.

What percent of graduates place in postgraduate training? N/A

NAPLEX First-Time Pass Rate: 84.21% (2020)

MPJE First-Time Pass Rate: 40.63% (2020)

Other: Pharmacy Early Assurance Program (EAP). For more information, visit: https://www.umes.edu/Pharmacy/Pages/Pharmacy-Early-Assurance-Program-(EAP)/

UNIVERSITY OF MARYLAND SCHOOL OF PHARMACY

Address: 20 North Pine St., Baltimore, MD 21201
Website: https://www.pharmacy.umaryland.edu/
Contact: https://www.pharmacy.umaryland.edu/requestinfo/
Phone: (410) 706-7650

COST OF ATTENDANCE

In-State Tuition and Fees: $32,642
Additional Expenses: N/A
Total: $32,642*

Out-of-State Tuition and Fees: $48,293
Additional Expenses: N/A
Total: $48,293*

*Note: These figures do not reflect estimated housing/living expenses.

Financial Aid: https://www.pharmacy.umaryland.edu/academics/
pharmd/tuition-and-financial-assistance/

ADDITIONAL INFORMATION

Interesting tidbit: Starting in their first year, PharmD students have various elective options to personalize their experience, and these opportunities continue into their advanced experiential rotation year as P4s. Also, the School of Pharmacy currently offers four pathway options, focused courses of elective study designed to enhance learning in a structured manner - Geriatrics and Palliative Care Pathway, Pharmacotherapy Pathway, Pharmapreneurship Pathway, and Research Pathway.

Important Updates due to COVID-19: Virtual Interview

Were tests required? No.

Are tests expected next year? No.

What international experiences are available? Global partnerships and learning opportunities abroad. For more information, visit: https://www.pharmacy.umaryland.edu/globalhealth/

What dual degree options exist? PharmD/JD, PharmD/MBA, PharmD/MPH, PharmD/MS, and PharmD/PhD. For more information, visit: https://www.pharmacy.umaryland.edu/academics/dualdegrees/

What service learning opportunities exist? Service learning through experiential education.

What percent of graduates place in postgraduate training? 41.7% (2019)

NAPLEX First-Time Pass Rate: 91.41% (2020)

MPJE First-Time Pass Rate: 78.13% (2020)

Other: Pathways in the following areas: Geriatrics and Palliative Care, Pharmacotherapy, Pharmapreneurship, and Research. For more information, visit: https://www.pharmacy.umaryland.edu/academics/dualdegrees/

ALABAMA

ARKANSAS

DELAWARE

DISTRICT OF COLUMBIA

FLORIDA

GEORGIA

KENTUCKY

LOUISIANA

MARYLAND

MISSISSIPPI

NORTH CAROLINA

OKLAHOMA

SOUTH CAROLINA

TENNESSEE

TEXAS

VIRGINIA

WEST VIRGINIA

SOUTH

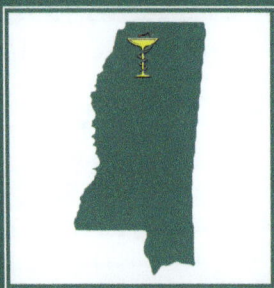

ALABAMA

ARKANSAS

DELAWARE

DISTRICT OF
COLUMBIA

FLORIDA

GEORGIA

KENTUCKY

LOUISIANA

MARYLAND

MISSISSIPPI

NORTH CAROLINA

OKLAHOMA

SOUTH CAROLINA

TENNESSEE

TEXAS

VIRGINIA

WEST VIRGINIA

UNIVERSITY OF MISSISSIPPI SCHOOL OF PHARMACY

Address: Thad Cochran Research Center, University Ave, University, MS 38677
Website: *https://pharmacy.olemiss.edu/*
Contact: *https://pharmacy.olemiss.edu/about-sop/contact-us/*
Phone: (662) 915-7265

COST OF ATTENDANCE

In-State Tuition and Fees: $25,476
Additional Expenses: $18,094
Total: $43,570

Out-of-State Tuition and Fees: $51,486
Additional Expenses: $18,094
Total: $69,580

Financial Aid: https://finaid.olemiss.edu/prospective-graduate/

ADDITIONAL INFORMATION

Interesting tidbit: First and second years of coursework are on the Oxford campus, while the third and fourth years of coursework is held at the University of Mississippi Medical Center in Jackson. School of Pharmacy students enrolled in the professional program (PharmD) will be awarded a B.S. in Pharmaceutical Sciences degree after the first professional year of study. Awarding of this degree not only signifies four years of college.

Important Updates due to COVID-19: Virtual Interview

Were tests required? No.

Are tests expected next year? No.

What international experiences are available? International summer abroad programs and coursework on Global Health & Pharmacy.

What dual degree options exist? No dual degree options listed.

What service learning opportunities exist? Local and regional outreach available.

What percent of graduates place in postgraduate training? N/A

NAPLEX First-Time Pass Rate: 91.75% (2020)

MPJE First-Time Pass Rate: 88.71% (2020)

Other: Early Entry program available to high school applicants. For more information, visit: https://pharmacy.olemiss.edu/earlyentry/

WILLIAM CAREY UNIVERSITY SCHOOL OF PHARMACY

Address: 19640 Highway 67, Biloxi, MS 39532
Website: *https://www.wmcarey.edu/School/Pharmacy*
Contact: *https://www.wmcarey.edu/page/pharmacy-contact-us*
Phone: (228) 702-1792

COST OF ATTENDANCE

Tuition and Fees: $41,000
Additional Expenses: N/A
Total: $41,000*

*Note: This figure does not reflect estimated housing/living expenses.

Financial Aid: https://www.wmcarey.edu/page/pharmacy-tuition-fees-financial-aid

ADDITIONAL INFORMATION

Interesting tidbit: William Carey's School of Pharmacy offers a two-year and ten months accelerated Doctor of Pharmacy program. The accelerated program model allows students to complete the PharmD degree faster and to start their pharmacy career sooner.

Important Updates due to COVID-19: Virtual Interview

Were tests required? No.

Are tests expected next year? No.

What international experiences are available? Global capstone course.

What dual degree options exist? No dual degree options listed.

What service learning opportunities exist? N/A

What percent of graduates place in postgraduate training? N/A*

NAPLEX First-Time Pass Rate: N/A*

MPJE First-Time Pass Rate: N/A*

*The inaugural class of the WCU School of Pharmacy graduated April 10, 2021. The school has not updated students' outcomes.

ALABAMA

ARKANSAS

DELAWARE

DISTRICT OF COLUMBIA

FLORIDA

GEORGIA

KENTUCKY

LOUISIANA

MARYLAND

MISSISSIPPI

NORTH CAROLINA

OKLAHOMA

SOUTH CAROLINA

TENNESSEE

TEXAS

VIRGINIA

WEST VIRGINIA

SOUTH

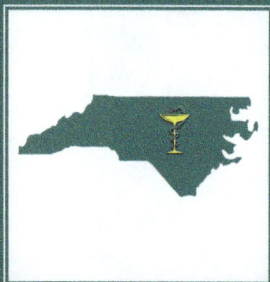

ALABAMA

ARKANSAS

DELAWARE

DISTRICT OF
COLUMBIA

FLORIDA

GEORGIA

KENTUCKY

LOUISIANA

MARYLAND

MISSISSIPPI

NORTH CAROLINA

OKLAHOMA

SOUTH CAROLINA

TENNESSEE

TEXAS

VIRGINIA

WEST VIRGINIA

CAMPBELL UNIVERSITY COLLEGE OF PHARMACY AND HEALTH SCIENCES

Address: 143 Main Street, Buies Creek, NC 27506
Website: *https://cphs.campbell.edu/*
Contact: *https://cphs.campbell.edu/about/contact-us/*
Phone: (800) 760-9734

COST OF ATTENDANCE

Tuition and Fees: $47,396
Additional Expenses: N/A
Total: $47,396*

*Note: This figure does not reflect estimated housing/living expenses.

Financial Aid: https://cphs.campbell.edu/admissions/scholarships/pharmd/

ADDITIONAL INFORMATION

Interesting tidbit: Campbell University's Doctor of Pharmacy program has won all three pharmacy competitions - ACCP Clinical Pharmacy Challenge, ASHP Clinical Skills Competition, and APhA Patient Counseling Competition.

Important Updates due to COVID-19: Virtual Interview

Were tests required? No.

Are tests expected next year? No.

What international experiences are available? N/A

What dual degree options exist? PharmD/MBA, PharmD/MPH, PharmD/MS in Clinical Research, PharmD/MS in Pharmaceutical Sciences, and PharmD/MS in Public Health. For more information, visit: https://cphs.campbell.edu/admissions/apply/pharmacy/

What service learning opportunities exist? N/A

What percent of graduates place in postgraduate training? 30% (2019)

NAPLEX First-Time Pass Rate: 93.00% (2020)

MPJE First-Time Pass Rate: 96.51% (2020)

Other: Early Assurance Guarantee Program available to first-year Campbell undergraduates. For more information, visit: https://cphs.campbell.edu/academic-programs/pharmacy/pre-pharmacy/pharmacy-scholar/

HIGH POINT UNIVERSITY FRED WILSON SCHOOL OF PHARMACY

Address: One University Parkway, High Point, NC 27268
Website: *http://www.highpoint.edu/pharmacy/*
Contact: *https://discover.highpoint.edu/register/inquiry*
Phone: (336) 841-9198

COST OF ATTENDANCE

Tuition and Fees: $40,812
Additional Expenses: N/A
Total: $40,812*

*Note: This figure does not reflect estimated housing/living expenses.

Financial Aid: http://www.highpoint.edu/financialplanning/professional-students/

ADDITIONAL INFORMATION

Interesting tidbit: The groundbreaking High Point University Integrated Learning Model weaves foundational basic science courses with practical clinical experiences throughout the PharmD program to develop stronger problem solving skills and the chance to combine classroom learning with real world application. HPU gives students the opportunity to apply the science they learned in the classroom in patient-care settings shortly afterwards, which enables them to better understand their coursework earlier in the curriculum.

Important Updates due to COVID-19: Virtual Interview

Were tests required? No.

Are tests expected next year? No.

What international experiences are available? N/A

What dual degree options exist? PharmD/MBA.

What service learning opportunities exist? N/A

What percent of graduates place in postgraduate training? N/A

NAPLEX First-Time Pass Rate: 88.89% (2020)

MPJE First-Time Pass Rate: 90.38% (2020)

Other: Early Assurance program available to high school applicants. For more information, visit: http://www.highpoint.edu/pharmacy/files/2019/01/Early-Assurance-2018.pdf

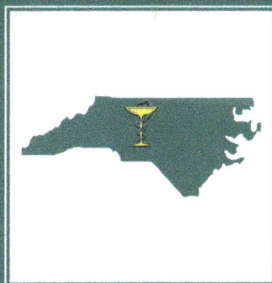

ALABAMA
ARKANSAS
DELAWARE
DISTRICT OF COLUMBIA
FLORIDA
GEORGIA
KENTUCKY
LOUISIANA
MARYLAND
MISSISSIPPI
NORTH CAROLINA
OKLAHOMA
SOUTH CAROLINA
TENNESSEE
TEXAS
VIRGINIA
WEST VIRGINIA

SOUTH

ALABAMA

ARKANSAS

DELAWARE

DISTRICT OF
COLUMBIA

FLORIDA

GEORGIA

KENTUCKY

LOUISIANA

MARYLAND

MISSISSIPPI

NORTH CAROLINA

OKLAHOMA

SOUTH CAROLINA

TENNESSEE

TEXAS

VIRGINIA

WEST VIRGINIA

UNIVERSITY OF NORTH CAROLINA ESHELMAN SCHOOL OF PHARMACY

Address: 301 Pharmacy Lane, CB 7355, Chapel Hill, NC 27599
Website: *https://pharmacy.unc.edu/*
Contact: *http://pharm2.sites.unc.edu/contact-us*
Phone: (919) 966-9786

Other locations: Asheville, NC

COST OF ATTENDANCE

In-State Tuition and Fees: $24,329
Additional Expenses: N/A
Total: $24,329*

Out-of-State Tuition and Fees: $46,890
Additional Expenses: N/A
Total: $46,890*

*Note: These figures do not reflect estimated housing/living expenses.

Financial Aid: https://studentaid.unc.edu/

Note: $100,000 in scholarships for first-year students. Applicants are considered for these scholarships through the supplemental application.

ADDITIONAL INFORMATION

Interesting tidbit: UNC Eshelman School of Pharmacy offers a dual campus model with campuses in Chapel Hill and Asheville. One school, two campuses, same degree. All students complete their PY1 foundational year on the Chapel Hill campus. During the PY1 year, students designate their choice for one of the campuses, each of which offers a distinct but comparable experience.

Important Updates due to COVID-19: Temporarily making the PCAT test an optional requirement for the 2020-2021 admissions cycle. Accept pass or credit grades for courses taken during the Spring 2020 and Fall 2020 semesters from institutions that put special grading accommodations in place.

Were tests required? No.

Are tests expected next year? Yes.

What international experiences are available? International rotations. For more information on other global initiatives, visit: https://pharmacy.unc.edu/global/

What dual degree options exist? PharmD/MBA and PharmD/MPH. For more information, visit: https://pharmacy.unc.edu/education/pharmd/program/

What service learning opportunities exist? Rural Pharmacy Health Certificate Program. For more information, visit: https://pharmacy.unc.edu/practice/rural-pharmacy-health-program/

What percent of graduates place in postgraduate training? 68% (2020)

NAPLEX First-Time Pass Rate: 98.46% (2020)

MPJE First-Time Pass Rate: 95.60% (2020)

Other: Assured Enrollment pathway available to UNC undergraduates. For more information, visit: https://admissions.unc.edu/pharmacy/

WINGATE UNIVERSITY SCHOOL OF PHARMACY

Address: 220 N Camden St., Wingate, NC 28174
Website: *https://www.wingate.edu/academics/graduate/pharmacy*
Contact: *https://www.wingate.edu/academics/graduate/pharmacy/ wusop-contact-us*
Phone: (704) 233-8633

Other locations: Hendersonville, NC

COST OF ATTENDANCE

Tuition and Fees: $35,400
Additional Expenses: N/A
Total: $ 35,400*

***Note:** This figure does not reflect estimated housing/living expenses.

Financial Aid: https://www.wingate.edu/admissions/financial-aid/ student-financial-aid

ADDITIONAL INFORMATION

Interesting tidbit: All classes, case studies, discussions and laboratory sessions are taught by faculty, not graduate students. All classes are supported fully with Web notes in advance of each session, which allows the student to listen to lectures and participate fully in discussions instead of busily penning notes.

Important Updates due to COVID-19: Accept online coursework beginning spring 2020 until normal operations resume. Accept Pass/Fail courses beginning spring 2020 until normal operations resume. Virtual Interview.

Were tests required? No.

Are tests expected next year? No.

What international experiences are available? Mission trips with faculty.

What dual degree options exist? PharmD/MBA. For more information, visit: https://www.wingate.edu/academics/graduate/ pharmacy/wusop-academics

What service learning opportunities exist? N/A

What percent of graduates place in postgraduate training? N/A

NAPLEX First-Time Pass Rate: 74.68% (2020)

MPJE First-Time Pass Rate: 95.77% (2020)

Other: Early Assurance program available to high school applicants. For more information, visit website and download Early Assurance information pamphlet: https://www.wingate. edu/academics/graduate/pharmacy/wusop-admissions

ALABAMA
ARKANSAS
DELAWARE
DISTRICT OF COLUMBIA
FLORIDA
GEORGIA
KENTUCKY
LOUISIANA
MARYLAND
MISSISSIPPI
NORTH CAROLINA
OKLAHOMA
SOUTH CAROLINA
TENNESSEE
TEXAS
VIRGINIA
WEST VIRGINIA

SOUTH

ALABAMA

ARKANSAS

DELAWARE

DISTRICT OF
COLUMBIA

FLORIDA

GEORGIA

KENTUCKY

LOUISIANA

MARYLAND

MISSISSIPPI

NORTH CAROLINA

OKLAHOMA

SOUTH CAROLINA

TENNESSEE

TEXAS

VIRGINIA

WEST VIRGINIA

SOUTHWESTERN OKLAHOMA STATE UNIVERSITY COLLEGE OF PHARMACY

Address: 100 Campus Dr., Weatherford, OK 73096
Website: *https://www.swosu.edu/academics/pharmacy/index.aspx*
Contact: *https://www.swosu.edu/about/contact.php*
Phone: (580) 774-3063

COST OF ATTENDANCE

In-State Tuition and Fees: $24,705
Additional Expenses: N/A
Total: $24,705*

Out-of-State Tuition and Fees: $40,500
Additional Expenses: N/A
Total: $40,500*

*Note: These figures do not reflect estimated housing/living expenses.

Financial Aid: https://bulldog.swosu.edu/student-services/financial-aid/index.php

ADDITIONAL INFORMATION

Interesting tidbit: SWOSU has the only Doctor of Pharmacy program in the nation that admits twice yearly. Students may apply for admission into the professional program for the fall and spring semesters.

Important Updates due to COVID-19: Virtual Interview

Were tests required? PCAT required.

Are tests expected next year? Yes.

What international experiences are available? N/A

What dual degree options exist? PharmD/MBA.

What service learning opportunities exist? Rural Health Center Medical Clinic. For more information, visit: https://bulldog.swosu.edu/academics/pharmacy/rhc/charitable-services.php

What percent of graduates place in postgraduate training? 32% (2018)

NAPLEX First-Time Pass Rate: 90.20 % (2020)

MPJE First-Time Pass Rate: 97.67% (2020)

Other: Degree specialization in Pharmacy Leadership. or more information, visit: https://bulldog.swosu.edu/academics/pharmacy/pliq/index.php

UNIVERSITY OF OKLAHOMA COLLEGE OF PHARMACY

Address: 1110 N. Stonewall Ave., Oklahoma City, OK 73117
Website: *https://pharmacy.ouhsc.edu/*
Contact: *https://pharmacy.ouhsc.edu/contact-us*
Phone: (405) 271-6484

COST OF ATTENDANCE

In-State Tuition and Fees: $23,960
Additional Expenses: N/A
Total: $23,960*

Out-of-State Tuition and Fees: $43,752
Additional Expenses: N/A
Total: $43,752*

*Note: These figures do not reflect estimated housing/living expenses.

Financial Aid: https://financialservices.ouhsc.edu/

ADDITIONAL INFORMATION

Interesting tidbit: The University of Oklahoma College of Pharmacy is one of only two colleges of pharmacy in the United States to offer a fully operational nuclear pharmacy on campus. It also operates the only nationally-certified Poison & Drug Information Center in the state. OUHSC also has the only National Cancer Institute-designated public cancer center in the state.

Important Updates due to COVID-19: Accept a Pass or a Satisfactory as acceptable for successful completion of any prerequisite courses they are enrolled in for Fall 2020 or Spring 2021.

Were tests required? No.

Are tests expected next year? No.

What international experiences are available? International rotation with sister pharmacy school in Clermont-Ferrand, France. Students may also travel during spring break with student organizations for mission trips.

What dual degree options exist? No dual degree options listed.

What service learning opportunities exist? Unity Clinic, a free mobile health clinic to help disadvantaged populations. Other opportunities include volunteer work in free flu clinics, tutoring program with Frederick A. Douglass High School, and working at the call center at the Oklahoma Center for Poison & Drug.

What percent of graduates place in postgraduate training? 25.6% (2020)

NAPLEX First-Time Pass Rate: 90.24% (2020)

MPJE First-Time Pass Rate: 86.11% (2020)

Other: PharmD Early Assurance Program (PEAP) available to high school applicants. For more information, visit: https://pharmacy.ouhsc.edu/programs/doctor-of-pharmacy/pharm-d-early-assurance-program-hs-seniors

Early Assurance also available to individuals with a non-science U.S. university bachelor degree. For more information, visit: https://pharmacy.ouhsc.edu/programs/doctor-of-pharmacy/nsbhpeap

Nuclear Pharmacy track available. For more information, visit: https://pharmacy.ouhsc.edu/programs/doctor-of-pharmacy/degreeoptions/nuclear

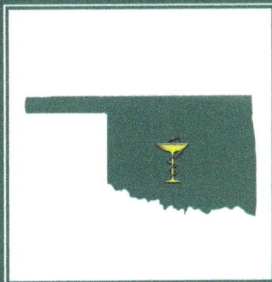

Degree options: ambulatory care, leadership, pediatrics, and research. For more information, visit: https://pharmacy.ouhsc.edu/programs/doctor-of-pharmacy/degreeoptions

ALABAMA

ARKANSAS

DELAWARE

DISTRICT OF COLUMBIA

FLORIDA

GEORGIA

KENTUCKY

LOUISIANA

MARYLAND

MISSISSIPPI

NORTH CAROLINA

OKLAHOMA

SOUTH CAROLINA

TENNESSEE

TEXAS

VIRGINIA

WEST VIRGINIA

SOUTH

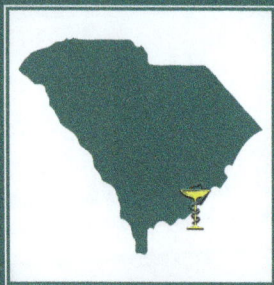

ALABAMA

ARKANSAS

DELAWARE

DISTRICT OF
COLUMBIA

FLORIDA

GEORGIA

KENTUCKY

LOUISIANA

MARYLAND

MISSISSIPPI

NORTH CAROLINA

OKLAHOMA

SOUTH CAROLINA

TENNESSEE

TEXAS

VIRGINIA

WEST VIRGINIA

MEDICAL UNIVERSITY OF SOUTH CAROLINA COLLEGE OF PHARMACY

Address: 280 Calhoun Street, Charleston, SC 29425
Website: *https://pharmacy.musc.edu/*
Contact: *https://pharmacy.musc.edu/students-and-admissions/prospective-students/request-more-information*
Phone: (843) 792-2300

COST OF ATTENDANCE

In-State Tuition and Fees: $26,045
Additional Expenses: N/A
Total: $26,045*

Out-of-State Tuition and Fees: $40,056
Additional Expenses: N/A
Total: $40,056*

*Note: These figures do not reflect estimated housing/living expenses.

Financial Aid: https://pharmacy.musc.edu/students-and-admissions/scholarships-and-financial-aid

ADDITIONAL INFORMATION

Interesting tidbit: The MUSC Medical Center and College of Pharmacy Residency Program offers one of the largest and most respected pharmacy residency programs in the country with 12 specialty tracks and typically 20 residents.

Important Updates due to COVID-19: Virtual Interview

Were tests required? No.

Are tests expected next year? No.

What international experiences are available? N/A

What dual degree options exist? PharmD/MBA, PharmD/MS in Health Informatics, and PharmD/PhD. For more information, visit: https://pharmacy.musc.edu/academic-programs/concurrent-degree-programs

What service learning opportunities exist? Service learning through student organizations and experiential education.

What percent of graduates place in postgraduate training? N/A

NAPLEX First-Time Pass Rate: 93.51% (2020)

MPJE First-Time Pass Rate: 87.23% (2020)

Other: Early Assurance Program available for high school applicants. For more information, visit: https://pharmacy.musc.edu/students-and-admissions/prospective-students/early-assurance-program

PRESBYTERIAN COLLEGE SCHOOL OF PHARMACY

Address: 307 North Broad St., Clinton, SC 29325
Website: *https://pharmacy.presby.edu/*
Contact: *https://pharmacy.presby.edu/admissions/request-information/*
Phone: (864) 938-3900

COST OF ATTENDANCE

Tuition and Fees: $39,600
Additional Expenses: N/A
Total: $39,600*

***Note:** This figure does not reflect estimated housing/living expenses.

Financial Aid: https://pharmacy.presby.edu/admissions/financial-aid/

ADDITIONAL INFORMATION

Interesting tidbit: Presbyterian College School of Pharmacy places a high value on advocacy, activism and outreach; therefore service learning is integrated throughout our pharmacy program. In 2020, the Presbyterian College School of Pharmacy received continued accreditation through 2028, the eight-year term being the longest in the School's history.

Important Updates due to COVID-19: Virtual Interview

Were tests required? No.

Are tests expected next year? No.

What international experiences are available? International rotations.

What dual degree options exist? No dual degree options listed.

What service learning opportunities exist? Service learning through experiential education. See international experiences.

What percent of graduates place in postgraduate training? 60% PGY1 match rate (2021)

NAPLEX First-Time Pass Rate: 95.65% (2020)

MPJE First-Time Pass Rate: 86.36% (2020)

Other: Early Entry Pre-Pharmacy available to high school applicants. For more information, visit: https://www.presby.edu/academics/undergraduate/academic-departments-programs/pre-health-sciences-program/pre-pharmacy/early-entry-pre-pharmacy/

Degree Plus Pre-Pharmacy available to Presbyterian College undergraduates. For more information, visit: https://www.presby.edu/academics/undergraduate/academic-departments-programs/pre-health-sciences-program/pre-pharmacy/degree-plus-pre-pharmacy/

ALABAMA
ARKANSAS
DELAWARE
DISTRICT OF COLUMBIA
FLORIDA
GEORGIA
KENTUCKY
LOUISIANA
MARYLAND
MISSISSIPPI
NORTH CAROLINA
OKLAHOMA
SOUTH CAROLINA
TENNESSEE
TEXAS
VIRGINIA
WEST VIRGINIA

SOUTH

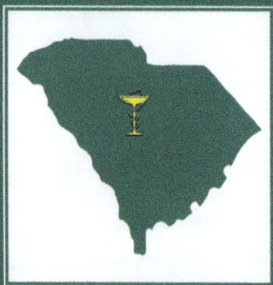

ALABAMA

ARKANSAS

DELAWARE

DISTRICT OF
COLUMBIA

FLORIDA

GEORGIA

KENTUCKY

LOUISIANA

MARYLAND

MISSISSIPPI

NORTH CAROLINA

OKLAHOMA

SOUTH CAROLINA

TENNESSEE

TEXAS

VIRGINIA

WEST VIRGINIA

UNIVERSITY OF SOUTH CAROLINA COLLEGE OF PHARMACY

Address: 715 Sumter St., Columbia, SC 29208
Website: *https://www.sc.edu/study/colleges_schools/pharmacy/index.php*
Contact: *https://www.sc.edu/study/colleges_schools/pharmacy/about/contact.php*
Phone: (803) 777-4151

COST OF ATTENDANCE

In-State Tuition and Fees: $24,240
Additional Expenses: N/A
Total: $24,240*

Out-of-State Tuition and Fees: $38,534
Additional Expenses: N/A
Total: $38,534*

*Note: These figures do not reflect estimated housing/living expenses.

Financial Aid: https://www.sc.edu/study/colleges_schools/pharmacy/about/tuition_and_scholarships/index.php

ADDITIONAL INFORMATION

Interesting tidbit: The UofSC PharmD students benefit from the College of Pharmacy's one-of-a-kind Kennedy Pharmacy Innovation Center, a specialized learning center that unites the study and practice of pharmacy with the exciting opportunities of entrepreneurship and innovation.

Important Updates due to COVID-19: Due to the COVID-19 pandemic, the UofSC College of Pharmacy will not require the PCAT for admission into the Doctor of Pharmacy (Pharm.D.) program for the 2021-2022 application cycle.

Were tests required? Yes.

Are tests expected next year? No.

What international experiences are available? Exchange programs and study abroad in locations such as Egypt, China, Qatar, Saudi Arabia, and Kuwait. For more information, visit: https://www.sc.edu/study/colleges_schools/pharmacy/student_experience/international_programs/index.php

What dual degree options exist? PharmD/MBA, PharmD/MPH or MHA, PharmD/MHIT, and PharmD/PhD. For more information, visit: https://www.sc.edu/study/colleges_schools/pharmacy/pharmacy_education/dual_degree_programs/index.php

What service learning opportunities exist? Service learning through experiential education, student organizations, and international opportunities. For more information, visit: https://www.sc.edu/study/colleges_schools/pharmacy/student_experience/index.php

What percent of graduates place in postgraduate training? 25% (2018)

NAPLEX First-Time Pass Rate: 87.63% (2020)

MPJE First-Time Pass Rate: 91.30% (2020)

Other: Early Assurance Program available to high school applicants. For more information, visit: https://www.sc.edu/study/colleges_schools/pharmacy/pharmacy_education/gamecock_pharmacy_assurance/index.php

BELMONT UNIVERSITY COLLEGE OF PHARMACY

Address: 1900 Belmont Blvd, Nashville, TN 37212
Website: *http://www.belmont.edu/pharmacy/index.html*
Contact: *Contact via phone or email: pharmacy@belmont.edu*
Phone: (615) 460-8122

COST OF ATTENDANCE

Tuition and Fees: $44,660
Additional Expenses: N/A
Total: $44,660*

*Note: These figures do not reflect estimated housing/living expenses.

Financial Aid: See "Scholarship Opportunities": http://www.belmont.edu/pharmacy/admission.html

ADDITIONAL INFORMATION

Interesting tidbit: BUCOP is located in Nashville, Tennessee - known as the U.S. healthcare capital. At Belmont, students learn in a student-centered Christian community of learning and service. With five areas of specialized concentration, students have the opportunity to choose the path that's right for them.

Important Updates due to COVID-19: Virtual Interview

Were tests required? No.

Are tests expected next year? No.

What international experiences are available? International mission trips.

What dual degree options exist? PharmD/MBA. For more information, visit: http://www.belmont.edu/pharmacy/academics/pharmacy-mba/index.html

What service learning opportunities exist? Service learning through student organizations and international mission trips.

What percent of graduates place in postgraduate training? 33% (2019)

NAPLEX First-Time Pass Rate: 88.37% (2020)

MPJE First-Time Pass Rate: 76.47% (2020)

Other: Early Assurance program available to high school applicants. For more information, visit: http://www.belmont.edu/pharmacy/earlyassurance.html

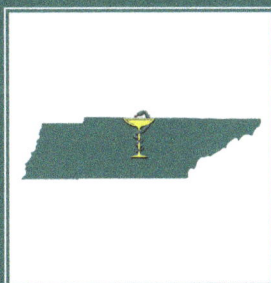

ALABAMA
ARKANSAS
DELAWARE
DISTRICT OF COLUMBIA
FLORIDA
GEORGIA
KENTUCKY
LOUISIANA
MARYLAND
MISSISSIPPI
NORTH CAROLINA
OKLAHOMA
SOUTH CAROLINA
TENNESSEE
TEXAS
VIRGINIA
WEST VIRGINIA

SOUTH

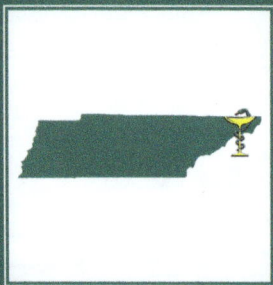

ALABAMA

ARKANSAS

DELAWARE

DISTRICT OF COLUMBIA

FLORIDA

GEORGIA

KENTUCKY

LOUISIANA

MARYLAND

MISSISSIPPI

NORTH CAROLINA

OKLAHOMA

SOUTH CAROLINA

TENNESSEE

TEXAS

VIRGINIA

WEST VIRGINIA

EAST TENNESSEE STATE UNIVERSITY BILL GATTON COLLEGE OF PHARMACY

Address: Gatton College of Pharmacy, Maple Ave, Johnson City, TN 37604
Website: *https://www.etsu.edu/pharmacy/*
Contact: *https://www.etsu.edu/pharmacy/contactus.php*
Phone: (423) 439-6338

COST OF ATTENDANCE

Tuition and Fees: $39,621
Additional Expenses: N/A
Total: $39,621*

*Note: This figure does not reflect estimated housing/living expenses.

Financial Aid: https://www.etsu.edu/pharmacy/administration/financial_aid/p1_budget.php

ADDITIONAL INFORMATION

Interesting tidbit: The mission of Bill Gatton College of Pharmacy is to train progressive pharmacists that improve healthcare, focusing on rural and under-served communities. Gatton students lead a national award-winning chapter of Generation Rx.

Important Updates due to COVID-19: Virtual Interview

Were tests required? No.

Are tests expected next year? No.

What international experiences are available? International rotations in Ireland, Scotland, Hungary, or Uganda. For more information, visit: https://www.etsu.edu/pharmacy/administration/experiential_education/globalexperiences.php

What dual degree options exist? PharmD/MBA and PharmD/MPH. For more information, visit: https://www.etsu.edu/pharmacy/academic_programs/dual_degree_programs.php

What service learning opportunities exist? Service learning through experiential education during APPE. Rural Health rotations available. For more information, visit: https://www.etsu.edu/pharmacy/administration/experiential_education/rural_health.php

What percent of graduates place in postgraduate training? 23.7% (2019)

NAPLEX First-Time Pass Rate: 80.95% (2020)

MPJE First-Time Pass Rate: 82.50% (2020)

Other: Early Admission Pathway available to high school applicants or current ETSU freshmen. For more information, visit: https://www.etsu.edu/pharmacy/admissions/early_admission_pathway.php

Research elective available. For more information, visit: https://www.etsu.edu/pharmacy/departments/pharmaceutical_sciences/research.php

LIPSCOMB UNIVERSITY COLLEGE OF PHARMACY AND HEALTH SCIENCES

Address: 1 University Park Dr., Nashville, TN 37204
Website: *https://www.lipscomb.edu/pharmacy*
Contact: *https://www.lipscomb.edu/directory*
Phone: (615) 966-7164

COST OF ATTENDANCE

Tuition and Fees: $40,842
Additional Expenses: N/A
Total: $40,842*

*Note: This figure does not reflect estimated housing/living expenses.

Financial Aid: See "Tuition & Aid": https://www.lipscomb.edu/academics/programs/pharmacy

ADDITIONAL INFORMATION

Interesting tidbit: Lipscomb is conveniently located in an area with over 300 health care corporations. Early in your first semester students will have the opportunity to begin introductory pharmacy practice experiences (IPPEs), which will allow them to work with some of the nation's best practitioners in all areas of pharmacy practice, such as hospitals, community pharmacies, and specialty pharmacies such as long-term care and nuclear pharmacies.

Important Updates due to COVID-19: Virtual Interview

Were tests required? No.

Are tests expected next year? No.

What international experiences are available? International rotations.

What dual degree options exist? PharmD/Master of Health Care Informatics and PharmD/Master of Management in Health Care. For more information, visit: https://www.lipscomb.edu/pharmacy/academic-programs

What service learning opportunities exist? Mission and Community Service Program. For more information, visit: https://www.lipscomb.edu/pharmacy/community

What percent of graduates place in postgraduate training? 26.4% (2019)

NAPLEX First-Time Pass Rate: 85.53% (2020)

MPJE First-Time Pass Rate: 78.85% (2020)

Other: Early Assurance pathway.

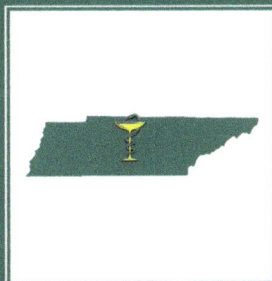

ALABAMA
ARKANSAS
DELAWARE
DISTRICT OF COLUMBIA
FLORIDA
GEORGIA
KENTUCKY
LOUISIANA
MARYLAND
MISSISSIPPI
NORTH CAROLINA
OKLAHOMA
SOUTH CAROLINA
TENNESSEE
TEXAS
VIRGINIA
WEST VIRGINIA

SOUTH

ALABAMA

ARKANSAS

DELAWARE

DISTRICT OF
COLUMBIA

FLORIDA

GEORGIA

KENTUCKY

LOUISIANA

MARYLAND

MISSISSIPPI

NORTH CAROLINA

OKLAHOMA

SOUTH CAROLINA

TENNESSEE

TEXAS

VIRGINIA

WEST VIRGINIA

SOUTH COLLEGE SCHOOL OF PHARMACY

Address: 3904 Lonas Dr., Knoxville, TN 37909
Website: *https://www.south.edu/programs/doctor-pharmacy/*
Contact: *https://www.south.edu/request-info/?program=doctor-pharmacy*
Phone: (865) 251-1800

COST OF ATTENDANCE

Tuition and Fees: $50,100
Additional Expenses: N/A
Total: $50,100*

*Note: This figure does not reflect estimated housing/living expenses.

Financial Aid: https://www.south.edu/programs/doctor-pharmacy/tuition-and-scholarships/

ADDITIONAL INFORMATION

Interesting tidbit: South College School of Pharmacy offers the only 3-year Doctor of Pharmacy program in the state of Tennessee. The mission of South College School of Pharmacy is to prepare pharmacy students to be proficient practitioners who deliver team-oriented, patient care with advocacy and compassion.

Important Updates due to COVID-19: Virtual Interview

Were tests required? No.

Are tests expected next year? No.

What international experiences are available? International rotations.

What dual degree options exist? No dual degree options listed.

What service learning opportunities exist? Service learning through student organizations and experiential education.

What percent of graduates place in postgraduate training? 5% (2020)

NAPLEX First-Time Pass Rate: 73.08% (2020)

MPJE First-Time Pass Rate: 84.62% (2020)

Other: South College Pharmacy Early Assurance Readiness Program (SPEAR) is available to high school applicants.

UNION UNIVERSITY COLLEGE OF PHARMACY

Address: 1050 Union University Dr., Jackson, TN 38305
Website: *https://www.uu.edu/programs/pharmacy/*
Contact: *https://www.uu.edu/contact-us.cfm*
Phone: (731) 668-1818

COST OF ATTENDANCE

Tuition and Fees: $38,800
Additional Expenses: N/A
Total: $38,800*

*Note: This figure does not reflect estimated housing/living expenses.

Financial Aid: https://www.uu.edu/financialaid/graduate/

ADDITIONAL INFORMATION

Interesting tidbit: Union University's overall commitment to integrating rigorous academics with a Christian worldview is exemplified in the credentials of the College of Pharmacy faculty. The UUCOP strives to provide a Christ-centered environment that focuses on the intellectual, spiritual, and moral development of students in committing themselves to the service and needs of society.

Important Updates due to COVID-19: Virtual Interview

Were tests required? No.

Are tests expected next year? No.

What international experiences are available? N/A

What dual degree options exist? PharmD/MBA. For more information, visit: https://www.uu.edu/programs/pharmacy/academics/pharmd-mba.cfm

What service learning opportunities exist? Service learning through curriculum and experiential education.

What percent of graduates place in postgraduate training? N/A

NAPLEX First-Time Pass Rate: 97.96% (2020)

MPJE First-Time Pass Rate: 79.41% (2020)

Other: Pharmacy Early Admission Program (PEAP) available to Union University freshmen. For more information, visit: https://www.uu.edu/programs/pharmacy/admissions/peap.cfm

Direct Admission Program available to undergraduate students at affiliated universities. For more information, visit: https://www.uu.edu/programs/pharmacy/admissions/direct-admission-program-partnerships.cfm

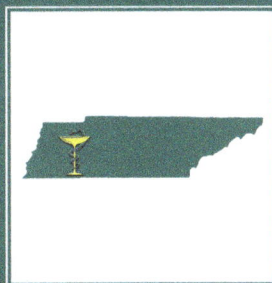

ALABAMA

ARKANSAS

DELAWARE

DISTRICT OF COLUMBIA

FLORIDA

GEORGIA

KENTUCKY

LOUISIANA

MARYLAND

MISSISSIPPI

NORTH CAROLINA

OKLAHOMA

SOUTH CAROLINA

TENNESSEE

TEXAS

VIRGINIA

WEST VIRGINIA

SOUTH

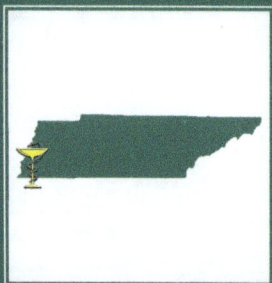

ALABAMA

ARKANSAS

DELAWARE

DISTRICT OF
COLUMBIA

FLORIDA

GEORGIA

KENTUCKY

LOUISIANA

MARYLAND

MISSISSIPPI

NORTH CAROLINA

OKLAHOMA

SOUTH CAROLINA

TENNESSEE

TEXAS

VIRGINIA

WEST VIRGINIA

UNIVERSITY OF TENNESSEE HEALTH SCIENCE CENTER COLLEGE OF PHARMACY

Address: 881 Madison Ave., Memphis, TN 38163
Website: *https://www.uthsc.edu/pharmacy/*
Contact: *http://futurepharmacist.uthsc.edu/inquiryform*
Phone: (901) 448-7053

Other locations: Knoxville, TN; Nashville, TN

COST OF ATTENDANCE

In-State Tuition and Fees: $22,370
Additional Expenses: N/A
Total: $22,370*

Out-of-State Tuition and Fees: $27,374
Additional Expenses: N/A
Total: $27,374*

*Note: These figures do not reflect estimated housing/living expenses.

Financial Aid: https://www.uthsc.edu/pharmacy/prospective-students/tuition-and-scholarships.php

ADDITIONAL INFORMATION

Interesting tidbit: The University of Tennessee Health Science Center offers three campus options across the state for students to complete the Doctor of Pharmacy program. All students begin their P1 year on the UTHSC Memphis campus. Following completion of their Memphis-based training, students may transfer to either the Knoxville or Nashville campus to complete the remainder of the professional program.

Important Updates due to COVID-19: Virtual Interview

Were tests required? No.

Are tests expected next year? No.

What international experiences are available? International rotations. For more information, visit: https://www.uthsc.edu/pharmacy/current-students/oel/appe.php#govappe

What dual degree options exist? PharmD/PhD, PharmD/MBA, PharmD/MPH, and PharmD/Masters in Health Informatics and Information Management or Certificate: https://www.uthsc.edu/pharmacy/current-students/academic-affairs/dual-degrees.php

What service learning opportunities exist? Service learning through experiential education during APPEs. Various opportunities for students both nationally and internationally. Government APPEs: Air Force (Alaska), Indian Health Service (Arizona, Montana, Wyoming), and US Army (Kentucky). For more information, visit: https://www.uthsc.edu/pharmacy/current-students/oel/appe.php#govappe

What percent of graduates place in postgraduate training? N/A

NAPLEX First-Time Pass Rate: 93.24% (2020)

MPJE First-Time Pass Rate: 89.62% (2020)

Other: Nuclear Pharmacy Certificate. For more information, visit: https://www.uthsc.edu/pharmacy/ce/nuclear-pharmacy.php

TEXAS A&M UNIVERSITY HEALTH SCIENCE CENTER IRMA LERMA RANGEL COLLEGE OF PHARMACY

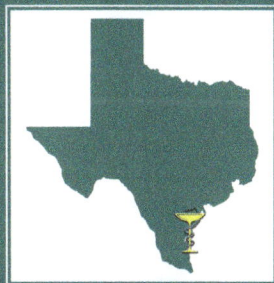

Address: 1010 W. Avenue B, Kingsville, TX 78363
Website: *https://pharmacy.tamu.edu/*
Contact: *https://pharmacy.tamu.edu/about/contact.html*
Phone: (361) 221-0604
Other Locations: College Station, TX

COST OF ATTENDANCE

In-State Tuition and Fees: $16,364
Additional Expenses: N/A
Total: $16,364*

Out-of-State Tuition and Fees: $56,360
Additional Expenses: N/A
Total: $56,360*

*Note: These figures do not reflect estimated housing/living expenses.

Financial Aid: https://pharmacy.tamu.edu/scholarships/

ADDITIONAL INFORMATION

Interesting tidbit: Rangel College of Pharmacy students can choose to enroll in Kingsville or College Station, receiving the same transformational education at either campus. One-third of classes, including all of the fourth year, will be spent training in clinics and hospitals.

Important Updates due to COVID-19: Virtual Interview

Were tests required? No.

Are tests expected next year? No.

What international experiences are available? International mission trips and global education through student organizations. For more information, visit: https://pharmacy.tamu.edu/current/student-organizations.html

What dual degree options exist? PharmD/MBA. For more information, visit: https://pharmacy.tamu.edu/pharmd/pharmd-mba.html

What service learning opportunities exist? Opioid Task Force, Health South Texas, and other partnerships where students may learn through community outreach. For more information, visit: https://pharmacy.tamu.edu/community/partnerships.html

Community Education: https://pharmacy.tamu.edu/community/community-education.html

What percent of graduates place in postgraduate training? 13% (2020)

NAPLEX First-Time Pass Rate: 85.19% (2020)

MPJE First-Time Pass Rate: 88.89% (2020)

Other: ASPIR2E Pre-Pharmacy Advanced Program (PPAP) available to prepare second-year undergraduate pre-pharmacy students in preparing them to become competitive applicants. For more information, visit: https://pharmacy.tamu.edu/aspire/pre-pharmacy-advanced.html

ALABAMA
ARKANSAS
DELAWARE
DISTRICT OF COLUMBIA
FLORIDA
GEORGIA
KENTUCKY
LOUISIANA
MARYLAND
MISSISSIPPI
NORTH CAROLINA
OKLAHOMA
SOUTH CAROLINA
TENNESSEE
TEXAS
VIRGINIA
WEST VIRGINIA

SOUTH

TEXAS SOUTHERN UNIVERSITY COLLEGE OF PHARMACY AND HEALTH SCIENCES

Address: 3100 Cleburne Street, Houston, TX 77004
Website: *http://www.tsu.edu/academics/colleges-and-schools/college-of-pharmacy-and-health-sciences/*
Contact: *http://www.tsu.edu/academics/colleges-and-schools/college-of-pharmacy-and-health-sciences/contact-us.html*
Phone: (713) 313-6700

COST OF ATTENDANCE

In-State Tuition and Fees: $18,113
Additional Expenses: N/A
Total: $18,113*

Out-of-State Tuition and Fees: $29,669
Additional Expenses: N/A
Total: $29,669*

*Note: These figures do not reflect estimated housing/living expenses.

Financial Aid: http://www.tsu.edu/admissions/financial-aid/index.html

ADDITIONAL INFORMATION

Interesting tidbit: Texas Southern University is heralded as a pioneer and has distinguished itself by producing a significant number of African American students who have obtained post-secondary and advanced degrees. Although initially established to educate African Americans, Texas Southern University has become one of the most diverse institutions in Texas.

Important Updates due to COVID-19: The 2020-2021 PCAT admission requirement is waived.

Were tests required? No.

Are tests expected next year? Yes.

What international experiences are available? N/A

What dual degree options exist? No dual degree options listed.

What service learning opportunities exist? Service learning through student organizations and experiential education.

What percent of graduates place in postgraduate training? N/A

NAPLEX First-Time Pass Rate: 83.08% (2020)

MPJE First-Time Pass Rate: 86.15% (2020)

TEXAS TECH UNIVERSITY HEALTH SCIENCES CENTER JERRY H. HODGE SCHOOL OF PHARMACY

Address: 3601 4th Street, Lubbock, TX 79424
Website: *https://www.ttuhsc.edu/pharmacy/default.aspx*
Contact: *https://www.ttuhsc.edu/pharmacy/contact.aspx*
Phone: (806) 414-9393

COST OF ATTENDANCE

In-State Tuition and Fees: $21,530
Additional Expenses: N/A
Total: $21,530*

Out-of-State Tuition and Fees: $33,591
Additional Expenses: N/A
Total: $33,591*

*Note: These figures do not reflect estimated housing/living expenses.

Financial Aid: https://www.ttuhsc.edu/pharmacy/prospective/moneytuitionandfees.aspx

ADDITIONAL INFORMATION

Interesting tidbit: TTUHSC-SOP was the first program in the nation to require all of its students to have laptop computers and to deliver materials and email services in support of coursework. The SOP also requires its students to complete more clinical training hours than any other pharmacy program in the country.

Important Updates due to COVID-19: Due to the ongoing COVID-19 pandemic, the PCAT will no longer be required for the remainder of Fall 2021 applicants.

Were tests required? No.

Are tests expected next year? Yes.

What international experiences are available? N/A

What dual degree options exist? PharmD/MBA. For more information, visit: https://www.ttuhsc.edu/pharmacy/mba/default.aspx

What service learning opportunities exist? Medication cleanouts, immunization clinics, health fairs, and more.

What percent of graduates place in postgraduate training? N/A

NAPLEX First-Time Pass Rate: 93.66% (2020)

MPJE First-Time Pass Rate: 87.97% (2020)

ALABAMA
ARKANSAS
DELAWARE
DISTRICT OF COLUMBIA
FLORIDA
GEORGIA
KENTUCKY
LOUISIANA
MARYLAND
MISSISSIPPI
NORTH CAROLINA
OKLAHOMA
SOUTH CAROLINA
TENNESSEE
TEXAS
VIRGINIA
WEST VIRGINIA

SOUTH

ALABAMA

ARKANSAS

DELAWARE

DISTRICT OF
COLUMBIA

FLORIDA

GEORGIA

KENTUCKY

LOUISIANA

MARYLAND

MISSISSIPPI

NORTH CAROLINA

OKLAHOMA

SOUTH CAROLINA

TENNESSEE

TEXAS

VIRGINIA

WEST VIRGINIA

UNIVERSITY OF HOUSTON COLLEGE OF PHARMACY

Address: 4849 Calhoun, Houston, TX 77204
Website: *https://www.uh.edu/pharmacy/*
Contact: *https://www.uh.edu/pharmacy/directory-home/*
Phone: (713) 743-1239

COST OF ATTENDANCE

In-State Tuition and Fees: $25,830
Additional Expenses: $20,470
Total: $46,300

Out-of-State Tuition and Fees: $45,024
Additional Expenses: $20,470
Total: $65,494

Financial Aid: https://www.uh.edu/pharmacy/prospective-students/pharmd/financial-aid/

ADDITIONAL INFORMATION

Interesting tidbit: In collaboration with its fellow Texas Medical Center institutions and elsewhere, UHCOP offers a range of clinical research opportunities and practice experiences (APPEs) in oncology, infectious disease, pediatrics, women's health, critical care, neurology, compounding and veterinary pharmacy. UH Pharm students also can pursue a variety of unique in-state and out-of-state experiential opportunities, including the Food and Drug Administration, the Centers for Disease Control and Prevention, and the Indian Health Service in Alaska and New Mexico.

Important Updates due to COVID-19: Temporarily suspend the PCAT requirement for the 2021 admission cycle.

Were tests required? No.

Are tests expected next year? Yes.

What international experiences are available? N/A

What dual degree options exist? PharmD/MBA and PharmD/PhD. For more information, visit: https://www.uh.edu/pharmacy/prospective-students/dual-programs/index-old.php

What service learning opportunities exist? N/A

What percent of graduates place in postgraduate training? 39.4% (2020)

NAPLEX First-Time Pass Rate: 92.26% (2020)

MPJE First-Time Pass Rate: 96.94% (2020)

Other: Certificate in Hispanic Healthcare. For more information, visit: https://www.uh.edu/pharmacy/prospective-students/pharmd/hispanic-healthcare-certificate/

UNIVERSITY OF NORTH TEXAS HEALTH SCIENCE CENTER UNT SYSTEM COLLEGE OF PHARMACY

Address: 3500 Camp Bowie Blvd., Fort Worth, TX 76107
Website: *https://www.unthsc.edu/college-of-pharmacy/*
Contact: *https://www.unthsc.edu/school-of-health-professions/contact-us/*
Phone: (817) 735-2003

COST OF ATTENDANCE

In-State Tuition and Fees: $22,956
Additional Expenses: N/A
Total: $22,956*

Out-of-State Tuition and Fees: $38,992
Additional Expenses: N/A
Total: $38,992*

***Note:** These figures do not reflect estimated housing/living expenses.

Financial Aid: https://www.unthsc.edu/financial-aid/application-and-eligibility/

ADDITIONAL INFORMATION

Interesting tidbit: the University of North Texas Health Science Center (UNTHSC)'s motto is "We make healthcare better." Doctors of pharmacy involved in disease and medication management make healthcare better by increasing safety, improving outcomes, and reducing costs.

Important Updates due to COVID-19: Virtual Interview

Were tests required? No.

Are tests expected next year? No.

What international experiences are available? N/A

What dual degree options exist? PharmD/MPH, PharmD/MS, and PharmD/PhD. For more information, visit:

What service learning opportunities exist? Service learning through experiential education.

What percent of graduates place in postgraduate training? 12% (2019)

NAPLEX First-Time Pass Rate: 86.81% (2020)

MPJE First-Time Pass Rate: 90.80% (2020)

Other: Early Assurance – PharmDirect program available to high school applicants and undergraduate students. For more information, visit: https://www.unthsc.edu/college-of-pharmacy/early-assurance-pharmdirect/

ALABAMA

ARKANSAS

DELAWARE

DISTRICT OF COLUMBIA

FLORIDA

GEORGIA

KENTUCKY

LOUISIANA

MARYLAND

MISSISSIPPI

NORTH CAROLINA

OKLAHOMA

SOUTH CAROLINA

TENNESSEE

TEXAS

VIRGINIA

WEST VIRGINIA

SOUTH

UNIVERSITY OF TEXAS AT AUSTIN COLLEGE OF PHARMACY

Address: 2409 University Ave., Austin, TX, 78712
Website: *https://pharmacy.utexas.edu/*
Contact: *https://pharmacy.utexas.edu/contact-us/*
Phone: (512) 471-1737

COST OF ATTENDANCE

In-State Tuition and Fees: $21,548
Additional Expenses: N/A
Total: $21,548*

Out-of-State Tuition and Fees: $49,240
Additional Expenses: N/A
Total: $49,240*

*Note: These figures do not reflect estimated housing/living expenses.

Financial Aid: https://pharmacy.utexas.edu/students/financial-aid/

ADDITIONAL INFORMATION

Interesting tidbit: UT Austin COP adheres to a new focus on the pharmacist as a provider of information rather than solely as a dispenser of drugs. Its PharmD curriculum is structured around an integrated approach to drug therapy management.

Important Updates due to COVID-19: Virtual Interview

Were tests required? PCAT required.

Are tests expected next year? Yes.

What international experiences are available? International exchange (UT-Pharmobility). For more information, visit: https://pharmacy.utexas.edu/students/programs-of-study/pharm-d-program/ut-pharmobility/

What dual degree options exist? PharmD/PhD. For more information, visit: http://sites.utexas.edu/adrgs/pharmdphd-honors-program/pharmd-ph-d-program/

What service learning opportunities exist? Service learning through student organizations, such as the Korean Community Health Screening, Men's Health Management Focus Group Initiative, and more. For more information, visit: https://pharmacy.utexas.edu/about/equity-diversity/outreach-cpc-sponsored-projects/

What percent of graduates place in postgraduate training? 40.47% (2019)

NAPLEX First-Time Pass Rate: 94.50% (2020)

MPJE First-Time Pass Rate: 93.20% (2020)

UNIVERSITY OF TEXAS AT EL PASO SCHOOL OF PHARMACY

Address: 1101 N. Campbell St., El Paso, TX 79902
Website: *https://www.utep.edu/pharmacy/*
Contact: *https://www.utep.edu/student-affairs/admissions/people/contact-us.html*
Phone: (915) 747-8519

COST OF ATTENDANCE

In-State Tuition and Fees: $19,000
Additional Expenses: N/A
Total: $19,000*

Out-of-State Tuition and Fees: $40,000
Additional Expenses: N/A
Total: $40,000*

*Note: These figures do not reflect estimated housing/living expenses.

Financial Aid: https://www.utep.edu/pharmacy/prospective-students/tuition-fees-and-expenses.html

ADDITIONAL INFORMATION

Interesting tidbit: Because the UTEP SOP is situated on the US-Mexico border, Spanish is required every semester of the first three years of the four year degree to increase and hone the technical Spanish skills of our students to best meet the needs of the local population and beyond. In addition, the School requires students to participate in short-term study abroad or study away experiences to expose them to different populations outside the region.

Important Updates due to COVID-19: PCAT requirement has been waived for Fall 2021 applicants.

Were tests required? No.

Are tests expected next year? Yes.

What international experiences are available? Pharmacy students are required to participate in short-term study abroad or study away experiences.

What dual degree options exist? No dual degree options listed.

What service learning opportunities exist? Study away experiences (e.g., addiction treatment centers in the country.)

What percent of graduates place in postgraduate training? 10% (2021)

NAPLEX First-Time Pass Rate: N/A*

MPJE First-Time Pass Rate: N/A*

*UTEP SOP graduated its inaugural class of 40 in 2021. There is no updated information available on students' outcomes.

ALABAMA
ARKANSAS
DELAWARE
DISTRICT OF COLUMBIA
FLORIDA
GEORGIA
KENTUCKY
LOUISIANA
MARYLAND
MISSISSIPPI
NORTH CAROLINA
OKLAHOMA
SOUTH CAROLINA
TENNESSEE
TEXAS
VIRGINIA
WEST VIRGINIA

SOUTH

ALABAMA

ARKANSAS

DELAWARE

DISTRICT OF
COLUMBIA

FLORIDA

GEORGIA

KENTUCKY

LOUISIANA

MARYLAND

MISSISSIPPI

NORTH CAROLINA

OKLAHOMA

SOUTH CAROLINA

TENNESSEE

TEXAS

VIRGINIA

WEST VIRGINIA

UNIVERSITY OF TEXAS AT TYLER BEN AND MAYTEE FISCH COLLEGE OF PHARMACY

Address: 3900 University Blvd., Tyler, TX 75799
Website: *https://www.uttyler.edu/pharmacy/*
Contact: *Contact via phone.*
Phone: (903) 565-5777

COST OF ATTENDANCE

In-State Tuition and Fees: $34,856
Additional Expenses: $13,448
Total: $48,304

Out-of-State Tuition and Fees: $16,974
Additional Expenses: $14,412
Total: $31,386

Financial Aid: https://www.uttyler.edu/financialaid/pharmacy/

ADDITIONAL INFORMATION

Interesting tidbit: Through the education of future pharmacists, the UT Tyler endeavors to advance public health and wellness in East Texas and beyond and to address the unmet health care needs of the rural and underserved populations through education and intervention.

Important Updates due to COVID-19: Virtual Interview

Were tests required? No.

Are tests expected next year? No.

What international experiences are available? No international service learning opportunities.

What dual degree options exist? No dual degree options listed.

What service learning opportunities exist? Immunizations, flu shots, volunteering at the local food bank, and more. Service learning through experiential education and student organizations.

What percent of graduates place in postgraduate training? N/A

NAPLEX First-Time Pass Rate: 69.32% (2020)

MPJE First-Time Pass Rate: 87.95% (2020)

UNIVERSITY OF THE INCARNATE WORD
FEIK SCHOOL OF PHARMACY

Address: 4301 Broadway, San Antonio, TX 78209
Website: *https://pharmacy.uiw.edu/*
Contact: *https://pharmacy.uiw.edu/about-us/contact-us.html*
Phone: (210) 883-1000

COST OF ATTENDANCE

Tuition and Fees: $41,892
Additional Expenses: N/A
Total: $41,892*

*Note: This figure does not reflect estimated housing/living expenses.

Financial Aid: https://pharmacy.uiw.edu/admissions/financial-assistance-and-scholarships.html

ADDITIONAL INFORMATION

Interesting tidbit: the Feik School of Pharmacy (FSOP) is the only faith-based School of Pharmacy in the state of Texas, whose mission is to support the core values of Faith, Truth, Service, Innovation, and Education. It is the first US pharmacy school to offer Spanish Certification.

Important Updates due to COVID-19: Virtual Interview

Were tests required? No.

Are tests expected next year? No.

What international experiences are available? Study abroad. For more information, visit: https://pharmacy.uiw.edu/student-life/study-abroad.html

What dual degree options exist? PharmD/MA in Administration (concentration in Healthcare Administration). For more information, visit: https://pharmacy.uiw.edu/academics/pharmd-and-maa-dual-degree.html

What service learning opportunities exist? Vaccinations clinic, Poison Prevention Awareness, and several other activities. For more information, visit: https://pharmacy.uiw.edu/student-life/service-opportunities.html

What percent of graduates place in postgraduate training? 9% (year unspecified)

NAPLEX First-Time Pass Rate: 96.25% (2020)

MPJE First-Time Pass Rate: 94.67% (2020)

Other: Direct Admit program available to high school applicants. For more information, visit: https://pharmacy.uiw.edu/admissions/direct-admit-program.html

ALABAMA
ARKANSAS
DELAWARE
DISTRICT OF COLUMBIA
FLORIDA
GEORGIA
KENTUCKY
LOUISIANA
MARYLAND
MISSISSIPPI
NORTH CAROLINA
OKLAHOMA
SOUTH CAROLINA
TENNESSEE
TEXAS
VIRGINIA
WEST VIRGINIA

SOUTH

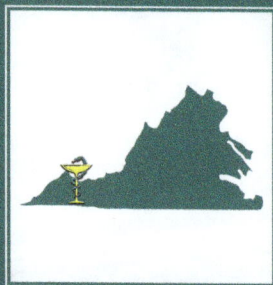

ALABAMA

ARKANSAS

DELAWARE

DISTRICT OF
COLUMBIA

FLORIDA

GEORGIA

KENTUCKY

LOUISIANA

MARYLAND

MISSISSIPPI

NORTH CAROLINA

OKLAHOMA

SOUTH CAROLINA

TENNESSEE

TEXAS

VIRGINIA

WEST VIRGINIA

APPALACHIAN COLLEGE OF PHARMACY

Address: 1060 Dragon Road, Oakwood, VA 24631
Website: *https://www.acp.edu/*
Contact: *https://www.acp.edu/contact-acp/*
Phone: (866) 935-7350

COST OF ATTENDANCE

Tuition and Fees: $37,500
Additional Expenses: $22,500
Total: $60,000

Financial Aid: https://www.acp.edu/scholarships-and-grants/

ADDITIONAL INFORMATION

Interesting tidbit: The Appalachian College of Pharmacy (ACP) is located in the heart of the central Appalachian Mountains. By bringing higher education and advances in healthcare to the region, ACP is well-positioned to be a catalyst for positive changes in economic development, education, and healthcare.

Important Updates due to COVID-19: Virtual Interview

Were tests required? No.

Are tests expected next year? No.

What international experiences are available? 1 week medical mission trip to El Salvador and a 5-week clinical rotation in the Dominican Republic.

What dual degree options exist? No dual degree options listed.

What service learning opportunities exist? Pharmacist in Community Service (PICS) Program involves Remote Area Medical (RAM) health fairs, the Health Wagon, Mountain Care Center, and more. For more information, visit: https://www.acp.edu/serving-the-underserved/

What percent of graduates place in postgraduate training? N/A

NAPLEX First-Time Pass Rate: 76.92% (2020)

MPJE First-Time Pass Rate: 63.33% (2020)

HAMPTON UNIVERSITY SCHOOL OF PHARMACY

Address: 121 William R. Harvey Way, Hampton, VA 23668
Website: *http://wp.hamptonu.edu/pharmacy/*
Contact: *http://wp.hamptonu.edu/pharmacy/contact-us-3/*
Phone: (757) 727-5071

COST OF ATTENDANCE

Tuition and Fees: $32,164
Additional Expenses: $17,790
Total: $49,954

Financial Aid: http://www.hamptonu.edu/apply/finaid.cfm

ADDITIONAL INFORMATION

*Please note the following: According to the Accreditation Council for Pharmacy Education (ACPE), as of August 1, 2020, Hampton University School of Pharmacy has had their accreditation status changed to "Withdrawn". Although Hampton University appealed, the decision to withdraw the accreditation by the ACPE was upheld. For more information, visit: https://www.acpe-accredit.org/faq-item/Hampton-University-School-of-Pharmacy-PharmD/

Interesting tidbit: HUSOP PharmD curriculum has been updated in the fall of 2019. The new curriculum continues to promote the success and growth of students, and enable them to adapt to new trends, ideas, and to innovate their own paths within the field of pharmacy.

Important Updates due to COVID-19: Virtual Interview

Were tests required? PCAT required.

Are tests expected next year? Yes.

What international experiences are available? N/A

What dual degree options exist? No dual degree options listed.

What service learning opportunities exist? Service learning through rotations as well as clubs and societies dedicated to volunteer work such as mobile clinics, immunization day, and local service trips.

What percent of graduates place in postgraduate training? 9.7% (2019)

NAPLEX First-Time Pass Rate: 55.00% (2020)

MPJE First-Time Pass Rate: 60.71% (2020)

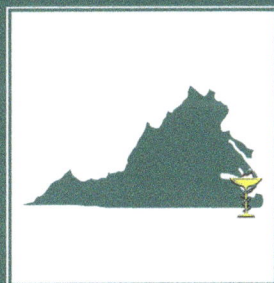

ALABAMA

ARKANSAS

DELAWARE

DISTRICT OF COLUMBIA

FLORIDA

GEORGIA

KENTUCKY

LOUISIANA

MARYLAND

MISSISSIPPI

NORTH CAROLINA

OKLAHOMA

SOUTH CAROLINA

TENNESSEE

TEXAS

VIRGINIA

WEST VIRGINIA

SOUTH

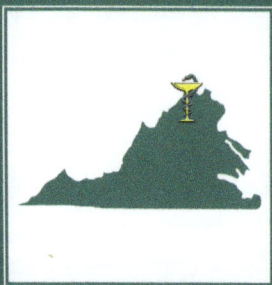

ALABAMA

ARKANSAS

DELAWARE

DISTRICT OF
COLUMBIA

FLORIDA

GEORGIA

KENTUCKY

LOUISIANA

MARYLAND

MISSISSIPPI

NORTH CAROLINA

OKLAHOMA

SOUTH CAROLINA

TENNESSEE

TEXAS

VIRGINIA

WEST VIRGINIA

SHENANDOAH UNIVERSITY BERNARD J. DUNN SCHOOL OF PHARMACY

Address: 1775 N Sector Ct, Winchester, VA 22601
Website: *https://www.su.edu/pharmacy/*
Contact: *https://www.su.edu/admissions/contact-us/*
Phone: (540) 665-4581

Other locations: Fairfax, VA

COST OF ATTENDANCE

Tuition and Fees: $37,610
Additional Expenses: N/A
Total: $37,610*

*Note: This figure does not reflect estimated housing/living expenses.

Financial Aid: https://www.su.edu/financial-aid/incoming-graduate-aid/

ADDITIONAL INFORMATION

Interesting tidbit: The Bernard J. Dunn School of Pharmacy leads the way in genetics-based pharmaceutical education and progressive instructional technology. Shenandoah's emphasis on pharmacogenomics prepares future pharmacists to utilize an individual's unique genetic composition to create personalized medicine and maximize drug safety and efficacy. Curricular materials are developed as web-based documents so that notes, slides, and lecture outlines can be available to you prior to classes and from any computer with Internet access.

Important Updates due to COVID-19: Virtual Interview

Were tests required? PCAT required.

Are tests expected next year? Yes.

What international experiences are available? Medical mission trips.

What dual degree options exist? PharmD/MBA, PharmD/MPH, and PharmD/MS in Pharmacogenomics. For more information, visit: https://www.su.edu/admissions/graduate-students/pharmacy-application-information/

What service learning opportunities exist? Service learning through student organizations, such as patient education, health fairs, immunization clinics, etc.

What percent of graduates place in postgraduate training? N/A

NAPLEX First-Time Pass Rate: 89.29% (2020)

MPJE First-Time Pass Rate: 81.58% (2020)

Other: 3+4 Early Assurance pathway available to high school students. For more information, visit: https://www.su.edu/admissions/future-freshmen/application-information/early-assurance-pathway-application-requirements/pharmacy-early-assurance-pathways-ea-pharmd/

VIRGINIA COMMONWEALTH UNIVERSITY AT THE MEDICAL COLLEGE OF VIRGINIA CAMPUS SCHOOL OF PHARMACY

Address: 410 N. 12th St., Richmond, VA 23298
Website: *https://pharmacy.vcu.edu/*
Contact: *https://pharmacy.vcu.edu/admissions/pharmd/contact-us/*
Phone: (804) 828-3000

COST OF ATTENDANCE

In-State Tuition and Fees: $31,866
Additional Expenses: N/A
Total: $31,866*

Out-of-State Tuition and Fees: $45,194
Additional Expenses: N/A
Total: $45,194*

*Note: These figures do not reflect estimated housing/living expenses.

Financial Aid: https://scholarships.pharmacy.vcu.edu/scholarships

ADDITIONAL INFORMATION

Interesting tidbit: In 1971, VCU was one of the first pharmacy schools in the nation to require that all students spend their final year in a practice setting under the supervision of faculty preceptors. To accommodate the growing student population and provide more educational and experiential diversity, the school opened two satellite campuses for third and fourth year Pharm.D. students - Inova Fairfax Campus (2007) and the University of Virginia Division (2012).

Important Updates due to COVID-19: PCAT is not required for the 2020-2021 cycle (optional).

Were tests required? No.

Are tests expected next year? Yes.

What international experiences are available? International Relief Efforts. For more information, visit: https://pharmacy.vcu.edu/community-outreach/

What dual degree options exist? PharmD/PhD, PharmD/MBA, PharmD/MBA, and PharmD/Certificate of Aging Studies. For more information, visit: https://pharmacy.vcu.edu/admissions/dual-degree/

What service learning opportunities exist? Community Health Screenings and engagement. For more information, visit: https://pharmacy.vcu.edu/community-outreach/

What percent of graduates place in postgraduate training? ~30% (year unspecified)

NAPLEX First-Time Pass Rate: 94.87% (2020)

MPJE First-Time Pass Rate: 81.05% (2020)

Other: Guaranteed Admit Program through VCU Honors College.

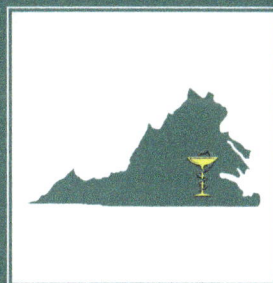

ALABAMA
ARKANSAS
DELAWARE
DISTRICT OF COLUMBIA
FLORIDA
GEORGIA
KENTUCKY
LOUISIANA
MARYLAND
MISSISSIPPI
NORTH CAROLINA
OKLAHOMA
SOUTH CAROLINA
TENNESSEE
TEXAS
VIRGINIA
WEST VIRGINIA

SOUTH

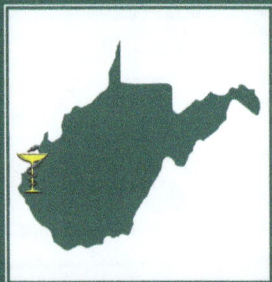

ALABAMA

ARKANSAS

DELAWARE

DISTRICT OF
COLUMBIA

FLORIDA

GEORGIA

KENTUCKY

LOUISIANA

MARYLAND

MISSISSIPPI

NORTH CAROLINA

OKLAHOMA

SOUTH CAROLINA

TENNESSEE

TEXAS

VIRGINIA

WEST VIRGINIA

MARSHALL UNIVERSITY SCHOOL OF PHARMACY

Address: 1 John Marshall Drive, Huntington, WV 25701
Website: *https://www.marshall.edu/pharmacy/*
Contact: *https://www.marshall.edu/pharmacy/about_us/contact-us/*
Phone: (304) 696-7302

COST OF ATTENDANCE

In-State Tuition and Fees: $20,854
Additional Expenses: $23,320
Total: $44,174

Out-of-State Tuition and Fees: $35,526
Additional Expenses: $23,320
Total: $58,846

Financial Aid: https://www.marshall.edu/pharmacy/student-info/current-students/scholarships/

ADDITIONAL INFORMATION

Interesting tidbit: There's no waiting until the third year for practice experience. By the second semester, students will be certified and in the field. Students will earn three certifications - Immunization (APhA) certification, Medication Therapy Management (APhA) certification, and Diabetes Management (APhA) certification- in the Marshall program at no added cost.

Important Updates due to COVID-19: Students will have their choice to attend either virtual or In person interviews starting on March 12th, 2021.

Were tests required? No.

Are tests expected next year? No.

What international experiences are available? International rotations

What dual degree options exist? PharmD/MBA and PharmD/MPH. For more information, visit: https://www.marshall.edu/pharmacy/academic-programs/

What service learning opportunities exist? Service learning through experiential education during APPEs.

What percent of graduates place in postgraduate training? N/A

NAPLEX First-Time Pass Rate: 85.71% (2020)

MPJE First-Time Pass Rate: 78.26% (2020)

Other: 3+4 Accelerated Pathways for Marshall undergraduate students. For more information, visit: https://www.marshall.edu/pharmacy/academic-partnerships/marshall-university-34-accelerated-pathways/

UNIVERSITY OF CHARLESTON SCHOOL OF PHARMACY

Address: 2300 MacCorkle Ave SE, Charleston, WV 25396
Website: *https://www.ucwv.edu/academics/schools/school-of-pharmacy/*
Contact: *Contact via phone.*
Phone: (304) 357-4889

COST OF ATTENDANCE

Tuition and Fees: $35,425
Additional Expenses: N/A
Total: $35,425*

***Note:** This figure does not reflect estimated housing/living expenses.

Financial Aid: https://www.ucwv.edu/academics/schools/school-of-pharmacy/affording-your-degree/

ADDITIONAL INFORMATION

Interesting tidbit: the University of Charleston School of Pharmacy (UCSOP) PharmD curriculum focuses on managing the healthcare problems of patients in rural and underserved communities. Being located in the capital city of WV provides students with advocacy/legislative opportunities to meet with federal, state and county policymakers who influence the level, extent, and scope of pharmacists' practice.

Important Updates due to COVID-19: Virtual Interview

Were tests required? Any Graduate-level standardized test (PCAT, GRE, MCAT, or DAT) accepted.

Are tests expected next year? Yes.

What international experiences are available? No international experiences.

What dual degree options exist? PharmD/MBA. For more information, visit: https://www.ucwv.edu/academics/schools/school-of-pharmacy/pharmacy-mba-program/

What service learning opportunities exist? Community outreach opportunities such as Immunization Education, Asthma/COPD Education, and more. For more information, visit: http://www.ucwv.edu/wp-content/uploads/2019/09/School-of-Pharmacy-Community-Outreach.pdf

What percent of graduates place in postgraduate training? N/A

NAPLEX First-Time Pass Rate: 64.44% (2020)

MPJE First-Time Pass Rate: 50.00% (2020)

Other: Pharmacy Direct Program available to University of Charleston undergraduate applicants.

ALABAMA
ARKANSAS
DELAWARE
DISTRICT OF COLUMBIA
FLORIDA
GEORGIA
KENTUCKY
LOUISIANA
MARYLAND
MISSISSIPPI
NORTH CAROLINA
OKLAHOMA
SOUTH CAROLINA
TENNESSEE
TEXAS
VIRGINIA
WEST VIRGINIA

SOUTH

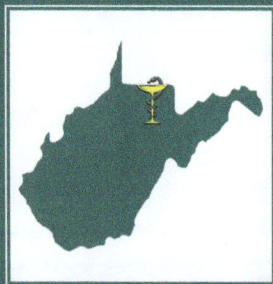

ALABAMA

ARKANSAS

DELAWARE

DISTRICT OF
COLUMBIA

FLORIDA

GEORGIA

KENTUCKY

LOUISIANA

MARYLAND

MISSISSIPPI

NORTH CAROLINA

OKLAHOMA

SOUTH CAROLINA

TENNESSEE

TEXAS

VIRGINIA

WEST VIRGINIA

WEST VIRGINIA UNIVERSITY SCHOOL OF PHARMACY

Address: 64 Medical Center Drive, Morgantown, WV 26506
Website: *https://pharmacy.wvu.edu/*
Contact: *https://pharmacy.wvu.edu/about/contact-us/*
Phone: (304) 293-1894

COST OF ATTENDANCE

In-State Tuition and Fees: $21,780
Additional Expenses: N/A
Total: $21,780*

Out-of-State Tuition and Fees: $43,164
Additional Expenses: N/A
Total: $43,164*

*Note: This figure does not reflect estimated housing/living expenses.

Financial Aid: https://pharmacy.hsc.wvu.edu/pharmaceutical-systems-and-policy/phd-program-in-health-services-and-outcomes-research/information-for-current-students/financial-assistance/

ADDITIONAL INFORMATION

Interesting tidbit: the School of Pharmacy offers five Areas of Emphasis (AoE) for students - Advanced Clinical Practice, College Teaching in Pharmacy, Geriatric Pharmacy, Global Health for Pharmacy, and Translational Pharmacy Research. The AoE Program provides students with the opportunity to concentrate their elective courses and one or more experiential rotations in a specific area of study within the pharmacy. Successful completion of an Area of Emphasis will be indicated on the student's transcript at graduation.

Important Updates due to COVID-19: In response to the ongoing pandemic, the PCAT is optional for the 2020-2021 and 2021-2022 admissions cycles.

Were tests required? No.

Are tests expected next year? No.

What international experiences are available? International rotations and global health area of concentration.

What dual degree options exist? PharmD/MBA. For more information, visit: https://pharmacy.hsc.wvu.edu/student-services/pharmd-program/pharmdmba-program/

What service learning opportunities exist? Service learning through experiential education and student organizations. For more information on the student organizations, visit: https://pharmacy.hsc.wvu.edu/student-services/pharmd-program/student-organizations/

What percent of graduates place in postgraduate training? 29% (2020)

NAPLEX First-Time Pass Rate: 92.54% (2020)

MPJE First-Time Pass Rate: 84.21% (2020)

Other: Direct Admit Pathway Program available to high school and WVU undergraduate applicants. For more information, visit: https://pharmacy.hsc.wvu.edu/student-services/pre-pharmacy/direct-admit-pathway-pre-pharmacy-program/

Areas of emphasis: Clinical/Residency, Geriatrics & Gerontology, Global Health, Research, and Teaching. For more information, visit: https://pharmacy.hsc.wvu.edu/student-services/pharmd-program/areas-of-emphasis-program

CHAPTER 5

REGION FOUR
WEST

ALASKA

ARIZONA

CALIFORNIA

COLORADO

HAWAII

IDAHO

MONTANA

NEVADA

NEW MEXICO

OREGON

UTAH

WASHINGTON

WYOMING

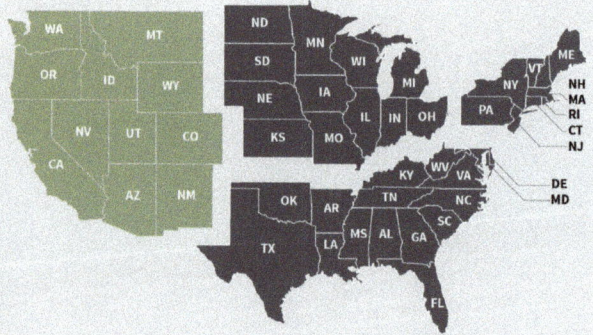

30 *Programs* | 13 *States*

PHARMACY PROGRAMS

Pharmacy School	Ave. GPA & PCAT (%) Early Decision (ED): Yes/No Int'l Students: Yes/No	Admissions Statistics	Science Req. Other than Gen Chem, OChem, Physics, Bio
Midwestern University - Glendale 19555 N 59th Ave., Glendale, AZ 85308	3.25 PCAT: Not Req. ED: Yes Int'l Student: Yes	(2019) Apps Received: 577 Interviews Offered: 275 Admission Offered: N/A Number Enrolled: 142 Admitted Rate: 24.6% (2020) Apps Received: 344 Interviews Offered: N/A Admission Offered: N/A Number Enrolled: 141 Admitted Rate: 41.0%	Human or Vertebrate Anatomy Stats. Calc. *This is an accelerated 3-year PharmD program.
University of Arizona 650 East Van Buren St., Phoenix, AZ 85004	3.44 PCAT: 62 ED: Yes Int'l Student: Yes	(2019) Apps Received: 198 Interviews Offered: N/A Admission Offered: N/A Number Enrolled: 139 Admitted Rate: 70.2% (2020) Apps Received: 228 Interviews Offered: N/A Admission Offered: N/A Number Enrolled: 126 Admitted Rate: 55.3%	Anatomy & Physio. Microbio. Calc. Stats.
American University of Health Sciences* 1600 E Hill St, Signal Hill, CA 90755	N/A PCAT: Not Req. ED: Yes Int'l Student: Yes	(2019) Apps Received: N/A Interviews Offered: N/A Admission Offered: N/A Number Enrolled: N/A Admitted Rate: N/A (2020) Apps Received: 114 Interviews Offered: N/A Admission Offered: N/A Number Enrolled: 25 Admitted Rate: 21.9%	Microbio. w/ Lab Human Physio. w/ Lab Stats. Calc. Psych./Sociology *This is an accelerated 3-year PharmD program.

Pharmacy School	Ave. GPA & PCAT (%) / Early Decision (ED): Yes/No / Int'l Students: Yes/No	Admissions Statistics	Science Req. Other than Gen Chem, OChem, Physics, Bio
California Health Sciences University 120 N. Clovis Avenue, Clovis, CA 93612	N/A PCAT: N/A ED: Yes Int'l Student: Yes	(2019) Apps Received: 536 Interviews Offered: N/A Admission Offered: N/A Number Enrolled: 66 Admitted Rate: 12.3% (2020) Apps Received: 224 Interviews Offered: N/A Admission Offered: N/A Number Enrolled: N/A** Admitted Rate: N/A **44 students in the incoming College of Pharmacy 2024 class cannot matriculate this fall as CHSU's pre-accreditation status was withdrawn by the ACPE.	Microbio. Physio. Anatomy Psych.
California Northstate University 9700 W. Taron Dr., Elk Grove, CA 95757	3.3 PCAT: Not Req. ED: Yes Int'l Student: Yes	(2019) Apps Received: 849 Interviews Offered: N/A Admission Offered: N/A Number Enrolled: 144 Admitted Rate: 16.9% (2020) Apps Received: 395 Interviews Offered: N/A Admission Offered: N/A Number Enrolled: 91 Admitted Rate: 23.0%	Biochem. or Cell & Molecular Bio. Microbio. Human Physio. Calc. Stats.

WEST

PHARMACY PROGRAMS

Pharmacy School	Ave. GPA & PCAT (%) / Early Decision (ED): Yes/No / Int'l Students: Yes/No	Admissions Statistics	Science Req. Other than Gen Chem, OChem, Physics, Bio
Chapman University* 9401 Jeronimo Rd Irvine, CA 92618	N/A PCAT: N/A ED: Yes Int'l Student: No	(2019) Apps Received: 314 Interviews Offered: N/A Admission Offered: N/A Number Enrolled: 60 Admitted Rate: 19.1% (2020) Apps Received: 248 Interviews Offered: N/A Admission Offered: N/A Number Enrolled: 82 Admitted Rate: 33.1%	Human Physio. w/ Lab Human Anatomy w/ Lab Microbio. Genetics or Molecular Bio. Calc. Stats. *This is an accelerated 3-year PharmD program.
Keck Graduate Institute (KGI) School of Pharmacy and Health Sciences 535 Watson Dr., Claremont, CA 91711	N/A PCAT: Not Req. ED: Yes Int'l Student: No	(2019) Apps Received: 432 Interviews Offered: N/A Admission Offered: N/A Number Enrolled: 69 Admitted Rate: 15.9% (2020) Apps Received: 248 Interviews Offered: N/A Admission Offered: N/A Number Enrolled: 82 Admitted Rate: 33.1%	Biochem. Microbio. Anatomy w/ Lab Physio. w/ Lab Calc. Stats. Psych./Sociology
Loma Linda University 24745 Stewart St., Loma Linda, CA 92350	3.4 PCAT: Not Req. ED: No Int'l Student: Yes	(2019) Apps Received: 312 Interviews Offered: N/A Admission Offered: N/A Number Enrolled: 77 Admitted Rate: 24.7% (2020) Apps Received: 301 Interviews Offered: N/A Admission Offered: N/A Number Enrolled: 74 Admitted Rate: 24.6%	Biochem. Social/Behav. Science

Pharmacy School	Ave. GPA & PCAT (%) / Early Decision (ED): Yes/No / Int'l Students: Yes/No	Admissions Statistics	Science Req. Other than Gen Chem, OChem, Physics, Bio
Marshall B. Ketchum University 2575 Yorba Linda Blvd, Fullerton, CA 92831	N/A PCAT: Optional ED: Yes Int'l Student: No	(2019) Apps Received: 434 Interviews Offered: N/A Admission Offered: N/A Number Enrolled: 58 Admitted Rate: 13.4% (2020) Apps Received: 239 Interviews Offered: N/A Admission Offered: N/A Number Enrolled: 53 Admitted Rate: 22.2%	Human Anatomy w/ Lab Human Physio. w/ Lab Calc. Social/Behav. Science
Touro University - California 1310 Club Dr., Vallejo, CA 94592	3.3 PCAT: Not Req. ED: Yes Int'l Student: No	(2019) Apps Received: 568 Interviews Offered: N/A Admission Offered: N/A Number Enrolled: 117 Admitted Rate: 20.6% (2020) Apps Received: 318 Interviews Offered: N/A Admission Offered: N/A Number Enrolled: 79 Admitted Rate: 24.8%	Human Physio. Microbio. w/ Lab Calc.
University of California, Irvine* 209 Steinhaus Hall, Bldg 502, Irvine, CA 92697	3.0 PCAT: Not Req. ED: No Int'l Student: N/A	**(2020)** Apps Received: N/A Interviews Offered: N/A Admission Offered: 60 Number Enrolled: N/A Admitted Rate: N/A	*This program is currently in precandidate status. There is limited data available, as this is a new program.

WEST

PHARMACY PROGRAMS

Pharmacy School	Ave. GPA & PCAT (%) Early Decision (ED): Yes/No Int'l Students: Yes/No	Admissions Statistics	Science Req. Other than Gen Chem, OChem, Physics, Bio
University of California, San Diego 9500 Gilman Drive, La Jolla, CA 92093	3.6 PCAT: Not Req. ED: No Int'l Student: No	(2019) Apps Received: 588 Interviews Offered: N/A Admission Offered: N/A Number Enrolled: 72 Admitted Rate: 12.2% (2020) Apps Received: 414 Interviews Offered: N/A Admission Offered: N/A Number Enrolled: 62 Admitted Rate: 15.0%	Calc. Human Behavior Cell and Molecular Bio.
University of California, San Francisco* 513 Parnassus Avenue, San Francisco, CA 94143	3.5 PCAT: Optional ED: No Int'l Student: Yes	(2019) Apps Received: 512 Interviews Offered: 250 Admission Offered: N/A Numbe Enrolled: 127 Admitted Rate: 24.8% (2020) Apps Received: 423 Interviews Offered: N/A Admission Offered: N/A Number Enrolled: 127 Admitted Rate: 30.0%	Microbio. w/ Lab Calc. Stats. *This is an accelerated, 3-year program.
University of Southern California 1985 Zonal Ave., Los Angeles, CA 90089	3.41 PCAT: Not Req. ED: Yes Int'l Student: Yes	(2019) Apps Received: 703 Interviews Offered: 436 Admission Offered: 351 Number Enrolled: 197 Admitted Rate: 28.0% (2020) Apps Received: 481 Interviews Offered: 336 Admission Offered: 362 Number Enrolled: 191 Admitted Rate: 39.7%	Human Physio. Microbio. Biochem. Stats.

Pharmacy School	Ave. GPA & PCAT (%) / Early Decision (ED): Yes/No / Int'l Students: Yes/No	Admissions Statistics	Science Req. Other than Gen Chem, OChem, Physics, Bio
University of the Pacific* 3601 Pacific Avenue, Stockton, CA 95211	3.4 PCAT: Not Req. ED: Yes Int'l Student: Yes	(2019) Apps Received: 794 Interviews Offered: 250-350 Admission Offered: N/A Number Enrolled: 92 Admitted Rate: 12% (2020) Apps Received: 529 Interviews Offered: N/A Admission Offered: N/A Number Enrolled: 194 Admitted Rate: 36.7%	Calc. Human Physio. Psych. *This is an accelerated 3-year PharmD program.
West Coast University 590 North Vermont Avenue, Los Angeles, CA 90004	N/A PCAT: Not Req. ED: Yes Int'l Student: Yes	(2019) Apps Received: 499 Interviews Offered: N/A Admission Offered: N/A Number Enrolled: 73 Admitted Rate: 14.6% (2020) Apps Received: 384 Interviews Offered: N/A Admission Offered: N/A Number Enrolled: 90 Admitted Rate: 23.4%	Human/Mammalian Physio. w/ Lab Calc. Stats. Psych./Sociology
Western University of Health Sciences 309 E. Second St., Pomona, CA 91766	3.4 PCAT: Not Req. ED: Yes Int'l Student: Yes	(2019) Apps Received: 604 Interviews Offered: 354 Admission Offered: N/A Number Enrolled: 115 Admitted Rate: 19% (2020) Apps Received: 519 Interviews Offered: N/A Admission Offered: N/A Number Enrolled: 120 Admitted Rate: 23.1%	Human Anatomy Human Physio. Microbio. Biochem., Molecular Bio., or Cell Bio.

WEST

Pharmacy School	Ave. GPA & PCAT (%) / Early Decision (ED): Yes/No / Int'l Students: Yes/No	Admissions Statistics	Science Req. Other than Gen Chem, OChem, Physics, Bio
Regis University 3333 Regis Blvd, Denver, CO 80221	3.1 PCAT: Optional ED: Yes Int'l Student: Yes	(2019) Apps Received: 406 Interviews Offered: N/A Admission Offered: N/A Number Enrolled: 62 Admitted Rate: 15.3% (2020) Apps Received: 263 Interviews Offered: N/A Admission Offered: N/A Number Enrolled: 53 Admitted Rate: 20.2%	Calc. Human Anatomy Human Physio. Cellular & Molecular Bio. w/ Lab Organismic Bio. w/ Lab Additional Bio. w/ Lab
University of Colorado 12850 East Montview Blvd., Aurora, CO 80045	3.4 PCAT: Not Req. ED: Yes Int'l Student: Yes	(2019) Apps Received: 629 Interviews Offered: N/A Admission Offered: N/A Number Enrolled: 143 Admitted Rate: 22.7% (2020) Apps Received: 516 Interviews Offered: N/A Admission Offered: N/A Number Enrolled: 106 Admitted Rate: 20.5%	Biochem. Microbio. Human Anatomy Human Physio. Calc.
University of Hawaii at Hilo 200 W. Kawili Street, Hilo, HI 96720	3.1 PCAT: Optional ED: Yes Int'l Student: Yes	(2019) Apps Received: 194 Interviews Offered: N/A Admission Offered: N/A Number Enrolled: 86 Admitted Rate: 44.3% (2020) Apps Received: 88 Interviews Offered: N/A Admission Offered: N/A Number Enrolled: 48 Admitted Rate: 54.5%	Calc. Human Anatomy & Physio. w/ Lab Microbio. w/ Lab

Pharmacy School	Ave. GPA & PCAT (%) / Early Decision (ED): Yes/No / Int'l Students: Yes/No	Admissions Statistics	Science Req. Other than Gen Chem, OChem, Physics, Bio
Idaho State University 921 S. 5th Ave., Pocatello, ID 83209	3.4 PCAT: Not Req. ED: Yes Int'l Student: Yes	(2019) Apps Received: 204 Interviews Offered: N/A Admission Offered: N/A Number Enrolled: 85 Admitted Rate: 41.7% (2020) Apps Received: 163 Interviews Offered: N/A Admission Offered: N/A Number Enrolled: 90 Admitted Rate: 55.2%	Biochem. Microbio. w/ Lab Anatomy & Physio. w/ Lab Calc. Stats.
University of Montana 341 Skaggs Building, Missoula, MT 59812	3.4 PCAT: 50 ED: Yes Int'l Student: Yes	(2019) Apps Received: 146 Interviews Offered: N/A Admission Offered: N/A Number Enrolled: 68 Admitted Rate: 46.6% (2020) Apps Received: 92 Interviews Offered: N/A Admission Offered: N/A Number Enrolled: 46 Admitted Rate: 50.0%	Human Anatomy & Physio. Calc. Cell & Molecular Bio. Stats.
Roseman University of Health Sciences* 11 Sunset Way, Henderson, NV 89014	3.5 PCAT: Optional ED: Yes Int'l Student: Yes	(2019) Apps Received: 625 Interviews Offered: N/A Admission Offered: N/A Number Enrolled: 210 Admitted Rate: 33.6% (2020) Apps Received: 310 Interviews Offered: N/A Admission Offered: N/A Number Enrolled: 208 Admitted Rate: 67.1%	Calc. Microbio. Human anatomy Human Physio. *This is an accelerated 3-year PharmD program.

WEST

PHARMACY PROGRAMS

Pharmacy School	Ave. GPA & PCAT (%) Early Decision (ED): Yes/No Int'l Students: Yes/No	Admissions Statistics	Science Req. Other than Gen Chem, OChem, Physics, Bio
University of New Mexico 2502 Marble NE Albuquerque, NM 87131-0001	3.2 PCAT: Not Req. ED: Yes Int'l Student: Yes	(2019) Apps Received: 136 Interviews Offered: N/A Admission Offered: N/A Number Enrolled: 70 Admitted Rate: 51.2% (2020) Apps Received: 88 Interviews Offered: N/A Admission Offered: N/A Number Enrolled: 72 Admitted Rate: 81.8%	Microbio. w/ Lab Human Anatomy & Physio. Molecular & Cell Bio. Genetics Stats. Calc
Oregon State University 203 Pharmacy Building, Corvallis, OR 97331	3.5 PCAT: Not Req. ED: Yes Int'l Student: Yes	(2019) Apps Received: 408 Interviews Offered: 150-200 Admission Offered: N/A Number Enrolled: 99 Admitted Rate: 24.3% (2020) Apps Received: 265 Interviews Offered: N/A Admission Offered: N/A Number Enrolled: 82 Admitted Rate: 30.9%	Anatomy & Physio. w/ Lab Biochem. Microbio. w/ Lab Calc. Stats.
Pacific University Oregon* 190 SE 8th Avenue, Hillsboro, OR 97123	3.3 PCAT: Not Req. ED: Yes Int'l Student: Yes	(2019) Apps Received: 612 Interviews Offered: 200 Admission Offered: N/A Number Enrolled: 100 Admitted Rate: 16.3% (2020) Apps Received: 529 Interviews Offered: N/A Admission Offered: N/A Number Enrolled: 103 Admitted Rate: 19.5%	Human Anatomy & Physio. w/ Lab Microbio. Calc. Psych. Social/Behav. Sciences *This is an accelerated 3-year PharmD program.

Pharmacy School	Ave. GPA & PCAT (%) / Early Decision (ED): Yes/No / Int'l Students: Yes/No	Admissions Statistics	Science Req. Other than Gen Chem, OChem, Physics, Bio
University of Utah 30 South 2000 East, Salt Lake City, UT 84112	3.5 PCAT: 84 ED: No Int'l Student: Yes	(2019) Apps Received: 228 Interviews Offered: N/A Admission Offered: N/A Number Enrolled: 61 Admitted Rate: 26.8% (2020) Apps Received: 178 Interviews Offered: N/A Admission Offered: N/A Number Enrolled: 53 Admitted Rate: 29.8%	Human Anatomy Human Physio. Microbio. Stats. Calc.
University of Washington 1959 NE Pacific St., Seattle, WA 98195	3.5 PCAT: Not Req. ED: Yes Int'l Student: Yes	(2019) Apps Received: 403 Interviews Offered: 200 Admission Offered: N/A Number Enrolled: 109 Admitted Rate: 27% (2020) Apps Received: 376 Interviews Offered: N/A Admission Offered: 163 Number Enrolled: 108 Admitted Rate: 28.7%	Biochem. Microbio. Anatomy & Physio. Calc. Stats.
Washington State University 412 E. Spokane Falls Blvd., Spokane, WA 99202	3.3 PCAT: Not Req. ED: Yes Int'l Student: No	(2019) Apps Received: 419 Interviews Offered: N/A Admission Offered: N/A Number Enrolled: 174 Admitted Rate: 41.5% (2020) Apps Received: 258 Interviews Offered: N/A Admission Offered: N/A Number Enrolled: 133 Admitted Rate: 51.6%	Stats. Calc. Microbio. w/ Lab Human Anatomy w/ Lab Physio. w/ Lab Biochem.

WEST

PHARMACY PROGRAMS

Pharmacy School	Ave. GPA & PCAT (%) / Early Decision (ED): Yes/No / Int'l Students: Yes/No	Admissions Statistics	Science Req. Other than Gen Chem, OChem, Physics, Bio
University of Wyoming 1000 E University Ave, Laramie, WY 82071	3.5 PCAT: Not Req. ED: Yes Int'l Student: Yes	(2019) Apps Received: 131 Interviews Offered: N/A Admission Offered: N/A Number Enrolled: 52 Admitted Rate: 39.7% (2020) Apps Received: 72 Interviews Offered: N/A Admission Offered: N/A Number Enrolled: 33 Admitted Rate: 45.8%	Animal Bio. w/ Lab Human Anatomy w/ Lab Human Systems Physio. w/ Lab Medical Microbio. w/ Lab Biochem. Calc. Stats.

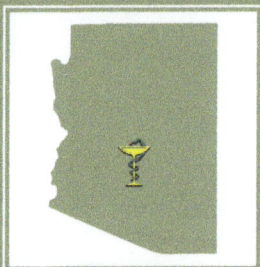

WA MT
OR ID WY
NV UT CO
CA
AZ NM

MIDWESTERN UNIVERSITY COLLEGE OF PHARMACY-GLENDALE

Address: 19555 N 59th Ave., Glendale, AZ 85308
Website: *https://www.midwestern.edu/academics/our-colleges/college-of-pharmacy*
Contact: *https://online.midwestern.edu/public/reqinfo.cgi*
Phone: (623) 572-3215

COST OF ATTENDANCE

Tuition and Fees: $65,036
Additional Expenses: $30,305
Total: $95,341

Financial Aid: https://www.midwestern.edu/admissions/tuition-and-financial-aid/financial-aid.xml

ADDITIONAL INFORMATION

Interesting tidbit: Midwestern University acknowledges that how and where students learn is as important as what they learn. Its Glendale, Arizona Campus, a 156-acre location that includes state-of-the-art facilities in a peaceful setting, is just 15 miles northwest of downtown Phoenix. Its campus and clinical environments provide students with the resources and atmosphere most conducive to maximizing their graduate healthcare education.

Important Updates due to COVID-19: Virtual Interview

Were tests required? No.

Are tests expected next year? No.

What international experiences are available? International service trips in the past.

What dual degree options exist? No dual degree options listed.

What service learning opportunities exist? Service learning through student organizations.

What percent of graduates place in postgraduate training? 33% (2020)

NAPLEX First-Time Pass Rate: 86.47% (2020)

MPJE First-Time Pass Rate: 88.43% (2020)

Other: Dual Acceptance Program. Students at affiliated colleges are eligible for this program. For more information, visit: https://www.midwestern.edu/academics/degrees-and-programs/doctor-of-pharmacy-az/dual-acceptance-program.xml

UNIVERSITY OF ARIZONA COLLEGE OF PHARMACY

Address: 1295 N. Martin, Tucson, AZ 85721
Website: *https://www.pharmacy.arizona.edu/*
Contact: *https://www.pharmacy.arizona.edu/academics/pharmd/contact*
Phone: (602) 827-2426
Other Locations: Phoenix, AZ

COST OF ATTENDANCE

In-State Tuition and Fees: $27,400
Additional Expenses: N/A
Total: $27,400*

Out-of-State Tuition and Fees: $47,600
Additional Expenses: N/A
Total: $47,600*

*Note: These figures do not reflect estimated housing/living expenses.

Financial Aid: https://www.pharmacy.arizona.edu/academics/pharmd/cost-and-financial-aid/scholarships

ADDITIONAL INFORMATION

Interesting tidbit: UA COP PharmD students will utilize knowledge of anatomy, physiology, and pathophysiology in clinical settings throughout their preparation where they will advance through a variety of experiential education opportunities including working in long-term care facilities, community care settings, hospitals and pharmacies.

Important Updates due to COVID-19: Waiving the requirement for the PCAT, health-care experience, and community service hours for 2020-2021 PharmCAS applicants.

Were tests required? No.

Are tests expected next year? Yes.

What international experiences are available? International rotations. For more information, visit: https://www.pharmacy.arizona.edu/academics/international-programs/pharmd-international-rotations

What dual degree options exist? PharmD/PhD, PHarmD/MPH, PharmD/MLS, PHarmD/JD, PharmD/MBA, and PharmD/MSN/FNP Cert. For more information, visit: https://www.pharmacy.arizona.edu/academics/pharmd-dual-degrees-certificates/dual-degrees

What service learning opportunities exist? Service learning through experiential education. Rural Health Professions Program available. For more information, visit: https://www.pharmacy.arizona.edu/academics/pharmd/pharmd-experiential-education/rural-health-professions-programs

What percent of graduates place in postgraduate training? PGY1 match rate of 65.3% (2021)

NAPLEX First-Time Pass Rate: 94.85% (2020)

MPJE First-Time Pass Rate: 91.11% (2020)

Other: International pharmacy program. For more information, visit: https://www.pharmacy.arizona.edu/academics/international-programs

Early Assurance Program available to high school applicants. For more information, visit: https://www.pharmacy.arizona.edu/academics/pharmd/admissions/early-assurance-program

ALASKA

ARIZONA

CALIFORNIA

COLORADO

HAWAII

IDAHO

MONTANA

NEVADA

NEW MEXICO

OREGON

UTAH

WASHINGTON

WYOMING

WEST

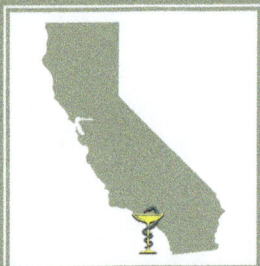

ALASKA

ARIZONA

CALIFORNIA

COLORADO

HAWAII

IDAHO

MONTANA

NEVADA

NEW MEXICO

OREGON

UTAH

WASHINGTON

WYOMING

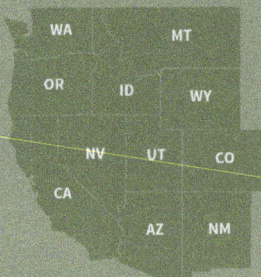

AMERICAN UNIVERSITY OF HEALTH SCIENCES SCHOOL OF PHARMACY*

Address: 1600 E Hill St, Signal Hill, CA 90755
Website: *https://www.auhs.edu/academics/pharmacy/*
Contact: *https://www.auhs.edu/admissions/contact/*
Phone: (562) 988-2278

COST OF ATTENDANCE

Tuition and Fees: $45,000
Additional Expenses: $18,856
Total: $63,856

Financial Aid: https://www.auhs.edu/admissions/financial-aid/

ADDITIONAL INFORMATION

*Please note the following: As of October 2021, American University of Health Sciences School of Pharmacy is currently a candidate for accreditation and will undergo a review for accreditation in the academic year of 2021-2022. For updates, please check: https://www.acpe-accredit.org/faq-item/American-University-of-Health-Sciences-School-of-Pharmacy-PharmD/

Interesting tidbit: Keeping in line with the vision of the University, PharmD students will be educated in a Christian-based environment. Students can fast track their careers with the school's three-year, year-round PharmD curriculum.

Important Updates due to COVID-19: Virtual Interview

Were tests required? No.

Are tests expected next year? No.

What international experiences are available? N/A

What dual degree options exist? No dual degree options listed.

What service learning opportunities exist? N/A

What percent of graduates place in postgraduate training? N/A

NAPLEX First-Time Pass Rate: N/A

MPJE First-Time Pass Rate: N/A

CALIFORNIA HEALTH SCIENCES UNIVERSITY COLLEGE OF PHARMACY*

Address: 120 N. Clovis Avenue, Clovis, CA 93612
Website: *https://pharmacy.chsu.edu/*
Contact: *https://my.chsu.edu/inquiryform*
Phone: (559) 325-3600

COST OF ATTENDANCE

Tuition and Fees: $45,000
Additional Expenses: $26,065
Total: $71,065

Financial Aid: https://pharmacy.chsu.edu/financial-aid-tuition/

ADDITIONAL INFORMATION

*Please note the following: The California Health Sciences University College of Pharmacy's Doctor of Pharmacy program has had its pre-accreditation status withdrawn by the Accreditation Council for Pharmacy Education. In cooperation with ACPE, the College is implementing a teach-out plan that will afford currently enrolled students in the Classes of 2021, 2022, and 2023, the same rights and privileges as graduates from a program holding ACPE Candidate status. However, Class of 2024 cannot matriculate.

Important Updates due to COVID-19: Virtual Interview

Were tests required? No.

Are tests expected next year? No.

What international experiences are available? No international rotations/service trips.

What dual degree options exist? No dual degree options listed.

What percent of graduates place in postgraduate training? N/A

What service learning opportunities exist? SAFE, Lock It Up, Community Engagement Day, California Blood Drive, etc.

Service learning through experiential education. For more information, visit: https://pharmacy.chsu.edu/office-of-experiential-education/

What percent of graduates place in postgraduate training? N/A

NAPLEX First-Time Pass Rate: 83.33% (2020)

CPJE First-Time Pass Rate: 38.5% (2020)

Other: CHSU has affiliation agreements with Fresno Pacific University, Bakersfield College, and Clovis Community College. For more information on these pathways, visit: https://pharmacy.chsu.edu/admissions-chsu-college-of-pharmacy/

Próspero Program available to 11th and 12th grade high school students and undergraduates. For more information, visit: https://pharmacy.chsu.edu/admissions-chsu-college-of-pharmacy/#pathways-to-chsu

ALASKA
ARIZONA
CALIFORNIA
COLORADO
HAWAII
IDAHO
MONTANA
NEVADA
NEW MEXICO
OREGON
UTAH
WASHINGTON
WYOMING

WEST

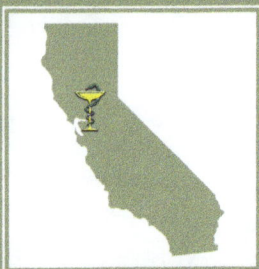

ALASKA

ARIZONA

CALIFORNIA

COLORADO

HAWAII

IDAHO

MONTANA

NEVADA

NEW MEXICO

OREGON

UTAH

WASHINGTON

WYOMING

CALIFORNIA NORTHSTATE UNIVERSITY COLLEGE OF PHARMACY

Address: 9700 W. Taron Dr., Elk Grove, CA 95757
Website: *https://pharmacy.cnsu.edu/*
Contact: *https://pharmacy.cnsu.edu/contact-cnucop*
Phone: (916) 686-7400

COST OF ATTENDANCE

Tuition and Fees: $49,000
Additional Expenses: $31,417
Total: $80,417

Financial Aid: http://www.cnsu.edu/student-financial-aid-office/student-financial-aid-officep

ADDITIONAL INFORMATION

Interesting tidbit: CNUCOP students are trained under an intensive curriculum that focuses on early clinical and disease-state integration and inter-professional education. Some of the top students in the PharmD program will have the opportunity to pursue the new, innovative PharmD-MD pathway, developed jointly with CNU's College of Medicine. This PharmD-MD pathway is the only one in California, as well as the first on the West Coast.

Important Updates due to COVID-19: Virtual Interview

Were tests required? No.

Are tests expected next year? No.

What international experiences are available? N/A

What dual degree options exist? PharmD/MBA. For more information, visit: https://pharmacy.cnsu.edu/executive-masters-of-business-administration-program-developing-exemplary-leaders

PharmD/MS in Pharmaceutical Sciences: https://pharmacy.cnsu.edu/academic-programs/mps-overview/mps-overview

What service learning opportunities exist? Service learning through experiential education. For more information, visit: https://pharmacy.cnsu.edu/department-of-experiential-education

What percent of graduates place in postgraduate training? N/A

NAPLEX First-Time Pass Rate: 81.8% (2020)

CPJE First-Time Pass Rate: 37% (2020)

Other: BS/PharmD program available to high school applicants. For more information, visit: http://healthsciences.cnsu.edu/programs-offered/bs-pharmd-combined-program/about

CHAPMAN UNIVERSITY SCHOOL OF PHARMACY

Address: 9401 Jeronimo Rd, Irvine, CA 92618
Website: *https://www.chapman.edu/pharmacy/index.aspx*
Contact: *https://go.chapman.edu/register/CUSP-info*
Phone: (714) 744-7650

COST OF ATTENDANCE

Tuition and Fees: $27,270
Additional Expenses: $60,227
Total: $87,497

Financial Aid: https://www.chapman.edu/students/tuition-and-aid/financial-aid/index.aspx

ADDITIONAL INFORMATION

Interesting tidbit: Chapman U Pharm.D. is a three-year, accelerated professional degree composed of eight, 15-week trimesters. Students receive an iPad Pro since exams are taken using the electronic device, and all textbooks are available free of charge in electronic format.

Important Updates due to COVID-19: Virtual Interview

Were tests required? No.

Are tests expected next year? No.

What international experiences are available? International service trips available for students in leadership positions in student organizations.

What dual degree options exist? No dual degree options listed.

What service learning opportunities exist? Service learning through experiential education and student organizations. For more information, visit: https://www.chapman.edu/pharmacy/academic-programs/pharmd/experiential-education.aspx

What percent of graduates place in postgraduate training? N/A

NAPLEX First-Time Pass Rate: 90.5% (2020)

CPJE First-Time Pass Rate: 50.0% (2020)

Other: Early Assurance Program available to high school students. For more information, visit: https://www.chapman.edu/pharmacy/academic-programs/undergraduate-programs/pre-pharmacy.aspx

ALASKA

ARIZONA

CALIFORNIA

COLORADO

HAWAII

IDAHO

MONTANA

NEVADA

NEW MEXICO

OREGON

UTAH

WASHINGTON

WYOMING

WEST

ALASKA

ARIZONA

CALIFORNIA

COLORADO

HAWAII

IDAHO

MONTANA

NEVADA

NEW MEXICO

OREGON

UTAH

WASHINGTON

WYOMING

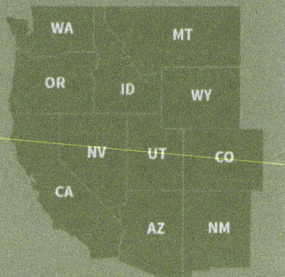

KECK GRADUATE INSTITUTE (KGI) SCHOOL OF PHARMACY AND HEALTH SCIENCES

Address: 535 Watson Dr., Claremont, CA 91711
Website: *https://www.kgi.edu/academics/school-of-pharmacy-and-health-sciences/overview/*
Contact: *https://www.kgi.edu/admissions-and-aid/request-info/*
Phone: (909) 607-7855

COST OF ATTENDANCE

Tuition and Fees: $48,400
Additional Expenses: $25,796
Total: $74,196

Financial Aid: https://www.kgi.edu/admissions-and-aid/tuition-financial-aid/funding-your-degree/

ADDITIONAL INFORMATION

Interesting tidbit: Along with a Doctor of Pharmacy degree, KGI graduates receive a certificate in one of four areas - Medication Therapy Outcomes (MTO), Healthcare Management (HCM), Health Information Technology (HIT) or Medical and Clinical Affairs (MCA).

Important Updates due to COVID-19: Virtual Interview

Were tests required? No.

Are tests expected next year? No.

What international experiences are available? International outreach trips (Mexico and Vietnam in the past).

What dual degree options exist? No dual degree options listed.

What service learning opportunities exist? Students volunteer to give immunizations in community health clinics.

What percent of graduates place in postgraduate training? 25% (2019)

NAPLEX First-Time Pass Rate: 92.3% (2020)

CPJE First-Time Pass Rate: 60.3% (2020)

Other: Certificates in the following areas: Medication Therapy Outcomes, Healthcare Management, Health Information Technology, and Medical & Clinical Affairs. For more information, visit: https://www.kgi.edu/academics/school-of-pharmacy-and-health-sciences/academic-programs/doctor-of-pharmacy/certificate-programs/

Community college to PharmD (6-year) available. For more information, visit: https://www.kgi.edu/academics/school-of-pharmacy-and-health-sciences/academic-programs/doctor-of-pharmacy/community-college-to-pharmd/

LOMA LINDA UNIVERSITY SCHOOL OF PHARMACY

Address: 24745 Stewart St., Loma Linda, CA 92350
Website: *https://pharmacy.llu.edu/*
Contact: *https://pharmacy.llu.edu/about/contact-location*
Phone: (909) 558-1300

COST OF ATTENDANCE

Tuition and Fees: $51,400
Additional Expenses: N/A
Total: $51,400*

*Note: This figure does not reflect estimated housing/living expenses.

Financial Aid: https://home.llu.edu/campus-and-spiritual-life/student-services/financial-life/financial-aid

ADDITIONAL INFORMATION

Interesting tidbit: The specific objective of the Doctor of Pharmacy (PharmD) degree program is to educate pharmacists in a Seventh-day Adventist Christian setting.

Important Updates due to COVID-19: Virtual Interview

Were tests required? No.

Are tests expected next year? No.

What international experiences are available? International mission trips.

What dual degree options exist? PharmD/MS in Health Informatics. For more information, visit: http://llucatalog.llu.edu/combined-degree-programs/pharmacy-health-informatics-pharmd-ms/

What service learning opportunities exist? N/A

What percent of graduates place in postgraduate training? N/A

NAPLEX First-Time Pass Rate: 88.9% (2020)

CPJE First-Time Pass Rate: 37.8% (2020)

ALASKA

ARIZONA

CALIFORNIA

COLORADO

HAWAII

IDAHO

MONTANA

NEVADA

NEW MEXICO

OREGON

UTAH

WASHINGTON

WYOMING

WEST

ALASKA

ARIZONA

CALIFORNIA

COLORADO

HAWAII

IDAHO

MONTANA

NEVADA

NEW MEXICO

OREGON

UTAH

WASHINGTON

WYOMING

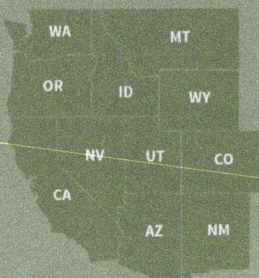

MARSHALL B. KETCHUM UNIVERSITY COLLEGE OF PHARMACY

Address: 2575 Yorba Linda Blvd, Fullerton, CA 92831
Website: *https://www.ketchum.edu/pharmacy*
Contact: *https://www.ketchum.edu/pharmacy/connect-us*
Phone: (714) 449-7400

COST OF ATTENDANCE

Tuition and Fees: $53,065
Additional Expenses: N/A
Total: $53,065*

*Note: This figure does not reflect estimated housing/living expenses.

Financial Aid: https://www.ketchum.edu/pharmacy/cost-aid

ADDITIONAL INFORMATION

Interesting tidbit: At MBKU, your required Capstone project can range from literature reviews to scientific bench research. Students seeking residency can utilize the Capstone to earn professional publication. Those not interested in residency can forego efforts to publish and focus their attention and energy on subjects that interest them more.

Important Updates due to COVID-19: Virtual Interview

Were tests required? PCAT is required if the applicant doesn't hold a bachelor's degree or an international applicant.

Are tests expected next year? PCAT is required if the applicant doesn't hold a bachelor's degree or an international applicant.

What international experiences are available? N/A

What dual degree options exist? No dual degree options listed.

What service learning opportunities exist? Service learning through experiential education.

What percent of graduates place in postgraduate training? N/A

NAPLEX First-Time Pass Rate: 69.6% (2020)

CPJE First-Time Pass Rate: 44.4% (2020)

TOURO UNIVERSITY - CALIFORNIA COLLEGE OF PHARMACY

Address: 1310 Club Dr., Vallejo, CA 94592
Website: *http://cop.tu.edu/*
Contact: *http://tu.edu/aboutus/contact.html*
Phone: (707) 638-5200

COST OF ATTENDANCE

Tuition and Fees: $48,600
Additional Expenses: $37,130
Total: $85,730

Financial Aid: http://studentservices.tu.edu/financialaid/index.html

ADDITIONAL INFORMATION

Interesting tidbit: Touro University California College of Pharmacy created the nation's first 2+2 Pharm.D. program, comprised of two years of experiences on campus, followed by two full years of hands-on clinical rotations at pharmacy practice sites.

Important Updates due to COVID-19: Only one letter of recommendation is required for the 2020-21 application cycle.

Were tests required? No.

Are tests expected next year? No.

What international experiences are available? N/A

What dual degree options exist? PharmD/MPH. For more information, visit: http://cop.tu.edu/programs_degrees/mph-dualdegree.html

What service learning opportunities exist? N/A

What percent of graduates place in postgraduate training? N/A

NAPLEX First-Time Pass Rate: 85.0% (2020)

CPJE First-Time Pass Rate: 58.3% (2020)

ALASKA

ARIZONA

CALIFORNIA

COLORADO

HAWAII

IDAHO

MONTANA

NEVADA

NEW MEXICO

OREGON

UTAH

WASHINGTON

WYOMING

WEST

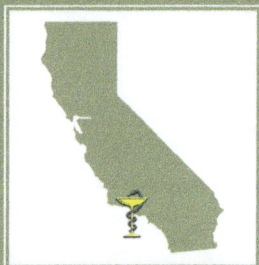

ALASKA

ARIZONA

CALIFORNIA

COLORADO

HAWAII

IDAHO

MONTANA

NEVADA

NEW MEXICO

OREGON

UTAH

WASHINGTON

WYOMING

UNIVERSITY OF CALIFORNIA, IRVINE SCHOOL OF PHARMACY*

Address: 209 Steinhaus Hall, Bldg 502, Irvine, CA 92697
Website: *https://pharmsci.uci.edu/pharm-d/*
Contact: *https://pharmsci.uci.edu/pharmd-request-information/*
Phone: (949) 824-1991

COST OF ATTENDANCE

In-State Tuition and Fees: $42,438
Additional Expenses: $6,594.96
Total: $49,032.96

Out-of-State Tuition and Fees: $54,683
Additional Expenses: $6,594.96
Total: $61,277.96

Financial Aid: https://pharmsci.uci.edu/pharm-d/

ADDITIONAL INFORMATION

*Please note the following: As of November 2021, University of California, Irvine is currently in pre-candidate status for accreditation and will undergo a review for accreditation in the academic year of 2021-2022. For updates, please check: https://www.acpe-accredit. org/faq-item/University-of-California-Irvine-School-of-Pharmacy-Pharmaceutical-Sciences-PharmD/

Interesting tidbit: UCI's PharmD program does not require nor consider the PCAT or GRE.

Important Updates due to COVID-19: A "PASS" grade is acceptable for coursework completed during Spring or Summer 2020. Online courses completed during Spring 2020 to Summer 2021 are acceptable.

Were tests required? No.

Are tests expected next year? No.

What international experiences are available? N/A

What dual degree options exist? No dual degree options listed.

What service learning opportunities exist? N/A

What percent of graduates place in postgraduate training? N/A

NAPLEX First-Time Pass Rate: N/A

MPJE First-Time Pass Rate: N/A

UNIVERSITY OF CALIFORNIA, SAN DIEGO SKAGGS SCHOOL OF PHARMACY & PHARMACEUTICAL SCIENCES

Address: 9500 Gilman Drive, La Jolla, CA 92093
Website: *https://pharmacy.ucsd.edu/*
Contact: *https://pharmacy.ucsd.edu/about/contact*
Phone: (858) 822-4900

COST OF ATTENDANCE

In-State Tuition and Fees: $41,419
Additional Expenses: $25,407
Total: $66,826

Out-of-State Tuition and Fees: $53,664
Additional Expenses: $25,407
Total: $79,071

Financial Aid: https://pharmacy.ucsd.edu/admissions/financial-aid-and-cost-study

ALASKA

ARIZONA

CALIFORNIA

COLORADO

HAWAII

IDAHO

MONTANA

NEVADA

NEW MEXICO

OREGON

UTAH

WASHINGTON

WYOMING

ADDITIONAL INFORMATION

Interesting tidbit: UC San Diego pharmacy and medical students develop a foundation in the biomedical sciences in common classes and shared volunteer community clinical experiences. The proximity of the UC San Diego Scripps Institution of Oceanography gives pharmacy students the opportunity to consider research in marine pharmacology and drugs of the sea.

Important Updates due to COVID-19: Virtual Interview

Were tests required? No.

Are tests expected next year? No.

What international experiences are available? Elective in Mexican healthcare systems. For more information, visit: https://pharmacy.ucsd.edu/index.php/admissions/electives-third-year-students

What dual degree options exist? PharmD/PhD. For more information, visit: https://pharmacy.ucsd.edu/degree-programs/dual-pharmd-phd-program

What service learning opportunities exist? Service learning through experiential education.

What percent of graduates place in postgraduate training? 47% (2020)

NAPLEX First-Time Pass Rate: 100% (2020)

CPJE First-Time Pass Rate: 66.7% (2020)

Other: BS/PharmD (7-year) available to UCSD undergraduate freshmen. For more information, visit: https://pharmacy.ucsd.edu/degree-programs/seven-year-bs-chemistrydoctor-pharmacy-program

WEST

WA MT
OR ID WY
NV UT CO
CA
AZ NM

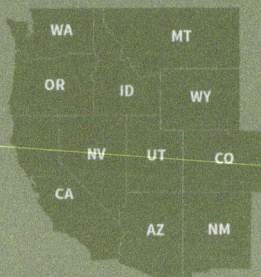

UNIVERSITY OF CALIFORNIA, SAN FRANCISCO SCHOOL OF PHARMACY

Address: 513 Parnassus Avenue, San Francisco, CA 94143
Website: *https://pharmacy.ucsf.edu/*
Contact: *https://pharmacy.ucsf.edu/about/contact*
Phone: (415) 353-7800

COST OF ATTENDANCE

In-State Tuition and Fees: $11,442
Additional Expenses: $42,125
Total: $53,567

Out-of-State Tuition and Fees: $23,687
Additional Expenses: $42,125
Total: $65,812

Financial Aid: https://pharmd.ucsf.edu/admissions/cost

ADDITIONAL INFORMATION

Interesting tidbit: The UCSF PharmD program shifted from a 4-yr program to a 3-year program with the 2018 entering class. The UCSF PharmD curriculum is designed for you to consistently apply scientific thinking across all coursework. Asking why, why not, how, and questioning the status quo will become your new norm.

Important Updates due to COVID-19: Accept pass/fail grades, without prejudice, for courses taken during the COVID-19 pandemic. Accept online courses/labs if they are offered by the school at which the candidate was enrolled prior to the current crisis. For students who are beyond undergraduate school, UCSF SOP accepts online courses/labs undertaken to meet prerequisites regardless of the institution, as long as it is regionally accredited.

Were tests required? No.

Are tests expected next year? No.

What international experiences are available? Global research projects available.

What dual degree options exist? PharmD/MS in Clinical Research: https://pharmacy.ucsf.edu/education/pharmd-mscr

PharmD/PhD: https://pharmacy.ucsf.edu/education/pharmd-phd

What service learning opportunities exist? Service learning through student organizations. For more information, visit: https://pharm.ucsf.edu/current/student-life-orgs

What percent of graduates place in postgraduate training? 75% (2020)

NAPLEX First-Time Pass Rate: 100% (2020)

CPJE First-Time Pass Rate: 65% (2020)

UNIVERSITY OF SOUTHERN CALIFORNIA SCHOOL OF PHARMACY

Address: 1985 Zonal Ave., Los Angeles, CA 90089
Website: *https://pharmacyschool.usc.edu/*
Contact: *https://pharmacyschool.usc.edu/contact/*
Phone: (323) 442-1369

COST OF ATTENDANCE

Tuition and Fees: $64,632
Additional Expenses: N/A
Total: $64,632*

*Note: This figure does not reflect estimated housing/living expenses.

Financial Aid: https://pharmacyschool.usc.edu/programs/pharmd/pharmdprogram/financing-your-pharmd-degree/

ADDITIONAL INFORMATION

Interesting tidbit: The USC School of Pharmacy established the nation's first Doctor of Pharmacy (PharmD) program in 1950 and it is the largest degree program within the School of Pharmacy. From the first clinical pharmacy program in the nation and the first pharmacy school to offer clinical clerkships, the School continues a tradition of leadership and innovation.

Important Updates due to COVID-19: Virtual Interview

Were tests required? No.

Are tests expected next year? No.

What international experiences are available? Clerkships, internships, service trips abroad, etc. For more information, visit: https://pharmacyschool.usc.edu/about/focus/globalization/

What dual degree options exist? PharmD/JD, PharmD/MBA, PharmD/MPH, PharmD/MS in Regulatory Science, PharmD/MS in Gerontology, PharmD/MS in Healthcare Decision Analysis, and PharmD/PhD. For more information, visit: https://pharmacyschool.usc.edu/programs/pharmd/

What service learning opportunities exist? Service learning through experiential education. For more information, visit: https://pharmacyschool.usc.edu/about/focus/experiential/

What percent of graduates place in postgraduate training? N/A

NAPLEX First-Time Pass Rate: 90.6% (2020)

CPJE First-Time Pass Rate: 52.8% (2020)

ALASKA

ARIZONA

CALIFORNIA

COLORADO

HAWAII

IDAHO

MONTANA

NEVADA

NEW MEXICO

OREGON

UTAH

WASHINGTON

WYOMING

WEST

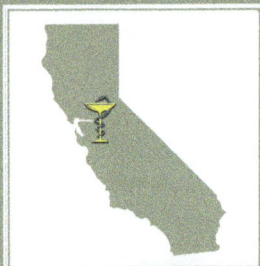

ALASKA

ARIZONA

CALIFORNIA

COLORADO

HAWAII

IDAHO

MONTANA

NEVADA

NEW MEXICO

OREGON

UTAH

WASHINGTON

WYOMING

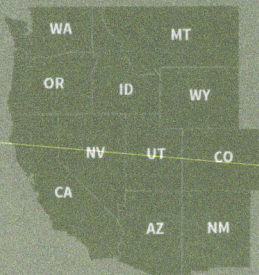

UNIVERSITY OF THE PACIFIC THOMAS J. LONG SCHOOL OF PHARMACY

Address: 3601 Pacific Avenue, Stockton, CA 95211
Website: *https://www.pacific.edu/academics/schools-and-colleges/thomas-j-long-school-of-pharmacy.html*
Contact: *https://www.pacific.edu/contact-us.html*
Phone: (209) 946-7415

COST OF ATTENDANCE

Tuition and Fees: $82,560
Additional Expenses: N/A
Total: $82,560*

*Note: This figure does not reflect housing/living expenses.

Financial Aid: https://admissions.pacific.edu/financial-aid/

ADDITIONAL INFORMATION

Interesting tidbit: University of the Pacific PharmD students collaborate with students from the physician assistant studies, speech-language pathology, physical therapy, dental surgery, and athletic training programs at Pacific.

Important Updates due to COVID-19: Virtual Interview

Were tests required? No.

Are tests expected next year? No.

What international experiences are available? Short service trips organized through student organizations.

What dual degree options exist? PharmD/PhD and PharmD/MS. For more information, visit: https://www.pacific.edu/academics/schools-and-colleges/thomas-j-long-school-of-pharmacy/academics/pharmaceutical-and-chemical-sciences.html

What service learning opportunities exist? Medicare Part D, Audiology Clinics, and Speech-Language Pathology Clinics. For more information, visit: https://www.pacific.edu/academics/schools-and-colleges/thomas-j-long-school-of-pharmacy/community-health-services.html

What percent of graduates place in postgraduate training? N/A

NAPLEX First-Time Pass Rate: 90.8% (2020)

CPJE First-Time Pass Rate: 47.2% (2020)

Other: Pre-Pharmacy Advantage Program available to first-time freshmen undergraduates. For more information, visit: https://www.pacific.edu/academics/schools-and-colleges/thomas-j-long-school-of-pharmacy/academics/pre-pharmacy-advantage-program.html

Pathway programs in partnership with UC Merced and Pepperdine University. For more information, visit: https://www.pacific.edu/academics/schools-and-colleges/thomas-j-long-school-of-pharmacy/academics/doctor-of-pharmacy/pathway-programs.html

WEST COAST UNIVERSITY SCHOOL OF PHARMACY

Address: 590 North Vermont Avenue, Los Angeles, CA 90004
Website: *https://westcoastuniversity.edu/programs/doctor-pharmacy.html*
Contact: *Contact form on the main page, see Website.*
Phone: (866) 508-2684

COST OF ATTENDANCE

Tuition and Fees: $65,679
Additional Expenses: N/A
Total: $65,679*

*Note: This figure does not reflect estimated housing/living expenses.

Financial Aid: https://westcoastuniversity.edu/admissions/financial-aid.html

ADDITIONAL INFORMATION

Interesting tidbit: West Coast University includes six campus locations in Southern California, Texas, and Florida. Its Doctor of Pharmacy program received candidacy status through Accreditation Council for Pharmacy Education (ACPE) in 2015 and full accreditation in 2018.

Important Updates due to COVID-19: Virtual Interview

Were tests required? No.

Are tests expected next year? No.

What international experiences are available? Global pharmacy rotation.

What dual degree options exist? No dual degree options listed.

What service learning opportunities exist? Service learning through experiential education.

What percent of graduates place in postgraduate training? N/A

NAPLEX First-Time Pass Rate: 82.4% (2020)

CPJE First-Time Pass Rate: 48.6% (2020)

ALASKA

ARIZONA

CALIFORNIA

COLORADO

HAWAII

IDAHO

MONTANA

NEVADA

NEW MEXICO

OREGON

UTAH

WASHINGTON

WYOMING

WEST

ALASKA

ARIZONA

CALIFORNIA

COLORADO

HAWAII

IDAHO

MONTANA

NEVADA

NEW MEXICO

OREGON

UTAH

WASHINGTON

WYOMING

WESTERN UNIVERSITY OF HEALTH SCIENCES COLLEGE OF PHARMACY

Address: 309 E. Second St., Pomona, CA 91766
Website: *https://www.westernu.edu/pharmacy/*
Contact: *https://www.westernu.edu/pharmacy/pharmacy-contact/*
Phone: (909) 469-5500

COST OF ATTENDANCE

Tuition and Fees: $51,585
Additional Expenses: $22,932
Total: $74,517

Financial Aid: https://prospective.westernu.edu/pharmacy/pharmd/tuition-scholarships/

ADDITIONAL INFORMATION

Interesting tidbit: Starting in P2, academic course work is delivered in individual blocks of instructional time, wherein each block builds upon the learning that has occurred in preceding blocks. This method of delivery occurs in the second year and the first half of the third year.

Important Updates due to COVID-19: Virtual Interview

Were tests required? No.

Are tests expected next year? No.

What international experiences are available? International rotations during APPEs. For more information on experiential education, visit: https://www.westernu.edu/pharmacy/pharmacy-oee/

What dual degree options exist? No dual degree options listed.

What service learning opportunities exist? Various types of outreach events such as the Rx5000 Walk/Run, Palomares Day, and more. For more information, visit: https://www.westernu.edu/pharmacy/pharmacy-outreach-events/

What percent of graduates place in postgraduate training? 18.9% (2020)

NAPLEX First-Time Pass Rate: 95.2% (2020)

CPJE First-Time Pass Rate: 65.2% (2020)

Other: Linkage Programs available in partnership with certain undergraduate institutions. For more information, visit: https://prospective.westernu.edu/undergraduate-linkage-programs/

REGIS UNIVERSITY RUECKERT-HARTMAN COLLEGE FOR HEALTH PROFESSIONS SCHOOL OF PHARMACY

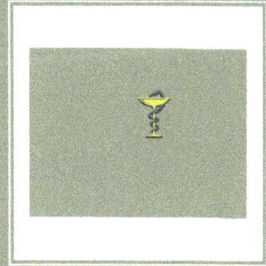

Address: 3333 Regis Blvd, Denver, CO 80221
Website: *https://www.regis.edu/academics/colleges-and-schools/ rueckert-hartman/pharmacy/index*
Contact: *https://www.regis.edu/request-info/index*
Phone: (303) 458-4900

COST OF ATTENDANCE

Tuition and Fees: $41,170
Additional Expenses: N/A
Total: $41,170*

*Note: This figure does not reflect estimated housing/living expenses.

Financial Aid: https://www.regis.edu/financial-aid/index

ADDITIONAL INFORMATION

Interesting tidbit: Regis' School of Pharmacy is one of only two pharmacy schools in the country using Team-Based Learning (TBL) as the primary teaching method and the only pharmacy school combining TBL with an integrated curriculum approach. TBL breaks away from the traditional lecture format, instead of focusing on teaching courses and concepts through experiential opportunities.

Important Updates due to COVID-19: Virtual Interview

Were tests required? No.

Are tests expected next year? No.

What international experiences are available? International rotations.

What dual degree options exist? PharmD/MS in Health Informatics. For more information, visit: https://www.regis.edu/academics/ majors-and-programs/graduate/pharmd-health-informatics-dual

PharmD/MS in Health Services Administration: https://www.regis. edu/academics/majors-and-programs/graduate/pharmd-hsa-dual

What service learning opportunities exist? Service learning through experiential education. For more information, visit: https:// www.regis.edu/academics/colleges-and-schools/rueckert-hartman/ pharmacy/experiential-learning

What percent of graduates place in postgraduate training? N/A

NAPLEX First-Time Pass Rate: 77.78% (2020)

MPJE First-Time Pass Rate: 77.78% (2020)

ALASKA

ARIZONA

CALIFORNIA

COLORADO

HAWAII

IDAHO

MONTANA

NEVADA

NEW MEXICO

OREGON

UTAH

WASHINGTON

WYOMING

WEST

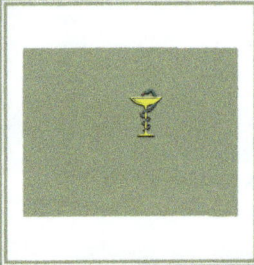

ALASKA

ARIZONA

CALIFORNIA

COLORADO

HAWAII

IDAHO

MONTANA

NEVADA

NEW MEXICO

OREGON

UTAH

WASHINGTON

WYOMING

UNIVERSITY OF COLORADO ANSCHUTZ MEDICAL CAMPUS SKAGGS SCHOOL OF PHARMACY AND PHARMACEUTICAL SCIENCES

Address: 12850 East Montview Blvd., Aurora, CO 80045
Website: *http://www.ucdenver.edu/academics/colleges/pharmacy/Pages/SchoolofPharmacy.aspx*
Contact: *http://www.ucdenver.edu/academics/colleges/pharmacy/AboutUs/Pages/ContactUs.aspx*
Phone: (303) 724-2882

COST OF ATTENDANCE

In-State Tuition and Fees: $32,470
Additional Expenses: N/A
Total: $32,470*

Out-of-State Tuition and Fees: $41,265
Additional Expenses: N/A
Total: $41,265*

*Note: These figures do not reflect estimated housing/living expenses.

Financial Aid: http://www.ucdenver.edu/academics/colleges/pharmacy/Admissions/PharmDProgram/TuitionFinancialAid/Pages/AwardsandScholarships.aspx

ADDITIONAL INFORMATION

Interesting tidbit: Skaggs PharmD students benefit from learning on the world-class CU Anschutz Medical Campus, the largest academic health center in the Rocky Mountain region. It is home to six health professional schools, over 60 centers and institutes, and two nationally ranked hospitals that treat more than 2 million adult and pediatric patients each year.

Important Updates due to COVID-19: As of April 2020, the University of Colorado accepts prerequisite coursework with a Pass grade taken in the spring and summer of 2020. The University of Colorado will accept online prerequisite coursework.

Were tests required? No.

Are tests expected next year? No.

What international experiences are available? International rotations.

What dual degree options exist? PharmD/MBA and PharmD/MPH. For more information, visit: http://www.ucdenver.edu/academics/colleges/pharmacy/AcademicPrograms/PharmDProgram/DualDegreePrograms/Pages/DualDegreePrograms.aspx

What service learning opportunities exist? All PharmD students required to participate in education partnership with Aurora Public Schools. Students also have the opportunity to do clinical pharmacy training in rural Colorado areas. For more information, visit: http://www.ucdenver.edu/academics/colleges/pharmacy/AcademicPrograms/PharmDProgram/ExperientialProgram/Pages/AuroraPublicSchoolsServiceLearning.aspx

What percent of graduates place in postgraduate training? N/A

NAPLEX First-Time Pass Rate: 91.5% (2020)

MPJE First-Time Pass Rate: 85.54% (2020)

Other: University of Colorado is currently implementing an Early Assurance pathway.

UNIVERSITY OF HAWAII AT HILO DANIEL K. INOUYE COLLEGE OF PHARMACY

Address: 200 W. Kawili Street, Hilo, HI 96720
Website: *https://pharmacy.uhh.hawaii.edu/*
Contact: *https://pharmacy.uhh.hawaii.edu/contact*
Phone: (808) 932-8120

COST OF ATTENDANCE

In-State Tuition and Fees: $24,096
Additional Expenses: $21,402
Total: $45,498

Out-of-State Tuition and Fees: $41,040
Additional Expenses: $21,402
Total: $62,442

Financial Aid: https://hilo.hawaii.edu/financialaid/

ADDITIONAL INFORMATION

Interesting tidbit: The College of Pharmacy was born out of Senator Daniel K. Inouye's vision that each neighbor island will harbor centers of excellence. The senator believed that every island in Hawai'i has its own potential and unique characteristics to add a specialty to the university system. For Hawai'i Island, it was to be the only College of Pharmacy in the Pacific region.

Important Updates due to COVID-19: Credit/Pass grades accepted for the Winter 2020/Spring 2020 terms.

Were tests required? No.

Are tests expected next year? No.

What international experiences are available? Rotations available in all four major islands, US territories of American Samoa, Guam, and Saipan, and mainland sites.

What dual degree options exist? No dual degree options listed.

What service learning opportunities exist? Service learning through experiential education. For more information, visit: https://pharmacy.uhh.hawaii.edu/academics/experiential-program

What percent of graduates place in postgraduate training? N/A

NAPLEX First-Time Pass Rate: 83.05% (2020)

MPJE First-Time Pass Rate: 60.71% (2020)

Other: Early Admission available to high school and undergraduate applicants. For more information, visit: https://pharmacy.uhh.hawaii.edu/admissions/pre-pharmacy-early-admission

ALASKA

ARIZONA

CALIFORNIA

COLORADO

HAWAII

IDAHO

MONTANA

NEVADA

NEW MEXICO

OREGON

UTAH

WASHINGTON

WYOMING

WEST

ALASKA

ARIZONA

CALIFORNIA

COLORADO

HAWAII

IDAHO

MONTANA

NEVADA

NEW MEXICO

OREGON

UTAH

WASHINGTON

WYOMING

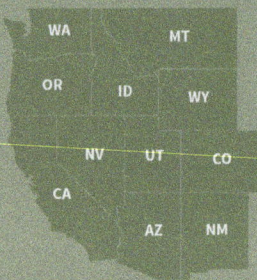

IDAHO STATE UNIVERSITY COLLEGE OF PHARMACY

Address: 921 S. 5th Ave., Pocatello, ID 83209
Website: *https://www.isu.edu/pharmacy/*
Contact: *https://www.isu.edu/pharmacy/leftsidebar/*
Phone: (208) 282-4597

Other locations: Anchorage, AK; Meridian, ID

COST OF ATTENDANCE

In-State Tuition and Fees: $19,248
Additional Expenses: N/A
Total: $19,248*

Out-of-State Tuition and Fees: $40,296
Additional Expenses: N/A
Total: $40,296*

Alaska Resident Tuition: $14,605
Additional Expenses: N/A
Total: $14,605*

*Note: These figures do not reflect estimated housing/living expenses.

Financial Aid: https://www.isu.edu/pharmacy/prospective-students/pharmd-program/cost/

ADDITIONAL INFORMATION

Interesting tidbit: TThe ISU College of Pharmacy is delivered synchronously in Pocatello and Meridian, Idaho, and Anchorage, Alaska. To meet the needs of the state of Idaho and Alaska, approximately 70% of each new class is comprised of Idaho or Alaska residents.

Important Updates due to COVID-19: Virtual Interview

Were tests required? No.

Are tests expected next year? No.

What international experiences are available? Informal/independent electives around global outreach.

What dual degree options exist? PharmD/MBA and PharmD/PhD. Students apply after completion of their PharmD first year.

What service learning opportunities exist? Immunization, classroom presentations to K-12, and more.

What percent of graduates place in postgraduate training? 28% (2020)

NAPLEX First-Time Pass Rate: 88.16% (2020)

MPJE First-Time Pass Rate: N/A

UNIVERSITY OF MONTANA COLLEGE OF HEALTH PROFESSIONS AND BIOMEDICAL SCIENCES SKAGGS SCHOOL OF PHARMACY

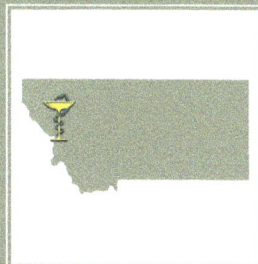

Address: 341 Skaggs Building, Missoula, MT 59812
Website: *http://health.umt.edu/pharmacy/*
Contact: *http://health.umt.edu/pharmacy/Contact%20Us/default.php*
Phone: (406) 243-4656

COST OF ATTENDANCE

In-State Tuition and Fees: $13,711
Additional Expenses: N/A
Total: $13,094*

Out-of-State Tuition and Fees: $33,537
Additional Expenses: N/A
Total: $31,958*

*Note: These figures do not reflect estimated housing/living expenses.

Financial Aid: http://health.umt.edu/pharmacy/Prospective%20 Students/Pharm.D.%20Program/Financial%20Aid%20and%20 Scholarships.php

ADDITIONAL INFORMATION

Interesting tidbit: Beginning in the academic year 2021-2022, the Skaggs School of Pharmacy will begin offering tuition awards of up to $15,000/year to out-of-state students who are committed to completing the PharmD degree at the University of Montana. The award is based on academic merit and awarded to high-achieving and academically strong out-of-state students.

Important Updates due to COVID-19: Virtual Interview

Were tests required? PCAT required.

Are tests expected next year? PCAT required.

What international experiences are available? International rotations and service trips.

What dual degree options exist? PharmD/MBA, PharmD/MPH, PharmD/MS, and PharmD/PhD.

What service learning opportunities exist? IPHARM program and immunizations. For more information on IPHARM, visit: https:// health.umt.edu/ipharm/

What percent of graduates place in postgraduate training? Residency match 79% (2019)

NAPLEX First-Time Pass Rate: 84.21% (2020)

MPJE First-Time Pass Rate: 71.43% (2020)

ALASKA

ARIZONA

CALIFORNIA

COLORADO

HAWAII

IDAHO

MONTANA

NEVADA

NEW MEXICO

OREGON

UTAH

WASHINGTON

WYOMING

WEST

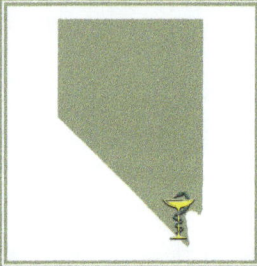

ALASKA

ARIZONA

CALIFORNIA

COLORADO

HAWAII

IDAHO

MONTANA

NEVADA

NEW MEXICO

OREGON

UTAH

WASHINGTON

WYOMING

ROSEMAN UNIVERSITY OF HEALTH SCIENCES COLLEGE OF PHARMACY

Address: 11 Sunset Way, Henderson, NV 89014
Website: *https://pharmacy.roseman.edu/*
Contact: *http://gopharmacy.roseman.edu/inquiryform*
Phone: (702) 968-2007

Other Locations: South Jordan, UT

COST OF ATTENDANCE

Tuition and Fees: $61,035
Additional Expenses: N/A
Total: $61,035*

*Note: This figure does not reflect estimated housing/living expenses.

Financial Aid: https://pharmacy.roseman.edu/admissions/financial-aid/

ADDITIONAL INFORMATION

Interesting tidbit: Courses are taught using a block model, where students are able to focus on one content area at a time. The block teaching model allows for greater focus and, subsequently, increases retention of course information. The classroom portion of the 3-year curriculum is completed in two years, and the third and final year of the program is dedicated to advanced pharmacy practice experiences.

Important Updates due to COVID-19: Virtual Interview

Were tests required? No.

Are tests expected next year? No.

What international experiences are available? Medical mission trips.

What dual degree options exist? PharmD/MBA. For more information, visit: https://pharmacy.roseman.edu/explore/pharmdmba-advantage/

What service learning opportunities exist? Drug Abuse Awareness and more. For more information, visit: https://pharmacy.roseman.edu/student-life/community-engagement/

What percent of graduates place in postgraduate training? N/A

NAPLEX First-Time Pass Rate: 85.49% (2020)

MPJE First-Time Pass Rate: 70.41% (2020)

UNIVERSITY OF NEW MEXICO COLLEGE OF PHARMACY

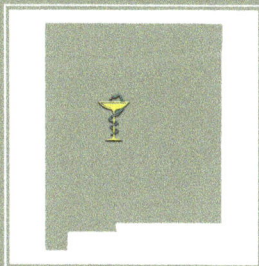

Address: 2502 Marble NE, Albuquerque, NM 87131-0001
Website: *https://hsc.unm.edu/college-of-pharmacy/*
Contact: *https://hsc.unm.edu/contacts.html*
Phone: (505) 272-3241

COST OF ATTENDANCE

In-State Tuition and Fees: $21,331
Additional Expenses: $24,568
Total: $45,899

Out-of-State Tuition and Fees: $44,750
Additional Expenses: $24,568
Total: $69,318

Financial Aid: https://hsc.unm.edu/pharmacy/programs/pharmd/tuition/financial-aid.html

ADDITIONAL INFORMATION

Interesting tidbit: PharmD students can choose to receive advanced training to become pharmacist clinicians at no extra cost. Or, students can choose advanced training to become an authorized nuclear pharmacist as part of their elective coursework. One of only three schools where students can complete the certification in nuclear pharmacy while earning a PharmD.

Important Updates due to COVID-19: Virtual Interview

Were tests required? No.

Are tests expected next year? No.

What international experiences are available? N/A

What dual degree options exist? PharmD/MBA and PharmD/MS. For more information, visit: https://hsc.unm.edu/college-of-pharmacy/education-and-admissions/pharmd-dual-degree.html

What service learning opportunities exist? Community outreach opportunities including Community Outreach Day, Generation Rx and Immunizations. For more information, visit: https://hsc.unm.edu/college-of-pharmacy/practice/community-outreach/index.html

What percent of graduates place in postgraduate training? N/A

NAPLEX First-Time Pass Rate: 92.75% (2020)

MPJE First-Time Pass Rate: 75.44% (2020)

Other: Early Assurance available to undergraduate applicants. For more information, visit: https://hsc.unm.edu/college-of-pharmacy/education-and-admissions/pharmd-early-assurance.html

Cooperative Pharmacy Program between New Mexico State University and UNM. For more information, visit: https://hsc.unm.edu/college-of-pharmacy/education-and-admissions/unm-nmsu-cooperative-pharmacy.html

ALASKA
ARIZONA
CALIFORNIA
COLORADO
HAWAII
IDAHO
MONTANA
NEVADA
NEW MEXICO
OREGON
UTAH
WASHINGTON
WYOMING

WEST

ALASKA

ARIZONA

CALIFORNIA

COLORADO

HAWAII

IDAHO

MONTANA

NEVADA

NEW MEXICO

OREGON

UTAH

WASHINGTON

WYOMING

OREGON STATE UNIVERSITY COLLEGE OF PHARMACY

Address: 203 Pharmacy Building, Corvallis, OR 97331
Website: *https://pharmacy.oregonstate.edu/*
Contact: *https://pharmacy.oregonstate.edu/email/node/145/ field_email*
Phone: (541) 737-3999

COST OF ATTENDANCE

In-State Tuition and Fees: $22,887
Additional Expenses: N/A
Total: $22,887*

Out-of-State Tuition and Fees: $33,544
Additional Expenses: N/A
Total: $33,544*

*Note: These figures do not reflect estimated housing/living expenses.

Financial Aid: https://pharmacy.oregonstate.edu/pharm-d-tuition-and-fees

ADDITIONAL INFORMATION

Interesting tidbit: Students spend the first two years of the Pharm.D. program in Corvallis on the main Oregon State University campus. This offers all the resources of a major research university and a classic collegiate experience. They spend the third year of the Pharm.D. program in Portland on the Oregon Health & Science University campus, offering all the benefits of a partnership with a renowned academic medical center. The fourth-year is entirely devoted to experiential education throughout the state of Oregon and beyond.

Important Updates due to COVID-19: Virtual Interview

Were tests required? No.

Are tests expected next year? No.

What international experiences are available? N/A

What dual degree options exist? PharmD/PhD: https://pharmacy.oregonstate.edu/pharmd_phd

PharmD/MBA: https://pharmacy.oregonstate.edu/mba-pharmacy-professionals

What service learning opportunities exist? N/A

What percent of graduates place in postgraduate training? 39.8% (2020)

NAPLEX First-Time Pass Rate: 96.20% (2020)

MPJE First-Time Pass Rate: 90.32% (2020)

Other: Early Assurance Program (EAP) available to high school seniors, college students, and post-baccalaureate students. For more information, visit: https://pharmacy.oregonstate.edu/eap-oregon-early-assurance-program

PACIFIC UNIVERSITY SCHOOL OF PHARMACY

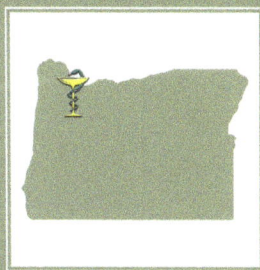

Address: 190 SE 8th Avenue, Hillsboro, OR 97123
Website: *https://www.pacificu.edu/academics/colleges/college-health-professions/school-pharmacy*
Contact: *https://www.pacificu.edu/contact-us*
Phone: (503) 352-7283

COST OF ATTENDANCE

Tuition and Fees: $51,640
Additional Expenses: $23,708
Total: $75,348

Financial Aid: https://www.pacificu.edu/pharmacy/apply-now/tuition-financial-aid

ADDITIONAL INFORMATION

Interesting tidbit: The Pacific University School of Pharmacy's 3-year PharmD curriculum is delivered in a modified block design, where students study one topic at a time before moving on to another content area. Students complete experiential components of the curriculum throughout their first and second didactic years. The third-year is devoted entirely to advanced clinical experience.

Important Updates due to COVID-19: Virtual Interview

Were tests required? No.

Are tests expected next year? No.

What international experiences are available? International rotations. For more information, visit: https://www.pacificu.edu/colleges/college-health-professions/school-pharmacy/global-pharmacy-education-research

What dual degree options exist? PharmD/MBA and PharmD/MS in Pharmaceutical Sciences. For more information, visit: https://www.pacificu.edu/academics/colleges/college-health-professions/school-pharmacy/pharmdms-degree-program

What service learning opportunities exist? Service learning through service organizations. Generation Rx, Operation Diabetes, Operation Immunization, and more. For more information, visit: https://www.pacificu.edu/pharmacy/student-organizations

What percent of graduates place in postgraduate training?

NAPLEX First-Time Pass Rate: 92.39% (2020)

MPJE First-Time Pass Rate: 86.67% (2020)

ALASKA

ARIZONA

CALIFORNIA

COLORADO

HAWAII

IDAHO

MONTANA

NEVADA

NEW MEXICO

OREGON

UTAH

WASHINGTON

WYOMING

WEST

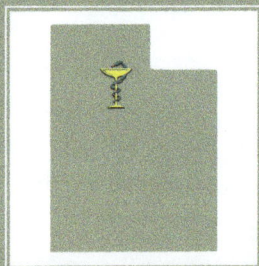

ALASKA

ARIZONA

CALIFORNIA

COLORADO

HAWAII

IDAHO

MONTANA

NEVADA

NEW MEXICO

OREGON

UTAH

WASHINGTON

WYOMING

UNIVERSITY OF UTAH COLLEGE OF PHARMACY

Address: 30 South 2000 East, Salt Lake City, UT 84112
Website: *https://pharmacy.utah.edu/*
Contact: *https://pharmacy.utah.edu/cop-information/about/contact-us.php*
Phone: (801) 581-6731

COST OF ATTENDANCE

In-State Tuition and Fees: $31,647
Additional Expenses: N/A
Total: $31,647*

Out-of-State Tuition and Fees: $60,770
Additional Expenses: N/A
Total: $60,770*

*Note: These figures do not reflect estimated housing/living expenses.

Financial Aid: https://pharmacy.utah.edu/student-information/pharmd-applicant/financial-aid.php

ADDITIONAL INFORMATION

Interesting tidbit: UofU PharmD program represents a collaborative effort of the four academic departments of the College of Pharmacy - departments of Medicinal Chemistry, Pharmaceutics and Pharmaceutical Chemistry, Pharmacology and Toxicology, and Pharmacotherapy.

Important Updates due to COVID-19: Accept prerequisite courses taken Pass/No Pass or Credit/No Credit during Winter 2020/Spring 2020/Summer 2020 terms.

Were tests required? Yes if an applicant does not hold a bachelor's degree.

Are tests expected next year? Yes if an applicant does hold a bachelor's degree.

What international experiences are available? International rotations and service trips

What dual degree options exist? PharmD/PhD. For more information, visit: https://pharmacy.utah.edu/student-information/pharmd-pathway/

What service learning opportunities exist? Community outreach such as mobile clinics, immunizations, etc.

What percent of graduates place in postgraduate training? N/A

NAPLEX First-Time Pass Rate: 87.72% (2020)

MPJE First-Time Pass Rate: 78.95% (2020)

Other: Early Assurance program available. For more information, visit: https://pharmacy.utah.edu/student-information/pharmd-applicant/

UNIVERSITY OF WASHINGTON SCHOOL OF PHARMACY

Address: 1959 NE Pacific St., Seattle, WA 98195
Website: *https://sop.washington.edu/*
Contact: *https://sop.washington.edu/pharmd/contact/*
Phone: (206) 543-6100

COST OF ATTENDANCE

In-State Tuition and Fees: $33,565
Additional Expenses: N/A
Total: $33,565*

Out-of-State Tuition and Fees: $55,804
Additional Expenses: N/A
Total: $55,804*

***Note:** These figures do not reflect estimated housing/living expenses.

Financial Aid: https://sop.washington.edu/pharmd/admissions/tuition-and-financial-aid/

ADDITIONAL INFORMATION

Interesting tidbit: UW School of Pharmacy provides scientific leadership through the development of innovative research programs in the biomedical sciences, conducts basic, translational and outcomes research, and makes informed decisions at preclinical, clinical and post-approval stages of drug discovery, development, and implementation. It ranks #2 nationally for federal research support among Schools of Pharmacy.

Important Updates due to COVID-19: Accept prerequisite courses graded as Pass/No Pass or Credit/No Credit versus a numerical/letter grade during terms where the pandemic has impacted instruction. All courses taken before the winter 2020 term must show a letter grade.

Were tests required? No.

Are tests expected next year? No.

What international experiences are available? International rotations and Global Medicines Program. For more information, visit: https://sop.washington.edu/department-of-pharmacy/research/global-medicines-program/

What dual degree options exist? PharmD/MBA: https://sop.washington.edu/pharmd/curriculum/concurrent-degree-info/pharmd-mba/

PharmD/PhD in Medicinal Chemistry or Pharmaceutics: https://sop.washington.edu/department-of-medicinal-chemistry/graduate-education-training-programs/phd-program/

PharmD/MS in Pharmaceutical Outcomes Research and Policy: https://sop.washington.edu/choice/graduate-education-training-programs/pharmd-ms-degree-program/

What service learning opportunities exist? Service learning through experiential education. For more information, visit: https://sop.washington.edu/pharmd/experiential-education/

What percent of graduates place in postgraduate training? 41% (2019)

NAPLEX First-Time Pass Rate: 97.94% (2020)
MPJE First-Time Pass Rate: 96.25% (2020)

ALASKA

ARIZONA

CALIFORNIA

COLORADO

HAWAII

IDAHO

MONTANA

NEVADA

NEW MEXICO

OREGON

UTAH

WASHINGTON

WYOMING

WEST

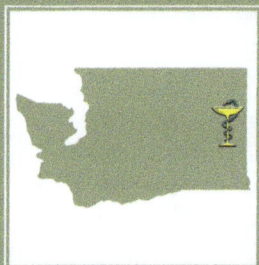

ALASKA

ARIZONA

CALIFORNIA

COLORADO

HAWAII

IDAHO

MONTANA

NEVADA

NEW MEXICO

OREGON

UTAH

WASHINGTON

WYOMING

WASHINGTON STATE UNIVERSITY COLLEGE OF PHARMACY AND PHARMACEUTICAL SCIENCES

Address: 412 E. Spokane Falls Blvd., Spokane, WA 99202
Website: *https://pharmacy.wsu.edu/*
Contact: *https://pharmacy.wsu.edu/request-info/*
Phone: (509) 368-6605
Other Locations: Yakima, Washington

COST OF ATTENDANCE

In-State Tuition and Fees: $26,072
Additional Expenses: N/A
Total: $26,072*

Out-of-State Tuition and Fees: $42,726
Additional Expenses: N/A
Total: $42,726*

*Note: These figures do not reflect estimated housing/living expenses.

Financial Aid: https://spokane.wsu.edu/studentaffairs/financial-services/scholarships/

ADDITIONAL INFORMATION

Interesting tidbit: Students spend the first three years of the Doctor of Pharmacy program on the WSU Health Sciences campus in Spokane or the WSU Doctor of Pharmacy program extension on the Pacific Northwest University of Health Sciences campus in Yakima. Applicants can indicate their campus of choice within the supplemental application, which will be considered on a space-available basis.

Important Updates due to COVID-19: VIrtual Interview

Were tests required? No.

Are tests expected next year? No.

What international experiences are available? International rotations. For more information, visit: https://pharmacy.wsu.edu/doctor-of-pharmacy/experiential-services/

What dual degree options exist? PharmD/MBA: https://pharmacy.wsu.edu/dual-degree-programs/pharm-d-mba/

PharmD/PhD: https://pharmacy.wsu.edu/dual-degree-programs/pharm-d-ph-d-program/

What service learning opportunities exist? Service learning through experiential education. For more information, visit: https://pharmacy.wsu.edu/doctor-of-pharmacy/experiential-services/

What percent of graduates place in postgraduate training? 44% (2020)

NAPLEX First-Time Pass Rate: 87.01% (2020)

MPJE First-Time Pass Rate: 85.09% (2020)

Other: Save-A-Seat program available to high school and current college students. For more information, visit: https://pharmacy.wsu.edu/doctor-of-pharmacy/admissions/save-a-seat-2/

UNIVERSITY OF WYOMING SCHOOL OF PHARMACY

Address: 1000 E University Ave, Laramie, WY 82071
Website: *http://www.uwyo.edu/pharmacy/*
Contact: *http://www.uwyo.edu/uw/people/index.html*
Phone: (307) 766-6120

COST OF ATTENDANCE

In-State Tuition and Fees: $17,917
Additional Expenses: $19,059
Total: $36,976

Out-of-State Tuition and Fees: $37,876
Additional Expenses: $19,059
Total: $56,935

Alumni Tuition and Fees: $26,877
Additional Expenses: $19,059
Total: $45,937

Financial Aid: http://www.uwyo.edu/pharmacy/pharmd-program/tuition-fees.html

ADDITIONAL INFORMATION

Interesting tidbit: The University of Wyoming School of Pharmacy is part of the Health Sciences Center located on the University of Wyoming campus. The UWYO School of Pharmacy utilizes the pharmacy patient care process throughout the four-year curriculum. This enables us to follow a practice-ready curriculum.

Important Updates due to COVID-19: The school of pharmacy does not accept online coursework, except for Covid-19 related exceptions and except for the following coursework: Statistics, Calculus, and Biochemistry.

Were tests required? No.

Are tests expected next year? No.

What international experiences are available? N/A

What dual degree options exist? PharmD/MBA. For more information, visit: http://www.uwyo.edu/pharmacy/pharmd-program/doctor-of-pharmacy-mba.html

What percent of graduates place in postgraduate training? N/A

What service learning opportunities exist? N/A

What percent of graduates place in postgraduate training? N/A

NAPLEX First-Time Pass Rate: 90.91% (2020)

MPJE First-Time Pass Rate: 80.95% (2020)

Other: Aspire program available to first-year undergraduates. For more information, visit: http://www.uwyo.edu/pharmacy/pharmd-program/aspire-program.html

ALASKA

ARIZONA

CALIFORNIA

COLORADO

HAWAII

IDAHO

MONTANA

NEVADA

NEW MEXICO

OREGON

UTAH

WASHINGTON

WYOMING

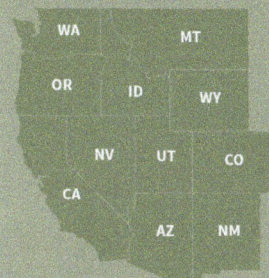

WEST

CHAPTER 6

REGION FIVE
U.S TERRITORIES

Pharmacy School	Ave. GPA & PCAT (%) Early Decision (ED): Yes/No Int'l Students: Yes/No	Admissions Statistics	Science Req. Other than Gen Chem, OChem, Physics, Bio
University of Puerto Rico Medical Sciences Campus School of Pharmacy, University of Puerto Rico Medical Sciences Campus, Centro Médico, San Juan, PR 00931	3.0 PCAT: N/A ED: No Int'l Student: No	**(2019)** Apps Received: 96 Interviews Offered: N/A Admission Offered: N/A Number Enrolled: 45 Admitted Rate: 46.9% **(2020)** Apps Received: 135 Interviews Offered: N/A Admission Offered: N/A Number Enrolled: 45 Admitted Rate: 33.3%	Calc. Anatomy & Physio.

UNIVERSITY OF PUERTO RICO MEDICAL SCIENCES CAMPUS SCHOOL OF PHARMACY

Address: School of Pharmacy, University of Puerto Rico Medical Sciences Campus, Centro Médico, San Juan, PR 00931
Website: *https://farmacia.rcm.upr.edu/academic-programs/doctor-of-pharmacy-program/*
Contact: *https://farmacia.rcm.upr.edu/contact/*
Phone: (787) 758-2525 Ext. 5422

COST OF ATTENDANCE

In-State Tuition and Fees: $15,876
Additional Expenses: N/A
Total: $15,876*

Out-of-State Tuition and Fees: $28,376
Additional Expenses: N/A
Total: $28,376*

*Note: These figures do not reflect estimated housing/living expenses.

Financial Aid: N/A.

ADDITIONAL INFORMATION

Interesting tidbit: Pharmacy was the first health profession program to be offered at the higher education level in Puerto Rico and the first to be accredited. The Doctor of Pharmacy program, as well as the Pharmacy Practice Residency program, were implemented in 2001.

Important Updates due to COVID-19: Virtual Interview

Were tests required? PCAT required.

Are tests expected next year? Yes.

What international experiences are available? No international options.

What dual degree options exist? No dual degree options listed.

What percent of graduates place in postgraduate training? 9.8% (2019)

NAPLEX First-Time Pass Rate: 95.24% (2020)

MPJE First-Time Pass Rate: N/A

What service learning opportunities exist? Service learning through experiential education. For more information, visit: https://farmacia.rcm.upr.edu/academic-programs/doctor-of-pharmacy-program/experiential-drph/

PUERTO RICO

PUERTO RICO

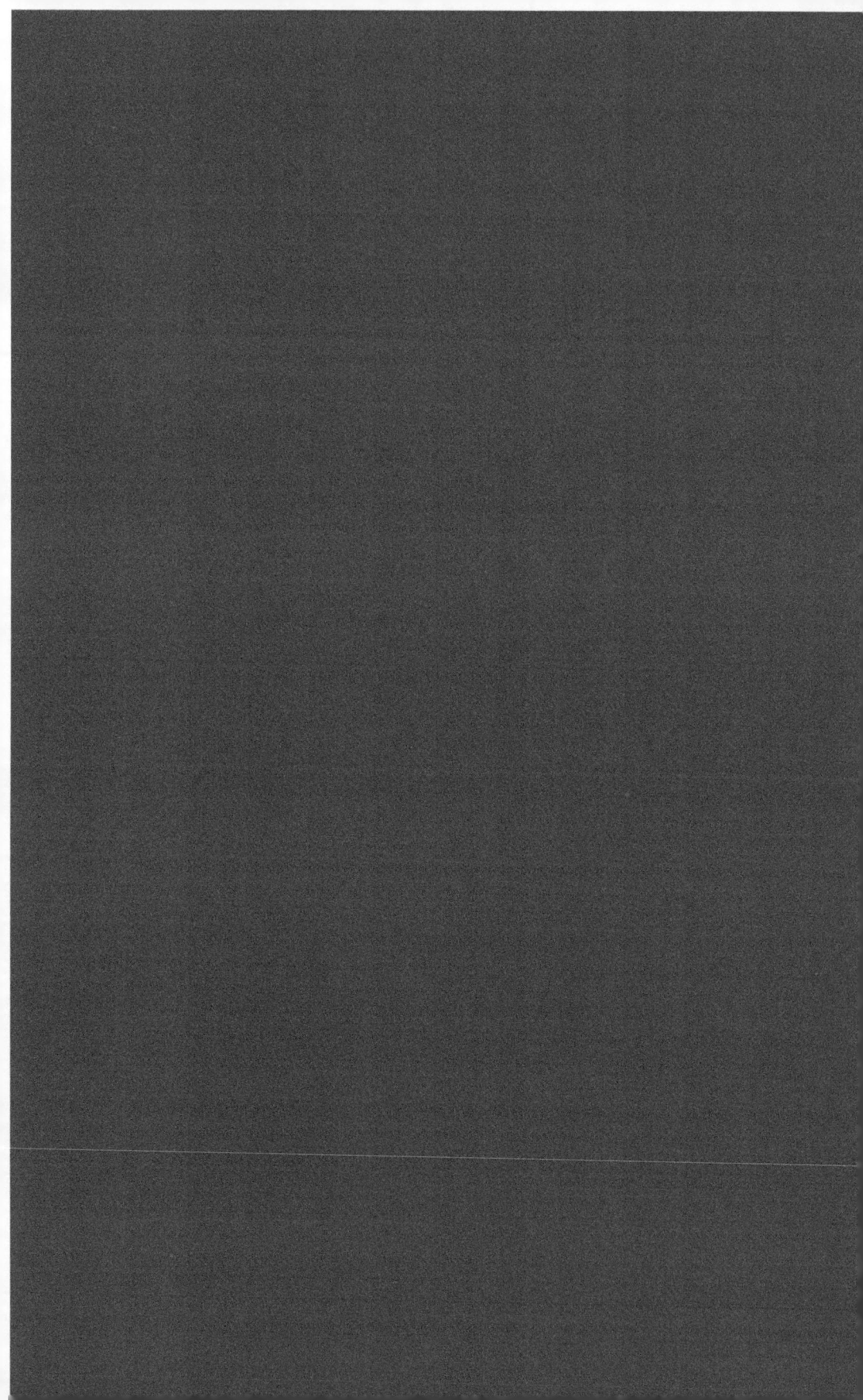

MEDICAL
SCHOOL LISTS

CHAPTER 7

PHARMACY SCHOOLS BY CITY/STATE

Pharmacy Schools	City	State	Website
Auburn University Harrison School of Pharmacy	Auburn	AL	https://pharmacy.auburn.edu/
Samford University McWhorter School of Pharmacy	Birmingham	AL	https://www.samford.edu/pharmacy/
University of Arkansas for Medical Sciences College of Pharmacy	Little Rock	AR	https://pharmacy.uams.edu/
Harding University College of Pharmacy	Searcy	AR	https://www.harding.edu/academics/colleges-departments/pharmacy
Midwestern University College of Pharmacy-Glendale	Glendale	AZ	https://www.midwestern.edu/academics/our-colleges/college-of-pharmacy%E2%80%93glendale.xml
University of Arizona College of Pharmacy	Tucson	AZ	https://www.pharmacy.arizona.edu/
Keck Graduate Institute (KGI) School of Pharmacy and Health Sciences	Claremont	CA	https://www.kgi.edu/academics/school-of-pharmacy-and-health-sciences/overview/
California Health Sciences University College of Pharmacy	Clovis	CA	https://pharmacy.chsu.edu/
California Northstate University College of Pharmacy	Elk Grove	CA	https://pharmacy.cnsu.edu/
Marshall B. Ketchum University College of Pharmacy	Fullerton	CA	https://www.ketchum.edu/pharmacy
Chapman University School of Pharmacy	Irvine	CA	https://www.chapman.edu/pharmacy/index.aspx
University of California, Irvine School of Pharmacy	Irvine	CA	https://pharmsci.uci.edu/pharm-d/
University of California, San Diego Skaggs School of Pharmacy & Pharmaceutical Sciences	La Jolla	CA	https://pharmacy.ucsd.edu/
Loma Linda University School of Pharmacy	Loma Linda	CA	https://pharmacy.llu.edu/
West Coast University School of Pharmacy	Los Angeles	CA	https://westcoastuniversity.edu/programs/doctor-pharmacy.html
University of Southern California School of Pharmacy	Los Angeles	CA	https://pharmacyschool.usc.edu/
Western University of Health Sciences College of Pharmacy	Pomona	CA	https://www.westernu.edu/pharmacy/

Pharmacy Schools	City	State	Website
University of California, San Francisco School of Pharmacy	San Francisco	CA	https://pharmacy.ucsf.edu/
American University of Health Sciences School of Pharmacy	Signal Hill	CA	https://www.auhs.edu/academics/pharmacy/
University of the Pacific Thomas J. Long School of Pharmacy	Stockton	CA	https://www.pacific.edu/academics/schools-and-colleges/thomas-j-long-school-of-pharmacy.html
Touro University - California College of Pharmacy	Vallejo	CA	http://cop.tu.edu/
University of Colorado Anschutz Medical Campus Skaggs School of Pharmacy and Pharmaceutical Sciences	Aurora	CO	http://www.ucdenver.edu/academics/colleges/pharmacy/Pages/SchoolofPharmacy.aspx
Regis University Rueckert-Hartman College for Health Professions School of Pharmacy	Denver	CO	https://www.regis.edu/academics/colleges-and-schools/rueckert-hartman/pharmacy/index
University of Connecticut School of Pharmacy	Storrs	CT	https://pharmacy.uconn.edu/
University of Saint Joseph School of Pharmacy and Physician Assistant Studies	West Hartford	CT	https://www.usj.edu/academics/academic-schools/sppas/
Howard University College of Pharmacy	Washington	DC	http://pharmacy.howard.edu/
Nova Southeastern University College of Pharmacy	Fort Lauderdale	FL	https://pharmacy.nova.edu/index.html
University of Florida College of Pharmacy	Gainesville	FL	https://pharmacy.ufl.edu/
Larkin University College of Pharmacy	Miami	FL	https://ularkin.org/pharmacy/
Florida Agricultural & Mechanical University College of Pharmacy and Pharmaceutical Sciences	Tallahassee	FL	https://pharmacy.famu.edu/
University of South Florida Health Taneja College of Pharmacy	Tampa	FL	https://health.usf.edu/pharmacy
Palm Beach Atlantic University Lloyd L. Gregory School of Pharmacy	West Palm Beach	FL	https://www.pba.edu/academics/schools/gregory-pharmacy/index.html
University of Georgia College of Pharmacy	Athens	GA	https://rx.uga.edu/

Pharmacy Schools	City	State	Website
Mercer University College of Pharmacy	Atlanta	GA	https://pharmacy.mercer.edu/
South University School of Pharmacy	Savannah	GA	https://www.southuniversity.edu/degree-programs/pharmacy
Philadelphia College of Osteopathic Medicine - Georgia School of Pharmacy	Suwanee	GA	https://www.pcom.edu/academics/programs-and-degrees/doctor-of-pharmacy/
University of Hawaii at Hilo Daniel K. Inouye College of Pharmacy	Hilo	HI	https://pharmacy.uhh.hawaii.edu/
Drake University College of Pharmacy and Health Sciences	Des Moines	IA	https://www.drake.edu/cphs/
University of Iowa College of Pharmacy	Iowa 52242	IA	https://pharmacy.uiowa.edu/
Idaho State University College of Pharmacy	Pocatello	ID	https://www.isu.edu/pharmacy/
University of Illinois at Chicago College of Pharmacy	Chicago	IL	https://pharmacy.uic.edu/
Chicago State University College of Pharmacy	Chicago	IL	https://www.csu.edu/collegeofpharmacy/
Southern Illinois University Edwardsville School of Pharmacy	Edwardsville	IL	https://www.siue.edu/pharmacy/
Midwestern University Chicago College of Pharmacy	IL 60515	IL	https://www.midwestern.edu/academics/degrees-and-programs/doctor-of-pharmacy-il.xml
Rosalind Franklin University of Medicine and Science College of Pharmacy	North Chicago	IL	https://www.rosalindfranklin.edu/academics/college-of-pharmacy/
Roosevelt University College of Pharmacy	Schaumburg	IL	https://www.roosevelt.edu/colleges/pharmacy
Butler University College of Pharmacy and Health Sciences	Indianapolis	IN	https://www.butler.edu/cophs
Manchester University College of Pharmacy, Natural and Health Sciences	North Manchester	IN	https://www.manchester.edu/academics/colleges/college-of-pharmacy-natural-health-sciences
Purdue University College of Pharmacy	West Lafayette	IN	https://www.pharmacy.purdue.edu/

Pharmacy Schools	City	State	Website
University of Kansas School of Pharmacy	Lawrence	KS	https://pharmacy.ku.edu/
University of Kentucky College of Pharmacy	Lexington	KY	https://pharmacy.uky.edu/
Sullivan University College of Pharmacy	Louisville	KY	https://www.sullivan.edu/colleges/college-of-pharmacy-and-health-sciences
University of Louisiana at Monroe College of Pharmacy	Monroe	LA	https://www.ulm.edu/pharmacy/
Xavier University of Louisiana College of Pharmacy	New Orleans	LA	https://www.xula.edu/collegeofpharmacy
MCPHS University School of Pharmacy - Boston	Boston	MA	https://www.mcphs.edu/
Northeastern University Bouvé College of Health Sciences School of Pharmacy	Boston	MA	https://bouve.northeastern.edu/pharmacy/
Western New England University College of Pharmacy	Springfield	MA	https://www1.wne.edu/pharmacy-and-health-sciences/
MCPHS University School of Pharmacy - Worcester	Worcester	MA	https://www.mcphs.edu/
University of Maryland School of Pharmacy	Baltimore	MD	https://www.pharmacy.umaryland.edu/
Notre Dame of Maryland University School of Pharmacy	Baltimore	MD	https://www.ndm.edu/colleges-schools/school-pharmacy
University of Maryland Eastern Shore School of Pharmacy and Health Professions	Princess Anne	MD	https://www.umes.edu/pharmacy/
Husson University School of Pharmacy	Bangor	ME	https://www.husson.edu/pharmacy/
University of New England College of Pharmacy	Portland	ME	https://www.une.edu/pharmacy
University of Michigan College of Pharmacy	Ann Arbor	MI	https://pharmacy.umich.edu/
Ferris State University College of Pharmacy	Big Rapids	MI	https://www.ferris.edu/pharmacy/
Wayne State University Eugene Applebaum College of Pharmacy and Health Sciences	Detroit	MI	https://cphs.wayne.edu/
University of Minnesota College of Pharmacy	Duluth	MN	https://www.pharmacy.umn.edu/

Pharmacy Schools	City	State	Website
University of Missouri-Kansas City School of Pharmacy	Kansas City	MO	https://pharmacy.umkc.edu/
St. Louis College of Pharmacy	St. Louis	MO	https://www.uhsp.edu/
William Carey University School of Pharmacy	Biloxi	MS	https://www.wmcarey.edu/School/Pharmacy
University of Mississippi School of Pharmacy	University	MS	https://pharmacy.olemiss.edu/
University of Montana College of Health Professions and Biomedical Sciences Skaggs School of Pharmacy	Missoula	MT	http://health.umt.edu/pharmacy/
Campbell University College of Pharmacy and Health Sciences	Buies Creek	NC	https://cphs.campbell.edu/
University of North Carolina Eshelman School of Pharmacy	Chapel Hill	NC	https://pharmacy.unc.edu/
High Point University Fred Wilson School of Pharmacy	High Point	NC	http://www.highpoint.edu/pharmacy/
Wingate University School of Pharmacy	Wingate	NC	https://www.wingate.edu/academics/graduate/pharmacy
North Dakota State University College of Health Professions School of Pharmacy	Fargo	ND	https://www.ndsu.edu/pharmacy/
University of Nebraska Medical Center College of Pharmacy	Omaha	NE	https://www.unmc.edu/pharmacy/
Creighton University School of Pharmacy and Health Professions	Omaha	NE	https://spahp.creighton.edu/
Fairleigh Dickinson University School of Pharmacy	Florham Park	NJ	https://view2.fdu.edu/academics/pharmacy/
Rutgers, the State University of New Jersey Ernest Mario School of Pharmacy	Piscataway	NJ	https://pharmacy.rutgers.edu/
University of New Mexico College of Pharmacy	Albuquerque	NM	https://hsc.unm.edu/college-of-pharmacy/
Roseman University of Health Sciences College of Pharmacy	Henderson	NV	https://pharmacy.roseman.edu/
Albany College of Pharmacy and Health Sciences School of Pharmacy and Pharmaceutical Sciences	Albany	NY	https://www.acphs.edu/

Pharmacy Schools	City	State	Website
Long Island University Arnold and Marie Schwartz College of Pharmacy and Health Sciences	Brooklyn	NY	https://liu.edu/Pharmacy
D'Youville College School of Pharmacy	Buffalo	NY	http://www.dyc.edu/academics/schools-and-departments/pharmacy/
University at Buffalo The State University of New York School of Pharmacy & Pharmaceutical Sciences	Buffalo	NY	http://pharmacy.buffalo.edu/
Binghamton University State University of New York School of Pharmacy and Pharmaceutical Sciences	Johnson City	NY	https://www.binghamton.edu/pharmacy-and-pharmaceutical-sciences/
Touro New York College of Pharmacy	New York	NY	https://tcop.touro.edu/
St. John's University College of Pharmacy and Health Sciences	Queens	NY	https://www.stjohns.edu/academics/programs/doctor-pharmacy
St. John Fisher College Wegmans School of Pharmacy	Rochester	NY	https://www.sjfc.edu/schools/school-of-pharmacy/
Ohio Northern University Raabe College of Pharmacy	Ada	OH	https://www.onu.edu/college-pharmacy
Cedarville University School of Pharmacy	Cedarville	OH	https://www.cedarville.edu/Academic-Schools-and-Departments/Pharmacy.aspx
University of Cincinnati James L. Winkle College of Pharmacy	Cincinnati	OH	https://pharmacy.uc.edu/
Ohio State University College of Pharmacy	Columbus	OH	https://pharmacy.osu.edu/
University of Findlay College of Pharmacy	Findlay	OH	https://www.findlay.edu/pharmacy/
Northeast Ohio Medical University College of Pharmacy	Rootstown	OH	https://www.neomed.edu/pharmacy/
University of Toledo College of Pharmacy and Pharmaceutical Sciences	Toledo	OH	https://www.utoledo.edu/pharmacy/
University of Oklahoma College of Pharmacy	Oklahoma City	OK	https://pharmacy.ouhsc.edu/

Pharmacy Schools	City	State	Website
Southwestern Oklahoma State University College of Pharmacy	Weatherford	OK	https://www.swosu.edu/academics/pharmacy/index.aspx
Oregon State University College of Pharmacy	Corvallis	OR	https://pharmacy.oregonstate.edu/
Pacific University School of Pharmacy	Hillsboro	OR	https://www.pacificu.edu/academics/colleges/college-health-professions/school-pharmacy
Lake Erie College of Osteopathic Medicine School of Pharmacy	Erie	PA	https://lecom.edu/academics/school-of-pharmacy/
Temple University School of Pharmacy	Philadelphia	PA	https://pharmacy.temple.edu/
Thomas Jefferson University Jefferson College of Pharmacy	Philadelphia	PA	https://www.jefferson.edu/university/pharmacy.html
University of the Sciences Philadelphia College of Pharmacy	Philadelphia	PA	https://www.usciences.edu/philadelphia-college-of-pharmacy/
Duquesne University School of Pharmacy	Pittsburg	PA	https://www.duq.edu/academics/schools/pharmacy
University of Pittsburgh School of Pharmacy	Pittsburgh	PA	https://www.pharmacy.pitt.edu/
Wilkes University Nesbitt School of Pharmacy	Wilkes-Barre	PA	https://www.wilkes.edu/academics/colleges/nesbitt-school-of-pharmacy/index.aspx
University of Puerto Rico Medical Sciences Campus School of Pharmacy	San Juan	PR	https://farmacia.rcm.upr.edu/academic-programs/doctor-of-pharmacy-program/
University of Rhode Island College of Pharmacy	Kingston	RI	https://web.uri.edu/pharmacy/
Medical University of South Carolina College of Pharmacy	Charleston	SC	https://pharmacy.musc.edu/
Presbyterian College School of Pharmacy	Clinton	SC	https://pharmacy.presby.edu/
University of South Carolina College of Pharmacy	Columbia	SC	https://www.sc.edu/study/colleges_schools/pharmacy/index.php

Pharmacy Schools	City	State	Website
South Dakota State University College of Pharmacy and Allied Health Professions	Brookings	SD	https://www.sdstate.edu/pharmacy-allied-health-professions
Union University College of Pharmacy	Jackson	TN	https://www.uu.edu/programs/pharmacy/
East Tennessee State University Bill Gatton College of Pharmacy	Johnson City	TN	https://www.etsu.edu/pharmacy/
South College School of Pharmacy	Knoxville	TN	https://www.south.edu/programs/doctor-pharmacy/
University of Tennessee Health Science Center College of Pharmacy	Memphis	TN	https://www.uthsc.edu/pharmacy/
Lipscomb University College of Pharmacy and Health Sciences	Nashville	TN	https://www.lipscomb.edu/pharmacy
Belmont University College of Pharmacy	Nashville	TN	http://www.belmont.edu/pharmacy/index.html
University of Texas at Austin College of Pharmacy	Austin	TX	https://pharmacy.utexas.edu/
University of Texas at El Paso School of Pharmacy	El Paso	TX	https://www.utep.edu/pharmacy/
University of North Texas Health Science Center UNT System College of Pharmacy	Fort Worth	tx	https://www.unthsc.edu/college-of-pharmacy/
University of Houston College of Pharmacy	Houston	TX	https://www.uh.edu/pharmacy/
Texas Southern University College of Pharmacy and Health Sciences	Houston	TX	http://www.tsu.edu/academics/colleges-and-schools/college-of-pharmacy-and-health-sciences/
Texas A & M University Health Science Center Irma Lerma Rangel College of Pharmacy	Kingsville	TX	https://pharmacy.tamu.edu/
Texas Tech University Health Sciences Center Jerry H. Hodge School of Pharmacy	Lubbock	TX	https://www.ttuhsc.edu/pharmacy/default.aspx
University of the Incarnate Word Feik School of Pharmacy	San Antonio	TX	https://pharmacy.uiw.edu/
University of Texas at Tyler Ben and Maytee Fisch College of Pharmacy	Tyler	TX	https://www.uttyler.edu/pharmacy/
University of Utah College of Pharmacy	Salt Lake City	UT	https://pharmacy.utah.edu/

Pharmacy Schools	City	State	Website
Hampton University School of Pharmacy	Hampton	VA	http://wp.hamptonu.edu/pharmacy/
Appalachian College of Pharmacy	Oakwood	VA	https://www.acp.edu/
Virginia Commonwealth University at the Medical College of Virginia Campus School of Pharmacy	Richmond	VA	https://pharmacy.vcu.edu/
Shenandoah University Bernard J. Dunn School of Pharmacy	Winchester	VA	https://www.su.edu/pharmacy/
University of Washington School of Pharmacy	Seattle	WA	https://sop.washington.edu/
Washington State University College of Pharmacy and Pharmaceutical Sciences	Spokane	WA	https://pharmacy.wsu.edu/
University of Wisconsin-Madison School of Pharmacy	Madison	WI	https://pharmacy.wisc.edu/
Concordia University Wisconsin School of Pharmacy	Mequon	WI	https://www.cuw.edu/academics/schools/pharmacy/index.html
Medical College of Wisconsin School of Pharmacy	Milwaukee	WI	https://www.mcw.edu/education/pharmacy-school
University of Charleston School of Pharmacy	Charleston	WV	https://www.ucwv.edu/academics/schools/school-of-pharmacy/
Marshall University School of Pharmacy	Huntington	WV	https://www.marshall.edu/pharmacy/
West Virginia University School of Pharmacy	Morgantown	WV	https://pharmacy.wvu.edu/
University of Wyoming School of Pharmacy	Laramie	WY	http://www.uwyo.edu/pharmacy/

CHAPTER 8

PHARMACY SCHOOL ADMISSIONS PREREQUISITES

ALABAMA

PharmD Schools	Required	Recommended	Notes
AUBURN UNIVERSITY HARRISON SCHOOL OF PHARMACY	Bio., Chem. w/ Lab, OChem. w/ Lab, Human Anatomy & Physio. or Upper-div Physio. (see Notes), Microbio., Calc., Stats., and Biochem.	Physics, Bio. Sciences (e.g., Genetics/Genomic Bio., Immunology, Physio., Cell Bio., and Comparative Anatomy), Chem. (e.g., Physical Chem., Analytical Chem., and Enzymology), and Advanced Math (beyond Calc. 1)	Upper-div Physio may include: Mammalian, Vertebrate, Human, or Animal Physiology. AP credits accepted per Auburn University's testing out policy.
SAMFORD UNIVERSITY MCWHORTER SCHOOL OF PHARMACY	Engl. Comp., Engl./ American Lit., Calc., Human Anatomy & Physio., Microbio., Chem., OChem., Elementary Stats., Public Speaking, World History/ Western Civilization/ U.S. History, Sociology/Psych., Other Liberal Arts (see Recommended), 2 Physical Activity Courses or 1 Lifetime Wellness Course.	Liberal Arts: Political Science, History, Lit., For. Lang., Philosophy, Psych., Sociology, Geography, Econ., Religion, and either Art, Music, or Drama Appreciation.	AP credits accepted for certain courses. Contact admissions for more information.

For the number of hours required for prerequisite courses, and for the most up-to-date information, please refer to the individual school websites.
*A.P. credit satisfies the requirement.
** When A.P. credit is awarded, upper-level coursework in the same subject area is required.
*** A.P. credit may satisfy the requirement on a case by case basis

ARKANSAS

PharmD Schools	Required	Recommended	Notes
HARDING UNIVERSITY COLLEGE OF PHARMACY	Chem. w/ Lab, OChem. w/ Lab, Biochem., Microbio. w/ Lab, Bio. (see Recommended) Calc., Stats., Speech/ Public Speaking, Engl. Comp., Econ, Psych./Sociology, and Other Electives.	Bio - Choose from: Human Anatomy & Physio., Genetics, Cell Bio., Immunology, Bio. 1, and Bio 2.	AP credits accepted as long as they are listed on undergraduate transcript.
UNIVERSITY OF ARKANSAS FOR MEDICAL SCIENCES COLLEGE OF PHARMACY	College Algebra, Chem. w/ Lab, OChem. w/ Lab, Bio. w/ Lab, Microbio. w/ Lab, Electives (see Notes), Engl. Comp./Writing, Communication/ Speech, Econ./ Accounting, Stats., Psych., Cultural Humanities (see Notes).	N/A	Electives - Choose from: Anatomy, Physio., Biochem., Cell Bio., Genetics, Quantitative Analysis, Physical Chem., Calc. 1, Physics 1, Critical Thinking, or Logic. Cultural Humanities - Choose from: World Cultures, World History, Anthropology, Sociology, For. Lang., and ASL. Maximum 8 AP semester hours accepted for core courses and 6 AP semester hours for non-core courses. AP credits must be listed on undergraduate transcript.

For the number of hours required for prerequisite courses, and for the most up-to-date information, please refer to the individual school websites.

*A.P. credit satisfies the requirement.

** When A.P. credit is awarded, upper-level coursework in the same subject area is required.

*** A.P. credit may satisfy the requirement on a case by case basis

ARIZONA

PharmD Schools	Required	Recommended	Notes
MIDWESTERN UNIVERSITY COLLEGE OF PHARMACY-GLENDALE	Engl. Comp., Bio. w/ Lab, Social Sciences, General Education Electives, Human or Vertebrate Anatomy, Chem. w/ Lab, OChem. w/ Lab, Physics, Stats., Calc., Speech, and Econ.	N/A	AP credits accepted as long as they are listed on undergraduate transcript.
UNIVERSITY OF ARIZONA COLLEGE OF PHARMACY	Chem., OChem., Anatomy & Physio., Bio., Microbio., Physics, Engl. Comp., Calc., Stats., Social Sciences, Traditional & Culture, Fine Arts/Lit., and Diversity Emphasis.	N/A	AP credits accepted for non-science coursework.

CALIFORNIA

PharmD Schools	Required	Recommended	Notes
AMERICAN UNIVERSITY OF HEALTH SCIENCES SCHOOL OF PHARMACY	Chem. w/ Lab, OChem. w/ Lab, Bio. w/ Lab, Microbio. w/ Lab, Human Physio. w/ Lab, Stats., Calc., Econ., Psych./Sociology, Public Speaking, Engl. Comp., and Humanities and Social/Behav. Sciences.	N/A	No listed information on AP credits. Contact admissions.
CALIFORNIA HEALTH SCIENCES UNIVERSITY COLLEGE OF PHARMACY	Chem. w/ Lab, OChem. w/ Lab, Bio. w/ Lab, Microbio., Physio., Anatomy, Psych., Econ., Calc., and Public Speaking.	N/A	AP credits accepted.

For the number of hours required for prerequisite courses, and for the most up-to-date information, please refer to the individual school websites.
*A.P. credit satisfies the requirement.
** When A.P. credit is awarded, upper-level coursework in the same subject area is required.
*** A.P. credit may satisfy the requirement on a case by case basis

CALIFORNIA NORTHSTATE UNIVERSITY COLLEGE OF PHARMACY	Chem. w/ Lab, OChem. w/ Lab, Biochem. or Cell & Molecular Bio., Bio. w/ Lab, Human Physio., Physics, Calc., Stats., Public Speaking, Engl. Comp., and General Education Requirements.	N/A	AP credits accepted as long as they are listed on undergraduate transcript. AP scores must be 3+ and will only count towards first course in a series of science courses (e.g., Chem. 1)
CHAPMAN UNIVERSITY SCHOOL OF PHARMACY	Bio. w/ Lab, Human Physio. w/ Lab, Microbio. Chem. w/ Lab, OChem. w/ Lab, Physics w/ Lab, Genetics or Molecular Bio., Calc., Stats., Psych./ Sociology, Econ., Speech, Engl. Comp., Human Anatomy w/ Lab, and Electives.	N/A	AP credit accepted for Bio., Physio., Psych., and Stats. if the score is 4+. AP credit accepted for Calc. with a score of 4+ on the Calc. AB exam or 3+ on the Calc. BC exam.
KECK GRADUATE INSTITUTE (KGI) SCHOOL OF PHARMACY AND HEALTH SCIENCES	Chem. w/ Lab, OChem. w/ Lab, Bio. w/ Lab, Biochem., Microbio., Anatomy w/ Lab, Physio. w/ Lab, Physics, Calc., Stats., Econ., Psych./ Sociology, Public Speaking, and Engl. Comp.	N/A	AP credits accepted as long as they are listed on undergraduate transcript.
LOMA LINDA UNIVERSITY SCHOOL OF PHARMACY	Bio. w/ Lab, Chem. w/ Lab, OChem. w/ Lab, Physics w/ Lab, Biochem., Engl. Comp./Writing, Humanities, and Social/Behav. Science.	N/A	AP scores 3+ may be used towards first term of one-year series prerequisite courses (e.g., Chem 1).

For the number of hours required for prerequisite courses, and for the most up-to-date information, please refer to the individual school websites.
*A.P. credit satisfies the requirement.
** When A.P. credit is awarded, upper-level coursework in the same subject area is required.
*** A.P. credit may satisfy the requirement on a case by case basis

MARSHALL B. KETCHUM UNIVERSITY COLLEGE OF PHARMACY	Bio. w/ Lab, Chem. w/ Lab, OChem. w/ Lab, Calc., Human Anatomy w/ Lab, Human Physio. w/ Lab, Engl. Comp., Social/ Behav. Science, Communication, Psych., and Econ.	Preferred communication coursework: Public Speaking and Interpersonal Communication	AP credit accepted for non-science coursework.
TOURO UNIVERSITY - CALIFORNIA COLLEGE OF PHARMACY	Chem. w/ Lab, OChem. w/ Lab, Human Physio., Microbio. w/ Lab, and Calc.	N/A	Two options for chemistry. In second option, Biochem. is accepted. See university site for more information. AP credits accepted as long as they are listed on undergraduate transcript.
UNIVERSITY OF CALIFORNIA, IRVINE SCHOOL OF PHARMACY & PHARMACEUTICAL SCIENCES	Bio., Biochem., Human Physio., Chem. w/Lab, OChem. w/Lab, Calc., Stats., English/ Writing, Macro- or Microecon., Psych., and Public Speaking or Debate.	N/A	AP credits accepted.
UNIVERSITY OF CALIFORNIA, SAN DIEGO SKAGGS SCHOOL OF PHARMACY & PHARMACEUTICAL SCIENCES	Engl. w/ Writing, Chem. w/ Lab, OChem. w/ Lab, Bio. w/ Lab (Cellular and Molecular and Whole Animal), Physics w/ Lab, Calc., Econ., Public Speaking, and Human Behavior.	N/A	AP credits accepted as long as they are listed on undergraduate transcript.

For the number of hours required for prerequisite courses, and for the most up-to-date information, please refer to the individual school websites.
*A.P. credit satisfies the requirement.
** When A.P. credit is awarded, upper-level coursework in the same subject area is required.
*** A.P. credit may satisfy the requirement on a case by case basis

UNIVERSITY OF CALIFORNIA, SAN FRANCISCO SCHOOL OF PHARMACY	Chem. w/ Lab, OChem. w/ Lab, Bio. w/ Lab, Physio., Microbio. w/ Lab, Calc., Stats., Engl. Comp., and Humanities/Social Sciences.	Human Physio. preferred.	AP credits accepted. See university website for details on score required and classes that can be substituted with AP credit.
UNIVERSITY OF SOUTHERN CALIFORNIA SCHOOL OF PHARMACY	Calc., Bio. w/ Lab, Human Physio., Microbio., Chem. w/ Lab, OChem. w/ Lab, Biochem., and Stats.	Physics courses that include thermodynamics and electromagnetism. Upper division course in Molecular or Cell Biology, Microecon., General Psych./Sociology, or Cultural Anthropology.	AP score of 3+ may be used towards first quarter or semester of a one-year series of pre-pharmacy courses (e.g., Chem 1).
UNIVERSITY OF THE PACIFIC THOMAS J. LONG SCHOOL OF PHARMACY	Calc., Physics w/ Lab, Chem. w/ Lab, OChem. w/ Lab, Bio. w/ Lab, Physio. w/ Lab, Engl. Comp., Public Speaking, Econ., and Psych.	Microbio.	AP credits (score 4+) accepted for non-science coursework: Physics, Calc., Econ., Engl., and certain General Education coursework.
WEST COAST UNIVERSITY SCHOOL OF PHARMACY	Chem. w/ Lab, OChem. w/ Lab, Bio. (and Cell Bio.), Physics w/ Lab, Econ., Calc., Stats., Speech Communication, Engl. Comp., Psych./ Sociology, and General Electives in Humanities and Social/Behav. Science.	N/A	AP credits accepted.

For the number of hours required for prerequisite courses, and for the most up-to-date information, please refer to the individual school websites.

*A.P. credit satisfies the requirement.

** When A.P. credit is awarded, upper-level coursework in the same subject area is required.

*** A.P. credit may satisfy the requirement on a case by case basis

WESTERN UNIVERSITY OF HEALTH SCIENCES COLLEGE OF PHARMACY	Engl., Chem. w/ Lab, OChem. w/ Lab, Human Anatomy, Human Physio., Microbio., Biochem./ Molecular Bio./ Cell Bio., Speech Communication, Calc., and Bio.	Medical Microbio.	AP credits accepted as long as they are listed on undergraduate transcript.

COLORADO

PharmD Schools	Required	Recommended	Notes
REGIS UNIVERSITY RUECKERT-HARTMAN COLLEGE FOR HEALTH PROFESSIONS SCHOOL OF PHARMACY	Engl. Comp., Speech Communications, Social Sciences, Religious Studies, Calc., Econ., Chem. w/ Lab, OChem. w/ Lab, Human Anatomy, Human Physio., Cellular & Molecular Bio. w/ Lab, Organismic Bio. w/ Lab, and Additional Bio. w/ Lab: Biochem., Cell Bio., Genetics & Genomics, Immunology, Microbio., or Molecular Bio.	Psychology and Sociology.	No listed information on AP credits. Contact admissions.

For the number of hours required for prerequisite courses, and for the most up-to-date information, please refer to the individual school websites.
*A.P. credit satisfies the requirement.
** When A.P. credit is awarded, upper-level coursework in the same subject area is required.
*** A.P. credit may satisfy the requirement on a case by case basis

UNIVERSITY OF COLORADO ANSCHUTZ MEDICAL CAMPUS SKAGGS SCHOOL OF PHARMACY AND PHARMACEUTICAL SCIENCES	Biochem., Bio. w/ Lab, Chem. w/ Lab, OChem. w/ Lab, Microbio., Human Anatomy, Human Physio., Calc., Physics, Econ., Engl. Comp., Public Speaking, Humanities/Social Science, and General Education.	N/A	AP credits accepted if itemized on verified PharmCAS transcripts, otherwise official scores must be sent directly to CU Pharmacy.

CONNECTICUT

PharmD Schools	Required	Recommended	Notes
UNIVERSITY OF CONNECTICUT SCHOOL OF PHARMACY	Bio. w/ Lab, Chem. w/ Lab, OChem. w/ Lab, Biochem., Microbio., Human Anatomy & Physio., Econ., Physics w/ Lab, Engl., Arts & Humanities, and Sociology.	N/A	AP credits accepted.
UNIVERSITY OF SAINT JOSEPH SCHOOL OF PHARMACY AND PHYSICIAN ASSISTANT STUDIES	Microbio. w/ Lab, Human Anatomy and Physio. w/ Lab, Chem. w/ Lab, OChem. w/ Lab, Physics w/ Lab, Calc., Stats., Engl. Comp., second Engl. course, Oral Communication, Econ., Health-related Science, Behav. Sciences, and Humanities/Fine Arts.	N/A	No listed information on AP credits. Contact admissions.

For the number of hours required for prerequisite courses, and for the most up-to-date information, please refer to the individual school websites.

*A.P. credit satisfies the requirement.

** When A.P. credit is awarded, upper-level coursework in the same subject area is required.

*** A.P. credit may satisfy the requirement on a case by case basis

D.C.

PharmD Schools	Required	Recommended	Notes
HOWARD UNIVERSITY COLLEGE OF PHARMACY	Chem. w/ Lab, Bio., OChem. w/ Lab, Calc., Physics w/ Lab, Speech, Humanities, Socio-Behav. Sciences, General Electives, Anatomy/Physio., Biochem., and Engl.	N/A	No listed information on AP credits. Contact admissions.

FLORIDA

PharmD Schools	Required	Recommended	Notes
FLORIDA AGRICULTURAL & MECHANICAL UNIVERSITY COLLEGE OF PHARMACY AND PHARMACEUTICAL SCIENCES	Bio. w/ Lab, Anatomy & Physio. w/ Lab, Chem. w/ Lab, OChem. w/ Lab, Freshman Communication, Pre-Calc., Calc., and Physics w/ Lab.	Humanities, Soc. Science, and General Education (e.g., Public Speaking, Intro to Stats., Health Modern Living, and Intro to Afro-American Studies).	AP credit accepted for some prerequisites. Typically, a score of 3+ is required. Contact admissions for more information.
LARKIN UNIVERSITY COLLEGE OF PHARMACY	Bio. w/ Lab, Anatomy & Physio., Chem. w/ Lab, OChem. w/ Lab, Physics, Engl., Calc., Stats., Speech/ Public Speaking, Advanced Science Courses (see Recommended), Econ., Humanities or Social/Behav. Sciences, and Psych./Sociology.	Advanced Science Courses: Immunology, Microbio., Biochem., Cell Bio., Molecular Bio., or Genetics.	AP credit accepted if score is 3+.

For the number of hours required for prerequisite courses, and for the most up-to-date information, please refer to the individual school websites.
*A.P. credit satisfies the requirement.
** When A.P. credit is awarded, upper-level coursework in the same subject area is required.
*** A.P. credit may satisfy the requirement on a case by case basis

NOVA SOUTHEASTERN UNIVERSITY COLLEGE OF PHARMACY	Bio. w/ Lab, Anatomy & Physio., Chem. w/ Lab, OChem. w/ Lab, Physics, Engl., Calc., Speech/ Public Speaking, Humanities, Social/ Behav. Sciences, Extra Soc./Behav. Sciences or Humanities (see Recommended), and Advanced Sciences (see Recommended).	Extra Soc./Behav. Sciences or Humanities: Ethics, Micro/Macroecon., and General/Life Science Stats. Advanced Sciences: Cellular or Molecular Bio., Microbio., Biochem., or Genetics.	No listed information on AP credits. Contact admissions.
PALM BEACH ATLANTIC UNIVERSITY LLOYD L. GREGORY SCHOOL OF PHARMACY	Engl., Econ., Elementary Stats., Calc., Chem. w/ Lab, OChem. w/ Lab, Bio. w/ Lab, Human Anatomy & Physio. w/ Lab, Microbio. w/ Lab, Biochem., Speech, and Humanities.	Micro or Macro Econ. Recommended.	AP credits accepted for some prerequisites.
UNIVERSITY OF FLORIDA COLLEGE OF PHARMACY	Engl. Comp., Analytical Geom. w/ Calc., Soc./ Behav. Sciences, Humanities, Chem. w/ Lab, Bio. w/ Lab, OChem. w/ Lab, Anatomy/Physio. w/ Lab, Biochem., Microbio., and Stats.	N/A	AP credit accepted.

For the number of hours required for prerequisite courses, and for the most up-to-date information, please refer to the individual school websites.

*A.P. credit satisfies the requirement.

** When A.P. credit is awarded, upper-level coursework in the same subject area is required.

*** A.P. credit may satisfy the requirement on a case by case basis

UNIVERSITY OF SOUTH FLORIDA HEALTH TANEJA COLLEGE OF PHARMACY	Engl., Calc., Biochem., Genetics, Psych./Sociology, Econ., Humanities and Arts and/ or Behav./Social Sciences, Stats., Bio. w/ Lab, Chem. w/ Lab, OChem. w/ Lab, Physics, Microbio., Human Anatomy & Physio., and Cell or Molecular Bio.	N/A	AP credit accepted if score is 3+.

GEORGIA

PharmD Schools	Required	Recommended	Notes
MERCER UNIVERSITY COLLEGE OF PHARMACY	Anatomy & Physio., Bio. w/ Lab, Microbio., Chem. w/ Lab, OChem. w/ Lab, Biochem., Calc., Stats., Engl. Comp./Writing, Communication/ Speech, Econ., Humanities Electives, and Soc./ Behav. Science Electives.	At least one elective must focus on cultural diversity (e.g., Sociology, Cultural Anthropology, Cultural Geography, World Lit., World Religions, Gender Studies, or Cultural Studies in a language other than applicant's native language).	AP credits accepted as long as they are listed on undergraduate transcript.
PHILADELPHIA COLLEGE OF OSTEOPATHIC MEDICINE - GEORGIA SCHOOL OF PHARMACY	Bio. w/ Lab, Chem. w/ Lab, OChem. w/ Lab, Physics w/ Lab, Calc., Stats., Engl. Comp., Econ., Speech, Soc./Behav. Science, Humanities, and Electives.	N/A	No listed information on AP credits. Contact admissions.

For the number of hours required for prerequisite courses, and for the most up-to-date information, please refer to the individual school websites.

*A.P. credit satisfies the requirement.

** When A.P. credit is awarded, upper-level coursework in the same subject area is required.

*** A.P. credit may satisfy the requirement on a case by case basis

SOUTH UNIVERSITY SCHOOL OF PHARMACY	Engl. Comp., Lit., Bio. w/ Lab, Microbio., Chem. w/ Lab, OChem. w/ Lab, Anatomy & Physio., Econ., Psych./ Sociology, Public Speaking, Calc., Stats., and Electives.	Lab recommended for Physics and Anatomy & Physio. Elective should be in the Humanities, Social/Behav. Sciences, or Arts.	No listed information on AP credits. Contact admissions.
UNIVERSITY OF GEORGIA COLLEGE OF PHARMACY	Engl. Comp., Calc., Stats., Communication/ Speech, Macro/ Microecon., Soc./ Behav. Sciences, World Languages & Culture, Chem. w/ Lab, OChem. w/ Lab, Bio. w/ Lab, Microbio., Biochem., and Anatomy & Physio.	N/A	AP credits accepted as long as they are listed on undergraduate transcript.

HAWAII

PharmD Schools	Required	Recommended	Notes
UNIVERSITY OF HAWAII AT HILO DANIEL K. INOUYE COLLEGE OF PHARMACY	Engl. Comp./Writing, Humanities, Soc./ Behav. Sciences, World Cultural Diversity, Econ., Communication/ Speech, Calc., Bio. w Lab, Human Anatomy & Physio. w/ Lab, Microbio. w/ Lab, Chem. w/ Lab, and OChem. w/ Lab.	N/A	AP credits accepted as long as they are listed on undergraduate transcript. AP credits cannot be used for lab components.

For the number of hours required for prerequisite courses, and for the most up-to-date information, please refer to the individual school websites.

*A.P. credit satisfies the requirement.

** When A.P. credit is awarded, upper-level coursework in the same subject area is required.

*** A.P. credit may satisfy the requirement on a case by case basis

IDAHO

PharmD Schools	Required	Recommended	Notes
IDAHO STATE UNIVERSITY COLLEGE OF PHARMACY	Bio. w/ Lab, Chem. w/ Lab, Stats., Calc., OChem. w/ Lab, Biochem., Physics/Biophysics, Microbio. w/ Lab, Econ., Anatomy & Physio. w/ Lab, and General Ed/ Electives.	N/A	AP credit accepted.

ILLINOIS

PharmD Schools	Required	Recommended	Notes
CHICAGO STATE UNIVERSITY COLLEGE OF PHARMACY	Engl. Comp., Bio. w/ Lab, Anatomy w/ Lab, Chem. w/ Lab, OChem. w/ Lab, Physics, Calc., Speech., Econ., Stats. (see Notes), Psych./Sociology, Additional Coursework (Social/ Behav. Sciences, Humanities, Fine Arts, For. Lang., Business or Comp. Sciences).	N/A	Stats. must include probability testing, population stats., and hypothesis testing up to simple regression. AP credits accepted as long as they are listed on undergraduate transcript.

For the number of hours required for prerequisite courses, and for the most up-to-date information, please refer to the individual school websites.
*A.P. credit satisfies the requirement.
** When A.P. credit is awarded, upper-level coursework in the same subject area is required.
*** A.P. credit may satisfy the requirement on a case by case basis

MIDWESTERN UNIVERSITY CHICAGO COLLEGE OF PHARMACY	Bio. w/ Lab, Human/ Vertebrate Anatomy, Soc./Behav. Science Electives, General Education Electives (see Recommended), Chem. w/ Lab, OChem. w/ Lab, Physics, Calc., Engl. Comp., Speech/ Public Speaking, Econ., and Stats. (General or Biostatistics).	General Education Electives: Art & Humanities, Additional Soc./ Behav. Sciences, For. Lang., Business, and Computer courses.	No listed information on AP credits. Contact admissions.
ROOSEVELT UNIVERSITY COLLEGE OF PHARMACY	Bio. w/ Lab, Chem. w/ Lab, OChem. w/ Lab, Physics, Anatomy & Physio. w/ Lab, Calc., Econ., Stats., Engl. Comp., Speech Communication, Humanities and/or Soc./Behav. Science Courses.	N/A	AP credits accepted as long as they are listed on undergraduate transcript and score is a 4+.
ROSALIND FRANKLIN UNIVERSITY OF MEDICINE AND SCIENCE COLLEGE OF PHARMACY	Bio. w/ Lab, Chem. w/ Lab, OChem. w/ Lab, Microbio., Anatomy or Anatomy & Physio. w/ Lab, Calc., Written Comm., Oral Comm., Stats., Social/Behav. Sci., Humanities, and Electives.	Spanish highly recommended.	AP credits may be accepted for certain prerequisites. Contact admissions for more information.

For the number of hours required for prerequisite courses, and for the most up-to-date information, please refer to the individual school websites.
*A.P. credit satisfies the requirement.
** When A.P. credit is awarded, upper-level coursework in the same subject area is required.
*** A.P. credit may satisfy the requirement on a case by case basis

| SOUTHERN ILLINOIS UNIVERSITY EDWARDSVILLE SCHOOL OF PHARMACY | Bio. w/ Lab, Anatomy & Physio. w/ Lab, Microbio./ Bacteriology, Chem. w/ Lab, OChem. w/ Lab, Calc., Stats., Physics w/ Lab, Engl. Comp., Speech/ Communication, Econ., Philosophy, and Behav./Soc. Sciences. | N/A | AP credits accepted as long as they are listed on undergraduate transcript. |
| UNIVERSITY OF ILLINOIS AT CHICAGO COLLEGE OF PHARMACY | Engl. Comp./Writing, Communication/ Speech, Additional course in Communication, Bio. w/ Lab, Anatomy & Physio., Microbio. w/ Lab, Chem. w/ Lab, Biochem., Physics, Calc., Stats., Social/ Behav. Science, and Humanities. | N/A | No listed information on AP credits. Contact admissions. |

INDIANA

PharmD Schools	Required	Recommended	Notes
BUTLER UNIVERSITY COLLEGE OF PHARMACY AND HEALTH SCIENCES	Chem. w/ Lab, OChem. w/ Lab, Cell Bio., Microbio. w/ Lab, Human Anatomy & Physio., and Calc.	N/A	Students seeking direct entry pathway may not count more than 3 courses through AP credits.
MANCHESTER UNIVERSITY COLLEGE OF PHARMACY, NATURAL AND HEALTH SCIENCES	Chem. w/ Lab, OChem. w/ Lab, Bio. w/ Lab, Microbio. w/ Lab, Physics, Stats., Calc., Communications/ Speech, Engl. Comp., Econ., Humanities, Social Science., Other Electives	At least one humanities/ social science electives should deal with primarily international culture.	AP credits accepted as long as they are listed on undergraduate transcript.

For the number of hours required for prerequisite courses, and for the most up-to-date information, please refer to the individual school websites.

*A.P. credit satisfies the requirement.

** When A.P. credit is awarded, upper-level coursework in the same subject area is required.

*** A.P. credit may satisfy the requirement on a case by case basis

	Anatomy & Physio. w/ Lab, Calc., Econ., Engl. Comp., Bio. w/ Lab, Chem. w/ Lab, Microbio. w/ Lab, OChem. w/ Lab, Physics w/ Lab, Immunology (preferred, also accept Cell Bio., Genetics, or Cancer Bio.), Biochem., Stats., and Speech Communications.	N/A	AP credits accepted.
PURDUE UNIVERSITY COLLEGE OF PHARMACY			

IOWA

PharmD Schools	Required	Recommended	Notes
DRAKE UNIVERSITY COLLEGE OF PHARMACY AND HEALTH SCIENCES	Chem. w/ Lab, OChem. w/ Lab, Bio. w/ Lab, Microbio. w/ Lab, Stats., Calc., Engl. Comp./Writing, and Public Speaking.	N/A	Must score 4+ on AP exams to obtain credit towards prerequisites.
UNIVERSITY OF IOWA COLLEGE OF PHARMACY	Engl. Comp.*, Chem., Calc.*, Stats.*, Bio., Physics, OChem., Anatomy, Physio., Microecon.*, Biochem., Microbio., and General Ed. Coursework*.	N/A	AP credit accepted.

For the number of hours required for prerequisite courses, and for the most up-to-date information, please refer to the individual school websites.

*A.P. credit satisfies the requirement.

** When A.P. credit is awarded, upper-level coursework in the same subject area is required.

*** A.P. credit may satisfy the requirement on a case by case basis

KANSAS

PharmD Schools	Required	Recommended	Notes
UNIVERSITY OF KANSAS SCHOOL OF PHARMACY	Chem., Calc., OChem., Microbio., Anatomy, Physio., Physics, Molecular/ Cell. Bio., Social Sciences/ Humanities, Engl., Public Speaking, and Stats.	N/A	AP credits accepted, although KU strongly recommends taking classroom-based credit in a college.

KENTUCKY

PharmD Schools	Required	Recommended	Notes
SULLIVAN UNIVERSITY COLLEGE OF PHARMACY	Engl. Comp., Chem. w/ Lab, OChem., Calc., Bio. w/ Lab, Microbio. w/ Lab, Human Anatomy & Physio., Econ., Public Speaking, Stats., and General Ed. Electives.	N/A	AP credits accepted for coursework, not for labs.
UNIVERSITY OF KENTUCKY COLLEGE OF PHARMACY	Bio. w/ Lab, Microbio. w/ Lab, Chem. w/ Lab, OChem. w/ Lab, Anatomy, Physio., Stats., Math, Business, Engl. Comp., Communication/ Speech, and Electives.	N/A	AP credits accepted for certain courses. Contact admissions.

For the number of hours required for prerequisite courses, and for the most up-to-date information, please refer to the individual school websites.

*A.P. credit satisfies the requirement.

** When A.P. credit is awarded, upper-level coursework in the same subject area is required.

*** A.P. credit may satisfy the requirement on a case by case basis

LOUISIANA

PharmD Schools	Required	Recommended	Notes
UNIVERSITY OF LOUISIANA AT MONROE COLLEGE OF PHARMACY	Engl. Comp., Physics w/ Lab, Stats., Econ., Public Speaking, Humanities, Social Sciences, Fine Arts, Microbio. w/ Lab, Anatomy and Physio. w/ Lab, Cell Bio./Cell Physio., Genetics, Calc., Chem. w/ Lab, OChem. w/ Lab, and Biochem.	N/A	AP credit accepted.
XAVIER UNIVERSITY OF LOUISIANA COLLEGE OF PHARMACY	Bio. w/ Lab, Microbio. w/ Lab, Chem. w/ Lab, OChem. w/ Lab, Physics w/ Lab, Calc., Biostats., Comp. & Rhetoric, Comp. & Lit., Public Speaking, Health Ethics, Psych./ Sociology, and Theology.	N/A	No listed information on AP credits. Contact admissions.

MAINE

PharmD Schools	Required	Recommended	Notes
HUSSON UNIVERSITY SCHOOL OF PHARMACY	Chem. w/ Lab, OChem. w/ Lab, Bio. w/ Lab, Human Anatomy and Physio. w/ Lab, Calc., Stats., Rhetoric & Comp., Econ., Intro to Psych/Sociology, Speech, Electives.	N/A	AP credit accepted only for non-Math, non-Chemistry, and non-Biology courses (e.g., History, Spanish, etc.)

For the number of hours required for prerequisite courses, and for the most up-to-date information, please refer to the individual school websites.
*A.P. credit satisfies the requirement.
** When A.P. credit is awarded, upper-level coursework in the same subject area is required.
*** A.P. credit may satisfy the requirement on a case by case basis

UNIVERSITY OF NEW ENGLAND COLLEGE OF PHARMACY	Cell Bio. w/ Lab, Human Anatomy & Physio. w/ Lab, Chem. w/ Lab, OChem. w/ Lab, Physics, Microbio., Calc., Stats. for Life Sciences, Engl. Comp., Social Science, Public Speaking, Humanities/Liberal Arts, Social/Global Awareness, and Gen. Ed.	N/A	AP credits accepted as long as they are listed on undergraduate transcript.

MARYLAND

PharmD Schools	Required	Recommended	Notes
NOTRE DAME OF MARYLAND UNIVERSITY SCHOOL OF PHARMACY	Engl., Speech/Public Speaking, Anatomy & Physio. w/ Lab, Physics, Psych./ Social Science/ Political Science, General Education (See Notes), Ethics, Econ., Calc., Stats., Chem. w/ Lab, OChem. w/ Lab, Bio. w/ Lab, and Microbio. w/ Lab.	Medical ethics preferred over Ethics. Biostats. preferred over Stats.	General Education may be divided among the following: Fine Arts, Religious Studies, Business, For. Lang., and Humanities. Science, Math, Physical Education, and Health Care coursework will not satisfy this requirement. AP credits accepted.

For the number of hours required for prerequisite courses, and for the most up-to-date information, please refer to the individual school websites.
*A.P. credit satisfies the requirement.
** When A.P. credit is awarded, upper-level coursework in the same subject area is required.
*** A.P. credit may satisfy the requirement on a case by case basis

252

UNIVERSITY OF MARYLAND EASTERN SHORE SCHOOL OF PHARMACY AND HEALTH PROFESSIONS	Chem. w/ Lab, OChem. w/ Lab, Bio. w/ Lab, Anatomy & Physio. w/ Lab, Microbio. w/ Lab, Physics w/ Lab, Calc., Stats., Public/Speaking/ Interpersonal Communication, Engl. Comp./Lit, Econ., Humanities/ Social Sciences (see Recommended).	Humanities/Social Sciences: Sociology, Psychology, Arts, Music, History. Introductory Biochem. course is strongly encouraged.	AP credits accepted for science coursework if score is 4+ and they are accepted for non-science coursework if score is 3+. They must be listed on the undergraduate transcript.
UNIVERSITY OF MARYLAND SCHOOL OF PHARMACY	Engl. Comp./Writing, Chem. w/ Lab, Communication/ Speech, Microecon., OChem. w/ Lab, Bio. w/ Lab, Calc., Physics w/ Lab, Microbio. w/ Lab, Stats., Human Anatomy & Physio., and Humanities.	N/A	AP credits accepted.

MASSACHUSETTS

PharmD Schools	Required	Recommended	Notes
MCPHS UNIVERSITY SCHOOL OF PHARMACY - BOSTON	N/A	N/A	This program is intended for high school applicants.

For the number of hours required for prerequisite courses, and for the most up-to-date information, please refer to the individual school websites.
*A.P. credit satisfies the requirement.
** When A.P. credit is awarded, upper-level coursework in the same subject area is required.
*** A.P. credit may satisfy the requirement on a case by case basis

MCPHS UNIVERSITY SCHOOL OF PHARMACY - WORCESTER	Bio. w/ Lab, Chem. w/ Lab, Microbio. w/ Lab, OChem. w/ Lab, Calc., Math or Computer Science Elective, Stats., and Physics w/ Lab. If you do not have a U.S. or Canadian Bachelor's Degree, additional coursework required: Engl. Comp., English Elective, Intro to Psych., Intro to Sociology, Intro to History or Political Science, Econ, Humanities Elective, Social Science Elective, and Behavioral Science elective.	N/A	AP credits accepted if score is above 4.
NORTHEASTERN UNIVERSITY BOUVÉ COLLEGE OF HEALTH SCIENCES SCHOOL OF PHARMACY	Chem. w/ Lab, Bio. w/ Lab, OChem. w/ Lab, Biochem., Calc./Stats., Physics, Arts/Humanities/ Social Sciences, and Human Physio. w/ Anatomy.	N/A	AP credits accepted as long as they are listed on undergraduate transcript.

For the number of hours required for prerequisite courses, and for the most up-to-date information, please refer to the individual school websites.
*A.P. credit satisfies the requirement.
** When A.P. credit is awarded, upper-level coursework in the same subject area is required.
*** A.P. credit may satisfy the requirement on a case by case basis

| WESTERN NEW ENGLAND UNIVERSITY COLLEGE OF PHARMACY | Bio. w/ Lab, Human Anatomy & Physio. w/ Lab, Chem. w/ Lab, OChem. w/ Lab, Microbio. w/ Lab, Physics w/ Lab, Calc., Stats., Engl. Comp., Econ., Psych., Public Speaking, Ethics, Social Science Elective or Public/ Population-based Health. | N/A | AP credits for non-science subjects accepted. |

MICHIGAN

PharmD Schools	Required	Recommended	Notes
FERRIS STATE UNIVERSITY COLLEGE OF PHARMACY	Chem. w/ Lab, OChem. w/ Lab, Biochem., Bio. w/ Lab, Anatomy & Physio., Microbio. w/ Lab, Genetics, Physics, Calc., Stats., Engl. Comp., Public Speaking/ Interpersonal Communication, Psych./Sociology, Econ., and cultural enrichment course.	N/A	AP credits accepted for certain coursework.
UNIVERSITY OF MICHIGAN COLLEGE OF PHARMACY	Bio.*, Biochem., Calc.*, Chem. w/ Lab*, OChem. w/ Lab, Engl. Comp., Genetics, Human Anatomy, Human Physio., Microbio. w/ Lab, Physics w/ Lab*, Stats.*, Humanities or For. Lang.*, and Social Science*.	Statistics involving ANOVA, chi square tests, and multiple regression comparisons strongly recommended.	AP credits accepted for certain coursework.

For the number of hours required for prerequisite courses, and for the most up-to-date information, please refer to the individual school websites.
*A.P. credit satisfies the requirement.
** When A.P. credit is awarded, upper-level coursework in the same subject area is required.
*** A.P. credit may satisfy the requirement on a case by case basis

WAYNE STATE UNIVERSITY EUGENE APPLEBAUM COLLEGE OF PHARMACY AND HEALTH SCIENCES	Microbio. w/ Lab, Anatomy & Physio., Chem. w/ Lab, OChem. w/ Lab, Calc., Physics w/ Lab, Biochem., Bio., College Writing, Oral Communication, Stats., and General Ed.	N/A	AP credits may be accepted.

MINNESOTA

PharmD Schools	Required	Recommended	Notes
UNIVERSITY OF MINNESOTA COLLEGE OF PHARMACY	Bio. w/ Lab*, Microbio., Human/ Comparative Anatomy, Human/ Comparative Physio., Advanced Bio., Calc.*, Stats.*, Chem. w/ Lab*, OChem. w/ Lab, Physics*, Soc./ Behav. Sciences*, Engl. Comp., and Communication.	N/A	AP credit accepted if listed on undergraduate transcript and score is 3+.

MISSISSIPPI

PharmD Schools	Required	Recommended	Notes
UNIVERSITY OF MISSISSIPPI SCHOOL OF PHARMACY	Engl. Comp., OChem. w/ Lab, Physics w/ Lab, Social Sciences, Humanities & Fine Arts, Bioethics, Biochem., Human Physio., Medical Microbio., Speech, Genetics, Calc., Chem. w/ Lab, Bio. w/ Lab, Stats., Microecon., and Human Anatomy.	N/A	AP credits accepted for non-science coursework.

For the number of hours required for prerequisite courses, and for the most up-to-date information, please refer to the individual school websites.

*A.P. credit satisfies the requirement.

** When A.P. credit is awarded, upper-level coursework in the same subject area is required.

*** A.P. credit may satisfy the requirement on a case by case basis

| WILLIAM CAREY UNIVERSITY SCHOOL OF PHARMACY | Engl. Comp., Public Speaking/Speech, General Education, Econ., Bio. w/ Lab, Anatomy & Physio. w/ Lab, Chem. w/ Lab, OChem. w/ Lab, Physics, Calc., Stats., and Social Sciences. | N/A | AP credits accepted on a case-by-case basis. |

MISSOURI

PharmD Schools	Required	Recommended	Notes
ST. LOUIS COLLEGE OF PHARMACY	Chem. w/ Lab, OChem. w/ Lab, Biochem., Bio. w/ Lab, Human Anatomy & Physio. w/ Lab, Microbio. w/ Lab, Calc., Stats., Physics w/ Lab, Engl. Comp./ College Writing, Public Speaking/ Communication., Psych./Sociology, Microecon./ Macroecon./Survey of Econ course, and General Liberal Arts/ Humanities.	N/A	No listed information on AP credits. Contact admissions.

For the number of hours required for prerequisite courses, and for the most up-to-date information, please refer to the individual school websites.

*A.P. credit satisfies the requirement.

** When A.P. credit is awarded, upper-level coursework in the same subject area is required.

*** A.P. credit may satisfy the requirement on a case by case basis

UNIVERSITY OF MISSOURI-KANSAS CITY SCHOOL OF PHARMACY	Chem. w/ Lab, Calc. w/ Analytical Geometry, Human Anatomy w/ Lab, Communication/ Speech, OChem. w/ Lab, Microbio. w/ Lab, Medical Terminology, Humanities (Course covering U.S. gov.), Bio., Engl. Comp., Physics w/ Lab, Cell Bio., and Stats.	N/A	AP scores must be sent from the testing agency to UMKC.

MONTANA

PharmD Schools	Required	Recommended	Notes
UNIVERSITY OF MONTANA COLLEGE OF HEALTH PROFESSIONS AND BIOMEDICAL SCIENCES SKAGGS SCHOOL OF PHARMACY	Human Anatomy & Physio., Chem. w/ Lab, Calc., College Writing, Cell & Molecular Bio., OChem. w/ Lab, Econ., Physics w/ Lab, Stats., Sociology/Psych., Public Speaking, and Electives.	N/A	AP credit accepted for certain coursework, such as Calc., Econ., Engl., Psych., and Stats.

NEBRASKA

PharmD Schools	Required	Recommended	Notes
CREIGHTON UNIVERSITY SCHOOL OF PHARMACY AND HEALTH PROFESSIONS	Bio. w/ Lab, Human Anatomy, Chem. w/ Lab, OChem. w/ Lab, Calc., Engl. Comp., Speech, Psych., Econ., and Electives from Humanities or Soc./Behav. Sciences.	N/A	AP credits accepted as long as they are listed on undergraduate transcript.

For the number of hours required for prerequisite courses, and for the most up-to-date information, please refer to the individual school websites.

*A.P. credit satisfies the requirement.

** When A.P. credit is awarded, upper-level coursework in the same subject area is required.

*** A.P. credit may satisfy the requirement on a case by case basis

UNIVERSITY OF NEBRASKA MEDICAL CENTER COLLEGE OF PHARMACY	Chem. w/ Lab, OChem. w/ Lab, Biochem., Physics w/ Lab, Quantitative Chem. Analysis or Physics 2, Bio. w/ Lab, Anatomy, Physio., Engl. Comp., Speech, Calc., Stats./Biostats., and General Ed.	N/A	AP credits accepted as long as they are listed on undergraduate transcript.

NEVADA

PharmD Schools	Required	Recommended	Notes
ROSEMAN UNIVERSITY OF HEALTH SCIENCES COLLEGE OF PHARMACY	Chem. w/ Lab, OChem. w/ Lab, Calc., Microbio., Human Anatomy, Human Physio., Engl. Comp., and Speech/ Communications.	Biochem. and Molecular Bio.	AP credits accepted for Calc. and Chem. if score is 3+.

NEW MEXICO

PharmD Schools	Required	Recommended	Notes
UNIVERSITY OF NEW MEXICO COLLEGE OF PHARMACY	Engl. Comp., Chem. w/ Lab, OChem. w/ Lab, Molecular & Cell Bio., Genetics, Microbio. w/ Lab, Anatomy & Physio., Econ., Calc., Stats., Physics, and Communications Elective	Biochem.	No listed information on AP credits. Contact admissions.

For the number of hours required for prerequisite courses, and for the most up-to-date information, please refer to the individual school websites.

*A.P. credit satisfies the requirement.

** When A.P. credit is awarded, upper-level coursework in the same subject area is required.

*** A.P. credit may satisfy the requirement on a case by case basis

NEW JERSEY

PharmD Schools	Required	Recommended	Notes
FAIRLEIGH DICKINSON UNIVERSITY SCHOOL OF PHARMACY	Bio. w/ Lab, Anatomy & Physio. w/ Lab, Chem. w/ Lab, OChem. w/ Lab, Physics w/ Lab, Biochem., Calc., Stats., Engl., and Free Electives.	Speech or Professional Communication and Econ.	AP credits accepted as long as they are listed on undergraduate transcript.
RUTGERS, THE STATE UNIVERSITY OF NEW JERSEY ERNEST MARIO SCHOOL OF PHARMACY	Bio w. Lab, Chem. w/ Lab, OChem. w/ Lab, Anatomy & Physio., Physics w/ Lab, Calc., Research Stats., Intro to Microecon., College-level Writing, and Humanities/Social Science electives.	N/A	Up to 8 AP credits accepted.

NEW YORK

PharmD Schools	Required	Recommended	Notes
ALBANY COLLEGE OF PHARMACY AND HEALTH SCIENCES SCHOOL OF PHARMACY AND PHARMACEUTICAL SCIENCES	Chem. w/ Lab, Bio. w/ Lab, OChem. w/ Lab, 200-level Bio., Stats. Calc., Microbio. w/ Lab, Physics w/ Lab, Public Speaking, Humanities, Social Science Elective, General Electives.	N/A	AP credits accepted as long as they are listed on undergraduate transcript.

For the number of hours required for prerequisite courses, and for the most up-to-date information, please refer to the individual school websites.
*A.P. credit satisfies the requirement.
** When A.P. credit is awarded, upper-level coursework in the same subject area is required.
*** A.P. credit may satisfy the requirement on a case by case basis

BINGHAMTON UNIVERSITY STATE UNIVERSITY OF NEW YORK SCHOOL OF PHARMACY AND PHARMACEUTICAL SCIENCES	Engl., Bio. w/ Lab*, Chem. w/ Lab*, OChem. w/ Lab, Microbio., Anatomy & Physio., Physics w/ Lab*, Calc.*, Stats.*, Econ., and Social/ Behav. Sciences.	Calc. 2, Physics 2, and Biochem.	AP credits accepted for starred subjects. Score of 4+ accepted for first course in sequence (e.g., Bio 1). Typically, score of 5+ accepted for second course in sequence (e.g., Bio 2). See website for more details.
D'YOUVILLE COLLEGE SCHOOL OF PHARMACY	Bio. w/ Lab, 200-level Bio., Chem. w/ Lab, OChem. w/ Lab, Physics w/ Lab, Calc., Stats., Engl. Comp., Humanities, Communication/ Speech, and Econ.	N/A	AP credits not accepted.
LONG ISLAND UNIVERSITY ARNOLD AND MARIE SCHWARTZ COLLEGE OF PHARMACY AND HEALTH SCIENCES	Contact admissions.	N/A	AP credits accepted as long as they are listed on undergraduate transcript.
ST. JOHN FISHER COLLEGE WEGMANS SCHOOL OF PHARMACY	Chem. w/ Lab, Bio. w/ Lab, Physics w/ Lab, OChem., Engl. Comp., Stats., Calc., Humanities/ Social Sciences, and Econ. (Microecon. preferred).	General Bio., Anatomy, Physio., and Microbio.	AP credits may not be used to fulfill science requirements.
ST. JOHN'S UNIVERSITY COLLEGE OF PHARMACY AND HEALTH SCIENCES	N/A	N/A	This program is intended for high school applicants.

For the number of hours required for prerequisite courses, and for the most up-to-date information, please refer to the individual school websites.

*A.P. credit satisfies the requirement.

** When A.P. credit is awarded, upper-level coursework in the same subject area is required.

*** A.P. credit may satisfy the requirement on a case by case basis

TOURO NEW YORK COLLEGE OF PHARMACY	Chem. w/ Lab, OChem. w/ Lab, Biochem., Human Anatomy w/ Lab or Anatomy & Physio. w/ Lab, Physio. w/ Lab or Anatomy and Physio. 2 w/ Lab, Microbio. w/ Lab, Calc., Econ., Physics w/ Lab, Engl. Comp., Public Speaking, Humanities, and Social/Behav. Science.	N/A	AP credits accepted as long as they are listed on undergraduate transcript.
UNIVERSITY AT BUFFALO THE STATE UNIVERSITY OF NEW YORK SCHOOL OF PHARMACY & PHARMACEUTICAL SCIENCES	Chem. w/ Lab*, OChem. w/ Lab,, Bio. w/ Lab*, Microbio., Biochem., Anatomy, Physio., Calc.*, Stats.*, Engl. Comp., and Social Science.	N/A	AP credits accepted if score is 4+.

NORTH CAROLINA

PharmD Schools	Required	Recommended	Notes
CAMPBELL UNIVERSITY COLLEGE OF PHARMACY AND HEALTH SCIENCES	Calc., Physics w/ Lab, Chem. w/ Lab, OChem. w/ Lab, Bio. w/ Lab, Microbio. w/ Lab, Human Anatomy & Physio. w/ Lab, Stats., Engl. Comp., Humanities/Fine Arts or Social/Behav. Science, and Electives (see Recommended).	Electives: Advanced biology or chemistry strongly encouraged. In addition, certain business electives may meet requirements for the dual PharmD/MBA.	No listed information on AP credits. Contact admissions.

For the number of hours required for prerequisite courses, and for the most up-to-date information, please refer to the individual school websites.
*A.P. credit satisfies the requirement.
** When A.P. credit is awarded, upper-level coursework in the same subject area is required.
*** A.P. credit may satisfy the requirement on a case by case basis

HIGH POINT UNIVERSITY FRED WILSON SCHOOL OF PHARMACY	Chem. w/ Lab, OChem. w/ Lab, Bio. w/ Lab, Physio. w/ Lab, Microbio. w/ Lab, Calc., Physics, Engl. Comp./Writing, Communication/ Speech, Social/ Behav. Sciences, and Electives as needed.	N/A	No listed information on AP credits. Contact admissions.
UNIVERSITY OF NORTH CAROLINA ESHELMAN SCHOOL OF PHARMACY	Chem. w/ Lab, Calc., Stats., OChem. w/ Lab, Bio. w/ Lab, Human Anatomy & Physio. w/ Lab, Microbio. w/ Lab, Physics w/ Lab, and Biochem.	N/A	AP credits accepted on a case-by-case basis.
WINGATE UNIVERSITY SCHOOL OF PHARMACY	Chem. w/ Lab, Calc., Stats., OChem. w/ Lab, Bio. w/ Lab, Anatomy & Physio. w/ Lab, Microbio. w/ Lab, Engl. Comp./ Writing, Humanities, Physics w/ Lab, and Electives.	N/A	AP credits accepted as long as they are listed on undergraduate transcript.

For the number of hours required for prerequisite courses, and for the most up-to-date information, please refer to the individual school websites.

*A.P. credit satisfies the requirement.

** When A.P. credit is awarded, upper-level coursework in the same subject area is required.

*** A.P. credit may satisfy the requirement on a case by case basis

NORTH DAKOTA

PharmD Schools	Required	Recommended	Notes
NORTH DAKOTA STATE UNIVERSITY COLLEGE OF HEALTH PROFESSIONS SCHOOL OF PHARMACY	Anatomy & Physio. w/ Lab, Bio. w/ Lab, Microbio. w/ Lab, Chem. w/ Lab, OChem. w/ Lab, Biochem., Physics, Microecon., Intercultural Communication, Stats., Calc., Engl. Comp./Writing, Communication/ Speech, Humanities Elective, and Wellness Elective.	N/A	AP credits accepted as long as they are listed on undergraduate transcript.

OHIO

PharmD Schools	Required	Recommended	Notes
CEDARVILLE UNIVERSITY SCHOOL OF PHARMACY	Engl. Comp., Speech, Chem. w/ Lab, OChem. w/ Lab, Calc., Physics w/ Lab, Bio. w/ Lab, Anatomy & Physio. w/ Lab, Microbio. w/ Lab, Cell Bio., and Advanced Physio. (see Notes).	N/A	Advanced Physio. not req. if Anatomy & Physio. courses are at the 3000 level. AP credits accepted.
NORTHEAST OHIO MEDICAL UNIVERSITY COLLEGE OF PHARMACY	Anatomy & Physio., Chem. w/ Lab, OChem. w/ Lab, Bio. w/ Lab, Microbio., Physics, Calc., Stats., Engl. Comp., and Additional Science Electives	Health Science Statistics	AP credits accepted as long as they are listed on undergraduate transcript.

For the number of hours required for prerequisite courses, and for the most up-to-date information, please refer to the individual school websites.
*A.P. credit satisfies the requirement.
** When A.P. credit is awarded, upper-level coursework in the same subject area is required.
*** A.P. credit may satisfy the requirement on a case by case basis

OHIO NORTHERN UNIVERSITY RAABE COLLEGE OF PHARMACY	Chem. w/ Lab, OChem. w/ Lab, Bio. w/ Lab, Anatomy & Physio. w/ Lab, Physics, Calc., Stats., Engl. Comp., Psych./Sociology, Communications/ Speech, and Humanities.	N/A	AP credits accepted as long as they are listed on undergraduate transcript.
OHIO STATE UNIVERSITY COLLEGE OF PHARMACY	Bio. w/ Lab, Chem. w/ Lab, OChem. w/ Lab, Physics w/ Lab, Calc., Human Anatomy w/ Lab, Microbio. w/ Lab, Stats., Biochem., and Human Physio.	N/A	AP credits may be accepted for certain courses. Contact admissions for more information.
UNIVERSITY OF CINCINNATI JAMES L. WINKLE COLLEGE OF PHARMACY	Engl. Comp./Writing, Stats., Chem. w/ Lab, Bio. w/ Lab, OChem. w/ Lab, Physics w/ Lab, Calc., Microbio., Anatomy & Physio., and Biochem.	N/A	AP credits may be accepted. Applicant should contact admissions for further information on which courses are accepted.
UNIVERSITY OF FINDLAY COLLEGE OF PHARMACY	Cell./Molecular Bio. w/ Lab, Immunology, Human Genetics w/ Lab, Microbio. w/ Lab, Chem. w/ Lab, OChem. w/ Lab, College Writing, Physics, Health Care Ethics, Engl. Comp./ Writing, Calc., and Stats & Data Analysis.	N/A	AP credits accepted. Contact admissions for more information.
UNIVERSITY OF TOLEDO COLLEGE OF PHARMACY AND PHARMACEUTICAL SCIENCES	Bio. w/ Lab, Chem. w/ Lab, OChem. w/ Lab, Physics, Calc., Intro to Physio. or Anatomy & Physio., Engl. Comp., and Stats.	N/A	AP credits accepted if sent by the testing agency.

For the number of hours required for prerequisite courses, and for the most up-to-date information, please refer to the individual school websites.

*A.P. credit satisfies the requirement.

** When A.P. credit is awarded, upper-level coursework in the same subject area is required.

*** A.P. credit may satisfy the requirement on a case by case basis

OKLAHOMA

PharmD Schools	Required	Recommended	Notes
SOUTHWESTERN OKLAHOMA STATE UNIVERSITY COLLEGE OF PHARMACY	Engl. Comp., American Gov., U.S. History, Computer Science, Calc., Bio. w/ Lab, Microbio. w/ Lab, Human Anatomy w/ Lab, Chem. w/ Lab, OChem. w/ Lab, Physics, Psych., Macroecon., World History/World Cultural Geography/ Humanities, Public Speaking, and Humanities coursework.	N/A	AP credits accepted.
UNIVERSITY OF OKLAHOMA COLLEGE OF PHARMACY	Calc., Physics, Chem. w/ Lab, OChem. w/ Lab, Bio., Engl., Microbio. w/ Lab, and Electives.	Electives: Stats., Computer Science, Diversity coursework, Econ., Communications, Behav. Science, and an additional Math course.	AP credits accepted as long as they are listed on undergraduate transcript.

For the number of hours required for prerequisite courses, and for the most up-to-date information, please refer to the individual school websites.
*A.P. credit satisfies the requirement.
** When A.P. credit is awarded, upper-level coursework in the same subject area is required.
*** A.P. credit may satisfy the requirement on a case by case basis

OREGON

PharmD Schools	Required	Recommended	Notes
OREGON STATE UNIVERSITY COLLEGE OF PHARMACY	Chem. w/ Lab, Bio. w/ Lab, Physics w/ Lab, OChem. w/ Lab, Microbio. w/ Lab, Human Physio., Human Anatomy, Biochem., Calc., Stats., and Public Health Care Delivery/Econ.	Medical Terminology, Medical Ethics, Bioethics, Scientific Reasoning, Advanced coursework in Writing or Language, and Additional social/biomedical science coursework: Cell & Molecular Bio., Genetics, Epidemiology, Physical Chem., Biostats., Ecology, Evolution, Virology, Immunology, Public Health, Bioinformatics, or Computer Skills.	No listed information on AP credits. Contact admissions.
PACIFIC UNIVERSITY SCHOOL OF PHARMACY	Bio. w/ Lab, Microbio., Anatomy & Physio. w/ Lab, Chem. w/ Lab, OChem. w/ Lab, Physics w/ Lab, Calc., Engl. Comp., Speech, Psych., Econ., Social/Behav. Sciences, and Humanities/Fine Arts.	Biochem., Molecular Bio., Genetics, Cell Bio., and Immunology.	AP credit (score 4+) is accepted for non-science coursework.

For the number of hours required for prerequisite courses, and for the most up-to-date information, please refer to the individual school websites.

*A.P. credit satisfies the requirement.

** When A.P. credit is awarded, upper-level coursework in the same subject area is required.

*** A.P. credit may satisfy the requirement on a case by case basis

PENNSYLVANIA

PharmD Schools	Required	Recommended	Notes
DUQUESNE UNIVERSITY SCHOOL OF PHARMACY	Bio. w/ Lab, Chem. w/ Lab, OChem. w/ Lab, Physics w/ Lab, Calc., Engl. Comp. and Lit., and Humanities.	N/A	No listed information on AP credits. Contact admissions.
LAKE ERIE COLLEGE OF OSTEOPATHIC MEDICINE SCHOOL OF PHARMACY	Bio. w/ Lab (see Recommended), Chem. w/ Lab, OChem. w/ Lab (see Notes), Math-based Physics or Physical Chem., Calc., Stats., Econ., Psych/Sociology/ Anthropology, Engl. (see Recommended), and Didactic Coursework in Math, Science or Humanities.	Bio.: Zoology, Genetics, Cell, Micro, Immunology, Molecular, Animal Physio., Vertebrate Anatomy, or health-foundational bio. Engl.: Writing (Technical Business, or Research).	AP credits accepted for coursework with a score of 3+. OChem. 2 may be substituted with Biochem. w/ Lab
TEMPLE UNIVERSITY SCHOOL OF PHARMACY	Calc., Chem. w/ Lab, Bio. w/ Lab, OChem. w/ Lab, Physics w/ Lab, Anatomy/ Physio., Analytical Reading/Writing Engl. Comp, Econ., Social Sciences, Humanities, and Stats.	N/A	No listed information on AP credits. Contact admissions.

For the number of hours required for prerequisite courses, and for the most up-to-date information, please refer to the individual school websites.
*A.P. credit satisfies the requirement.
** When A.P. credit is awarded, upper-level coursework in the same subject area is required.
*** A.P. credit may satisfy the requirement on a case by case basis

THOMAS JEFFERSON UNIVERSITY JEFFERSON COLLEGE OF PHARMACY	Anatomy & Physio. 1 and 2 or Anatomy w/ Lab and Physio. w/ Lab, Calc., Microbio. w/ Lab, Engl. Comp., Soc. Sci., Humanities, Bio. w/ Lab, Chem. w/ Lab, OChem. w/ Lab, and Algebra or Calc.-based Physics w/ Lab.	N/A	AP credits accepted as long as they are listed on undergraduate transcript.
UNIVERSITY OF PITTSBURGH SCHOOL OF PHARMACY	Bio. w/ Lab, Chem. w/ Lab, OChem. w/ Lab, Calc. (Analytic Geom. & Calc.), Stats., Engl. Comp., Humanities and Social Sciences.	N/A	AP credits accepted for certain coursework. Contact admissions for more information.
UNIVERSITY OF THE SCIENCES PHILADELPHIA COLLEGE OF PHARMACY	Bio. w/ Lab, Chem. w/ Lab, Calc., Writing-Intensive Engl., Soc./Behav. Science, OChem. w/ Lab, Physics w/ Lab, Human Anatomy & Physio., Microbio. w/ Lab, Stats., Intro. to Communications or Public Speaking, and Econ.	N/A	AP credits accepted for certain courses. For more information, visit: https://www.usciences.edu/admission/prior-learning-credits-by-exam-details.html
WILKES UNIVERSITY NESBITT SCHOOL OF PHARMACY	Chem. w/ Lab, OChem. w/ Lab, Bio. w/ Lab, Physics w/ Lab, Calc., Stats., Microecon., and Oral Communications.	N/A	No listed information on AP credits. Contact admissions.

For the number of hours required for prerequisite courses, and for the most up-to-date information, please refer to the individual school websites.

*A.P. credit satisfies the requirement.

** When A.P. credit is awarded, upper-level coursework in the same subject area is required.

*** A.P. credit may satisfy the requirement on a case by case basis

PUERTO RICO

PharmD Schools	Required	Recommended	Notes
UNIVERSITY OF PUERTO RICO MEDICAL SCIENCES CAMPUS SCHOOL OF PHARMACY	Engl. Comp./ Writing, Spanish, Communication/ Speech, Humanities, Social Sciences, Pre-Calc., Calc., Chem., OChem., Bio., Physics w/ Lab, Psych., Econ., and Anatomy and Physio.	N/A	AP credits accepted for English and Spanish prerequisites.

RHODE ISLAND

PharmD Schools	Required	Recommended	Notes
UNIVERSITY OF RHODE ISLAND COLLEGE OF PHARMACY	N/A	N/A	This program is intended for high school applicants.

SOUTH CAROLINA

PharmD Schools	Required	Recommended	Notes
MEDICAL UNIVERSITY OF SOUTH CAROLINA COLLEGE OF PHARMACY	Chem. w/ Lab, OChem. w/ Lab, Physics, Calc., Stats., Bio. w/ Lab, Engl. Comp., Engl. Lit., Speech/ Verbal Skills/Public Speaking, Econ., Psych., Human Anatomy, Human Physio., Liberal Arts Electives, and Microbio.	Microecon. preferred.	Microbio. will not be accepted as a biology prereq. No listed information on AP credits. Contact admissions.

For the number of hours required for prerequisite courses, and for the most up-to-date information, please refer to the individual school websites.
*A.P. credit satisfies the requirement.
** When A.P. credit is awarded, upper-level coursework in the same subject area is required.
*** A.P. credit may satisfy the requirement on a case by case basis

		N/A	
PRESBYTERIAN COLLEGE SCHOOL OF PHARMACY	Bio. w/ Lab, Microbio. w/ Lab, Humanities, Engl., Psych./Sociology, Public Speaking, Human Anatomy & Physio., Chem. w/ Lab, OChem. w/ Lab, Physics, Stats., Calc., and Econ.	N/A	AP credits accepted as long as they are listed on undergraduate transcript.
UNIVERSITY OF SOUTH CAROLINA COLLEGE OF PHARMACY	Chem. w/ Lab, Physics, Calc., Stats., Bio. w/ Lab, Engl. Comp., Speech/ Communication, Social/Behav. Science, Psych., Anatomy & Physio., Liberal Art Electives, and Microbio.	N/A	AP credits accepted.

SOUTH DAKOTA

PharmD Schools	Required	Recommended	Notes
SOUTH DAKOTA STATE UNIVERSITY COLLEGE OF PHARMACY AND ALLIED HEALTH PROFESSIONS	Chem. w/ Lab, OChem. w/ Lab, Bio. w/ Lab, Calc., Microbio. w/ Lab, Human Anatomy w/ Lab, Human Physio. w/ Lab, Econ., Engl. Comp., Speech, and Stats.	N/A	AP credits accepted.

For the number of hours required for prerequisite courses, and for the most up-to-date information, please refer to the individual school websites.

*A.P. credit satisfies the requirement.

** When A.P. credit is awarded, upper-level coursework in the same subject area is required.

*** A.P. credit may satisfy the requirement on a case by case basis

TENNESSEE

PharmD Schools	Required	Recommended	Notes
BELMONT UNIVERSITY COLLEGE OF PHARMACY	Bio. w/ Lab, Chem. w/ Lab, OChem. w/ Lab, Physics, Calc., Stats., Engl. Comp./Writing, Communication/ Speech, Soc./Behav. Science, Humanities, and Electives.	N/A	AP credits accepted.
EAST TENNESSEE STATE UNIVERSITY BILL GATTON COLLEGE OF PHARMACY	Bio. w/ Lab, Microbio. w/ Lab, Bio. Elective, Chem. w/ Lab, OChem. w/ Lab, Physics w/ Lab, Calc., Stats., Econ., Engl. Comp./Writing, Communication/ Speech, Additional Writing-Intensive course, Social Sciences/Humanities Electives, and General Electives (see Recommended).	Science coursework recommended for general electives.	AP credits accepted if applicant takes coursework in a higher level within the same discipline.
LIPSCOMB UNIVERSITY COLLEGE OF PHARMACY AND HEALTH SCIENCES	Chem. w/ Lab, Speech Communication, Econ., Social Science/Humanities Electives, General Electives (see Recommended), OChem. w/ Lab, Microbio. w/ Lab, Bio. w/ Lab, Stats., Calc., and Engl. Comp.	General Electives: Coursework in Bio., Chem., or Math recommended	No listed information on AP credits. Contact admissions.

For the number of hours required for prerequisite courses, and for the most up-to-date information, please refer to the individual school websites.
*A.P. credit satisfies the requirement.
** When A.P. credit is awarded, upper-level coursework in the same subject area is required.
*** A.P. credit may satisfy the requirement on a case by case basis

SOUTH COLLEGE SCHOOL OF PHARMACY	Bio. w/ Lab, Anatomy & Physio. w/ Lab, Chem. w/ Lab, OChem. w/ Lab, Microbio. w/ Lab, Calc., Stats., Engl. Comp., Speech Communication, Econ., Humanities Electives, and Social/Behav. Sciences Electives.	N/A	AP credits accepted.
UNION UNIVERSITY COLLEGE OF PHARMACY	Bio. or Zoology w/ Lab, Chem. w/ Lab, OChem. w/ Lab, Human Anatomy & Physio. w/ Lab, Physics w/ Lab, Microbio. w/ Lab, Calc., Stats., Written Comp., Communications/ Speech, Humanities Electives, and Social Sciences Electives.	Biochem., Immunology, Genetics, and second semester of Physics.	Applicants should take laboratories when available. No listed information on AP credits. Contact admissions.
UNIVERSITY OF TENNESSEE HEALTH SCIENCE CENTER COLLEGE OF PHARMACY	Bio./Zoology w/ Lab, Microbio. w/ Lab, Chem. w/ Lab, OChem. w/ Lab, Anatomy & Physio. w/ Lab, Calc., Stats., Communication/ Speech, Engl. Comp., Social Sciences, and Humanities.	N/A	No listed information on AP credits. Contact admissions.

For the number of hours required for prerequisite courses, and for the most up-to-date information, please refer to the individual school websites.

*A.P. credit satisfies the requirement.

** When A.P. credit is awarded, upper-level coursework in the same subject area is required.

*** A.P. credit may satisfy the requirement on a case by case basis

TEXAS

PharmD Schools	Required	Recommended	Notes
TEXAS A & M UNIVERSITY HEALTH SCIENCE CENTER IRMA LERMA RANGEL COLLEGE OF PHARMACY	Calc., Physics w/ Lab, Engl. Comp., Bio. w/ Labs, Chem. w/ Labs, Microbio. w/ Lab, Molecular Bio. or Genetics, OChem. w/ Lab, Speech Communication, Stats., Art, Humanities, Sociology/Psych./ Econ/Comp. Sci, History, and Political Science.	N/A	AP credits accepted as long as they are listed on undergraduate transcript.
TEXAS SOUTHERN UNIVERSITY COLLEGE OF PHARMACY AND HEALTH SCIENCES	Bio. w/ Lab, Human Anatomy & Physio. w/ Lab, Microbio. w/ Lab, Chem. w/ Lab, OChem. w/ Lab, Stats., Calc., Physics w/ Lab, Engl., Public Speaking, Computer Science, Soc./Behav. Sciences, Fine Art, US History, and Political Science.	N/A	No listed information on AP credits. Contact admissions.
TEXAS TECH UNIVERSITY HEALTH SCIENCES CENTER JERRY H. HODGE SCHOOL OF PHARMACY	Bio. w/ Lab, Microbio. w/ Lab, Chem. w/ Lab, OChem. w/ Lab, Physics w /Lab, Speech, Engl. Comp., Humanities/Social Sciences, Econ., Calc., and Stats.	N/A	AP credits accepted as long as they are listed on undergraduate transcript.

For the number of hours required for prerequisite courses, and for the most up-to-date information, please refer to the individual school websites.
*A.P. credit satisfies the requirement.
** When A.P. credit is awarded, upper-level coursework in the same subject area is required.
*** A.P. credit may satisfy the requirement on a case by case basis

UNIVERSITY OF HOUSTON COLLEGE OF PHARMACY	Bio. w/ Lab, Microbio. w/ Lab, Genetics, Chem. w/ Lab, OChem. w/ Lab, Calc., Stats., Physics, Psych./Sociology, Government/ Political Science, American History, Engl., Language/ Philosophy/Culture, Creative Arts, and Writing.	N/A	AP credits accepted.
UNIVERSITY OF NORTH TEXAS HEALTH SCIENCE CENTER UNT SYSTEM COLLEGE OF PHARMACY	Bio. w/ Lab, Microbio. w/ Lab, Human Anatomy & Physio. w/ Lab, Genetics, Chem. w/ Lab, OChem. w/ Lab, Physics w/ Lab, Calc., Stats., Engl. Comp., Literature, US History, Political Science, Fine Arts/ Humanities Elective, Public Speaking, and Social & Behav. Science Elective.	N/A	AP credits accepted as long as they are listed on undergraduate transcript.
UNIVERSITY OF TEXAS AT AUSTIN COLLEGE OF PHARMACY	Bio., Chem. w/ Lab, OChem. w/ Lab, Genetics, Microbio. w/ Lab, Physics w/ Lab, Stats., Engl. Comp./Writing, Literature, US History, American Government, Visual/ Performing Arts, and Social/Behav. Science.	N/A	AP credits accepted. However, UT Austin strongly recommends all math and science coursework be completed at the college level.

For the number of hours required for prerequisite courses, and for the most up-to-date information, please refer to the individual school websites.

*A.P. credit satisfies the requirement.

** When A.P. credit is awarded, upper-level coursework in the same subject area is required.

*** A.P. credit may satisfy the requirement on a case by case basis

UNIVERSITY OF TEXAS AT EL PASO SCHOOL OF PHARMACY	Engl. Comp./ Writing, Calc., Stats., Bio. w/ Lab, Human Anatomy & Physio. w/ Lab, Genetics, Chem. w/ Lab, OChem. w/ Lab, Biochem., Microbio. w/ Lab, Physics w/ Lab, Spanish, and Texas Core Curriculum Standards.	N/A	No listed information on AP credits. Contact admissions.
UNIVERSITY OF TEXAS AT TYLER BEN AND MAYTEE FISCH COLLEGE OF PHARMACY	Chem. w/ Lab, Bio. w/ Lab, Communication/ Speech, Microbio. w/ Lab, OChem. w/ Lab, Calc., and Human Anatomy & Physio. w/ Lab.	N/A	AP credits accepted for certain courses. Contact admissions for more information.
UNIVERSITY OF THE INCARNATE WORD FEIK SCHOOL OF PHARMACY	Chem. w/ Lab, OChem. w/ Lab, Bio. w/ Lab, Microbio. w/ Lab, Human Anatomy & Physio. w/ Lab, Physics w/ Lab, Calc., Stats., Engl. Comp., Social/ Behav. Sciences, Fine Arts, Literature, Philosophy, and Communication/ Speech.	N/A	AP credits accepted.

For the number of hours required for prerequisite courses, and for the most up-to-date information, please refer to the individual school websites.
*A.P. credit satisfies the requirement.
** When A.P. credit is awarded, upper-level coursework in the same subject area is required.
*** A.P. credit may satisfy the requirement on a case by case basis

UTAH

PharmD Schools	Required	Recommended	Notes
UNIVERSITY OF UTAH COLLEGE OF PHARMACY	Human Anatomy, Human Physio., Chem. w/ Lab, OChem. w/ Lab, Calc., Physics, Stats., Microbio., and Public Speaking.	N/A	AP credit accepted for Calc., Chem., Physics, and Stats. only.

VIRGINIA

PharmD Schools	Required	Recommended	Notes
APPALACHIAN COLLEGE OF PHARMACY	Bio. w/ Lab, Advanced Bio., Chem. w/ Lab, OChem. w/ Lab, Physics w/ Lab, Human Anatomy/ Physio., Microbio., Engl. Comp., Math, Calc., Social/ Behav. Sciences, Humanities, Computer Science, and Other Electives.	College Stats. and Public Speaking.	AP credits accepted.
HAMPTON UNIVERSITY SCHOOL OF PHARMACY	Engl., Pre-Calc., Calc., Bio. w/ Lab, Chem. w/ Lab, Health, Speech, History, OChem. w/ Lab, Physics w/ Lab, Humanities, Social Science, Microbio. (Lab pref.), Microbio./ Immunology, Genetics, Human Anatomy w/ Lab, Human Physio. w/ Lab, and Stats.	Medical terminology and Medical Microbio.	AP credits not accepted.

For the number of hours required for prerequisite courses, and for the most up-to-date information, please refer to the individual school websites.

*A.P. credit satisfies the requirement.

** When A.P. credit is awarded, upper-level coursework in the same subject area is required.

*** A.P. credit may satisfy the requirement on a case by case basis

SHENANDOAH UNIVERSITY BERNARD J. DUNN SCHOOL OF PHARMACY	Engl. Comp., Communication/ Speech, Bio. w/ Lab, Chem. w/ Lab, OChem. w/ Lab, Physics w/ Lab, Stats., Calc., Bio. Elective, Econ., Microbio., Humanities, Social/ Behav. Science, and Human Anatomy & Physio.	N/A	AP credits accepted for non-science coursework. If AP credits are accepted for a science course, the university will accept upper-level coursework in its place (e.g., cell biology may count for Bio. 1 if AP credit was given for Bio. 1)
VIRGINIA COMMONWEALTH UNIVERSITY AT THE MEDICAL COLLEGE OF VIRGINIA CAMPUS SCHOOL OF PHARMACY	Bio. w/ Lab, Human Anatomy (lab preferred), Human Physio., Microbio. (lab preferred), Biochem., Chem. w/ Lab, OChem. w/ Lab, Physics w/ Lab, Calc., Stats., and Engl.	N/A	AP credits may excuse certain coursework (English, Calc., Stats., General Ed, and Physics) if the score is 3+. However, AP credit will not be recognized in terms of meeting the 70 semester hours requirement. For instance, a student may utilize an AP score for English to satisfy the requirement, however these credits must be replaced with additional electives.

For the number of hours required for prerequisite courses, and for the most up-to-date information, please refer to the individual school websites.
*A.P. credit satisfies the requirement.
** When A.P. credit is awarded, upper-level coursework in the same subject area is required.
*** A.P. credit may satisfy the requirement on a case by case basis

WASHINGTON

PharmD Schools	Required	Recommended	Notes
UNIVERSITY OF WASHINGTON SCHOOL OF PHARMACY	Biochem., Bio. w/ Lab, Humanities Electives, Soc. Science Electives, Chem. w/ Lab, OChem. w/ Lab, Microbio. w/ Lab, Engl. Comp., Calc., Stats., Interpersonal Communications, Microecon., and Anatomy & Physio.	N/A	AP credit accepted for Chem., Calc., Stats., and Econ.
WASHINGTON STATE UNIVERSITY COLLEGE OF PHARMACY AND PHARMACEUTICAL SCIENCES	Engl. Comp., Philosophy, Psych., Microecon., Stats., Calc., Bio. w/ Lab, Chem. w/ Lab, OChem. w/ Lab, Microbio. w/ Lab, Human Anatomy w/ Lab, Physio. w/ Lab, and Advanced Engl. Comp.	N/A	AP credits accepted as long as they are listed on undergraduate transcript.

WEST VIRGINIA

PharmD Schools	Required	Recommended	Notes
MARSHALL UNIVERSITY SCHOOL OF PHARMACY	Engl. Comp./Writing, Calc., Stats., Bio. w/ Lab, Chem. w/ Lab, Human Anatomy w/ Lab, Human Physio. w/ Lab, Microbio. w/ Lab, OChem. w/ Lab, Physics w/ Lab, and Social Science Elective.	N/A	AP credits accepted as long as they are listed on undergraduate transcript.

For the number of hours required for prerequisite courses, and for the most up-to-date information, please refer to the individual school websites.

*A.P. credit satisfies the requirement.

** When A.P. credit is awarded, upper-level coursework in the same subject area is required.

*** A.P. credit may satisfy the requirement on a case by case basis

UNIVERSITY OF CHARLESTON SCHOOL OF PHARMACY	Human Anatomy w/ Lab, Human Physio. w/ Lab, Bio. w/ Lab, Chem. w/ Lab, OChem. w/ Lab, Microbio. w/ Lab, Calc., Stats., Engl. Comp., Psych./ Sociology, History or Political Science, and Econ.	N/A	AP credits accepted as long as they are listed on undergraduate transcript.
WEST VIRGINIA UNIVERSITY SCHOOL OF PHARMACY	Engl. Comp./Writing, Communication/ Speech, General Education, Econ., Stats., Calc., Bio. w/ Lab, Microbio., Chem. w/ Lab, OChem. w/ Lab, Biochem., and Physio.	N/A	AP credits accepted.

WISCONSIN

PharmD Schools	Required	Recommended	Notes
CONCORDIA UNIVERSITY WISCONSIN SCHOOL OF PHARMACY	Chem. w/ Lab, Bio. w/ Lab, OChem. w/ Lab, Physics w/ Lab, 1+ Advanced Science Electives (see Recommended), Calc., Engl. Comp./Writing, Communication/ Speech, Econ., Stats., and General Education Electives.	Advanced Science Electives: Physics 2, Physio., Anatomy, Microbio., Biochem., Cell Bio., Molecular Bio., Genetics, or other advanced science coursework.	AP credits accepted as long as they are listed on undergraduate transcript.

For the number of hours required for prerequisite courses, and for the most up-to-date information, please refer to the individual school websites.
*A.P. credit satisfies the requirement.
** When A.P. credit is awarded, upper-level coursework in the same subject area is required.
*** A.P. credit may satisfy the requirement on a case by case basis

MEDICAL COLLEGE OF WISCONSIN SCHOOL OF PHARMACY	Bio. w/ Lab, Advanced Bio., Chem. w/ Lab, OChem. w/ Lab, Stats., Calc., Physics, Econ., Engl. Comp., Public Speaking, and General Education Electives.	Bio: Anatomy, Physio, Biochem., Genetics, Microbio., Molecular Genetics. Stats.: Biostats. or Business Stats. Physics: with lab recommended. Econ.: Micro./ Macroecon., Business Econ., International Econ., or Intro to Econ. Engl. Comp.: English, Linguistics, or Writing. Public Speaking: Speech, Public Speaking, Interpersonal, or Group Communication. General Education Electives: Humanities, Social, and Behav. Sciences.	AP credits accepted as long as they are listed on undergraduate transcript.
UNIVERSITY OF WISCONSIN-MADISON SCHOOL OF PHARMACY	Calc., Chem. w/ Lab, OChem. w/ Lab, Bio. w/ Lab, Physics w/ Lab, Microbio., Human Physio. or Anatomy & Physio., Stats., Engl. Comp., Social Sciences, U.S. Diversity/Ethnic Studies, Humanities, and Additional Elective Coursework.	N/A	AP credits accepted as long as they are listed on undergraduate transcript.

For the number of hours required for prerequisite courses, and for the most up-to-date information, please refer to the individual school websites.
*A.P. credit satisfies the requirement.
** When A.P. credit is awarded, upper-level coursework in the same subject area is required.
*** A.P. credit may satisfy the requirement on a case by case basis

WYOMING

PharmD Schools	Required	Recommended	Notes
UNIVERSITY OF WYOMING SCHOOL OF PHARMACY	Bio. w/ Lab, Animal Bio. w/ Lab, Chem. w/ Lab, OChem. w/ Lab, Human Anatomy w/ Lab, Human Systems Physio. w/ Lab, Medical Microbio. w/ Lab, Calc., Stats., and Biochem.	N/A	No listed information on AP credits. Contact admissions.

CHAPTER 9

TOP 30 PHARMACY SCHOOLS

Rank	School
#1	University of North Carolina - Chapel Hill
#2	UC San Francisco
#3	University of Michigan - Ann Arbor
#4	University of Minnesota
#5	University of Florida
#6	University of Kentucky
#7	Ohio State University
#8	Purdue University
#9	University of Illinois - Chicago
#10	University of Texas - Austin
#11	University of Washington
#12	University of Wisconsin - Madison
#13	University of Pittsburgh
#14	University at Buffalo - SUNY
#15	University of Maryland - Baltimore
#16	University of Southern California
#17	University of Utah
#18	UC San Diego
#19	University of Iowa
#20	University of Arizona
#21	University of Colorado - Denver
#22	University of Tennessee Health Science Center
#23	Virginia Commonwealth University
#24	Rutgers University
#25	University of Georgia
#26	University of Kansas
#27	University of Mississippi
#28	University of Nebraska Medical Center
#29	University of Connecticut
#30	University of Cincinnati

CHAPTER 10

PHARMACY SCHOOLS BY AVERAGE PCAT SCORE

PharmD Schools	Avg. PCAT Comp. %
Rosalind Franklin University of Medicine and Science College of Pharmacy	43
University of the Incarnate Word Feik School of Pharmacy	43
Drake University College of Pharmacy and Health Sciences	50
Shenandoah University Bernard J. Dunn School of Pharmacy	50
West Virginia University School of Pharmacy	50
University of Montana College of Health Professions and Biomedical Sciences Skaggs School of Pharmacy	52
North Dakota State University College of Health Professions School of Pharmacy	54
University of Missouri-Kansas City School of Pharmacy	56
Southern Illinois University Edwardsville School of Pharmacy	60
University of Louisiana at Monroe College of Pharmacy	60
Binghamton University State University of New York School of Pharmacy and Pharmaceutical Sciences	61
University of Cincinnati James L. Winkle College of Pharmacy	61
Ferris State University College of Pharmacy	63
University of Oklahoma College of Pharmacy	63
University of South Florida Health Taneja College of Pharmacy	65
University of Arkansas for Medical Sciences College of Pharmacy	67
Texas Tech University Health Sciences Center Jerry H. Hodge School of Pharmacy	68
University of South Carolina College of Pharmacy	70
Virginia Commonwealth University at the Medical College of Virginia Campus School of Pharmacy	70
Wayne State University Eugene Applebaum College of Pharmacy and Health Sciences	70
Chapman University School of Pharmacy	72
University of Georgia College of Pharmacy	72
University of Nebraska Medical Center College of Pharmacy	72
University of Utah College of Pharmacy	74
University of Minnesota College of Pharmacy	75
University of Wisconsin-Madison School of Pharmacy	78
University of Houston College of Pharmacy	79
University of Michigan College of Pharmacy	79
Ohio State University College of Pharmacy	80
University of North Carolina Eshelman School of Pharmacy	89
St. John Fisher College Wegmans School of Pharmacy	~65

PharmD Schools	Avg. PCAT Comp. %
Philadelphia College of Osteopathic Medicine - Georgia School of Pharmacy	36 (Optional)
Midwestern University Chicago College of Pharmacy	43+ (rec.)
Fairleigh Dickinson University School of Pharmacy	50 PCAT/GRE opt.
Hampton University School of Pharmacy	50-60
University of Iowa College of Pharmacy	60-65
University of Kansas School of Pharmacy	65th percentile
University of Illinois at Chicago College of Pharmacy	70-80
University of Pittsburgh School of Pharmacy	70+
Albany College of Pharmacy and Health Sciences School of Pharmacy and Pharmaceutical Sciences	N/A
Cedarville University School of Pharmacy	N/A
Chicago State University College of Pharmacy	N/A
Creighton University School of Pharmacy and Health Professions	N/A
D'Youville College School of Pharmacy	N/A
Duquesne University School of Pharmacy	N/A
Harding University College of Pharmacy	N/A
High Point University Fred Wilson School of Pharmacy	N/A
Husson University School of Pharmacy	N/A
Lake Erie College of Osteopathic Medicine School of Pharmacy	N/A
Larkin University College of Pharmacy	N/A
Long Island University Arnold and Marie Schwartz College of Pharmacy and Health Sciences	N/A
MCPHS University School of Pharmacy - Boston	N/A
MCPHS University School of Pharmacy - Worcester	N/A
Medical College of Wisconsin School of Pharmacy	N/A
Medical University of South Carolina College of Pharmacy	N/A
Midwestern University College of Pharmacy-Glendale	N/A
Northeast Ohio Medical University College of Pharmacy	N/A
Nova Southeastern University College of Pharmacy	N/A
Palm Beach Atlantic University Lloyd L. Gregory School of Pharmacy	N/A
Roosevelt University College of Pharmacy	N/A
Roseman University of Health Sciences College of Pharmacy	N/A
Rutgers, the State University of New Jersey Ernest Mario School of Pharmacy	N/A
South Dakota State University College of Pharmacy and Allied Health Professions	N/A

PharmD Schools	Avg. PCAT Comp. %
Southwestern Oklahoma State University College of Pharmacy	N/A
St. Louis College of Pharmacy	N/A
Sullivan University College of Pharmacy	N/A
Texas A & M University Health Science Center Irma Lerma Rangel College of Pharmacy	N/A
Texas Southern University College of Pharmacy and Health Sciences	N/A
University at Buffalo The State University of New York School of Pharmacy & Pharmaceutical Sciences	N/A
University of Arizona College of Pharmacy	N/A
University of Charleston School of Pharmacy	N/A
University of Connecticut School of Pharmacy	N/A
University of Florida College of Pharmacy	N/A
University of Maryland Eastern Shore School of Pharmacy and Health Professions	N/A
University of Maryland School of Pharmacy	N/A
University of Mississippi School of Pharmacy	N/A
University of New England College of Pharmacy	N/A
University of New Mexico College of Pharmacy	N/A
University of North Texas Health Science Center UNT System College of Pharmacy	N/A
University of Puerto Rico Medical Sciences Campus School of Pharmacy	N/A
University of Saint Joseph School of Pharmacy and Physician Assistant Studies	N/A
University of Texas at Austin College of Pharmacy	N/A
University of Texas at El Paso School of Pharmacy	N/A
University of Toledo College of Pharmacy and Pharmaceutical Sciences	N/A
University of Wyoming School of Pharmacy	N/A
Wilkes University Nesbitt School of Pharmacy	N/A
William Carey University School of Pharmacy	N/A
Belmont University College of Pharmacy	Not Req.
Butler University College of Pharmacy and Health Sciences	Not req.
California Health Sciences University College of Pharmacy	Not req.
California Northstate University College of Pharmacy	Not req.
East Tennessee State University Bill Gatton College of Pharmacy	Not req.
Florida Agricultural & Mechanical University College of Pharmacy and Pharmaceutical Sciences	Not req.

PharmD Schools	Avg. PCAT Comp. %
Howard University College of Pharmacy	Not req.
Idaho State University College of Pharmacy	Not req.
Keck Graduate Institute (KGI) School of Pharmacy and Health Sciences	Not req.
Lipscomb University College of Pharmacy and Health Sciences	Not Req.
Loma Linda University School of Pharmacy	Not req.
Manchester University College of Pharmacy, Natural and Health Sciences	Not req.
Notre Dame of Maryland University School of Pharmacy	Not req.
Ohio Northern University Raabe College of Pharmacy	Not req.
Oregon State University College of Pharmacy	Not req.
Pacific University School of Pharmacy	Not req.
Purdue University College of Pharmacy	Not req.
Samford University McWhorter School of Pharmacy	Not req.
South University School of Pharmacy	Not req.
St. John's University College of Pharmacy and Health Sciences	Not req.
Temple University School of Pharmacy	Not req.
Thomas Jefferson University Jefferson College of Pharmacy	Not req.
Touro University - California College of Pharmacy	Not req.
University of California, Irvine School of Pharmacy	Not req.
University of California, San Diego Skaggs School of Pharmacy & Pharmaceutical Sciences	Not req.
University of Findlay College of Pharmacy	Not req.
University of Kentucky College of Pharmacy	Not req.
University of Rhode Island College of Pharmacy	Not req.
University of Southern California School of Pharmacy	Not req.
University of Tennessee Health Science Center College of Pharmacy	Not Req.
University of Texas at Tyler Ben and Maytee Fisch College of Pharmacy	Not req.
University of the Pacific Thomas J. Long School of Pharmacy	Not req.
University of the Sciences Philadelphia College of Pharmacy	Not req.
University of Washington School of Pharmacy	Not req.
Washington State University College of Pharmacy and Pharmaceutical Sciences	Not req.
West Coast University School of Pharmacy	Not req.
Western New England University College of Pharmacy	Not req.
Western University of Health Sciences College of Pharmacy	Not req.

PharmD Schools	Avg. PCAT Comp. %
Xavier University of Louisiana College of Pharmacy	Not req.
American University of Health Sciences School of Pharmacy	Optional
Appalachian College of Pharmacy	Optional
Auburn University Harrison School of Pharmacy	Optional
Campbell University College of Pharmacy and Health Sciences	Optional
Concordia University Wisconsin School of Pharmacy	Optional
Marshall B. Ketchum University College of Pharmacy	Optional
Marshall University School of Pharmacy	Optional
Mercer University College of Pharmacy	Optional
Northeastern University Bouvé College of Health Sciences School of Pharmacy	Optional
Presbyterian College School of Pharmacy	Optional
Regis University Rueckert-Hartman College for Health Professions School of Pharmacy	Optional
South College School of Pharmacy	Optional
Touro New York College of Pharmacy	Optional
Union University College of Pharmacy	Optional
University of California, San Francisco School of Pharmacy	Optional
University of Colorado Anschutz Medical Campus Skaggs School of Pharmacy and Pharmaceutical Sciences	Optional
University of Hawaii at Hilo Daniel K. Inouye College of Pharmacy	Optional
Wingate University School of Pharmacy	Optional

CHAPTER 11

PHARMACY SCHOOLS BY COST OF ATTENDANCE

PharmD Schools	In-State Tuition	Out-of-State Tuition	Out-of-State COA
Texas Southern University College of Pharmacy and Health Sciences	$16,293.00	$27,033.00	$27,033.00
University of Tennessee Health Science Center College of Pharmacy	$22,370.00	$27,374.00	$27,374.00
University of Toledo College of Pharmacy and Pharmaceutical Sciences	$18,489.00	$27,849.00	$27,849.00
University of Puerto Rico Medical Sciences Campus School of Pharmacy	$15,876.00	$28,376.00	$28,376.00
North Dakota State University College of Health Professions School of Pharmacy	$19,617.00	$28,669.00	$28,669.00
Texas Tech University Health Sciences Center Jerry H. Hodge School of Pharmacy	$18,323.00	$30,608.00	$30,608.00
South Dakota State University College of Pharmacy and Allied Health Professions	$20,127.00	$31,328.00	$31,328.00
University of Texas at Tyler Ben and Maytee Fisch College of Pharmacy	$8,316.00	$16,974.00	$31,386.00
University of Nebraska Medical Center College of Pharmacy	$25,274.00	$31,594.00	$31,594.00
University of Montana College of Health Professions and Biomedical Sciences Skaggs School of Pharmacy	$13,094.00	$31,958.00	$31,958.00
Southern Illinois University Edwardsville School of Pharmacy	$27,598.00	$32,418.00	$32,418.00
Palm Beach Atlantic University Lloyd L. Gregory School of Pharmacy	$32,474.00	$32,474.00	$32,474.00
Wingate University School of Pharmacy	$33,566.00	$33,566.00	$33,566.00
University of Charleston School of Pharmacy	$33,950.00	$33,950.00	$33,950.00
Marshall University School of Pharmacy	$21,148.00	$34,774.00	$34,774.00
University of Rhode Island College of Pharmacy	$22,464.00	$35,582.00	$35,582.00
Cedarville University School of Pharmacy	$35,682.00	$35,682.00	$35,682.00
University of Florida College of Pharmacy	$23,690.00	$36,000.00	$36,000.00
Xavier University of Louisiana College of Pharmacy	$36,098.00	$36,098.00	$36,098.00
Shenandoah University Bernard J. Dunn School of Pharmacy	$36,890.00	$36,890.00	$36,890.00

PharmD Schools	In-State Tuition	Out-of-State Tuition	Out-of-State COA
University of Cincinnati James L. Winkle College of Pharmacy	$24,418.00	$37,346.00	$37,346.00
Regis University Rueckert-Hartman College for Health Professions School of Pharmacy	$37,416.00	$37,416.00	$37,416.00
Hampton University School of Pharmacy	$37,588.00	$37,588.00	$37,588.00
University of South Florida Health Taneja College of Pharmacy	$19,904.00	$37,649.00	$37,649.00
Presbyterian College School of Pharmacy	$37,700.00	$37,700.00	$37,700.00
D'Youville College School of Pharmacy	$37,842.00	$37,842.00	$37,842.00
Union University College of Pharmacy	$37,850.00	$37,850.00	$37,850.00
University of Michigan College of Pharmacy	$32,220.00	$37,856.00	$37,856.00
Temple University School of Pharmacy	$35,310.00	$37,878.00	$37,878.00
Nova Southeastern University College of Pharmacy	$33,474.00	$38,251.00	$38,251.00
Mercer University College of Pharmacy	$38,484.00	$38,484.00	$38,484.00
Harding University College of Pharmacy	$39,030.00	$39,030.00	$39,030.00
Southwestern Oklahoma State University College of Pharmacy	$23,778.00	$39,114.00	$39,114.00
Concordia University Wisconsin School of Pharmacy	$39,149.00	$39,149.00	$39,149.00
University of Pittsburgh School of Pharmacy	$34,432.00	$39,340.00	$39,340.00
Ohio Northern University Raabe College of Pharmacy	$39,360.00	$39,360.00	$39,360.00
MCPHS University School of Pharmacy - Boston	$39,500.00	$39,500.00	$39,500.00
Ferris State University College of Pharmacy	$28,500.00	$28,500.00	$39,500.00
East Tennessee State University Bill Gatton College of Pharmacy	$39,684.00	$39,684.00	$39,684.00
Idaho State University College of Pharmacy	$19,238.00	$39,740.00	$39,740.00
University of Colorado Anschutz Medical Campus Skaggs School of Pharmacy and Pharmaceutical Sciences	$31,375.00	$39,870.00	$39,870.00

PharmD Schools	In-State Tuition	Out-of-State Tuition	Out-of-State COA
Chicago State University College of Pharmacy	$27,918.00	$39,906.00	$39,906.00
University of Texas at El Paso School of Pharmacy	$19,000.00	$40,000.00	$40,000.00
Medical University of South Carolina College of Pharmacy	$26,045.00	$40,056.00	$40,056.00
Samford University McWhorter School of Pharmacy	$40,066.00	$40,066.00	$40,066.00
University of the Incarnate Word Feik School of Pharmacy	$40,104.00	$40,104.00	$40,104.00
Wilkes University Nesbitt School of Pharmacy	$40,162.00	$40,162.00	$40,162.00
Thomas Jefferson University Jefferson College of Pharmacy	$40,178.00	$40,178.00	$40,178.00
Rosalind Franklin University of Medicine and Science College of Pharmacy	$40,661.00	$40,661.00	$40,661.00
Lipscomb University College of Pharmacy and Health Sciences	$40,842.00	$40,842.00	$40,842.00
Binghamton University State University of New York School of Pharmacy and Pharmaceutical Sciences	$30,285.00	$30,285.00	$40,975.00
William Carey University School of Pharmacy	$41,000.00	$41,000.00	$41,000.00
Notre Dame of Maryland University School of Pharmacy	$41,500.00	$41,500.00	$41,500.00
Fairleigh Dickinson University School of Pharmacy	$41,534.00	$41,534.00	$41,534.00
High Point University Fred Wilson School of Pharmacy	$41,556.00	$41,556.00	$41,556.00
University of Arkansas for Medical Sciences College of Pharmacy	$22,290.00	$41,570.00	$41,570.00
Husson University School of Pharmacy	$41,764.00	$41,764.00	$41,764.00
Albany College of Pharmacy and Health Sciences School of Pharmacy and Pharmaceutical Sciences	$41,780.00	$41,780.00	$41,780.00
University of South Carolina College of Pharmacy	$27,840.00	$42,048.00	$42,048.00
Drake University College of Pharmacy and Health Sciences	$42,186.00	$42,186.00	$42,186.00
Auburn University Harrison School of Pharmacy	$22,362.00	$42,522.00	$42,522.00

PharmD Schools	In-State Tuition	Out-of-State Tuition	Out-of-State COA
Campbell University College of Pharmacy and Health Sciences	$42,860.00	$42,860.00	$42,860.00
Belmont University College of Pharmacy	$43,040.00	$43,040.00	$43,040.00
Oregon State University College of Pharmacy	$26,560.00	$43,264.00	$43,264.00
University of Oklahoma College of Pharmacy	$23,960.00	$43,752.00	$43,752.00
University of the Sciences Philadelphia College of Pharmacy	$43,824.00	$43,824.00	$43,824.00
Virginia Commonwealth University at the Medical College of Virginia Campus School of Pharmacy	$31,054.00	$44,044.00	$44,044.00
University of New Mexico College of Pharmacy	$21,771.00	$44,199.00	$44,199.00
University of Findlay College of Pharmacy	$44,628.00	$44,628.00	$44,628.00
Butler University College of Pharmacy and Health Sciences	$45,040.00	$45,040.00	$45,040.00
University of Iowa College of Pharmacy	$28,599.00	$45,075.00	$45,075.00
University of Illinois at Chicago College of Pharmacy	$29,698.00	$45,216.00	$45,216.00
Western New England University College of Pharmacy	$45,366.00	$45,366.00	$45,366.00
University of Maryland School of Pharmacy	$26,730.00	$46,384.00	$46,384.00
West Coast University School of Pharmacy	$46,735.00	$46,735.00	$46,735.00
Touro University - California College of Pharmacy	$47,120.00	$47,120.00	$47,120.00
Midwestern University Chicago College of Pharmacy	$47,550.00	$47,550.00	$47,550.00
University of Arizona College of Pharmacy	$27,471.00	$47,598.00	$47,598.00
Ohio State University College of Pharmacy	$24,261.00	$47,957.00	$47,957.00
Medical College of Wisconsin School of Pharmacy	$48,463.00	$48,463.00	$48,463.00
South College School of Pharmacy	$48,600.00	$48,600.00	$48,600.00

PharmD Schools	In-State Tuition	Out-of-State Tuition	Out-of-State COA
University of Kansas School of Pharmacy	$26,405.00	$48,640.00	$48,640.00
University of Texas at Austin College of Pharmacy	$21,548.00	$49,240.00	$49,240.00
South University School of Pharmacy	$49,296.00	$49,296.00	$49,296.00
St. John's University College of Pharmacy and Health Sciences	$49,416.00	$49,416.00	$49,416.00
Pacific University School of Pharmacy	$49,667.00	$49,667.00	$49,667.00
California Northstate University College of Pharmacy	$50,160.00	$50,160.00	$50,160.00
University of Louisiana at Monroe College of Pharmacy	$24,069.00	$36,169.00	$50,239.00
Marshall B. Ketchum University College of Pharmacy	$50,545.00	$50,545.00	$50,545.00
Rutgers, the State University of New Jersey Ernest Mario School of Pharmacy	$18,607.00	$39,649.00	$50,689.00
Larkin University College of Pharmacy	$51,097.00	$51,097.00	$51,097.00
Roosevelt University College of Pharmacy	$51,920.00	$51,920.00	$51,920.00
University of Saint Joseph School of Pharmacy and Physician Assistant Studies	$52,200.00	$52,200.00	$52,200.00
Loma Linda University School of Pharmacy	$52,500.00	$52,500.00	$52,500.00
University of Kentucky College of Pharmacy	$28,338.00	$52,631.00	$52,631.00
Wayne State University Eugene Applebaum College of Pharmacy and Health Sciences	$27,379.00	$52,697.00	$52,697.00
MCPHS University School of Pharmacy - Worcester	$53,100.00	$53,100.00	$53,100.00
University of North Carolina Eshelman School of Pharmacy	$27,451.00	$53,908.00	$53,908.00
University of Missouri-Kansas City School of Pharmacy	$25,436.00	$54,067.00	$54,067.00
Florida Agricultural & Mechanical University College of Pharmacy and Pharmaceutical Sciences	$25,228.00	$36,322.00	$54,108.00

PharmD Schools	In-State Tuition	Out-of-State Tuition	Out-of-State COA
University of Washington School of Pharmacy	$32,712.00	$54,324.00	$54,324.00
Purdue University College of Pharmacy	$22,810.00	$41,612.00	$54,402.00
University of Wyoming School of Pharmacy	$18,340.00	$37,176.00	$54,468.00
University of California, San Diego Skaggs School of Pharmacy & Pharmaceutical Sciences	$42,849.00	$55,094.00	$55,094.00
West Virginia University School of Pharmacy	$21,786.00	$43,170.00	$55,603.00
Washington State University College of Pharmacy and Pharmaceutical Sciences	$22,572.00	$39,226.00	$55,832.00
St. John Fisher College Wegmans School of Pharmacy	$41,466.00	$41,466.00	$56,716.00
Texas A & M University Health Science Center Irma Lerma Rangel College of Pharmacy	$16,293.00	$16,293.00	$56,754.00
Manchester University College of Pharmacy, Natural and Health Sciences	$40,846.00	$40,846.00	$57,069.00
University of Houston College of Pharmacy	$20,962.00	$37,666.00	$57,650.00
St. Louis College of Pharmacy	$38,606.00	$38,606.00	$57,740.00
University at Buffalo The State University of New York School of Pharmacy & Pharmaceutical Sciences	$29,272.00	$39,962.00	$58,442.00
Roseman University of Health Sciences College of Pharmacy	$58,582.00	$58,582.00	$58,582.00
University of Minnesota College of Pharmacy	$29,826.00	$42,762.00	$58,634.00
University of Georgia College of Pharmacy	$18,528.00	$39,236.00	$58,924.00
University of Utah College of Pharmacy	$31,110.00	$59,653.00	$59,653.00
Duquesne University School of Pharmacy	$59,688.00	$59,688.00	$59,688.00
Lake Erie College of Osteopathic Medicine School of Pharmacy	$28,840.00	$28,840.00	$60,251.00
University of California, Irvine School of Pharmacy	$42,438.00	$54,683.00	$61,277.96
University of Maryland Eastern Shore School of Pharmacy and Health Professions	$32,761.00	$62,085.00	$62,085.00

PharmD Schools	In-State Tuition	Out-of-State Tuition	Out-of-State COA
Midwestern University College of Pharmacy-Glendale	$62,696.00	$62,696.00	$62,696.00
Appalachian College of Pharmacy	$40,500.00	$40,500.00	$63,000.00
University of California, San Francisco School of Pharmacy	$50,981.00	$63,226.00	$63,226.00
University of Hawaii at Hilo Daniel K. Inouye College of Pharmacy	$24,590.00	$41,534.00	$63,468.00
American University of Health Sciences School of Pharmacy	$63,503.00	$63,503.00	$63,503.00
University of New England College of Pharmacy	$44,005.00	$44,005.00	$63,605.00
Creighton University School of Pharmacy and Health Professions	$39,450.00	$39,450.00	$64,473.00
University of Southern California School of Pharmacy	$64,632.00	$64,632.00	$64,632.00
University of North Texas Health Science Center UNT System College of Pharmacy	$19,906.00	$35,942.00	$65,316.00
Philadelphia College of Osteopathic Medicine - Georgia School of Pharmacy	$40,890.00	$40,890.00	$65,444.00
University of Wisconsin-Madison School of Pharmacy	$27,812.00	$45,024.00	$66,828.00
Northeast Ohio Medical University College of Pharmacy	$26,448.00	$37,758.00	$67,388.00
Howard University College of Pharmacy	$32,775.00	$32,775.00	$67,698.00
Keck Graduate Institute (KGI) School of Pharmacy and Health Sciences	$47,990.00	$47,990.00	$70,726.00
University of Mississippi School of Pharmacy	$25,308.00	$51,000.00	$70,872.00
Sullivan University College of Pharmacy	$53,000.00	$53,000.00	$71,707.00
University of Connecticut School of Pharmacy	$30,666.00	$58,838.00	$72,096.00
California Health Sciences University College of Pharmacy	$47,772.00	$47,772.00	$73,444.00
Western University of Health Sciences College of Pharmacy	$75,117.00	$75,117.00	$75,117.00
Chapman University School of Pharmacy	$78,510.00	$78,510.00	$78,510.00
University of the Pacific Thomas J. Long School of Pharmacy	$81,094.00	$81,094.00	$81,094.00

PharmD Schools	In-State Tuition	Out-of-State Tuition	Out-of-State COA
Touro New York College of Pharmacy	$41,940.00	$41,940.00	$90,137.00
Northeastern University Bouvé College of Health Sciences School of Pharmacy	N/A	N/A	N/A
Long Island University Arnold and Marie Schwartz College of Pharmacy and Health Sciences	N/A	N/A	N/A

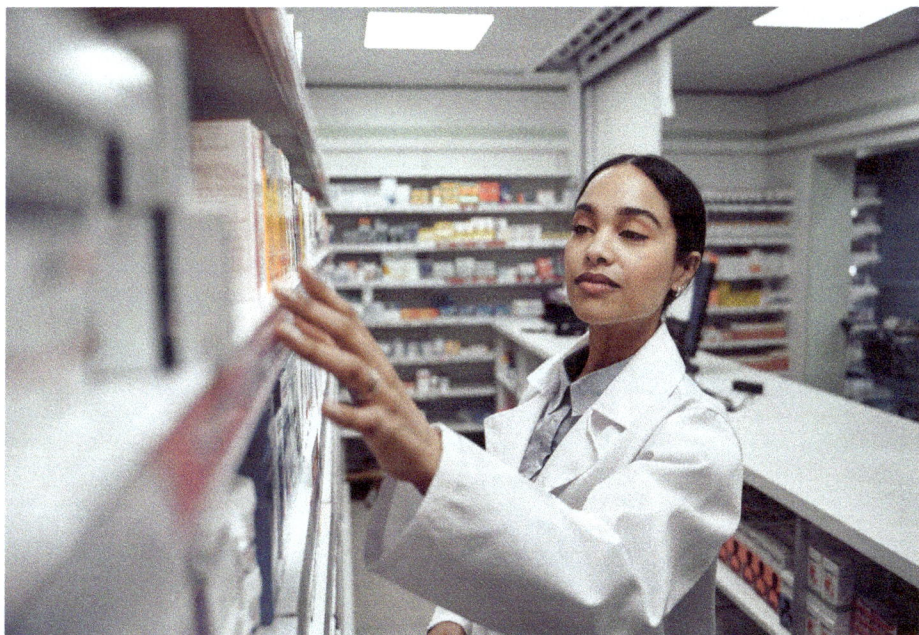

CHAPTER 12

PHARMACY SCHOOLS BY NUMBER OF INCOMING STUDENTS

PharmD Schools	# Enrolled in 2020
American University of Health Sciences School of Pharmacy	25
Husson University School of Pharmacy	33
University of Wyoming School of Pharmacy	33
Harding University College of Pharmacy	39
Union University College of Pharmacy	41
Cedarville University School of Pharmacy	42
University of New England College of Pharmacy	42
Medical College of Wisconsin School of Pharmacy	44
University of Findlay College of Pharmacy	44
University of Puerto Rico Medical Sciences Campus School of Pharmacy	45
University of Montana College of Health Professions and Biomedical Sciences Skaggs School of Pharmacy	46
Chicago State University College of Pharmacy	48
Sullivan University College of Pharmacy	48
University of Hawaii at Hilo Daniel K. Inouye College of Pharmacy	48
University of Maryland Eastern Shore School of Pharmacy and Health Professions	49
University of Charleston School of Pharmacy	50
Western New England University College of Pharmacy	51
William Carey University School of Pharmacy	51
Notre Dame of Maryland University School of Pharmacy	52
Marshall B. Ketchum University College of Pharmacy	53
Regis University Rueckert-Hartman College for Health Professions School of Pharmacy	53
University of Utah College of Pharmacy	53
Marshall University School of Pharmacy	54
Concordia University Wisconsin School of Pharmacy	55
Touro New York College of Pharmacy	55
Presbyterian College School of Pharmacy	56
Roosevelt University College of Pharmacy	56
University of Texas at El Paso School of Pharmacy	57
D'Youville College School of Pharmacy	58
University of Oklahoma College of Pharmacy	58
High Point University Fred Wilson School of Pharmacy	60
University of California, Irvine School of Pharmacy	60

PharmD Schools	# Enrolled in 2020
University of Saint Joseph School of Pharmacy and Physician Assistant Studies	60
University of California, San Diego Skaggs School of Pharmacy & Pharmaceutical Sciences	62
Rosalind Franklin University of Medicine and Science College of Pharmacy	63
University of Nebraska Medical Center College of Pharmacy	63
South Dakota State University College of Pharmacy and Allied Health Professions	65
University of Connecticut School of Pharmacy	65
West Virginia University School of Pharmacy	65
Medical University of South Carolina College of Pharmacy	67
Wilkes University Nesbitt School of Pharmacy	67
Lipscomb University College of Pharmacy and Health Sciences	68
Thomas Jefferson University Jefferson College of Pharmacy	68
Manchester University College of Pharmacy, Natural and Health Sciences	69
Texas Southern University College of Pharmacy and Health Sciences	70
Appalachian College of Pharmacy	72
University of New Mexico College of Pharmacy	72
Southwestern Oklahoma State University College of Pharmacy	73
Campbell University College of Pharmacy and Health Sciences	74
Loma Linda University School of Pharmacy	74
North Dakota State University College of Health Professions School of Pharmacy	74
Shenandoah University Bernard J. Dunn School of Pharmacy	74
Southern Illinois University Edwardsville School of Pharmacy	74
Palm Beach Atlantic University Lloyd L. Gregory School of Pharmacy	75
University of Arkansas for Medical Sciences College of Pharmacy	75
University of Texas at Tyler Ben and Maytee Fisch College of Pharmacy	75
Wingate University School of Pharmacy	75
South University School of Pharmacy	76
Drake University College of Pharmacy and Health Sciences	77
East Tennessee State University Bill Gatton College of Pharmacy	78
Howard University College of Pharmacy	79
Touro University - California College of Pharmacy	79

PharmD Schools	# Enrolled in 2020
Chapman University School of Pharmacy	82
Keck Graduate Institute (KGI) School of Pharmacy and Health Sciences	82
Oregon State University College of Pharmacy	82
University of Cincinnati James L. Winkle College of Pharmacy	83
University of Louisiana at Monroe College of Pharmacy	84
University of Michigan College of Pharmacy	85
Fairleigh Dickinson University School of Pharmacy	86
Florida Agricultural & Mechanical University College of Pharmacy and Pharmaceutical Sciences	87
Larkin University College of Pharmacy	87
University of North Texas Health Science Center UNT System College of Pharmacy	88
Belmont University College of Pharmacy	90
Idaho State University College of Pharmacy	90
West Coast University School of Pharmacy	90
Binghamton University State University of New York School of Pharmacy and Pharmaceutical Sciences	91
California Northstate University College of Pharmacy	91
Northeast Ohio Medical University College of Pharmacy	92
University of South Florida Health Taneja College of Pharmacy	92
University of the Incarnate Word Feik School of Pharmacy	92
University of Toledo College of Pharmacy and Pharmaceutical Sciences	94
Wayne State University Eugene Applebaum College of Pharmacy and Health Sciences	96
Ferris State University College of Pharmacy	97
South College School of Pharmacy	99
University of Iowa College of Pharmacy	100
Pacific University School of Pharmacy	103
Virginia Commonwealth University at the Medical College of Virginia Campus School of Pharmacy	103
University of Colorado Anschutz Medical Campus Skaggs School of Pharmacy and Pharmaceutical Sciences	106
Midwestern University Chicago College of Pharmacy	108
University of Washington School of Pharmacy	108
University of Mississippi School of Pharmacy	109

PharmD Schools	# Enrolled in 2020
Butler University College of Pharmacy and Health Sciences	110
Northeastern University Bouvé College of Health Sciences School of Pharmacy	110
University of South Carolina College of Pharmacy	110
Texas A & M University Health Science Center Irma Lerma Rangel College of Pharmacy	112
University of Pittsburgh School of Pharmacy	115
University of Houston College of Pharmacy	120
University of the Sciences Philadelphia College of Pharmacy	120
Western University of Health Sciences College of Pharmacy	120
Mercer University College of Pharmacy	122
University at Buffalo The State University of New York School of Pharmacy & Pharmaceutical Sciences	125
University of Maryland School of Pharmacy	125
University of Texas at Austin College of Pharmacy	125
University of Arizona College of Pharmacy	126
Samford University McWhorter School of Pharmacy	127
University of California, San Francisco School of Pharmacy	127
University of Wisconsin-Madison School of Pharmacy	128
Ohio Northern University Raabe College of Pharmacy	129
University of North Carolina Eshelman School of Pharmacy	130
University of Rhode Island College of Pharmacy	130
St. Louis College of Pharmacy	131
University of Kansas School of Pharmacy	132
Washington State University College of Pharmacy and Pharmaceutical Sciences	133
Ohio State University College of Pharmacy	137
University of Kentucky College of Pharmacy	140
Creighton University School of Pharmacy and Health Professions	141
Midwestern University College of Pharmacy-Glendale	141
Lake Erie College of Osteopathic Medicine School of Pharmacy	143
Duquesne University School of Pharmacy	145
University of Georgia College of Pharmacy	146
University of Missouri-Kansas City School of Pharmacy	146
University of Minnesota College of Pharmacy	147
Auburn University Harrison School of Pharmacy	148

PharmD Schools	# Enrolled in 2020
Purdue University College of Pharmacy	148
Temple University School of Pharmacy	152
Texas Tech University Health Sciences Center Jerry H. Hodge School of Pharmacy	157
Xavier University of Louisiana College of Pharmacy	158
Albany College of Pharmacy and Health Sciences School of Pharmacy and Pharmaceutical Sciences	173
University of Illinois at Chicago College of Pharmacy	176
University of Southern California School of Pharmacy	191
University of the Pacific Thomas J. Long School of Pharmacy	194
University of Tennessee Health Science Center College of Pharmacy	198
St. John Fisher College Wegmans School of Pharmacy	200
St. John's University College of Pharmacy and Health Sciences	200
MCPHS University School of Pharmacy - Worcester	201
Philadelphia College of Osteopathic Medicine - Georgia School of Pharmacy	203
Roseman University of Health Sciences College of Pharmacy	208
Rutgers, the State University of New Jersey Ernest Mario School of Pharmacy	214
Nova Southeastern University College of Pharmacy	219
University of Florida College of Pharmacy	248
MCPHS University School of Pharmacy - Boston	287
California Health Sciences University College of Pharmacy	N/A
Hampton University School of Pharmacy	N/A
Long Island University Arnold and Marie Schwartz College of Pharmacy and Health Sciences	N/A

CHAPTER 13

DENTAL SCHOOLS BY CITY/STATE

Dental Schools	City	State	Website
University of Alabama at Birmingham School of Dentistry	Birmingham	AL	https://www.uab.edu/dentistry/home/
Midwestern University College of Dental Medicine-Arizona	Glendale	AZ	https://www.midwestern.edu/academics/our-colleges/college-of-dental-medi-cine%E2%80%93arizona.xml
Arizona School of Dentistry & Oral Health	Mesa	AZ	https://www.atsu.edu/arizona-school-of-dentistry-and-oral-health
California North State College of Dental Medicine	Elk Grove	CA	http://dentalmedicine.cnsu.edu/
Loma Linda University School of Dentistry	Loma Linda	CA	https://dentistry.llu.edu/
Herman Ostrow School of Dentistry of USC	Los Angeles	CA	https://dentistry.usc.edu/
University of California, Los Angeles, School of Dentistry	Los Angeles	CA	https://www.dentistry.ucla.edu/
Western University of Health Sciences College of Dental Medicine	Pomona	CA	https://www.westernu.edu/dentistry/
University of California, San Francisco, School of Dentistry	San Francisco	CA	https://dentistry.ucsf.edu/
University of the Pacific Arthur A. Dugoni School of Dentistry	San Francisco	CA	https://www.dental.pacific.edu/
University of Colorado School of Dental Medicine	Aurora	CO	http://www.ucdenver.edu/academics/colleges/dentalmedicine/Pages/DentalMedicine.aspx
University of Connecticut School of Dental Medicine	Farmington	CT	https://dentalmedicine.uconn.edu/
Howard University College of Dentistry	Washington	DC	http://healthsciences.howard.edu/education/colleges/dentistry
Lake Erie College of Osteopathic Medicine School of Dental Medicine	Bradenton	FL	https://lecom.edu/academics/school-of-dental-medicine/
Nova Southeastern University College of Dental Medicine	Davie	FL	https://dental.nova.edu/index.html

Dental Schools	City	State	Website
University of Florida College of Dentistry	Gainesville	FL	https://dental.ufl.edu/
Dental College of Georgia at Augusta University	Augusta	GA	https://www.augusta.edu/dentalmedicine/
The University of Iowa College of Dentistry & Dental Clinics	Iowa City	IA	https://www.dentistry.uiowa.edu/
Southern Illinois University School of Dental Medicine	Alton	IL	http://www.siue.edu/dental/
University of Illinois at Chicago College of Dentistry	Chicago	IL	https://dentistry.uic.edu/
Midwestern University College of Dental Medicine-Illinois	Downers Grove	IL	https://www.midwestern.edu/academics/our-colleges/college-of-dental-medicine%E2%80%93illinois.xml
Indiana University School of Dentistry	Indianapolis	IN	https://dentistry.iu.edu/
University of Kentucky College of Dentistry	Lexington	KY	https://dentistry.uky.edu/
University of Louisville School of Dentistry	Louisville	KY	https://louisville.edu/dentistry
Louisiana State University Health New Orleans School of Dentistry	New Orleans	LA	https://www.lsusd.lsuhsc.edu/
Boston University Henry M. Goldman School of Dental Medicine	Boston	MA	http://www.bu.edu/dental/
Harvard School of Dental Medicine	Boston	MA	https://hsdm.harvard.edu/
Tufts University School of Dental Medicine	Boston	MA	https://dental.tufts.edu/
University of Maryland School of Dentistry	Baltimore	MD	https://www.dental.umaryland.edu/
University of New England College of Dental Medicine	Portland	ME	https://www.une.edu/dentalmedicine
University of Michigan School of Dentistry	Ann Arbor	MI	https://www.dent.umich.edu/
University of Detroit Mercy School of Dentistry	Detroit	MI	https://dental.udmercy.edu/
University of Minnesota School of Dentistry	Minneapolis	MN	https://www.dentistry.umn.edu/

Dental Schools	City	State	Website
University of Missouri-Kansas City School of Dentistry	Kansas City	MO	https://dentistry.umkc.edu/
Missouri School of Dentistry & Oral Health	Kirksville	MO	https://www.atsu.edu/missouri-school-of-dentistry-and-oral-health
University of Mississippi Medical Center School of Dentistry	Jackson	MS	https://www.umc.edu/sod/SOD_Home.html
University of North Carolina at Chapel Hill Adams School of Dentistry	Chapel Hill	NC	https://www.dentistry.unc.edu/
East Carolina University School of Dental Medicine	Greenville	NC	https://www.ecu.edu/cs-dhs/dental/
University of Nebraska Medical Center College of Dentistry	Lincoln	NE	https://www.unmc.edu/dentistry/
Creighton University School of Dentistry	Omaha	NE	https://dentistry.creighton.edu/
Rutgers, The State University of New Jersey, School of Dental Medicine	Newark	NJ	http://sdm.rutgers.edu/
University of Nevada, Las Vegas, School of Dental Medicine	Las Vegas	NV	https://www.unlv.edu/dental
University at Buffalo School of Dental Medicine	Buffalo	NY	http://dental.buffalo.edu/
Touro College of Dental Medicine at New York Medical College	Hawthorne	NY	https://dental.touro.edu/
Columbia University College of Dental Medicine	New York	NY	https://www.dental.columbia.edu/
NYU College of Dentistry	New York	NY	https://dental.nyu.edu/
Stony Brook University School of Dental Medicine	Stony Brook	NY	https://dentistry.stonybrookmedicine.edu/
Case Western Reserve University School of Dental Medicine	Cleveland	OH	https://case.edu/dental/
The Ohio State University College of Dentistry	Columbus	OH	https://dentistry.osu.edu/
University of Oklahoma College of Dentistry	Oklahoma City	OK	https://dentistry.ouhsc.edu/

Dental Schools	City	State	Website
Oregon Health & Science University School of Dentistry	Portland	OR	https://www.ohsu.edu/school-of-dentistry
The Maurice H. Kornberg School of Dentistry, Temple University	Philadelphia	PA	https://dentistry.temple.edu/
University of Pennsylvania School of Dental Medicine	Philadelphia	PA	https://www.dental.upenn.edu/
University of Pittsburgh School of Dental Medicine	Pittsburgh	PA	https://www.dental.pitt.edu/
University of Puerto Rico School of Dental Medicine	San Juan	PR	https://dental.rcm.upr.edu/
Medical University of South Carolina James B. Edwards College of Dental Medicine	Charleston	SC	https://dentistry.musc.edu/
University of Tennessee Health Science Center College of Dentistry	Memphis	TN	https://www.uthsc.edu/dentistry/
Meharry Medical College School of Dentistry	Nashville	TN	https://home.mmc.edu/school-of-dentistry/
Texas A&M College of Dentistry	Dallas	TX	https://dentistry.tamu.edu/
Texas Tech University Health Sciences Center El Paso Woody L. Hunt School of Dental Medicine	El Paso	TX	https://elpaso.ttuhsc.edu/sdm/
The University of Texas School of Dentistry at Houston	Houston	TX	https://dentistry.uth.edu/
UT Health San Antonio School of Dentistry	San Antonio	TX	https://www.uthscsa.edu/academics/dental
University of Utah School of Dentistry	Salt Lake City	UT	https://dentistry.utah.edu/
Roseman University of Health Sciences College of Dental Medicine – South Jordan, Utah	South Jordan	UT	https://dental.roseman.edu/
Virginia Commonwealth University School of Dentistry	Richmond	VA	https://dentistry.vcu.edu/
University of Washington School of Dentistry	Seattle	WA	https://dental.washington.edu/

Dental Schools	City	State	Website
Marquette University School of Dentistry	Milwaukee	WI	https://www.marquette.edu/dentistry/
West Virginia University School of Dentistry	Morgantown	WV	https://dentistry.wvu.edu/

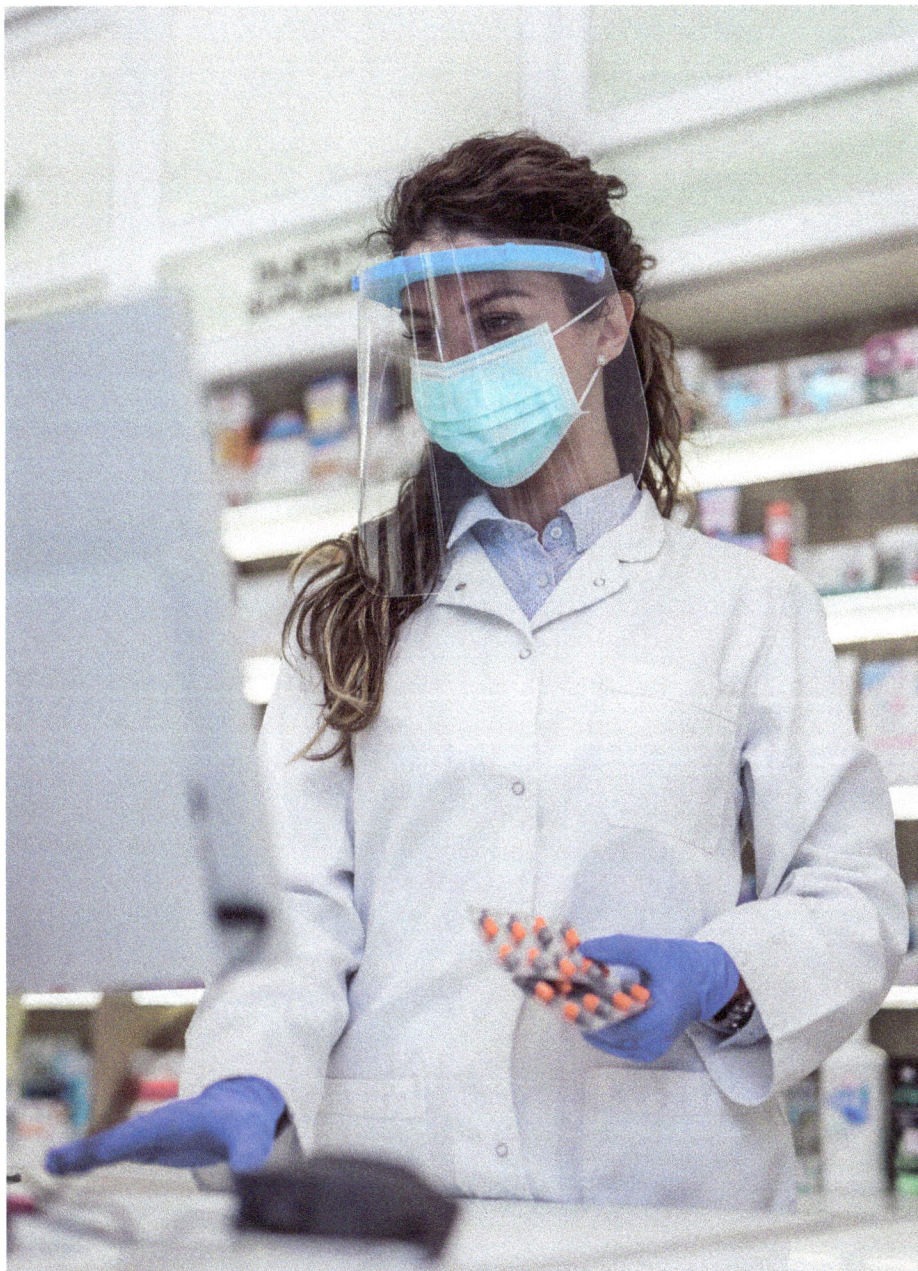

CHAPTER 14

MEDICAL SCHOOLS BY CITY/STATE

MD Schools	City	State	Website
University of Alabama School of Medicine	Birmingham	AL	*https://www.uab.edu/medicine/home/*
University of South Alabama College of Medicine	Mobile	AL	*https://www.southalabama.edu/colleges/com/*
University of Arkansas for Medical Sciences College of Medicine	Little Rock	AR	*https://medicine.uams.edu/*
The University of Arizona College of Medicine – Phoenix	Phoenix	AZ	*https://phoenixmed.arizona.edu/*
The University of Arizona College of Medicine – Tucson	Tucson	AZ	*https://medicine.arizona.edu/*
California University of Science and Medicine – School of Medicine	Colton	CA	*https://www.cusm.org/*
California Northstate University College of Medicine	Elk Grove	CA	*https://medicine.cnsu.edu/*
University of California, Irvine School of Medicine	Irvine	CA	*https://www.som.uci.edu/*
University of California, San Diego School of Medicine	La Jolla	CA	*https://medschool.ucsd.edu/Pages/default.aspx*
Loma Linda University School of Medicine	Loma Linda	CA	*https://medicine.llu.edu/*
David Geffen School of Medicine at UCLA	Los Angeles	CA	*https://medschool.ucla.edu/*
Keck School of Medicine of the University of Southern California	Los Angeles	CA	*https://keck.usc.edu/*
Kaiser Permanente School of Medicine	Pasadena	CA	*https://medschool.kp.org/*
University of California, Riverside School of Medicine	Riverside	CA	*https://medschool.ucr.edu/*

MD Schools	City	State	Website
University of California, Davis School of Medicine	Sacramento	CA	*https://health. ucdavis.edu/ medschool/*
University of California, San Francisco School of Medicine	San Francisco	CA	*https://medschool. ucsf.edu/*
Stanford University School of Medicine	Stanford	CA	*http://med.stanford. edu/*
University of Colorado School of Medicine	Aurora	CO	*https://medschool. cuanschutz.edu/*
University of Connecticut School of Medicine	Farmington	CT	*https://medicine. uconn.edu/*
Frank H. Netter MD School of Medicine at Quinnipiac University	Hamden	CT	*https://www.qu.edu/ schools/medicine. html*
Yale School of Medicine	New Haven	CT	*https://medicine. yale.edu/*
Georgetown University School of Medicine	Washington	DC	*https://som. georgetown.edu/*
Howard University College of Medicine	Washington	DC	*https://medicine. howard.edu/*
The George Washington University School of Medicine and Health Sciences	Washington	DC	*https://smhs.gwu. edu/*
Charles E. Schmidt College of Medicine at Florida Atlantic University	Boca Raton	FL	*http://med.fau.edu/*
Nova Southeastern University Dr. Kiran C. Patel College of Allopathic Medicine	Davie	FL	*https://md.nova.edu/ index.html*
University of Florida College of Medicine	Gainesville	FL	*https://med.ufl.edu/*

MD Schools	City	State	Website
Florida International University Herbert Wertheim College of Medicine	Miami	FL	https://medicine.fiu.edu/
University of Miami Leonard M. Miller School of Medicine	Miami	FL	https://med.miami.edu/
University of Central Florida College of Medicine	Orlando	FL	https://med.ucf.edu/
The Florida State University College of Medicine	Tallahassee	FL	https://med.fsu.edu/
USF Health Morsani College of Medicine	Tampa	FL	https://health.usf.edu/medicine
Emory University School of Medicine	Atlanta	GA	https://www.med.emory.edu/
Morehouse School of Medicine	Atlanta	GA	https://www.msm.edu/
Medical College of Georgia at Augusta University	Augusta	GA	https://www.augusta.edu/mcg/
Mercer University School of Medicine	Macon	GA	https://medicine.mercer.edu/
John A. Burns School of Medicine University of Hawaii at Manoa	Honolulu	HI	https://jabsom.hawaii.edu/
University of Iowa Roy J. and Lucille A. Carver College of Medicine	Iowa City	IA	https://medicine.uiowa.edu/
Carle Illinois College of Medicine	Champaign	IL	https://medicine.illinois.edu/
Northwestern University Feinberg School of Medicine	Chicago	IL	https://www.feinberg.northwestern.edu/
Rush Medical College of Rush University Medical Center	Chicago	IL	https://www.rushu.rush.edu/rush-medical-college

MD Schools	City	State	Website
University of Chicago Division of the Biological Sciences, The Pritzker School of Medicine	Chicago	IL	https://pritzker.uchicago.edu/
University of Illinois College of Medicine	Chicago	IL	https://medicine.uic.edu/
Loyola University Chicago Stritch School of Medicine	Maywood	IL	https://ssom.luc.edu/
Chicago Medical School at Rosalind Franklin University of Medicine and Science	North Chicago	IL	https://www.rosalindfranklin.edu/academics/chicago-medical-school/
Southern Illinois University School of Medicine	Springfield	IL	https://www.siumed.edu/
Indiana University School of Medicine	Indianapolis	IN	https://medicine.iu.edu/
University of Kansas School of Medicine	Kansas City	KS	http://www.kumc.edu/school-of-medicine.html
University of Kentucky College of Medicine	Lexington	KY	https://med.uky.edu/
University of Louisville School of Medicine	Louisville	KY	http://louisville.edu/medicine
LSU Health Sciences Center School of Medicine in New Orleans	New Orleans	LA	https://www.medschool.lsuhsc.edu/
Tulane University School of Medicine	New Orleans	LA	https://medicine.tulane.edu/
Louisiana State University School of Medicine in Shreveport	Shreveport	LA	https://www.lsuhs.edu/our-schools/school-of-medicine
Boston University School of Medicine	Boston	MA	https://www.bumc.bu.edu/busm/
Harvard Medical School	Boston	MA	https://hms.harvard.edu/

MD Schools	City	State	Website
Tufts University School of Medicine	Boston	MA	*https://medicine. tufts.edu/*
University of Massachusetts Medical School	North Worcester	MA	*https://www. umassmed.edu/*
Johns Hopkins University School of Medicine	Baltimore	MD	*https://www. hopkinsmedicine. org/som/*
University of Maryland School of Medicine	Baltimore	MD	*https://www. medschool. umaryland.edu/*
Uniformed Services University of the Health Sciences, F. Edward Hébert School of Medicine	Bethesda	MD	*https://www.usuhs. edu/medschool*
University of Michigan Medical School	Ann Arbor	MI	*https://medicine. umich.edu/ medschool/home*
Wayne State University School of Medicine	Detroit	MI	*https://www.med. wayne.edu/*
Michigan State University College of Human Medicine	East Lansing	MI	*http:// humanmedicine. msu.edu/*
Western Michigan University Homer Stryker M.D. School of Medicine	Kalamazoo	MI	*https://med.wmich. edu/*
Central Michigan University College of Medicine	Mt Pleasant	MI	*https://www.cmich. edu/colleges/med/ Pages/default.aspx*
Oakland University William Beaumont School of Medicine	Rochester	MI	*https://oakland.edu/ medicine/*
University of Minnesota Medical School	Minneapolis	MN	*https://med.umn. edu/*
Mayo Clinic Alix School of Medicine	Rochester	MN	*https://college.mayo. edu/academics/ school-of-medicine/*
University of Missouri-Columbia School of Medicine	Columbia	MO	*https://medicine. missouri.edu/*

MD Schools	City	State	Website
University of Missouri-Kansas City School of Medicine	Kansas City	MO	https://med.umkc.edu/
Saint Louis University School of Medicine	St. Louis	MO	https://www.slu.edu/medicine/index.php
Washington University in St. Louis School of Medicine	St. Louis	MO	https://medicine.wustl.edu/
University of Mississippi School of Medicine	Jackson	MS	https://www.umc.edu/som/SOM_Home.html
University of North Carolina School of Medicine	Chapel Hill	NC	https://www.med.unc.edu/
Duke University School of Medicine	Durham	NC	https://medschool.duke.edu/
The Brody School of Medicine at East Carolina University	Greenville	NC	https://medicine.ecu.edu/
Wake Forest School of Medicine of Wake Forest Baptist Medical Center	Winston-Salem	NC	https://school.wakehealth.edu/
University of North Dakota School of Medicine and Health Sciences	Grand Forks	ND	https://med.und.edu/
Creighton University School of Medicine	Omaha	NE	https://medschool.creighton.edu/
University of Nebraska College of Medicine	Omaha	NE	https://www.unmc.edu/com/
Geisel School of Medicine at Dartmouth	Hanover	NH	https://geiselmed.dartmouth.edu/
Cooper Medical School of Rowan University	Camden	NJ	https://cmsru.rowan.edu/
Rutgers, Robert Wood Johnson Medical School	New Brunswick	NJ	http://rwjms.rutgers.edu/

MD Schools	City	State	Website
Rutgers New Jersey Medical School	Newark	NJ	http://njms.rutgers.edu/
Hackensack-Meridian School of Medicine at Seton Hall University	Nutley	NJ	https://www.shu.edu/medicine/
University of New Mexico School of Medicine	Albuquerque	NM	https://hsc.unm.edu/school-of-medicine/
University of Nevada, Las Vegas School of Medicine	Las Vegas	NV	https://www.unlv.edu/medicine
University of Nevada, Reno School of Medicine	Reno	NV	https://med.unr.edu/
Albany Medical College	Albany	NY	https://www.amc.edu/Academic/index.cfm
Albert Einstein College of Medicine	Bronx	NY	https://www.einstein.yu.edu/
State University of New York Downstate Medical Center College of Medicine	Brooklyn	NY	https://www.downstate.edu/college-of-medicine/
Jacobs School of Medicine and Biomedical Sciences at the University at Buffalo	Buffalo	NY	http://medicine.buffalo.edu/
New York University Long Island School of Medicine	Mineola	NY	https://medli.nyu.edu/
Columbia University Vagelos College of Physicians and Surgeons	New York	NY	https://www.ps.columbia.edu/
CUNY School of Medicine	New York	NY	https://www.ccny.cuny.edu/csom
Donald and Barbara Zucker School of Medicine at Hofstra/Northwell	New York	NY	https://medicine.hofstra.edu/

MD Schools	City	State	Website
Icahn School of Medicine at Mount Sinai	New York	NY	https://icahn.mssm.edu/
New York University Grossman School of Medicine	New York	NY	https://med.nyu.edu/our-community/about-us
Weill Cornell Medicine	New York	NY	https://weill.cornell.edu/
University of Rochester School of Medicine and Dentistry	Rochester	NY	https://www.urmc.rochester.edu/smd.aspx
Renaissance School of Medicine at Stony Brook University	Stony Brook	NY	https://renaissance.stonybrookmedicine.edu/
State University of New York Upstate Medical University College of Medicine	Syracuse	NY	https://www.upstate.edu/com/
New York Medical College	Valhalla	NY	https://www.nymc.edu/
University of Cincinnati College of Medicine	Cincinnati	OH	https://www.med.uc.edu/
Case Western Reserve University School of Medicine	Cleveland	OH	https://case.edu/medicine/
The Ohio State University College of Medicine	Columbus	OH	https://medicine.osu.edu/
Boonshoft School of Medicine Wright State University	Dayton	OH	https://medicine.wright.edu/
Northeast Ohio Medical University College of Medicine	Rootstown	OH	https://www.neomed.edu/
The University of Toledo College of Medicine and Life Sciences	Toledo	OH	https://www.utoledo.edu/med/
University of Oklahoma College of Medicine	Oklahoma City	OK	https://medicine.ouhsc.edu/

MD Schools	City	State	Website
Oregon Health & Science University School of Medicine	Portland	OR	*https://www.ohsu.edu/school-of-medicine*
Penn State College of Medicine	Hershey	PA	*https://med.psu.edu/*
Drexel University College of Medicine	Philadelphia	PA	*https://drexel.edu/medicine/*
Lewis Katz School of Medicine at Temple University	Philadelphia	PA	*https://medicine.temple.edu/*
Sidney Kimmel Medical College at Thomas Jefferson University	Philadelphia	PA	*https://www.jefferson.edu/university/skmc.html*
The Raymond and Ruth Perelman School of Medicine at the University of Pennsylvania	Philadelphia	PA	*https://www.med.upenn.edu/*
University of Pittsburgh School of Medicine	Pittsburgh	PA	*https://www.medschool.pitt.edu/*
Geisinger Commonwealth School of Medicine	Scranton	PA	*https://www.geisinger.edu/education*
Universidad Central del Caribe School of Medicine	Bayamon	PR	*http://www.uccaribe.edu/medicine/*
San Juan Bautista School of Medicine	Caguas	PR	*https://www.sanjuanbautista.edu/*
Ponce Health Sciences University School of Medicine	Ponce	PR	*https://www.psm.edu/school-of-medicine/*
University of Puerto Rico School of Medicine	San Juan	PR	*https://md.rcm.upr.edu/md-program/*
The Warren Alpert Medical School of Brown University	Providence	RI	*https://medical.brown.edu/*
Medical University of South Carolina College of Medicine	Charleston	SC	*https://medicine.musc.edu/*

MD Schools	City	State	Website
University of South Carolina School of Medicine, Columbia	Columbia	SC	https://www.sc.edu/study/colleges_schools/medicine/index.php
University of South Carolina School of Medicine, Greenville	Greenville	SC	https://www.sc.edu/study/colleges_schools/medicine_greenville/index.php
University of South Dakota Sanford School of Medicine	Sioux Falls	SD	https://www.usd.edu/medicine
East Tennessee State University James H. Quillen College of Medicine	Johnson City	TN	https://www.etsu.edu/com/
University of Tennessee Health Science Center College of Medicine	Memphis	TN	https://www.uthsc.edu/medicine/
Meharry Medical College School of Medicine	Nashville	TN	https://home.mmc.edu/
Vanderbilt University School of Medicine	Nashville	TN	https://medschool.vanderbilt.edu/
The University of Texas at Austin Dell Medical School	Austin	TX	https://dellmed.utexas.edu/
Texas A&M University Health Science Center College of Medicine	Bryan	TX	https://medicine.tamu.edu/
The University of Texas Southwestern Medical School	Dallas	TX	https://www.utsouthwestern.edu/education/medical-school/
The University of Texas Rio Grande Valley School of Medicine	Edinburg	TX	https://www.utrgv.edu/school-of-medicine/
Paul L. Foster School of Medicine Texas Tech University Health Sciences Center	El Paso	TX	https://elpaso.ttuhsc.edu/som/

MD Schools	City	State	Website
TCU and UNTHSC School of Medicine	Fort Worth	TX	*https://mdschool.tcu.edu/*
The University of Texas Medical Branch at Galveston School of Medicine	Galveston	TX	*https://som.utmb.edu/*
Baylor College of Medicine	Houston	TX	*https://www.bcm.edu/*
McGovern Medical School at The University of Texas Health Science Center at Houston	Houston	TX	*https://med.uth.edu/*
University of Houston College of Medicine	Houston	TX	*https://www.uh.edu/medicine/*
Texas Tech University Health Sciences Center School of Medicine	Lubbock	TX	*https://www.ttuhsc.edu/medicine/default.aspx*
The University of Texas Health Science Center at San Antonio Joe R. and Teresa Lozano Long School of Medicine	San Antonio	TX	*http://som.uthscsa.edu/*
University of Utah School of Medicine	Salt Lake City	UT	*https://medicine.utah.edu/*
University of Virginia School of Medicine	Charlottesville	VA	*https://med.virginia.edu/*
Eastern Virginia Medical School	Norfolk	VA	*https://www.evms.edu/*
Virginia Commonwealth University School of Medicine	Richmond	VA	*https://medschool.vcu.edu/*
Virginia Tech Carilion School of Medicine	Roanoke	VA	*https://medicine.vtc.vt.edu/*
The Robert Larner, M.D. College of Medicine at the University of Vermont	Burlington	VT	*http://www.med.uvm.edu/*

MD Schools	City	State	Website
University of Washington School of Medicine	Seattle	WA	https://www.uwmedicine.org/school-of-medicine
Washington State University Elson S. Floyd College of Medicine	Spokane	WA	https://medicine.wsu.edu/
University of Wisconsin School of Medicine and Public Health	Madison	WI	https://www.med.wisc.edu/
Medical College of Wisconsin	Milwaukee	WI	https://www.mcw.edu/
Marshall University Joan C. Edwards School of Medicine	Huntington	WV	https://jcesom.marshall.edu/
West Virginia University School of Medicine	Morgantown	WV	https://medicine.hsc.wvu.edu/

326

CHAPTER 15

OSTEOPATHIC MEDICAL SCHOOLS BY CITY/STATE

DO Schools	City	State	Website
Edward Via College of Osteopathic Medicine (VCOM - Auburn Campus)	Auburn	AL	https://www.vcom.edu/
Alabama College of Osteopathic Medicine (ACOM)	Dothan	AL	https://www.acom.edu/
Arkansas College of Osteopathic Medicine (ARCOM)	Fort Smith	AR	https://acheedu.org/arcom/
New York Institute of Technology College of Osteopathic Medicine at Arkansas State (NYITCOM)	Jonesboro	AR	https://www.nyit.edu/arkansas
Midwestern University Arizona College of Osteopathic Medicine (MWU/AZCOM)	Glendale	AZ	https://www.midwestern.edu/academics/our-colleges/arizona-college-of-osteopathic-medicine.xml
A.T. Still University, School of Osteopathic Medicine in Arizona (ATSU-SOMA)	Mesa	AZ	https://www.atsu.edu/school-of-osteopathic-medicine-arizona
California Health Sciences University College of Osteopathic Medicine (CHSU-COM)	Clovis	CA	https://osteopathic.chsu.edu/
Western University of Health Sciences College of Osteopathic Medicine of the Pacific (WesternU/COMP)	Pomona	CA	https://www.westernu.edu/osteopathic/
Touro University College of Osteopathic Medicine-California (TUCOM)	Vallejo	CA	http://com.tu.edu/
Rocky Vista University College of Osteopathic Medicine (RVUCOM)	Parker	CO	http://www.rvu.edu/rvu-su/college-of-osteopathic-medicine/
Lake Erie College of Osteopathic Medicine-Bradenton (LECOM-Bradenton)	Bradenton	FL	https://lecom.edu/
Nova Southeastern University Dr. Kiran C. Patel College of Osteopathic Medicine (NSU-KPCOM-Clearwater)	Clearwater	FL	https://osteopathic.nova.edu/index.html
Nova Southeastern University Dr. Kiran C. Patel College of Osteopathic Medicine (NSU-KPCOM)	Fort Lauderdale	FL	https://osteopathic.nova.edu/index.html
Philadelphia College of Osteopathic Medicine South Georgia (PCOM South Georgia)	Moultrie	GA	https://www.pcom.edu/south-georgia/

DO Schools	City	State	Website
Philadelphia College of Osteopathic Medicine Georgia (PCOM Georgia)	Suwanee	GA	https://www.pcom.edu/campuses/georgia-campus/
Des Moines University College of Osteopathic Medicine (DMU-COM)	Des Moines	IA	https://www.dmu.edu/do/
Idaho College of Osteopathic Medicine (ICOM)	Meridian	ID	https://www.idahocom.org/
Midwestern University Chicago College of Osteopathic Medicine (MWU/CCOM)	Downers Grove	IL	https://www.midwestern.edu/academics/degrees-and-programs/doctor-of-osteopathic-medicine-il.xml
Marian University College of Osteopathic Medicine (MU-COM)	Indianapolis	IN	https://www.marian.edu/osteopathic-medical-school
University of Pikeville Kentucky College of Osteopathic Medicine (UP-KYCOM)	Pikeville	KY	https://www.upike.edu/osteopathic-medicine/
Edward Via College of Osteopathic Medicine-Monroe Campus (VCOM - Monroe Campus)	Monroe	LA	https://www.vcom.edu/louisiana
University of New England College of Osteopathic Medicine (UNECOM)	Biddeford	ME	https://www.une.edu/com
Michigan State University College of Osteopathic Medicine (MSUCOM-MUC)	Clinton Twp	MI	https://com.msu.edu/
Michigan State University College of Osteopathic Medicine (MSUCOM-DMC)	Detroit	MI	https://com.msu.edu/
Michigan State University College of Osteopathic Medicine (MSUCOM)	East Lansing	MI	https://com.msu.edu/
Minnesota College of Osteopathic Medicine	Gaylord	MN	N/A
Kansas City University of Medicine and Biosciences College of Osteopathic Medicine (KCU-COM)	Kansas City	MO	http://www.kcumb.edu/programs/college-of-osteopathic-medicine
A. T. Still University Kirksville College of Osteopathic Medicine (ATSU-KCOM)	Kirksville	MO	https://www.atsu.edu/kirksville-college-of-osteopathic-medicine

DO Schools	City	State	Website
William Carey University College of Osteopathic Medicine (WCUCOM)	Hattiesburg	MS	https://www.wmcarey.edu/College/Osteopathic-Medicine
Campbell University Jerry M. Wallace School of Osteopathic Medicine (CUSOM)	Lillington	NC	https://medicine.campbell.edu/
Rowan University School of Osteopathic Medicine (RowanSOM)	Stratford	NJ	https://som.rowan.edu/
Burrell College of Osteopathic Medicine (BCOM)	Las Cruces	NM	https://bcomnm.org/
Kansas City University of Medicine and Biosciences College of Osteopathic Medicine (KCU-COM-Joplin)	Joplin	NO	http://www.kcumb.edu/programs/college-of-osteopathic-medicine
Touro University Nevada College of Osteopathic Medicine (TUNCOM)	Henderson	NV	https://tun.touro.edu/programs/osteopathic-medicine/
Lake Erie College of Osteopathic Medicine - Elmira (LECOM-Elmira)	Elmira	NY	https://lecom.edu/
Touro College of Osteopathic Medicine (TouroCOM-Middletown)	Middletown	NY	https://tourocom.touro.edu/
Touro College of Osteopathic Medicine (TouroCOM-Harlem)	New York	NY	https://tourocom.touro.edu/
New York Institute of Technology College of Osteopathic Medicine (NYITCOM)	Old Westbury	NY	https://www.nyit.edu/medicine
Ohio University Heritage College of Osteopathic Medicine (OU-HCOM)	Athens	OH	https://www.ohio.edu/medicine/
Ohio University Heritage College of Osteopathic Medicine in Dublin (OU-HCOM-Dublin)	Dublin	OH	https://www.ohio.edu/medicine/
Ohio University Heritage College of Osteopathic Medicine in Cleveland (OU-HCOM-Cleveland)	Warrensville Heights	OH	https://www.ohio.edu/medicine/
Oklahoma State University Center for Health Sciences College of Osteopathic Medicine - Tahlequah (OSU-COM Tahlequah)	Tahlequah	OK	https://health.okstate.edu/com/index.html

DO Schools	City	State	Website
Oklahoma State University Center for Health Sciences College of Osteopathic Medicine (OSU-COM)	Tulsa	OK	https://health.okstate.edu/com/index.html
Western University of Health Sciences College of Osteopathic Medicine of the Pacific-Northwest (WesternU/COMP-Northwest)	Lebanon	OR	https://www.westernu.edu/northwest/
Lake Erie College of Osteopathic Medicine-Erie (LECOM)	Erie	PA	https://lecom.edu/
Lake Erie College of Osteopathic Medicine - Seton Hill (LECOM-Seton Hill)	Greensburg	PA	https://lecom.edu/
Philadelphia College of Osteopathic Medicine (PCOM)	Philadelphia	PA	https://www.pcom.edu/
Edward Via College of Osteopathic Medicine-Carolinas Campus (VCOM - Carolinas Campus)	Spartanburg	SC	https://www.vcom.edu/carolinas
Lincoln Memorial University DeBusk College of Osteopathic Medicine (LMU-DCOM)	Harrogate	TN	https://www.lmunet.edu/debusk-college-of-osteopathic-medicine/index.php
Lincoln Memorial University DeBusk College of Osteopathic Medicine - Knoxville (LMU-DCOM Knoxville)	Knoxville	TN	https://www.lmunet.edu/debusk-college-of-osteopathic-medicine/index.php
University of North Texas Health Science Center Texas College of Osteopathic Medicine (UNTHSC/TCOM)	Fort Worth	TX	https://www.unthsc.edu/texas-college-of-osteopathic-medicine/
Sam Houston State University College of Osteopathic Medicine	Huntsville	TX	https://www.shsu.edu/academics/osteopathic-medicine/
University of the Incarnate Word School of Osteopathic Medicine (UIWSOM)	San Antonio	TX	https://osteopathic-medicine.uiw.edu/
Rocky Vista University College of Osteopathic Medicine (RVUCOM-SU Campus)	Ivins	UT	http://www.rvu.edu/rvu-su/college-of-osteopathic-medicine/
Noorda College of Osteopathic Medicine	Provo	UT	https://noordacom.org/

DO Schools	City	State	Website
Edward Via College of Osteopathic Medicine (VCOM-Virginia Campus)	Blacksburg	VA	https://www.vcom.edu/virginia
Liberty University College of Osteopathic Medicine (LUCOM)	Lynchburg	VA	https://www.liberty.edu/lucom/
Pacific Northwest University of Health Sciences College of Osteopathic Medicine (PNWU-COM)	Yakima	WA	https://www.pnwu.edu/
West Virginia School of Osteopathic Medicine (WVSOM)	Lewisburg	WV	https://www.wvsom.edu/

CHAPTER 16

PHYSICIAN ASSISTANT SCHOOLS BY CITY/STATE

Physician Assistant	City	State	Website
University of Washington - MEDEX Northwest, Anchorage	Anchorage	AK	https://depts.washington.edu/medex/pa-program/
University of Alabama at Birmingham	Birmingham	AL	http://www.uab.edu/shp/cds/physician-assistant
Samford University	Homewood	AL	https://www.samford.edu/healthprofessions/master-of-science-in-physician-assistant-studies
University of South Alabama	Mobile	AL	https://www.southalabama.edu/colleges/alliedhealth/pa/
Faulkner University	Montgomery	AL	https://www.faulkner.edu/graduate/graduate-degrees/physican-assistant-studies-ms-pas/
University of Arkansas	Little Rock	AR	http://healthprofessions.uams.edu/programs/physicianassistant/
Harding University	Searcy	AR	http://www.harding.edu/PAprogram/
Midwestern University - Glendale	Glendale	AZ	https://www.midwestern.edu/academics/degrees-and-programs/master-of-medical-sciences-in-physician-assistant-studies-az.xml
A.T. Still University - Arizona School of Health Sciences	Mesa	AZ	https://www.atsu.edu/physician-assistant-degree
Northern Arizona University	Phoenix	AZ	http://www.nau.edu/pa
University of Southern California	Alhambra	CA	https://keck.usc.edu/physician-assistant-program/
Marshall B. Ketchum University	Fullerton	CA	https://www.ketchum.edu/pa-studies
Chapman University	Irvine	CA	https://www.chapman.edu/crean/academic-programs/graduate-programs/physician-assistant/index.aspx
University of La Verne	La Verne	CA	https://artsci.laverne.edu/physician-assistant/

Physician Assistant	City	State	Website
Loma Linda University	Loma Linda	CA	http://www.llu.edu/allied-health/sahp/pa
Charles R. Drew University	Los Angeles	CA	https://www.cdrewu.edu/cosh/PA
Samuel Merritt University	Oakland	CA	http://www.samuelmerritt.edu/physician_assistant
Western University of Health Sciences	Pomona	CA	http://prospective.westernu.edu/physician-assistant/welcome-14/
California Baptist University	Riverside	CA	https://calbaptist.edu/programs/master-of-science-physician-assistant-studies/
University of California, Davis	Sacramento	CA	https://health.ucdavis.edu/nursing/admissions/programs/mhs-pa.html
University of the Pacific	Sacramento	CA	http://pacific.edu/PAprogram
California State University, Monterey Bay	Salinas	CA	http://csumb.edu/mspa
Point Loma Nazarene University	San Diego	CA	https://www.pointloma.edu/graduate-studies/programs/physician-assistant-ms-m#applicationinformation
Dominican University of California	San Rafael	CA	https://www.dominican.edu/directory/physician-assistant-studies
Stanford University	Stanford	CA	https://med.stanford.edu/pa
Touro University California	Vallejo	CA	http://cehs.tu.edu/paprogram/
Southern California University of Health Sciences	Whittier	CA	https://www.scuhs.edu/academics/csih/master-of-science-physician-assistant-program/
Red Rocks Community College	Arvada	CO	https://www.rrcc.edu/physician-assistant
University of Colorado	Aurora	CO	http://www.ucdenver.edu/academics/colleges/medicalschool/education/degree_programs/PAProgram/Pages/Home.aspx

Physician Assistant	City	State	Website
Colorado Mesa University	Grand Junction	CO	https://www.coloradomesa.edu/kinesiology/graduate/pa-program/index.html
Rocky Vista University	Parker	CO	https://www.rvu.edu/admissions/mpas/
Yale University	New Haven	CT	http://www.paprogram.yale.edu/
University of Bridgeport	Bridgeport	CT	http://www.bridgeport.edu/academics/schools-colleges/physician-assistant-institute/physician-assistant-ms
Sacred Heart University	Fairfield	CT	https://www.sacredheart.edu/majors--programs/physician-assistant-studies---mpas/
Quinnipiac University	Hamden	CT	http://www.quinnipiac.edu/gradphysicianasst
University of Saint Joseph	West Hartford	CT	https://www.usj.edu/academics/academic-schools/sppas/physician-assistant-studies/admissions/
George Washington University	Washington	DC	https://smhs.gwu.edu/physician-assistant/
Keiser University	Fort Lauderdale	FL	https://www.keiseruniversity.edu/master-of-science-in-physician-assistant/
Nova Southeastern University - Fort Lauderdale	Fort Lauderdale	FL	http://www.nova.edu/chcs/pa/fortlauderdale/index.html
Nova Southeastern University - Orlando	Fort Lauderdale	FL	https://healthsciences.nova.edu/pa/orlando/index.html
Florida Gulf Coast University	Fort Myers	FL	https://www2.fgcu.edu/mariebcollege/HS/MPAS/index.html
Nova Southeastern University - Fort Myers	Fort Myers	FL	https://healthsciences.nova.edu/pa/fort-myers/index.html
University of Florida	Gainesville	FL	https://pap.med.ufl.edu/
Nova Southeastern University - Jacksonville	Jacksonville	FL	https://healthsciences.nova.edu/pa/jacksonville/index.html

Physician Assistant	City	State	Website
Barry University - Miami	Miami	FL	http://www.barry.edu/physician-assistant/
Barry University - St. Petersburg	Miami	FL	http://www.barry.edu/physician-assistant/
Florida International University Herbert Wertheim College of Medicine	Miami	FL	https://medicine.fiu.edu/academics/degrees-and-programs/master-in-physician-studies/index.html
Miami Dade College	Miami	FL	http://www.mdc.edu/physicianassistantas/
AdventHealth University	Orlando	FL	https://www.ahu.edu/academics/ms-physician-assistant
South University, West Palm Beach	Royal Palm Beach	FL	https://www.southuniversity.edu/west-palm-beach/physician-assistant-ms
Gannon University - Ruskin	Ruskin	FL	https://www.gannon.edu/academic-offerings/health-professions-and-sciences/graduate/master-of-physician-assistant-science/admission-requirements/
Florida State University	Tallahassee	FL	https://med.fsu.edu/index.cfm?page=pa.home
South University, Tampa	Tampa	FL	http://www.southuniversity.edu/tampa/areas-of-study/physician-assistant/physician-assistant-master-of-science-ms
University of South Florida	Tampa	FL	https://health.usf.edu/medicine/pa/
University of Tampa	Tampa	FL	https://www.ut.edu/graduate-degrees/physician-assistant-medicine-program
Emory University	Atlanta	GA	http://med.emory.edu/pa/
Mercer University	Atlanta	GA	http://chp.mercer.edu/academics-departments/physician-assistant-studies/
Morehouse School of Medicine	Atlanta	GA	http://www.msm.edu//physicianassistantprogram/index.php

Physician Assistant	City	State	Website
South College - Atlanta	Atlanta	GA	https://www.south.edu/programs/master-health-science-physician-assistant-studies/atlanta/
Augusta University	Augusta	GA	https://www.augusta.edu/alliedhealth/pa/
Brenau University	Gainesville	GA	https://www.brenau.edu/healthsciences/physician-assistant-studies/
South University, Savannah	Savannah	GA	https://www.southuniversity.edu/savannah/areas-of-study/physician-assistant/physician-assistant-master-of-science-ms
PCOM - Georgia	Suwanee	GA	https://www.pcom.edu/academics/programs-and-degrees/physician-assistant-studies/georgia.html
University of Washington - MEDEX Northwest, Kona	Kealakekua	HI	https://depts.washington.edu/medex/pa-program/
St. Ambrose University	Davenport	IA	http://www.sau.edu/master-of-physician-assistant-studies
Des Moines University	Des Moines	IA	https://www.dmu.edu/pa/
University of Dubuque	Dubuque	IA	http://www.dbq.edu/Academics/OfficeofAcademicAffairs/GraduatePrograms/MasterofScienceinPhysician-AssistantStudies/
University of Iowa	Iowa City	IA	http://www.medicine.uiowa.edu/pa/
Northwestern College	Orange City	IA	https://www.nwciowa.edu/graduate/physician-assistant
Idaho State University - Caldwell	Caldwell	ID	https://www.isu.edu/pa/
Idaho State University - Meridian	Meridian	ID	https://www.isu.edu/pa/
Idaho State University - Pocatello	Meridian	ID	https://www.isu.edu/pa/
Southern Illinois University	Carbondale	IL	https://www.siumed.edu/paprogram
Northwestern University	Chicago	IL	http://www.feinberg.northwestern.edu/sites/pa/

Physician Assistant	City	State	Website
Rush University	Chicago	IL	http://www.rushu.rush.edu/pa-program
Midwestern University - Downers Grove	Downers Grove	IL	https://www.midwestern.edu/admissions/apply/master-of-medical-sciences-in-physician-assistant-studies-in-downers-grove.xml
Rosalind Franklin University of Medicine	North Chicago	IL	https://www.rosalindfranklin.edu/academics/college-of-health-professions/degree-programs/physician-assistant-practice-ms/
Dominican University of Illinois	River Forest	IL	https://www.dom.edu/admission/graduate/health-sciences-programs/mmspas
Trine University	Angola	IN	http://www.trine.edu/academics/majors-and-minors/graduate/master-physician-assistant-studies/index.aspx
University of Evansville	Evansville	IN	https://www.evansville.edu/majors/physicianassistant/
University of Saint Francis	Fort Wayne	IN	http://pa.sf.edu/
Franklin College	Franklin	IN	https://franklincollege.edu/academics/graduate-programs/master-science-physician-assistant/
Butler University	Indianapolis	IN	http://www.butler.edu/physician-assistant/
Indiana University School of Health and Human Sciences	Indianapolis	IN	https://shhs.iupui.edu/admissions/graduate-professional/master-physician-assistant-studies.html
Indiana State University	Terre Haute	IN	https://www.indstate.edu/health/program/pa
Valparaiso University	Valparaiso	IN	https://www.valpo.edu/physician-assistant-program/programs/admission/
Wichita State University	Wichita	KS	http://www.wichita.edu/thisis/home/?u=pa

Physician Assistant	City	State	Website
University of Kentucky - Lexington	Lexington	KY	http://www.uky.edu/chs/academic-programs/physician-assistant-studies
Sullivan University	Louisville	KY	https://www.sullivan.edu/programs/master-of-science-in-physician-assistant
University of Kentucky - Morehead	Morehead	KY	https://www.uky.edu/chs/academic-programs/physician-assistant-studies
University of the Cumberlands	Williamsburg	KY	http://gradweb.ucumberlands.edu/medicine/mpas/overview
University of the Cumberlands, Northern Kentucky Campus	Williamsburg	KY	https://www.ucumberlands.edu/academics/graduate/programs/master-science-physician-assistant-studies
Franciscan Missionaries of Our Lady University	Baton Rouge	LA	https://www.franu.edu/academics/academic-programs/physician-assistant-studies
Lousiana State University - New Orleans	New Orleans	LA	http://alliedhealth.lsuhsc.edu/pa/
Xavier University of Louisiana	New Orleans	LA	https://www.xula.edu/physician-assistant-program-about
Louisiana State University Health Sciences Center Shreveport	Shreveport	LA	https://lsuhscshreveportedu.finalsite.com/departments/allied-health-professions-departments/physician-assistant
Boston University School of Medicine	Boston	MA	http://bu.edu/paprogram
MCPHS - Boston	Boston	MA	https://www.mcphs.edu/academics/school-of-physician-assistant-studies/physician-assistant/physician-assistant-studies-mpas
MGH Institute of Health Professions	Boston	MA	http://www.mghihp.edu/academics/school-of-health-and-rehabilitation-sciences/physician-assistant-studies/default.aspx

Physician Assistant	City	State	Website
Northeastern University	Boston	MA	https://bouve.northeastern.edu/physician-assistant/ms/
Tufts University	Boston	MA	https://medicine.tufts.edu/education/physician-assistant
Bay Path University	East Longmeadow	MA	https://www.baypath.edu/academics/graduate-programs/physician-assistant-studies-ms/
Springfield College	Springfield	MA	https://springfield.edu/programs/physician-assistant-studies
Westfield State University	Westfield	MA	https://www.westfield.ma.edu/academics/master-of-science-in-physician-assistant-studies/
MCPHS - Worcester	Worcester	MA	https://www.mcphs.edu/academics/school-of-physician-assistant-studies/physician-assistant/physican-assistant-studies-mpas-accelerated
University of Maryland Baltimore/Ann Arundel Community College	Arnold	MD	https://graduate.umaryland.edu/mshs-pa-umb/
Towson University CCBC - Essex	Baltimore	MD	https://www.towson.edu/chp/departments/health-sciences/grad/physician-assistant/
Frostburg State University	Hagerstown	MD	https://www.frostburg.edu/academics/majorminors/graduate/ms-physician-assistant/index.php
University of Maryland Eastern Shore	Princess Anne	MD	http://www.umes.edu/pa
University of New England	Portland	ME	http://www.une.edu/wchp/pa
Concordia University Ann Arbor	Ann Arbor	MI	https://www.cuaa.edu/academics/programs/physician-assistant-masters/index.html#overview
University of Detroit Mercy	Detroit	MI	http://healthprofessions.udmercy.edu/academics/pa/grad.php

Physician Assistant	City	State	Website
Wayne State Unversity	Detroit	MI	http://www.pa.cphs.wayne.edu/
University of Michigan - Flint	Flint	MI	https://www.umflint.edu/physician-assistant-ms/
Grand Valley State University - Grand Rapids	Grand Rapids	MI	http://www.gvsu.edu/pas
Western Michigan University	Kalamazoo	MI	http://www.wmich.edu/pa
Central Michigan University	Mount Pleasant	MI	https://www.cmich.edu/colleges/CHP/hp_academics/srms/physician_assistant/Pages/PA-Program-at-CMU.aspx
Grand Valley State University - Traverse City	Traverse City	MI	https://www.gvsu.edu/pas/traverse-city-campus-89.htm
Eastern Michigan University	Ypsilanti	MI	http://www.emich.edu/pa
College of St. Scholastica	Duluth	MN	http://www.css.edu/graduate/masters-doctoral-and-professional-programs/areas-of-study/ms-physician-assistant.html
Augsburg University	Minneapolis	MN	http://www.augsburg.edu/pa/
Mayo Clinic School of Health Sciences	Rochester	MN	https://college.mayo.edu/academics/health-sciences-education/physician-assistant-program-minnesota/
Saint Catherine University	Saint Paul	MN	https://www.stkate.edu/academic-programs/gc/physician-assistant-studies-mpas
Bethel University	St. Paul	MN	https://www.bethel.edu/graduate/academics/physician-assistant/
Stephens College	Columbia	MO	https://www.stephens.edu/academics/graduate-programs/master-in-physician-assistant-studies/
University of Missouri-Kansas City	Kansas City	MO	http://med.umkc.edu/pa/

Physician Assistant	City	State	Website
Saint Louis University	Saint Louis	MO	https://www.slu.edu/doisy/degrees/graduate/physician-assistant-mms.php
Missouri State University	Springfield	MO	http://www.missouristate.edu/pas
Mississippi College	Clinton	MS	http://www.mc.edu/academics/departments/pa/
Mississippi State University - Meridian	Meridian	MS	https://www.meridian.msstate.edu/academics/physician-assistant/
Rocky Mountain College	Billings	MT	http://pa.rocky.edu/
Gardner-Webb University	Boiling Springs	NC	https://gardner-webb.edu/academic-programs-and-resources/colleges-and-schools/health-sciences/schools-and-departments/physician-assistant-studies/index
Wake Forest University - Boone	Boone	NC	http://www.wakehealth.edu/Physician-Assistant-Program/
Campbell University	Buies Creek	NC	https://cphs.campbell.edu/academic-programs/physician-assistant/master-physician-assistant-practice/
UNC-Chapel Hill	Chapel Hill	NC	http://www.med.unc.edu/ahs/unc-pa
Duke University	Durham	NC	http://pa.duke.edu/
Elon University	Elon	NC	https://www.elon.edu/u/academics/health-sciences/physician-assistant/
Methodist University	Fayetteville	NC	http://www.methodist.edu/paprogram
East Carolina University	Greenville	NC	http://www.ecu.edu/pa
Wingate University - Hendersonville	Hendersonville	NC	https://www.wingate.edu/academics/hendersonville/physician-assistant
High Point University	High Point	NC	http://www.highpoint.edu/physicianassistant/
Pfeiffer University	Misenheimer	NC	https://www.pfeiffer.edu/mspas
Wingate University	Wingate	NC	http://pa.wingate.edu/

Physician Assistant	City	State	Website
Wake Forest University - Winston Salem	Winston-Salem	NC	http://www.wakehealth.edu/Physician-Assistant-Program/
University of North Dakota	Grand Forks	ND	http://med.und.edu/physician-assistant/index.cfm
University of Nebraska Medical Center - Kearney	Kearney	NE	https://www.unmc.edu/alliedhealth/education/pa/
Union College	Lincoln	NE	http://www.ucollege.edu/pa
College of Saint Mary	Omaha	NE	http://www.csm.edu/academics/health-human-services/master-science-degree-physician-assistant-studies
Creighton University	Omaha	NE	https://medschool.creighton.edu/program/physician-assistant-mpas
University of Nebraska Medical Center - Omaha	Omaha	NE	https://www.unmc.edu/alliedhealth/education/pa/
MCPHS - Manchester	Manchester	NH	https://www.mcphs.edu/academics/school-of-physician-assistant-studies/physician-assistant/physican-assistant-studies-mpas-accelerated
Franklin Pierce University	West Lebanon	NH	http://www.franklinpierce.edu/academics/gradstudies/programs_of_study/mpas/index.htm
Saint Elizabeth University	Morristown	NJ	https://cse.smartcatalogiq.com/en/2019-2020/academic-catalog/academic-programs/physician-assistant/ms-in-physician-assistant
Seton Hall University	Nutley	NJ	https://www.shu.edu/academics/ms-physician-assistant.cfm
Kean University	Union	NJ	https://www.kean.edu/academics/programs/physician-assistant-studies-ms

Physician Assistant	City	State	Website
Thomas Jefferson University - New Jersey	Voorhees	NJ	https://www.jefferson.edu/university/health-professions/departments/physician-assistant-studies/degrees-programs/graduate/ms-new-jersey.html
Monmouth University	West Long Branch	NJ	https://www.monmouth.edu/graduate/ms-physician-assistant/
Rutgers University	West Piscataway	NJ	https://shp.rutgers.edu/physician-assistant/master-of-science-physician-assistant-program/
University of New Mexico	Albuquerque	NM	http://goto.unm.edu/pa
University of St. Francis	Albuquerque	NM	http://www.stfrancis.edu/academics/physician-assistant-studies
Touro University Nevada	Henderson	NV	https://tun.touro.edu/programs/physician-assistant-studies/
University of Nevada, Reno	Reno	NV	https://med.unr.edu/physician-assistant
Albany Medical College	Albany	NY	https://www.amc.edu/academic/PhysicianAssistant/index.cfm
Daemen College	Amherst	NY	https://www.daemen.edu/academics/areas-study/physician-assistant/physician-assistant-studies-ms
Mercy College	Bronx	NY	https://www.mercy.edu/degrees-programs/ms-physician-assistant
Long Island University	Brooklyn	NY	https://www.liu.edu/Brooklyn/Academics/Schools/School-of-Health-Professions/Dept/Physician-Assistant/MS-PAS
SUNY Downstate Medical Center	Brooklyn	NY	https://sls.downstate.edu/admissions/chrp/pa/index.html
Canisius College	Buffalo	NY	https://www.canisius.edu/academics/programs/physician-assistant

Physician Assistant	City	State	Website
D'Youville College	Buffalo	NY	http://www.dyc.edu/academics/pa/
Touro College - Long Island	Central Islip	NY	https://shs.touro.edu/programs/physician-assistant/physician-assistant-long-island/
Touro College - NUMC	East Meadow	NY	https://shs.touro.edu/programs/physician-assistant/physician-assistant-long-island/
Hofstra University	Hempstead	NY	https://www.hofstra.edu/academics/colleges/nursing-physician-assistant/physician-assistant/
Ithaca College	Ithaca	NY	https://www.ithaca.edu/academics/school-health-sciences-and-human-performance/graduate-programs/physician-assistant-studies
CUNY York College	Jamaica	NY	http://www.york.cuny.edu/academics/departments/health-professions/physician-assistant
Pace University - Lenox Hill Hospital, NYC	New York	NY	http://www.pace.edu/college-health-professions/explore-programs/physician-assistant-program
The CUNY School of Medicine	New York	NY	https://www.ccny.cuny.edu/csom/
Touro College Manhattan	New York	NY	https://shs.touro.edu/programs/physician-assistant/physician-assistant-manhattan/
Weil Cornell Graduate School of Medical Sciences	New York	NY	https://gradschool.weill.cornell.edu/programs/health-sciences-physician-assistants
Yeshiva University, Katz School of Science and Health	New York	NY	https://www.yu.edu/katz/programs/graduate/physician-assistant
New York Institute of Technology	Old Westbury	NY	http://www.nyit.edu/pa

Physician Assistant	City	State	Website
Pace University - Pleasantville	Pleasantville	NY	https://www.pace.edu/college-health-professions/graduate-degree-programs/physician-assistant-program-pleasantville
Clarkson University	Potsdam	NY	http://www.clarkson.edu/pa
Marist College	Poughkeepsie	NY	http://www.marist.edu/science/physassist/
St. John's University	Queens	NY	https://www.stjohns.edu/academics/programs/physician-assistant-master-science
Rochester Institute of Technology	Rochester	NY	http://www.rit.edu/healthsciences/graduate-programs/physician-assistant
Stony Brook University Southhampton	Southampton	NY	https://healthtechnology.stonybrookmedicine.edu/programs/pa/elpa
St. Bonaventure University	St. Bonaventure	NY	https://www.sbu.edu/academics/physician-assistant-studies
Wagner College	Staten Island	NY	http://wagner.edu/physician-assistant/
Stony Brook University Health Science Center	Stony Brook	NY	https://healthtechnology.stonybrookmedicine.edu/programs/pa/elpa
Le Moyne College	Syracuse	NY	https://www.lemoyne.edu/pa
SUNY Upstate Medical Center	Syracuse	NY	http://www.upstate.edu/chp/programs/pa/index.php
University of Mount Union	Alliance	OH	https://www.mountunion.edu/physician-assistant-studies
Ashland University	Ashland	OH	https://www.ashland.edu/conhs/majors/master-science-physician-assistant-studies
Baldwin Wallace University	Berea	OH	https://www.bw.edu/graduate/physician-assistant/
Mount St. Joseph University	Cincinnati	OH	http://www.msj.edu/PA

Physician Assistant	City	State	Website
Case Western Reserve University	Cleveland	OH	http://case.edu/medicine/physician-assistant/
Ohio Dominican University	Columbus	OH	http://www.ohiodominican.edu/academics/graduate/physician-assistant-program
University of Dayton	Dayton	OH	https://udayton.edu/education/departments_and_programs/pa/index.php
Ohio University	Dublin	OH	https://www.ohio.edu/chsp/rcs/pa/
University of Findlay	Findlay	OH	https://www.findlay.edu/healthprofessions/physicianassistant-ma/
Kettering College	Kettering	OH	http://kc.edu/academics/physician-assistant/
Marietta College	Marietta	OH	https://www.marietta.edu/pa-program
Lake Erie College	Painesville	OH	http://www.lec.edu/pa
Mercy College of Ohio	Toledo	OH	https://mercycollege.edu/academics/programs/graduate/physician-assistant-studies
University of Toledo	Toledo	OH	http://www.utoledo.edu/med/grad/pa/
Northeastern State University	Muskogee	OK	https://academics.nsuok.edu/healthprofessions/Degree-Programs/Graduate/Physician-Assistant-Studie
Oklahoma City University	Oklahoma City	OK	https://www.okcu.edu/physician-assistant/home
University of Oklahoma - Oklahoma City	Oklahoma City	OK	https://medicine.ouhsc.edu/Prospective-Students/Degree-Programs/Physician-Associate-Program
Oklahoma State University Center for Health Sciences	Tulsa	OK	https://medicine.okstate.edu/pa/index.html
University of Oklahoma - Tulsa	Tulsa	OK	http://www.ou.edu/tulsa/community_medicine/scm-pa-program
Pacific University	Hillsboro	OR	http://www.pacificu.edu/pa
George Fox University	Newberg	OR	https://www.georgefox.edu/pa/index.html

Physician Assistant	City	State	Website
Oregon Health & Science University	Portland	OR	https://www.ohsu.edu/school-of-medicine/physician-assistant
DeSales University	Center Valley	PA	https://www.desales.edu/academics/graduate-studies/master-of-science-in-physician-assistant-studies-(mspas)
Misericordia University	Dallas	PA	https://www.misericordia.edu/page.cfm?p=655
Salus University	Elkins Park	PA	http://www.salus.edu/Colleges/Health-Sciences/Physician-Assistant.aspx
Gannon University - Erie, PA	Erie	PA	http://www.gannon.edu/academic-departments/physician-assistant-department/
Mercyhurst University	Erie	PA	https://www.mercyhurst.edu/academics/physician-assistant-studies-program
Arcadia University	Glenside	PA	https://www.arcadia.edu/academics/programs/physician-assistant
Seton Hill University	Greensburg	PA	https://www.setonhill.edu/academics/graduate-programs/physician-assistant-ms/
Thiel College	Greenville	PA	https://www.thiel.edu/graduate-degrees/physician-assistant
Penn State University	Hershey	PA	https://med.psu.edu/physician-assistant
Lock Haven University	Lock Haven	PA	https://paportal.lhup.edu/PA/
Saint Francis University	Loretto	PA	https://www.francis.edu/Physician-Assistant-Science/
Drexel University	Philadelphia	PA	http://drexel.edu/cnhp/academics/departments/Physician-Assistant/
Philadelphia College of Osteopathic Medicine (PCOM)	Philadelphia	PA	https://www.pcom.edu/academics/programs-and-degrees/physician-assistant-studies/

Physician Assistant	City	State	Website
Temple University Lewis Katz School of Medicine	Philadelphia	PA	https://medicine.temple.edu/education/physician-assistant-program
Thomas Jefferson University - City Center	Philadelphia	PA	https://www.jefferson.edu/university/health-professions/departments/physician-assistant-studies/degrees-programs/graduate/ms-center-city.html
Thomas Jefferson University - East Falls	Philadelphia	PA	https://www.jefferson.edu/university/health-professions/departments/physician-assistant-studies/degrees-programs/graduate/ms-east-falls/applying.html
University of the Sciences	Philadelphia	PA	https://www.usciences.edu/samson-college-of-health-sciences/physician-assistant-studies/index.html
Chatham University	Pittsburgh	PA	http://www.chatham.edu/mpas/
Duquesne University	Pittsburgh	PA	http://www.duq.edu/academics/schools/health-sciences/academic-programs/physician-assistant
University of Pittsburgh	Pittsburgh	PA	https://www.shrs.pitt.edu/PAProgram
Marywood University	Scranton	PA	http://www.marywood.edu/pa-program
Slippery Rock University	Slippery Rock	PA	http://www.sru.edu/academics/graduate-programs/physician-assistant-studies-master-of-science
West Chester University	West Chester	PA	https://www.wcupa.edu/healthSciences/physicianAssistant/default.aspx?gclid=EAIaIQobCh-MInYy7kYO36wIVAeWzCh-2qzAkbEAAYASAAEgItF-vD_BwE
King's College	Wilkes-Barre	PA	https://www.kings.edu/academics/undergraduate_majors/physicianassistant

Physician Assistant	City	State	Website
Pennsylvania College of Technology	Williamsport	PA	https://www.pct.edu/academics/nhs/physician-assistant/physician-assistant-studies
San Juan Bautista School of Medicine	Caguas	PR	https://www.sanjuanbautista.edu/education/programs/pa-program.html
Johnson & Wales University	Providence	RI	http://www.jwu.edu/PA
Bryant University	Smithfield	RI	http://gradschool.bryant.edu/health-sciences.htm
Charleston Southern University	Charleston	SC	http://www.csuniv.edu/pa
Medical University of South Carolina	Charleston	SC	https://education.musc.edu/students/enrollment/bulletin/colleges-and-degrees/health-professions/ms-in-physician-assistant
Presbyterian College	Clinton	SC	https://www.presby.edu/academics/graduate-professional/physician-assistant-program/
University of South Carolina SOM	Columbia	SC	http://www.southalabama.edu/alliedhealth/pa
North Greenville University	Greer	SC	http://www.ngu.edu/pa-medicine.php
University of South Dakota	Vemillion	SD	http://www.usd.edu/pa
Lincoln Memorial University	Harrogate	TN	https://www.lmunet.edu/school-of-medical-sciences/pa-harrogate/index.php
Lincoln Memorial University - Knoxville	Knoxville	TN	https://www.lmunet.edu/school-of-medical-sciences/pa-knoxville/index.php
South College - Knoxville	Knoxville	TN	https://www.south.edu/programs/master-health-science-physician-assistant-studies/knoxville/
Christian Brothers University	Memphis	TN	https://www.cbu.edu/pa
University of Tennessee Health Science Center	Memphis	TN	http://www.uthsc.edu/allied/pa

Physician Assistant	City	State	Website
Milligan University	Milligan	TN	http://www.milligan.edu/pa
Lipscomb University	Nashville	TN	https://www.lipscomb.edu
South College - Nashville	Nashville	TN	https://www.south.edu/programs/master-health-science-physician-assistant-studies/nashville/
Trevecca Nazarene University	Nashville	TN	https://www.trevecca.edu/programs/physician-assistant
Bethel University (TN)	Paris	TN	https://www.bethelu.edu/academics/degrees-and-programs/physician-assistant-studies
Hardin-Simmons University	Abilene	TX	https://www.hsutx.edu/pa
University of Mary Hardin-Baylor	Belton	TX	https://go.umhb.edu/graduate/physician-assistant/home
University of Texas Southwestern Medical Center	Dallas	TX	http://www.utsouthwestern.edu/pa
University of Texas Rio Grande Valley	Edinburgh	TX	https://www.utrgv.edu/pa/
U.S. Army Medical Center of Excellence IPAP	Fort Sam Houston	TX	https://medcoe.army.mil/ipap
University of North Texas HS Center Fort Worth	Fort Worth	TX	https://www.unthsc.edu/school-of-health-professions/physician-assistant-studies/
University of Texas Medical Branch at Galveston	Galveston	TX	http://shp.utmb.edu/PhysicianAssistantStudies/
Baylor College of Medicine	Houston	TX	https://www.bcm.edu/education/school-of-health-professions/physician-assistant-program
University of Texas Health Science Center - Laredo	Laredo	TX	https://www.uthscsa.edu/academics/health-professions/programs/physician-assistant-studies-ms/laredo-pa-extension-program

Physician Assistant	City	State	Website
Texas Tech University Health Sciences Center	Midland	TX	https://www.ttuhsc.edu/health-professions/master-physician-assistant-studies/
University of Texas Health Science Center - San Antonio	San Antonio	TX	http://www.uthscsa.edu/shp/pa/
University of Utah	Salt Lake City	UT	https://medicine.utah.edu/dfpm/physician-assistant-studies/program/
Rocky Mountain University of Health Professions	South Provo	UT	https://rm.edu/academics/master-of-physician-assistant-studies/
South University, Richmond	Glen Allen	VA	https://www.southuniversity.edu/richmond/physician-assistant-ms
James Madison University	Harrisonburg	VA	http://www.healthsci.jmu.edu/PA/
Shenandoah University - Loudoun	Leesburg	VA	https://www.su.edu/physician-assistant/masters-of-science-in-physician-assistant-studies/
University of Lynchburg	Lynchburg	VA	http://www.lynchburg.edu/graduate/physician-assistant-medicine/
Emory & Henry College	Marion	VA	http://www.ehc.edu/academics/programs/school-health-sciences/shs-programs/school-health-sciences-graduate-programs/physician-assistant-pa/
Eastern Virginia Medical School (early assurance, too)	Norfolk	VA	http://www.evms.edu/education/masters_programs/physician_assistant_program/
Mary Baldwin University	Roanoke	VA	https://go.marybaldwin.edu/health_sciences/pas/
Radford University Carilion	Roanoke	VA	https://www.radford.edu/content/grad/home/academics/graduate-programs/pa.html
Shenandoah Universityn - Winchester	Winchester	VA	https://www.su.edu/physician-assistant/masters-of-science-in-physician-assistant-studies/

Physician Assistant	City	State	Website
University of Washington - MEDEX Northwest, Seattle	Seattle	WA	https://depts.washington.edu/medex/pa-program/
University of Washington - MEDEX Northwest, Spokane	Spokane	WA	https://depts.washington.edu/medex/pa-program/
University of Washington - MEDEX Northwest, Tacoma	Tacoma	WA	https://depts.washington.edu/medex/pa-program/
University of Wisconsin - La Crosse	La Crosse	WI	https://www.uwlax.edu/grad/physician-assistant-studies/
University of Wisconsin-Madison	Madison	WI	https://www.med.wisc.edu/education/physician-assistant-pa-program/
Concordia University - Wisconsin	Mequon	WI	https://www.cuw.edu/academics/programs/physician-assistant-masters/
Marquette University	Milwaukee	WI	http://www.marquette.edu/physician-assistant
Caroll University	Waukesha	WI	http://www.carrollu.edu/gradprograms/physasst/admission.asp
University of Charleston	Charleston	WV	http://www.ucwv.edu/pa/
Marshall University Joan C. Edwards School of Medicine	Huntington	WV	https://jcesom.marshall.edu/students/physician-assistant-program/
West Virginia University	Morgantown	WV	https://medicine.hsc.wvu.edu/physician-assistant-studies/
Alderson-Broaddus University	Philippi	WV	http://ab.edu/academics/master-of-science-in-physician-assistant-studies/
West Liberty University	West Liberty	WV	http://www.westliberty.edu/physician-assistant/

CHAPTER 17

VETERINARY MEDICAL SCHOOLS BY CITY/STATE

Vet Schools	City	State	Website
Auburn University College of Veterinary Medicine	Auburn	AL	https://www.vetmed.auburn.edu/
Tuskegee University School of Veterinary Medicine	Tuskegee	AL	https://www.tuskegee.edu/programs-courses/colleges-schools/cvm
Midwestern University College of Veterinary Medicine	Glendale	AZ	https://www.midwestern.edu/academics/our-colleges/college-of-veterinary-medicine.xml
University of Arizona College of Veterinary Medicine	Oro Valley	AZ	https://vetmed.arizona.edu/
University of California, Davis School of Veterinary Medicine	Davis	CA	https://www.vetmed.ucdavis.edu/
Western University of Health Sciences College of Veterinary Medicine	Pomona	CA	https://www.westernu.edu/veterinary/
Colorado State University College of Veterinary Medicine and Biomedical Sciences	Fort Collins	CO	https://vetmedbiosci.colostate.edu/dvm/
University of Florida College of Veterinary Medicine	Gainesville	FL	https://education.vetmed.ufl.edu/
University of Georgia College of Veterinary Medicine	Athens	GA	https://vet.uga.edu/
Iowa State University College of Veterinary Medicine	Ames	IA	https://vetmed.iastate.edu/
University of Illinois College of Veterinary Medicine	Urbana	IL	https://vetmed.illinois.edu/
Purdue University College of Veterinary Medicine	West Lafayette	IN	https://www.purdue.edu/vet/
Kansas State University College of Veterinary Medicine	Manhattan	KS	https://www.vet.k-state.edu/
Louisiana State University School of Veterinary Medicine	Baton Rouge	LA	https://www.lsu.edu/vetmed/
Tufts University School of Veterinary Medicine	North Grafton	MA	https://vet.tufts.edu/
Michigan State University College of Veterinary Medicine	East Lansing	MI	https://cvm.msu.edu/
University of Minnesota College of Veterinary Medicine	St. Paul	MN	https://vetmed.umn.edu/
University of Missouri - Columbia College of Veterinary Medicine	Columbia	MO	https://cvm.missouri.edu/

Vet Schools	City	State	Website
Mississippi State University College of Veterinary Medicine	Mississippi State	MS	https://www.vetmed.msstate.edu/
North Carolina State University College of Veterinary Medicine	Raleigh	NC	https://cvm.ncsu.edu/
Cornell University College of Veterinary Medicine	Ithica	NY	https://www.vet.cornell.edu/
Long Island University School of Veterinary Medicine	Brookville	NY	https://liu.edu/vetmed
Ohio State University College of Veterinary Medicine	Columbus	OH	https://vet.osu.edu/
Oklahoma State University College of Veterinary Medicine	Stillwater	OK	https://vetmed.okstate.edu/
Oregon State University College of Veterinary Medicine	Corvallis	OR	https://vetmed.oregonstate.edu/
University of Pennsylvania School of Veterinary Medicine	Philadelphia	PA	https://www.vet.upenn.edu/
Lincoln Memorial University College of Veterinary Medicine	Harrogate	TN	https://www.lmunet.edu/college-of-veterinary-medicine/index.php
University of Tennessee College of Veterinary Medicine	Knoxville	TN	https://vetmed.tennessee.edu/
Texas A&M University College of Veterinary Medicine & Biomedical Sciences	College Station	TX	https://vetmed.tamu.edu/
Texas Tech University School of Veterinary Medicine	Amarillo	TX	https://www.depts.ttu.edu/vetschool/
Virginia Tech Virginia-Maryland College of Veterinary Medicine	Blacksburg	VA	http://www.vetmed.vt.edu/
Washington State University College of Veterinary Medicine	Pullman	WA	https://www.vetmed.wsu.edu/
University of Wisconsin-Madison School of Veterinary Medicine	Madison	WI	https://www.vetmed.wisc.edu/

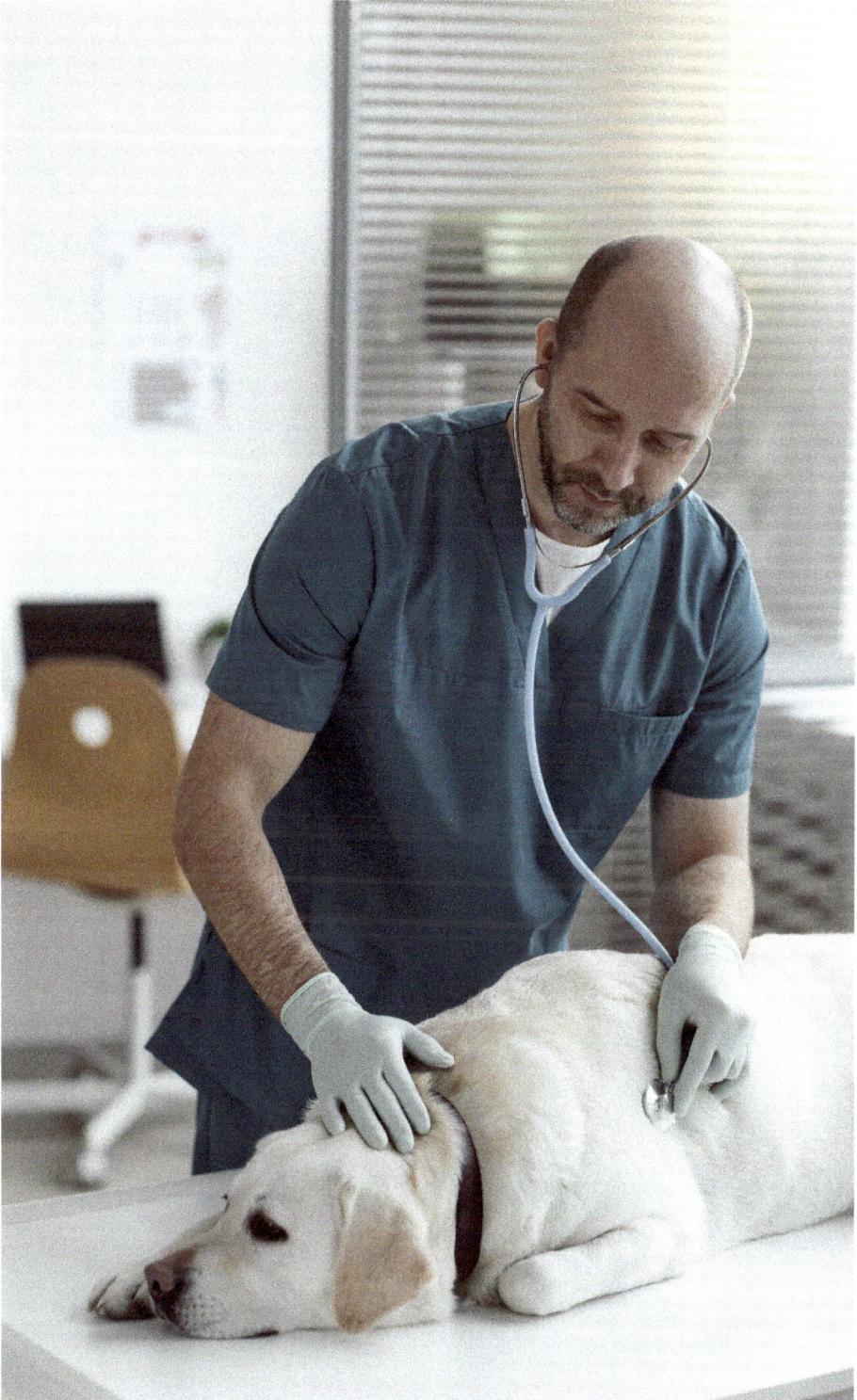

COMPREHENSIVE HEALTH CARE SERIES

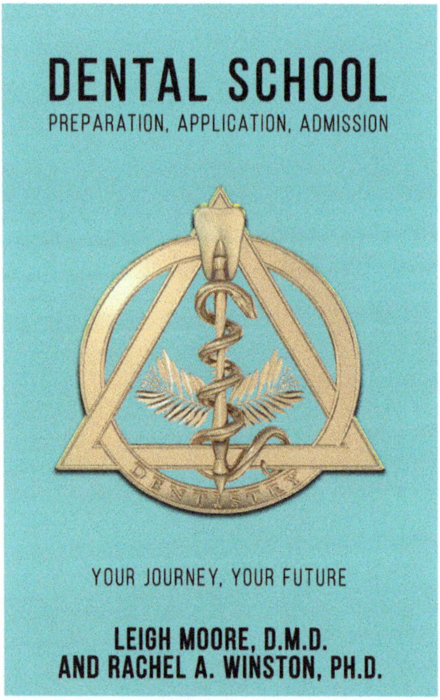
DENTAL SCHOOL
PREPARATION, APPLICATION, ADMISSION
YOUR JOURNEY, YOUR FUTURE
LEIGH MOORE, D.M.D.
AND RACHEL A. WINSTON, PH.D.

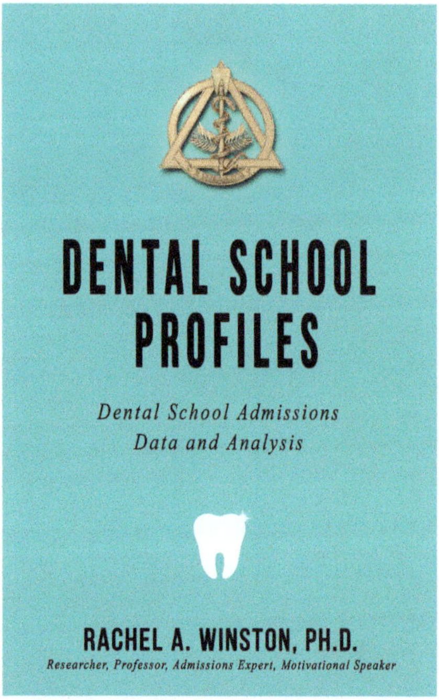
DENTAL SCHOOL
PROFILES
Dental School Admissions
Data and Analysis
RACHEL A. WINSTON, PH.D.
Researcher, Professor, Admissions Expert, Motivational Speaker

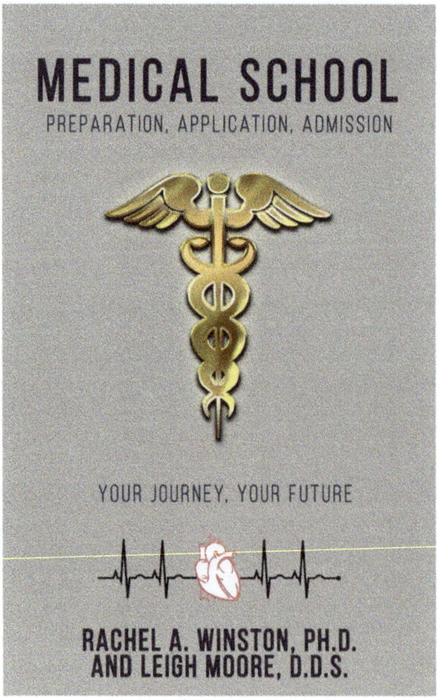
MEDICAL SCHOOL
PREPARATION, APPLICATION, ADMISSION
YOUR JOURNEY, YOUR FUTURE
RACHEL A. WINSTON, PH.D.
AND LEIGH MOORE, D.D.S.

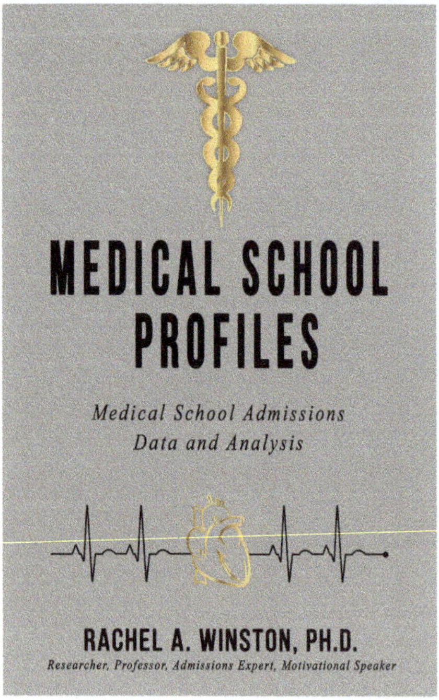
MEDICAL SCHOOL
PROFILES
Medical School Admissions
Data and Analysis
RACHEL A. WINSTON, PH.D.
Researcher, Professor, Admissions Expert, Motivational Speaker

VET SCHOOL
PREPARATION, APPLICATION, ADMISSION

YOUR JOURNEY, YOUR FUTURE

RACHEL A. WINSTON, PH.D.
Researcher, Professor, Admissions Expert, Motivational Speaker

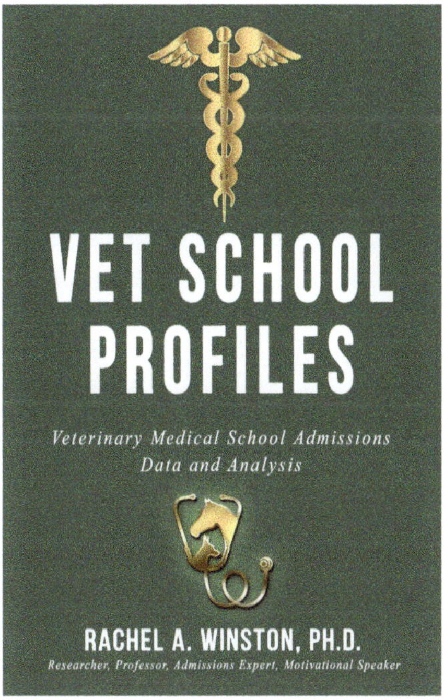

VET SCHOOL PROFILES

Veterinary Medical School Admissions Data and Analysis

RACHEL A. WINSTON, PH.D.
Researcher, Professor, Admissions Expert, Motivational Speaker

PHYSICIAN ASST. (PA) SCHOOL
PREPARATION, APPLICATION, ADMISSION

YOUR JOURNEY, YOUR FUTURE

RACHEL A. WINSTON, PH.D.
Researcher, Professor, Admissions Expert, Motivational Speaker

PHYSICIAN ASST. SCHOOL PROFILES

P.A. School Admissions Data and Analysis

RACHEL A. WINSTON, PH.D.
Researcher, Professor, Admissions Expert, Motivational Speaker

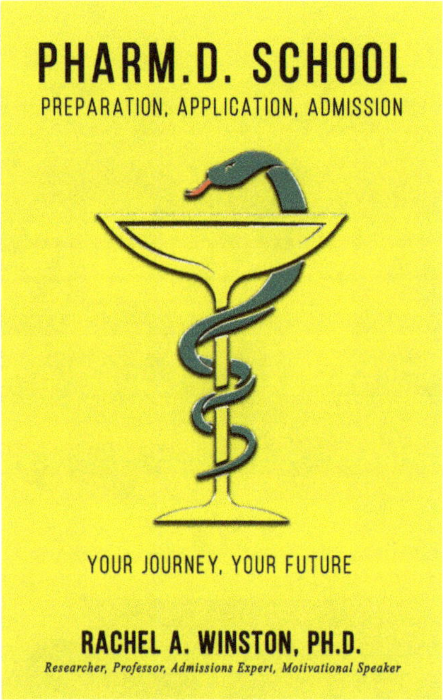

PHARM.D. SCHOOL
PREPARATION, APPLICATION, ADMISSION

YOUR JOURNEY, YOUR FUTURE

RACHEL A. WINSTON, PH.D.
Researcher, Professor, Admissions Expert, Motivational Speaker

PHARM.D. SCHOOL PROFILES

Pharmacy School Admissions Data and Analysis

RACHEL A. WINSTON, PH.D.
Researcher, Professor, Admissions Expert, Motivational Speaker

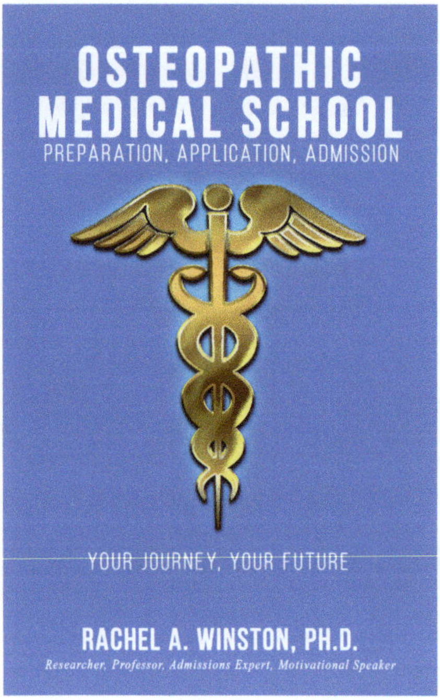

OSTEOPATHIC MEDICAL SCHOOL
PREPARATION, APPLICATION, ADMISSION

YOUR JOURNEY, YOUR FUTURE

RACHEL A. WINSTON, PH.D.
Researcher, Professor, Admissions Expert, Motivational Speaker

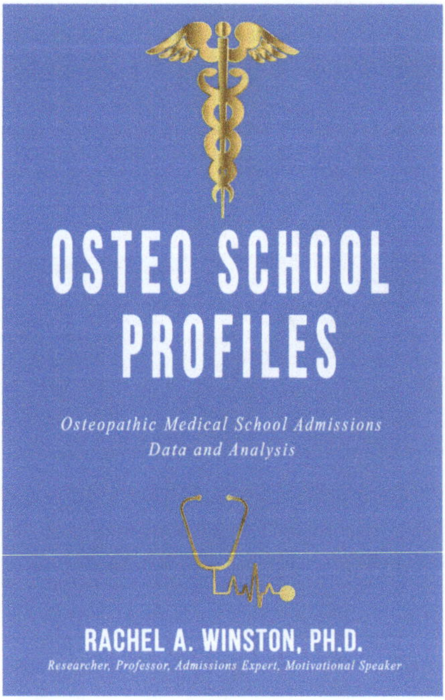

OSTEO SCHOOL PROFILES

Osteopathic Medical School Admissions Data and Analysis

RACHEL A. WINSTON, PH.D.
Researcher, Professor, Admissions Expert, Motivational Speaker

Is Medical School Your Goal?

FROM

HIGH SCHOOL
TO
MEDICAL SCHOOL

The Ultimate Guide to
BS/MD Programs

Rachel A. Winston, Ph.D.
Researcher, Professor, Admissions Expert, Motivational Speaker

This comprehensive healthcare series is designed in full color to aid the growing number of applicants seeking clear, comprehensive materials. As a college admissions expert and former UCLA College Counseling Certificate Program faculty member, Dr. Winston is dedicated to helping students obtain the information they need.

FOR MORE INFORMATION

bsmdguide.com
medschoolexpert.com

Purchase books at Lizard-publishing.com

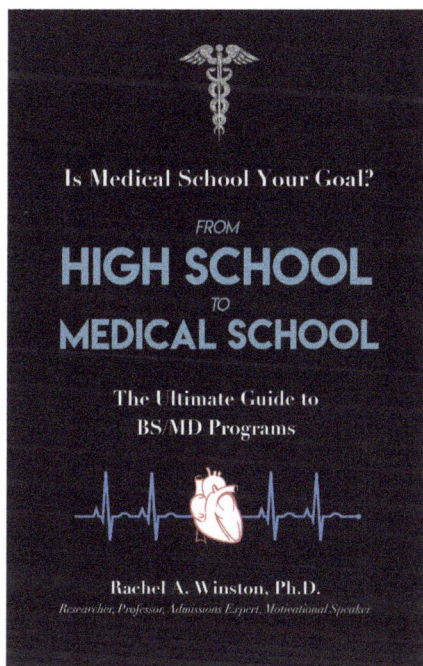

SERVICES OFFERED BY LIZARD EDUCATION:

- College Counseling
- Admissions News/Resources
- Essay Support and Editing
- Interview Preparation
- Road Trips to Visit Colleges
- Career Planning/Majors/Resumes
- BS/MD, BS/DO, BS/JD, BS/DDS
- Medical School
- Graduate School (Masters & Doctorate)
- Film Studio and Editing
- Portfolio Assistance/SlideRoom
- Athletics Recruiting/Highlight Films
- International Admissions/Visa/TOEFL
- Financial Aid and Scholarships
- UCs, Ivy Leagues, and Colleges Nationwide
- Book Publishing
- Engineering, Robotics, STEM
- Art Portfolios

Email: collegeguide@yahoo.com
Website: collegelizard.com

LIZARD

INDEX

D

E

F

H

I

K

L

366

U

V

W

X